FAMILIES IN CANADA TODAY

FAMILIES IN CANADA TODAY

Recent Changes and Their Policy Consequences

MARGRIT EICHLER

Ontario Institute for
Studies in Education
Toronto

Canadian Cataloguing in Publication Data

Eichler, Margrit, 1942-
Families in Canada today

Bibliography: p.
Includes index.
ISBN 0-7715-5692-6

1. Family - Canada. 2. Canada - Social conditions - 1965- * I. Title.

HQ560.E42 306.8'5'0971 C82-095216-8

Co-ordinating Editor: Joan Kerr

Editor: Kathy Austin

Cover Design: Alex Pandi

ISBN 0-7715-5692-6

1 2 3 4 5 IG 87 86 85 84 83

Written, printed, and bound in Canada

DEDICATED TO

Grete Brischke Eichler and Wolfgang Eichler,

with thanks

More Gage Books in Sociology

CANADIAN SOCIETY

Growth and Dualism – Roderic Beaujot and Kevin McQuillan

Canadian Society – Bernard R. Blishen, Frank E. Jones, Kaspar D. Naegele, and John Porter

Prophecy and Protest – Samuel D. Clark, J. Paul Grayson, and Linda M. Grayson

The Measure of Canadian Society – John Porter

THE FAMILY

Courtship, Marriage and the Family in Canada – G. N. Ramu

The Canadian Family – K. Ishwaran

SEX AND SEX ROLES

Secret Oppression – Constance Backhouse and Leah Cohen

The Sexes – R. N. Whitehurst and G. V. Booth

MINORITIES AND RACISM

Ethnicity and Human Rights in Canada – Evelyn Kallen

DEVIANCE AND CRIMINOLOGY

Police Command – Brian A. Grosman

Policing in Canada – William Kelly and Nora Kelly

Crime and You – A. M. Kirkpatrick and W. T. McGrath

Crime and Its Treatment in Canada – W. T. McGrath

Hookers, Rounders & Desk Clerks – Robert Prus and Styllianoss Irini

Roadhustler – Robert C. Prus and C. R. D. Sharper

Policeman – Claude L. Vincent

EDUCATION

Education, Change and Society – Richard A. Carlton, Louise A. Colley, and Neil J. MacKinnon

Contents

Preface

It may seem somewhat presumptuous to try to write a textbook on Canadian families given the state of our knowledge at the present time. In some way, I suppose it is. Nevertheless, I felt it would be useful as well as interesting to give it a try, knowing full well that there would be problems in the execution. Interesting it certainly was, and useful I hope it will be, at least to a modest degree. That is all one can aim for, in any case.

The intent of the book is twofold: one intent is to bring together as much of the available information on Canadian families as I could scratch together, and the other intent is to try to refocus family literature and research in a number of ways.

In order to present the available information, I not only consulted academic publications, but also unpublished work (to the degree that I could discover it and, when discovered, get a hold of it), government reports (to the degree that I could get access to them), statistical information, some of my own data collected in two separate projects, some information from the mass media, where it seemed relevant, and, indeed, information from every other source that I could discover. It is possible that I have overlooked some important publications, but I did try to gain an overview of the Canadian literature. No such attempt was made concerning the American literature or literature from still other countries, although I did occasionally draw on such works, where it seemed relevant and helpful.

The intent to refocus our research attention manifests itself in the discussion of four biasses which I see as threads that go through the literature: the monolithic, conservative, sexist, and microstructural biasses. To put this into positive terms, the first concern is to encourage a differentiated as opposed to a uniform view of families. That means that the focus is on the diversity of family types rather than on universalities or uniformities. This is reflected in the title of the book which does not talk about "the" Canadian family, but instead about Canadian *families*.

The second concern is to put forward the notion that there have been very major changes within Canadian families in the recent past and that this should become a central factor in our research. The focus is therefore on change rather than on stability, on historical differences rather than on continuities, and on the current situation rather than on the past.

The third concern arises from the premise that women and men experience the same families differently, due to their different structural positions. To represent this dual perspective consistently is therefore one of the aims of the book. Sometimes this was not possible due to lack of information; however, the important point is to constantly remind ourselves that such a dual perspective is something we should strive for, at least in terms of the questions we raise. A similar point could be made with respect to age: the same families are also experienced differently depending on one's status as a dependent child, adult, or senior citizen. However, carrying this second perspective systematically through the book has not been attempted, although the issue is occasionally alluded to: it would have meant writing another book, and one for which information would have been even more difficult to obtain.

Lastly, a major concern of the book is to try to integrate policy questions into our discussion about families. This includes an examination of how policies may influence behaviours within families, as well as an examination of the notions of families on which our current major relevant policies are based, and whether these notions are accurate. The focus is therefore on societal rather than on interpersonal issues, on the interactions of government, law, and other institutions with families rather than on the internal workings of families, on structural rather than on psychological variables.

Given the intent of the book to refocus our thinking, it was inevitable that in many cases needed information would simply not be available. New approaches require new theories which are based on new questions which can only be answered adequately with new data. However, new data will not be generated unless we first change the theoretical framework within which we have been operating. I decided early on not to let myself be impeded by this dilemma, and therefore proceeded, whenever I ran against the problem of lack of information, not only to describe how little we *do* know but also to point out the much larger questions that we *should* know about but do not.

It is my most deeply cherished hope that the many questions that are posed in the book — more so than the few answers that are suggested — will lead other researchers to address some of them, so that we can start filling the holes, the outlines of which have been described. In this sense, this book is not an ordinary textbook, for it raises more questions than it answers. Perhaps, however, this is the appropriate manner in which to approach families today — with uncertainty rather than with certainty.

Acknowledgements

A large number of people were helpful during the writing of this book, and I am sincerely grateful for the help I received without which the book could not have been written.

In the fall of 1980, during a sabbatical leave, I spent three months at the Office of the Coordinator for the Status of Women. During this time I collected a fair amount of information that has been incorporated into this book. I would like to thank Maureen O'Neill for inviting me to spend time in her office, thereby facilitating access to some of the government publications I drew from. In particular, Barbara Hicks was of enormous help, supplying me with large amounts of materials and useful leads.

During the conception and writing of this book I discussed various aspects of it with a number of people, including Christine Blain, Louise Dulude, Robert Glossop, Doris Guayatt, Louise Holmes, Harry McKay, Michael Mendelson, Nicole Morgan, Johanne Pes, Julyan Reid, Hilda Scott, and Carole Swan. Needless to say, we did not always agree, but the discussions were invariably helpful in clarifying my own thinking.

Statistics Canada was a very important resource, and both the staff in Ottawa as well as the staff in the regional office in Toronto have been very helpful. In particular, Gail Oja and Sylvia Wargon, as well as Doug Newton and Colin Geitzler were of assistance in finding information. John Gordon's help was simply outstanding.

Several students provided, at different points in time, some research assistance: Marisa Uribe, Kate Rousmanier, and Linda Yanz. I used drafts of chapters as a discussion basis in several seminars, and received as a consequence some very valuable feedback and criticism from the students. The contributions of Penny Gross, Maureen Killoran and Wendy Wyles have been incorporated into the text, and several student papers (which are individually cited in the text) have been utilized.

In an attempt to get access to recent Canadian materials, I wrote about 150–200 letters to individuals, asking for copies of their unpublished papers, references, lists of publications, and the like. The response was excellent: many people sent me information which was very helpful. I cannot possibly acknowledge all of these individuals, but want to mention Gordon Cressy, David Cruikshank, Julien D. Payne, and Benjamin Schlesinger as particularly helpful. A fair number of the papers and articles I received are cited in the text; however, due to space limitations, several planned sections had to be eliminated and therefore not all the materials I received are actually mentioned. Nevertheless, they were extremely useful and important, and I want in particular to thank those people who sent me such materials. In addition, Suzanne Campbell allowed me to rifle through the files of the Vanier Institute of the Family, and Frieda Forman of the Women's Resource Centre at OISE was, as usual, inexhaustible in her co-operation.

Several people read parts of the manuscript and commented upon it. In particular, I want to thank Monica Boyd, Robert Glossop, Jonah Goldstein, Louise Holmes, Meg Luxton, Jennifer Stoddard, and Kathleen Storrie for performing this invaluable service for me. As a consequence, several errors were eliminated, although sadly others may possibly remain. Even though every effort has been made to be as factually correct as possible, some errors are probably unavoidable in a book that draws on several different specialized literatures.

I have used data, most of them previously unpublished, from the Participation of Women Project (see Appendix 1). This forms part of an international study which also involves Tamara Dobrin, Pompiliu Gregorescu, Renata Siemienska, and Mino Vianello. Various aspects of the study were funded by SSHRCC grants #410-78-0300 and #410-78-0302 as well as OISE grant #3474.

As is usual, the manuscript has gone through several drafts, and therefore retypings. Several people worked at different times on typing different chapters, but Gail Buckland and Vivian Crossman did the bulk of the work, always in excellent form, and often under difficult conditions.

Finally, the people at Gage have been pleasant to work with: Bruce Conron as the initial contact who convinced me to write the book, Joan Kerr as Co-ordinating Editor, and Kathy Austin, an editor with whom it was a pleasure to work.

List of Tables

List of Figures

List of Charts

CHAPTER 1

Beyond the Monolithic Bias in Family Literature

Introduction

We are living in a time of rapid social change. In the field of medicine, for example, we are witnessing the creation of new life forms in laboratories, conception outside the uterus, organ transplants from living and dead donors, the establishment of sperm banks, the birth of a child from the sperm of a dead donor. Advances in microelectronics have started to create a revolution — in the workplace and in individual living habits — that can only be compared with the industrial revolution. Wives and mothers are joining the work force, thereby redefining the roles of males and females, adults and children.

It would therefore be totally unreasonable to expect that the one structure within which the large majority of people spend most of their lives — namely the family — would not also change drastically, if for no other reason than that we have all been touched, in one way or another, by these external changes.

Families themselves have undergone numerous internal changes. Until fairly recently, marriage was seen as a lifelong commitment. Now, it has become a volitional union, rather than an automatic one. Likewise, it is now often a conscious decision for couples to have children, rather than an automatic consequence of fertility. The prevalence of divorce affects in a fundamental sense all families, whether or not they *experience* divorce themselves.

Change, then, is everywhere evident, and most clearly experienced in the personal struggles of people who try to determine a path through an area they thought was well charted, but where suddenly the signposts have disappeared. However, when one looks over the sociology of the family literature, and the family literature more broadly defined, one does not gain this impression of change. This is due to the fact that the family literature suffers from four pervasive biasses. With some exceptions, of course, the family literature suffers from a monolithic bias, a conservative bias, a sexist bias, and a microstructural bias.

The *monolithic bias* expresses itself in a tendency to treat the family as a monolithic structure, and in an emphasis on uniformity of experience and universality of structure and functions rather than on diversity of experiences, structures, and functions.

The *conservative bias* expresses itself in the tendency to either largely ignore recent changes, or to treat them as ephemeral, rather than comprehending them as central and fundamental. This results in using analytic frameworks which are totally inadequate for newly emergent situations. An example of this type of thinking would be the tendency to regard reconstituted families as basically the same as families based on first marriages, and to try and analyze them in terms which were developed for this type of family. Two other manifestations of the conservative bias exist in a tendency to ignore the ugly aspects of familial relationships (such as wife battering, or child abuse and incest) and to treat children as passive, rather than active members of the family.

The *sexist bias* expresses itself in methodological practices and theoretical perspectives that tend to assume (a) that there is a natural differentiation of functions within families on the basis of sex, and (b) that there is uniformity of experience for all members in the same family. This leads to an overestimation of actual functional differentiation, and to an incapacity to understand the diverse experiences of members of the same familial unit.

Lastly, the *microstructural bias* expresses itself in a tendency to treat families as encapsulated units, in which we can explain behaviors simply by looking at what happens within that unit, rather than by trying to understand in what manner familial behaviors are partially affected by extraneous factors. It also leads to a neglect of policy issues, and to a neglect to incorporate important legal or policy changes (such as the changes in family law that took place in 1978 in various provinces) into a comprehensive analysis.

In the first part of the book, each of these biasses will be examined in detail and ways will be proposed to overcome them. This chapter will deal with ways to overcome the monolithic bias.

A very simple way in which to learn about how a phenomenon is conceptualized is to look at definitions. First, then, we will consider some of the prevalent definitions of the family.

Definitions of the Family

Probably the most famous and most widely used definition of the family is that of Murdock. It has exerted a powerful influence on the sociology of the family. He defines the family as

> a social group characterized by common residence, economic cooperation, and reproduction. It includes adults of both sexes, at least two of whom maintain a socially approved sexual relationship, and one or more children, own or adopted, of the sexually cohabiting adults.[1]

A modern reformulation of this classic functional definition of the family is, for instance, Rose Laub Coser's definition of the family as

> a group manifesting the following organizational attributes: It finds its origin in marriage; it consists of husband, wife, and children born in their wedlock, though other relatives may find their place close to this nuclear group, and the group is united by moral, legal, economic, religious and social rights and obligations (including sexual rights and prohibitions as well as such socially patterned feelings as love, attraction, piety, and awe).[2]

As a last example, another often-quoted definition of the family has been provided by Stephens, who defines marriage as

> a socially legitimate sexual union, begun with a public announcement and undertaken with some idea of permanence; it is assumed with a more or less explicit marriage contract, which spells out reciprocal rights and obligations between spouses and their future children.[3]

Stephens then goes on to define the family as

> a social arrangement based on marriage and the marriage contract, including recognition of the rights and duties of parenthood, common residence for husband, wife and children, and reciprocal economic obligations between husband and wife.[4]

What is of interest in our context is not only what (or who) is defined as part of a family, but also what (or who) is defined as *not* part of a family.

If we apply these definitions to the Canadian reality of today, we would, according to Coser and Stephens, but not according to Murdock, exclude common-law couples. None of the definitions except Coser's is able to incorporate commuting couples, or families whose children are elsewhere, such as at boarding schools or in institutions. Most importantly, none of these definitions include lone-parent families[5] or remarriage families in which one or both of the adults may have children with whom they maintain contact but who live in the household of an ex-spouse. Yet all of these groupings are to some degree recognized as families in Canada at the present time.

Using the terminology of the preceding three definitions, and applying it to present-day Canadian reality, a definition of the family which intends to describe those units which are presently called families could read as follows:

A family is a social group which may or may not include adults of both sexes (e.g., lone-parent families), may or may not include one or more children (e.g., childless couples), who may or may not have been born in their wedlock (e.g., adopted children, or children by one adult partner of a previous union). The relationship of the adults may or may not have its origin in marriage (e.g., common-law couples), they may or may not share a common residence (e.g., commuting couples). The adults may or may not cohabit sexually,[6] and the relationship may or may not involve such socially patterned feelings as love, attraction, piety, and awe.

This is not a very useful or satisfying definition, really, but a rather realistic one. (It is not offered as a definition to be used.) It must be noted that we have not even included familial groups which do exist at present but which are not generally recognized as families, such as homosexual couples with or without children and group arrangements.

The boundaries of contemporary families, then, must be recognized as fluid. Nevertheless, in spite of the difficulty of coming up with a good cut-and-dried definition of the family, if we ask ourselves, or anybody else, who is their family, most people will be able to give a clear and unambiguous answer. For instance, they may say, "my family consists of my spouse, my children, my parents, and Aunt Sally." However, they may not list Uncle Herbert, because there is very little interaction with him.

Likewise, if we look into various laws and policies, we will find some very concrete definitions of the family that define, *for a particular purpose,* who is and who is not part of a family, independent of the feelings of the people involved. Canadian law prohibits, for instance, marriage between family members. These regulations stem back to the Scriptures and canon law, were eventually codified by the Statutes of Henry VIII in 1540, and were listed by Archbishop Parker in 1563. (CCH Canadian Ltd., 1981, p. 1031, par. 2155). At present, a man in Canada is prohibited from marrying the following relatives: grandmother, grandfather's wife, wife's grandmother, aunt, uncle's wife, wife's aunt, mother, stepmother, wife's mother, daughter, wife's daughter, son's wife, sister, granddaughter, grandson's wife, wife's granddaughter, niece, nephew's wife (CCH Canadian Ltd., 1981, pp. 601–02, par. 1195). The restrictions on two further categories of marriage partners — wife's niece and brother's wife — were lifted by the Canadian Parliament in 1970. The table for women corresponds exactly to that for men. The relationships set forth in the tables include those by whole or half blood, whether legitimate or illegitimate. Most provinces have incorporated the tables into their marriage acts.

For purposes of matrimonial property division and mutual support obligations, the Ontario Family Law Reform Act of 1978 actually uses *two* definitions of spouse: for the first part of the law, which deals with family property, "spouse" refers to the legally married partner of a person; for the second part, which deals with support obligations, "spouse" includes in addition a cohabitant provided the partners have either cohabited for no less than five years, or they were "in a relationship of some permanence" (but presumably less than five years) and they have a child together (Ontario: Family Law Reform Act, 1978).

For tax purposes, a family comprises individuals who can be claimed as dependants (e.g., a dependent child), legally married couples, but not common-law couples; the latter cannot claim the exemptions that are available to legally married couples. This is in direct contradiction to the family law, which gives a limited recognition to common-law couples.

For social welfare purposes, any man and woman who reside together are treated as a couple, and a woman will be disentitled from benefits because she lives with a man.

The Canadian census defines the family as a group of persons consisting

> of a husband and wife (with or without children who have never been married, regardless of age) or a parent with one or more children never married, living in the same dwelling. A family may consist, also, of a man or woman living with a guardianship child or ward under 21 years of age for whom no pay was received.[7]

An economic family, finally, is defined as a group of individuals sharing a common dwelling unit and related by blood, marriage, or adoption. It is therefore a broader definition than the census family definition, since it may include married or previously married adult children (cf. Cloutier and Smith, 1980).

No two of these definitions cover all the same people. In other words, we are not only dealing with a multiplicity of family types, but also with a multiplicity of family definitions.

At least one author has advocated to abandon "the kinship-based view of family" altogether in favour of the notion of persons "living together" (Ball, 1974:35). Others have chosen to talk primarily about "familial relationships" (c.f., e.g., The Vanier Institute of the Family, 1977) rather than about "the family." The major problem with the concept is not the noun "family," but the article "the." As soon as we put forward a conception that there is such a thing as "the" family, we are by implication ruling out other similar kinds of groupings as non-family. This is a rather arbitrary process which is, however, unfortunately frequently engaged in. Nevertheless, specificity is often needed for a clear analysis. The tack here pursued will therefore be to explicitly acknowledge that there are a great variety of different family types co-existing at the present time, and that to speak of "the" family is therefore misleading in most cases. A better usage is to speak about families in the plural, or about familial relationships where that is appropriate. For specific purposes, specific designations are called for and will be used (e.g., the divorced family, the widowed family, the remarriage family, the husband-wife family, etc.).

For a systematic discussion, however, a uniform conceptual framework is necessary. We have already noted that families vary greatly in their structure (some have children, some do not, some have a husband and wife, others do not, etc.). Families also vary greatly in terms of experiences they provide for their members, ranging from the most emotionally satisfying to the most exploitative, brutal, and frightening types of interactions. If we do not wish to start out with a categorization of families, which would be highly restrictive, an alternative approach is to identify dimensions of familial interactions.

This can be done easily by reconceptualizing those aspects of families which were presented as universally applicable *functions* of families in the first three definitions cited in this chapter as *dimensions* of familial interactions.

Dimensions of Familial Interactions[8]

For our purposes, the most important dimensions of familial interactions are the following: the procreative dimension; the socialization dimension; the sexual dimension; the residential dimension; the economic dimension; the emotional dimension.

It must be noted that this is not an exhaustive list. One extremely important dimension which is not included is the legal dimension. The reason for ignoring it here is that it cross-cuts all other dimensions. Besides, it represents an extraneous factor, while the other dimensions are largely internal to a family system.[9] The same applies to the time dimension. Other dimensions which are important but not dealt with here include a social dimension (interactions with friends, acquaintances, etc.) and a religious and ethical dimension. This discussion is limited to those dimensions which are considered the most important ones.

Within each dimension, various degrees of interaction can be identified. In the following paragraphs, each dimension will be briefly described. This discussion will be followed by a schematic representation of continua of possible types of interactions within each dimension of familial interaction here considered.

Procreative dimension. Procreative interaction ranges from a couple having child(ren) with each other and only with each other, over one or both of them having child(ren) with other partners plus having child(ren) together, to their having children only with other partners or having none at all.

Socialization dimension. Interaction in the socialization dimension ranges from both parents being involved in the socialization of the children, over only one of them being involved (e.g., in the case of a divorce in which only one parent has custody and the other does not even have visitation rights), to neither of them being involved (e.g., when the child has been given up for adoption) or when there are no children to socialize.

Sexual dimension. Sexual interaction ranges from a marital couple having sex only with each other, over having sex together as well as with other partners, to having sex only with other persons or being celibate.

Residential dimension. Residential interaction ranges from all family members sharing the same residence day and night, to all or some of them living in completely separate residences, with a multiplicity of intermediate arrangements.

Economic dimension. Economic co-operation can refer to a wide variety of possible relationships. As far as familial interactions are concerned, the most important economic relationship regards support obligations and actual provision of support (i.e., a sociological rather than a legal definition of support) between family members. Economic co-operation in this sense, then, ranges from one family member being totally responsible for the support of all family members, to a family in which all members are totally economically independent (e.g., by purchasing their own food and shelter or by paying their share of any joint expenses). In between are various degrees of partial support responsibilities: for instance, one person being responsible for some but not all family members (e.g., when a husband-father provides for himself and his children, but his wife pays for her own expenses including her part of the shelter and food when shared), or one family member being only partially responsible for some other family members, such as when spouses pay their own expenses and share all expenses related to the support of children.

Emotional dimension. Emotional interaction ranges from all family members being positively emotionally involved with each other, to being negatively emotionally involved or not being emotionally involved at all. Emotional involvement may also be asymmetrical — one person may love a family member who is emotionally uninvolved or negative towards that person; (e.g., an emotionally absent parent/ spouse, an autistic child).

Schematic Representation of Dimensions of Familial Interaction

To gain a clearer view of the possible forms of familial interactions it is useful to present the various possibilities schematically.[10] Within each dimension, the types of interactions are presented in descending order of intensity, from the most intense form of interaction to the least intense form (non-interaction).

FIGURE 1.1
Dimensions of Familial Interaction

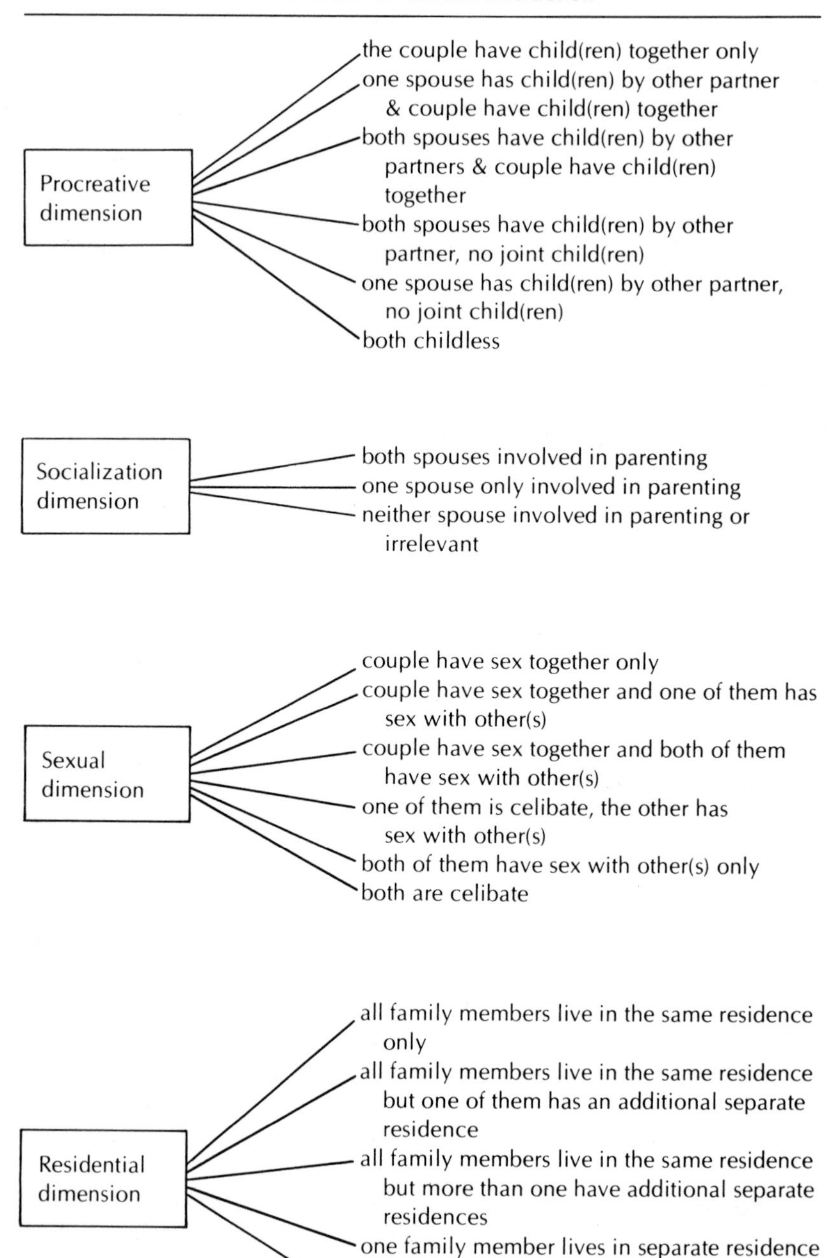

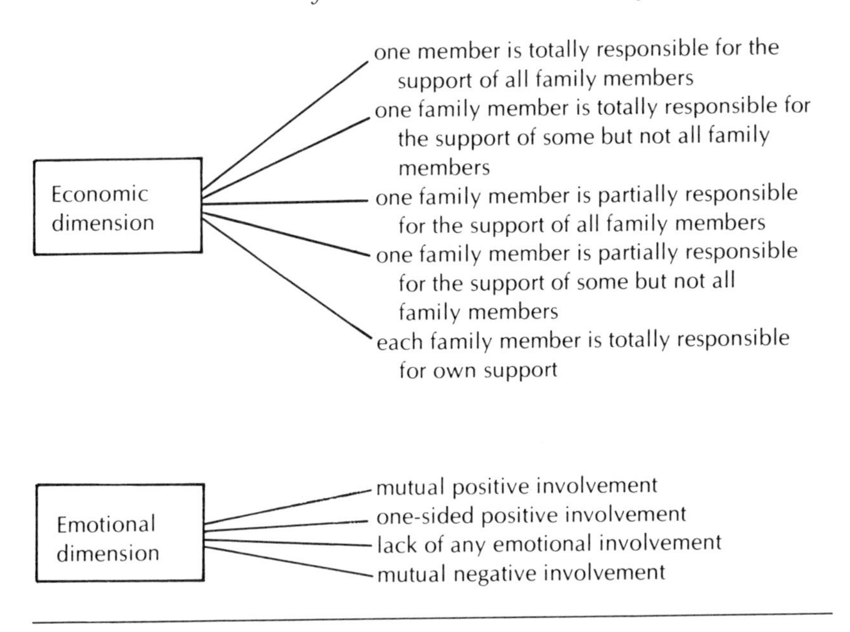

These dimensions of familial interactions, as outlined in Figure 1.1, provide us with an analytic framework within which family structures, functions, problems, and other characteristics can be meaningfully discussed. They also allow us to criticize the prevailing monolithic approach to families and to develop an alternative approach: the dimensional approach. In the following, the monolithic and the dimensional approaches to families will be formally defined, and the consequences of following either approach will be specified.

The Monolithic vs. the Dimensional[11] Approach to Families

Definition of the Monolithic and Dimensional Approaches

The monolithic approach to families is characterized by the assumption that high interaction in one dimension coincides with high interaction in all other dimensions of familial interplay. In other words, when two people are married it is assumed that either they will eventually have children together where there are none as yet, or that any children that are present are the biological children of the marital partners. It is further assumed that both parents are involved in the socialization of children, that the marital partners have sex only with each other, that all family members live in the same residence, that either one (and occasionally two) members of the family are totally responsible for the support of all family members, and that familial relations are characterized by mutual positive emotional involvement.

By contrast, the dimensional approach to families is characterized by the assumption that interaction in any of the dimensions identified can vary independently. For instance, a couple may be high in interaction in the procreative dimension (i.e., they have a child or children together) but they may be low on the socialization dimension (e.g., only one of them is involved in parenting the children). That is, while congruence between dimensions is *assumed* in the monolithic approach, this assumption is converted into an empirical question in the dimensional approach.

Consequences of a Monolithic vs. a Dimensional Approach to Families

Consequences of the monolithic versus the dimensional approach can be summarized as follows: The monolithic approach makes (1) an assumption of congruence which leads to (2) a bias in the data collection process, which leads to (3) an underestimation of the incidence of non-congruence and (4) inappropriate categorizations, which in turn, lead to (5) a misidentification of what constitutes "problem" families, and inappropriate questions.

By contrast the dimensional approach (1) examines empirically the degree of congruence and incongruence concerning the various dimensions, thereby (2) uncovering the prevailing bias in data collection and (3) the resulting underestimation of non-congruence. It leads further to (4) a critical examination of currently accepted categorizations and an attempt to develop more appropriate ones, (5) a redefinition of what constitutes a "problem" family, and the re-posing of questions.

For the rest of this chapter, we will outline each of the consequences of both approaches in broad strokes.

Assumption of Congruence vs. Empirical Examination of Degree of Congruence or Incongruence

An assumption of congruence takes two forms: either we assume we know about interaction in all dimensions here specified simply because a couple is married, or else we assume that because there is high interaction in one dimension there must also be high interaction in the other dimensions. An examination of non-congruence therefore also takes two forms: either an examination of the degree to which married couples do *not* exhibit a high degree of interaction in any of the dimensions here specified, or an examination of the degree to which high interaction in one dimension (e.g., the procreative or sexual dimension) is or is not associated with a high degree of interaction in any of the other dimensions (irrespective of marital status).

In order to streamline the discussion here we will focus only on the first type of congruence or incongruence. Chapter 7 will be devoted exclusively to the most important manifestation of the second type of incongruence, namely a discrepancy between spousal and parental roles, which implies a non-congruence between the socialization and the procreative and residential dimensions. The discussion here will be quite brief, since many of the points will be picked up later in more detail.

Familial interaction in the emotional dimension. Perhaps the most pervasive (and probably the most dangerous) assumption regarding familial interaction concerns the emotional dimension. There is a general notion that family members provide love and emotional support for each other. The family is characterized as a "haven in a heartless world" (Lasch, 1977), although seen as under increasing attack from outside agencies which have significantly eroded its capacity to function as a refuge. Duberman (1977:21), for example, argues that the present-day family in the United States "provides a setting in which the individual can freely express personality needs and expect to receive understanding, consideration, and love." A recent Ontario policy report makes an assumption that "the" family shields its members "from physical harm, whether from natural phenomena or human violence" and satisfies the "emotional needs in family members through the provision of love, services, resources and time" (Ontario, 1979:9–10).

Unfortunately, this is a romantic view of the family which often does not correspond to reality. Violence is a sad truth in many families, and negating its existence makes the lot of those who are assaulted by their husbands or fathers or other family members even worse. Most of the spousal violence that takes place within families is wife battering, rather than husband battering. A recent study found that of all the cases in the Family Court of the City of Toronto dealing with adults in 1979, 54 percent dealt with spousal violence, and of those cases, 95 percent were cases of wife battering, rather than husband battering, and that furthermore where there was an assault on a husband by a wife, this tended to be less severe — but also to be more severely dealt with in the court — than a case of a wife assaulted by her husband (Kincaid, 1981: Chapter 6).

In order to assess to what degree sociology textbooks on the family discuss the possibility of violence within families, a quick survey of eighteen recent family texts (all of them either first published or republished in the 1970s) was conducted.[12] Of the eighteen texts,[13] only three mention violence in any form at all. Blood (1972) briefly discusses the possibility of physical abuse under the heading of conflict resolution[14] and associates violence strongly with lack of education. "The violent quarrels, which are also heavily concentrated among the poorly educated people might be labelled a physical form of attack on the spouse or on dishes and other smashables" (Blood, 1972:78–79).

Reiss (1980:244--246) has a one and a half page discussion on "Violence and Marriage" which treats marital violence as a generic issue.[15] Lastly, Folkman and Clatworthy (1972:346–347) discuss the "battered child syndrome" under the heading of "the unwanted child."

All other authors indicated no reference to any form of familial violence whatsoever in either the table of contents or the index.[16] It seems no exaggeration to state that, by and large, violence within families is not dealt with in our textbooks.

Once we free ourselves from the assumption deriving from a monolithic approach to family studies that all family members interact in a positive emotional manner with each other, we are left with an empirical question as to the type of emotional interaction between family members. There is no doubt that in the best of cases families do all the things they are supposed to do: they provide emotional sustenance, shelter their members from the effects of unfriendly institutions, provide emotional intimacy, closeness, security, love. However, unfortunately, there is also no doubt that much too often, far from being a haven of security and love, they constitute a brutal, exploitative environment in which the worst forms of physical and emotional intimidation and abuse take place.

Steinmetz and Straus (1974:3) argue that "it would be hard to find a group or institution in American society in which violence is more of an everyday occurrence than it is within the family." A recent Canadian study estimates that "Every year, one in ten Canadian women who are married or in a relationship with a live-in lover are battered" (McLeod, 1980:21).

There is no indication that physical violence between spouses is limited to the poorly educated, as suggested by Blood (see Kincaid, 1981). It apparently cross-cuts all strata of society, although physical abuse among the lower strata is more likely to come to the attention of the relevant authorities and therefore there is a tendency to associate family violence with these groups.

Another form of familial violence is child abuse. One relevant U.S. estimate shows that as much as one-third of the population may experience some form of childhood sexual abuse (reported in MacFarlane, 1978:86). The 1978 Ontario Report of the Task Force on Child Abuse starts out with the observation, "It is impossible to avoid the conclusion that the present arrangement of services are not effective in protecting children from child abuse."

Overall, then, there is no doubt that emotional relationships between family members run the entire gamut from the most tender, emotionally satisfying, positive involvements to the most frightening, abusive, physically and mentally harmful relationships.

So far, we have dealt only with one dimension of familial interaction, the emotional one. Similar points can be made for all other dimensions.

Familial interactions in the procreative and socialization dimensions. The procreative and socialization dimensions are here dealt with together because several of the assumptions made in the monolithic approach stretch across both dimensions.

According to the monolithic approach, a married couple is expected to desire and eventually have children together. Where there are already children in a family, another assumption is that both parents are equally involved in the socialization process. There is, however, a conflicting assumption which co-exists: that the mother is (and should be) more involved in the socialization of the children than the father. The solution for reconciling these two conflicting assumptions is found by postulating that the roles fathers and mothers play in the socialization of the children are equally important, but fundamentally different: the father provides the male role model through his breadwinning function (here we have entered into the economic dimension) while the mother does everything else.

Out of the assumption that parents are equally (although in different ways) involved in the socialization of their children comes another assumption: namely that any children who live with a married couple are the biological children of both these marital partners, and that, by consequence, any children who do not live with a married couple, are not the biological children of either of these partners.

The dimensional approach, by contrast, converts all these assumptions into empirical questions. The widespread assumption that married couples must necessarily want to have children has been identified as "pro-natalist pressure" (Veevers, 1979). The involvement of parents in the socialization process is seen as ranging potentially from the involvement of both to non-interaction for one or both of the parents. In one of the few studies which has been conducted which questions the degree of involvement of parents in the socialization of their children, Cohen (1977) found a set of families in Britain which were structurally intact, but in which the fathers were, in effect, absent most of the time, and only minimally involved in socializing their children. Such questioning involves the recognition that earning money is an economic activity, *not* a socialization activity, and that fathers who act merely as breadwinners contribute to the family economically, but not, by virtue of their breadwinning, to the socialization of the children.

Finally, the assumption that any children present are biological children of a couple mixes the residential with the procreative and socialization dimension. It is increasingly untrue that children live with both their parents, due to the increase in divorces and remarriages. For the United States, it has been estimated that approximately 45 percent of the children born in the mid-70s will, before they reach age 18, have lived in a one-parent household (U.S. Department of Commerce, 1979:3). To put this figure into historical perspective, it is instructive to look at some past figures for marital disruption. Bane (1979:279) has calculated the percentage of children experiencing some form of marital disruption before the age of 18 in the period from 1910 to 1960. Taking all cases of disruption together, she found that in the decade of 1901 to 1910, 28.9 percent of all children in the U.S. experienced a marital disruption before they had reached the age of 18, as compared to 24.7 percent in the decade 1951–1960. In other words, between 1901 to 1960 the experience of marital disruption actually *decreased*, but even at its lowest point still a quarter of all children in the U.S. experienced a marital disruption before they had reached age 18. This rather striking fact is, of course, explained by changes in mortality rates. While the most important reason for marital disruption in the 1901–1910 decade was death of a parent (22.6 percent out of a total of 28.9 percent), in the 1951--1960 decade death of father or mother accounted for only 8.6 percent (out of a total of 24.7 percent) of all cases.[17] The largest amount of the difference is made up by rising divorce figures.

Unfortunately, no comparable Canadian statistics are available. While Canadian divorce rates are considerably lower than American divorce rates, it can reasonably be expected that marital disruption as experienced by children due to the death of a parent would be comparable for the two countries.

Neither should we assume that a parent, simply because he (occasionally she) is divorced and not sharing a residence with his (or her) children, is not involved in their socialization. Ahrons (1980), interviewing forty-one divorced parents with joint custody arrangements, found that about half of her sample reported that they were more involved with their children at the time of the interview than either at the time of separation or in the marriage prior to the time when they were considering divorce. Other parents, on the other hand, reported lesser involvement.

Jacobson (1978:357) examined the amount of time spent by parents with their children after separation. "Experience for the child can range from massive loss of the father to no loss at all. In most situations studied, children had contact with both parents at the time of the interview.[18] In eight cases,[19] fathers were reported to spend the same or more time with their children after the marital separation."

Finally, Dominic and Schlesinger (1980), interviewing nine "weekend fathers" found that they all stated that the quality of time spent with their children had improved since the separation.

Obviously, then, the assumptions deriving from the monolithic approach need to be empirically investigated rather than accepted at face value.

Familial interaction in the sexual dimension. According to the monolithic model, marital couples have sex only with each other. In fact, there is, of course, a high amount of extra- and non-marital sexual activity, although studies tend to be none too reliable, due to the prevalence of convenience samples. In one representative Canadian study, conducted in 1976 and containing probably the most accurate information on sexual behavior in Canada at that time, it was found that 4 percent of married men and 2.7 percent of married women never had coitus (Report of the Committee on the Operation of the Abortion Law, 1977: 329 and 331). Since it is unclear who the sexual partners of the sexually active population were, according to this survey a minimum of 4 percent of Canadian couples had no sexual relations together, but potentially the figure might be much higher. Again, rather than making assumptions about behaviour, it seems appropriate to investigate the behaviour instead.

Familial interaction in the residential dimension. According to the monolithic approach, we would expect all members of a nuclear family — husband, wife, and dependent children — to live in one residence. Turning this assumption into a question — In how many families do all family members share a residence all the time? — we find no representative data, but bits of information that suggest that there may be more discrepancies than are usually suggested in the literature. There are at least four categories of families which exhibit different types of residential patterns.

We have already touched on the discrepancies between the procreative, socialization, and residential dimensions in one of the previous sections. Children who visit their non-custodial parent regularly (or who are parented in turn by both their divorced parents in a situation of joint custody) are likely to have two residences. Even though *legally* they may have only one residence (with their custodial parent) if they have a room with their other parent and regularly spend time there, this should be regarded as a secondary residence.

Second, substantial numbers of people are regularly taken away from their primary residence due to requirements of their jobs; for example, people in the long distance transportation business, seasonal workers in remote areas, (loggers in logging camps), and others.

Third, there are a minority of couples who maintain two regular residences and both or one of them regularly commute (see, for example, Ngai, 1974, and Gross, 1980). However, figures on the frequency of this type of arrangement are unavailable.

Lastly, there is one other variation within the residential dimension that is not usually regarded as such but probably should be: children who attend some form of day care centre or who are taken care of in somebody else's home. These children do not have unrestricted access to their primary residence, their home, during the time in which they are being cared for by a day care worker outside of their home. While adults and school-age children may also spend considerable portions of time out of their home and residence, there is one crucial difference between these absences: adults and school-age children spend time away from their homes because of extrinsic reasons (school, work, amusement, etc.) which pull them from the home, while day care children are pushed out of the home because there is nobody to take care of them during certain times of the day. Since children eat, play, and normally sleep at their place of day care, it seems meaningful to conceptualize their day care place as a second residence for them.

In addition, there are the children who attend boarding school and family members who for some reason or other live (for an extended or shorter period of time) in some sort of institution. Overall, again, it seems appropriate to convert an assumption of co-residence into a question about the various types of residential living arrangements that can be found.

Familial interaction in the economic dimension. With respect to the economic dimension, finally, there is a growing awareness that we are shifting from a situation in which *one* family member tended to be formally responsible for the economic well-being of all other family members to one where *two* members are formally responsible. This is, however, very imperfectly integrated into the family literature as a whole. In this particular dimension, therefore, it is not so much the fact of a shift in economic co-operation which has gone unnoticed, but rather the lack of integration of the change into our overall understanding of families.

So far, we have only looked at one consequence of using a monolithic approach to families, namely the tendency to make an assumption that for a married couple interaction in all dimensions of familial interaction here considered will always be at the highest level, and that furthermore there is congruence between the levels of interaction across the various dimensions. By converting these assumptions into questions (using the dimensional approach), it can be seen that they are unwarranted.

Another consequence of using a monolithic approach is a bias in the data collection process.

Bias in Data Collection

It has already been noted several times that exact information of the type necessary for a dimensional approach to familial interaction is not presently available. For instance, with respect to the residential dimension, Kirschner and Walum (1978:514) have noted that due to the U.S. Bureau of Census 1970 definition of a married couple as a "husband and wife enumerated as members of the same household," "it is impossible to find out the incidence of two-location families." The same holds true for families in Canada. People are listed as living in one residence only, and if family members do not live in the same residence, they are not counted as family, since according to the census definition quoted above, a census family consists of family members *living in the same dwelling*.

The same problem is operative with respect to all other dimensions. For instance, with respect to the emotional dimension, the Report of the Standing Senate Committee on Health, Welfare and Science, *Child at Risk* (1980:38, par. 97) notes: "The extent of the problem is not known. Many cases are never detected. Many of those noticed are not reported. It is therefore impossible to find accurate statistics of child abuse." Van Stolk (1975:213) likewise states: "Statistically, in most provinces and states, the battered child hardly exists."

The same is true for incest and wife battering. There has so far never been a representative study on the prevalence of these crimes, so that we are left with shaky estimates as our best basis for information.

As far as discrepancies between the procreative, residential, and socialization dimensions are concerned, the most basic information is simply not being collected. For instance, our vital statistics on marriage do record previous civil status, so that we can figure out how many brides and bridegrooms were previously married, but they do not collect information on parental status, which would allow us to deduce how many children live with a biological parent and her or his new spouse. Overall, there is at present in Canada no accurate data source for finding out how many children do not live with both their biological parents. (This question will be dealt with in detail in Chapter 7.)

With respect to the socialization dimension alone, we do not know in what proportion of families both the parents are actively involved in the socialization of their children, and in how many families it is carried out by one parent (and occasionally by neither). Nor do we know in how many families in which the parents do not live together the children are nevertheless socialized by both of them.

With respect to behaviour in the sexual dimension, again, our knowledge is most sketchy. What we need is a representative survey of the entire range of sexual behaviour, including such aspects as incest. This does not, at present, exist.

Comparatively speaking, the best data are available for the economic dimension, and even here they are sketchy because either respondents tend to be treated as individuals only, irrespective of their family status, or the income is treated as "family income" irrespective of whether it is generated by one, two, or more earners. Either way, the available information does not easily lend itself to an understanding of familial interactions in this area. Nor do we have any solid information on how money decisions within families are made, and on what type of purchases money is spent by type and number of income earners. (See Chapter 6 for a discussion of this issue.)

Overall, then, the assumption of congruence that stems from a monolithic conception of the family leads to a bias in data collection. By contrast, once we start taking a dimensional approach, new questions become possible. The posing of the questions is comparatively simple; the answering of them is, at present, often impossible, because the data are *not* available. First, we must free ourselves of the conception of congruence in degree of interaction in dimensions of familial interaction; then we can pose new questions, and eventually, new answers will emerge.

The bias in data collection leads directly to an underestimation of the degree of non-congruence.

Underestimation of non-congruence. By its very nature, the process of underestimation of a phenomenon can only be demonstrated when it is at least partially overcome. It will be impossible to demonstrate the degree to which we underestimate the existence of variations in residential patterns, for example, until we begin collecting this information on some systematic basis.

Of the examples of non-congruence cited already, violence among family members has recently received some attention in a number of American and other studies. It is now obvious that it is a very widespread phenomenon that may affect, in some form or other (wife battering, husband battering, child battering, parent battering, incest with minors, physical violence, emotional violence, etc.), a very substantial proportion of families — possibly as many as half. Until the early 1970s, when the first books on this issue appeared, the assumption was that any of the forms of violence among family members was a very rare and deviant occurrence of little general applicability, since it only happened among socially marginal people. In this way, the monolithic image can be perpetuated — if we do not question the assumptions, they continue to be accepted as true.

We have already seen that only very sketchy information on possible non-congruities is currently available. At a minimum, however, we can avoid the trap of assuming that just because a non-congruity is not yet well documented, it does not exist. Empirically documenting the degree of congruity and non-congruity within and between dimensions must currently be seen as one of the more important tasks that needs to be done in the area of family studies. Prior to being able to do so, however, we must recognize that the way in which we currently categorize families is, in some cases, detrimental to observing non-congruities. In the following, we will briefly consider four concepts which are particularly problematic.

Inappropriate Categorizations

Most of the categorizations of families currently in use refer to some aspect of the organizational structure of a family; for example, husband-wife family, nuclear family, intact family, unbroken family, complete family (all referring to husband, wife, and children), extended family (referring to a family involving more relatives than those constituting a nuclear family), single-parent, one-parent, or lone-parent family (referring to a family where one parent has custody of his or her children who live with this parent), the uncompleted family unit (referring to an unwed mother and her child[ren]), the reconstituted family (involving at least one spouse who was previously married and divorced), and so on. Where families deviate from the organizational structure of a nuclear or extended family, they are usually considered under the heading of "family disorganization." Eshleman (1978:619–658), for one, discusses in a chapter on "Marital Crisis: Disorganization and Reorganization" primarily divorce and remarriage. This seems a rather typical approach.

Here, we will only briefly discuss four particularly important concepts: the husband-wife family, the one-parent family, the head of household, and family income.

The concept of the husband-wife family. The husband-wife family refers to one in which a husband and wife are living in the same household, with or without children. In principle (and in contrast to the other three concepts to be considered shortly), there is nothing wrong with the concept whatsoever, as long as we simply take it for what it is, namely a structural description of *one* aspect of a family structure. It is only in its use that the concept becomes problematic.

On the one hand, the concept of the husband-wife family makes no distinction between marriages which are first marriages or subsequent marriages for one or both partners, and depending on the context, this may inappropriately suggest that there are no great structural differences between different types of husband-wife families, when in fact remarriage is an extremely important variable.

Secondly, and more importantly, since families are for statistical purposes rarely if ever classified on the basis of parental relationships, this concept does not allow us to differentiate between families in which children are the children of both husband and wife, and families in which they are the children of only one of the marital partners. It is in this context that the concept becomes particularly troubling. The concept of the husband-wife family is a correlate to the concept of the one-parent family, and the latter is commonly associated with problems while the former is commonly seen as unproblematic.

Were we to classify families not only on the basis of the relationships between adults, but also on the basis of relationships between adults and children, we might be able to estimate better how many children in Canada are currently not living together with both their parents in the same household. The concept of the husband-wife family obfuscates this issue when it is used as the major categorization for families, to be compared to the number of one-parent families, which is, of course, a much more problematic concept.

The concept of the one-parent family. While there is nothing wrong with the concept of the husband-wife family *per se*, and problems emerge only through the overextended use of the concept, the concept of the one-parent (or lone-parent or single-parent) family is in and of itself inappropriate.

A so-called one-parent family may come into being by several different avenues: through an unmarried woman giving birth to a child whom she raises herself; through a single person adopting a child; through a two-parent family being split through separation, divorce, desertion, or death, It is thus a concept that covers a fairly wide range of situations. What is important in our context is that only a few of them refer to situations in which we are dealing with a true one-parent family situation, namely, one in which one parent is truly absent, and these are: birth of a child to an unmarried woman when the father is unknown (e.g., conceived through artificial donor insemination) or unreachable (e.g., a soldier who has returned to his native country); death of one parent; adoption of a child by a single adult; or desertion of a family by one parent such that his or her whereabouts are unknown. All other cases of so-called one-parent families involve, in fact, two parents. However, they do not conform to the monolithic model of a family in that one of the parents does not share a residence with the rest of the family, presumably does not have regular sexual relations with the other parent, most likely has only partial responsibility for the economic well-being of the other family members which he or she may or may not choose to fulfill, and usually is not legally married to the other parent. In other words, the parents exhibit low interaction in all dimensions except for the procreative one, and as a consequence, they are often treated in the literature as if they also had low or no interaction in the socialization dimension — which may or may not be true.

As a consequence of identifying families in which only one parent has custody as "one-parent families" we do not know how many divorced or unmarried parents manage to maintain a close input into the socialization dimension. We will only be able to investigate this question when we redefine families with divorced and unmarried persons as just that, without making the assumption that a cessation or absence of spousal roles must necessarily imply a total withdrawal of one parent from the socialization of the children. Conversely, according to a recent time budget study, fathers in one-job husband-wife families spent an average of six minutes per workday on child-care (Meissner et al., 1975:434, Table iv). The degree to which fathers in so-called two-parent families actually do participate in the socialization process of their children must therefore likewise be regarded as an open question. Upon investigation, it might turn out that many so-called two-parent, unbroken, intact, complete families are, in fact, broken or incomplete one-parent families as far as the socialization dimension is concerned.

The concept becomes particularly important in its unfortunate policy connotations. By officially classifying families in which the parents do not live together as one-parent families, even though two parents are alive and potentially available to look after the children, policies tend to focus on the custodial parent only and to completely neglect the non-custodial parent. Instead of trying to integrate the absent parent to the greatest degree possible into the socialization of the children, they usually treat the individual as a non-parent, merely because there is no marriage between this parent and the custodial parent. How this practice is currently carried on will be further considered in the chapters on legal and governmental practices (Chapters 9 and 10, respectively).

The neglect of seeing divorced fathers as parents is carried over into the data collection process. We may recognize an incongruity between the procreative and socialization dimensions in the case of a man who has married a divorced mother, but we tend to forget that the reverse incongruity exists for the biological father, since we have previously defined him as a "non-father." The same applies, although to a much lesser degree, to non-custodial mothers.

Recognizing the limitations of the one-parent family concept, Jacobson (1978:342) explicitly rejects the use of the term one-parent family "as marital separation of parents does not automatically imply that only one parent is available to the child." (One may add that neither does marital stability automatically imply that two parents are available to the child.) In order to overcome this problem, Levitin (1979) and Weiss (1979) both use the term single-parent household instead. While this is better, I prefer the term *one-parent household*, since single usually means "never married" — which may or may not be the case in a one-parent household.

The concept of the head of household. Another miscategorization which is derived from the monolithic model of the family is the concept of "head of household" which is automatically given to the father-husband of every family or to the mother when an adult male is absent. This term derives from the economic dimension of the monolithic family model according to which one adult — normally the father-husband — is totally responsible for the economic support of his family. In fact, however, husband-fathers are no longer solely legally, socially, or economically responsible for their families. Instead, this responsibility is increasingly shared by spouses. To continue to use this term, therefore, distorts actual economic and legal relationships.

In its last census, Statistics Canada no longer employed the concept of head of household. However, the use of the term is still widespread, and should be wholly discarded except where it provides an accurate description of actual economic, legal, and social relationships.

The concept of family income. As in the case of the last two examples, the concept of family income in most instances misrepresents actual circumstances. The majority of income in Canada is *not* family income, but is, instead, income of individuals who tend to be members of families. An exception is the child tax credit, which is based on the notion of family income, although it is payable to an individual (the mother).

"Family income," then, refers mostly to the sum of all incomes of members of the same family (family here being usually restricted to those family members who share the same household). It is important to realize that this is not identical with income that accrues to the family as a unit, since individual income is under the control of the income earner. Economists *assume* that income that is paid to one family member benefits all family members, but this remains an assumption. While in many cases it is probably a correct assumption, in others it is likely inappropriate. It tells us nothing about who disposes of income for what purposes, since information on how money within families is spent is exceedingly sparse (cf. Gagné, 1980). Although most provinces now allocate some aspect of matrimonial property to both spouses in the case of marriage breakdown (Huddart, 1981), nevertheless, this does not entitle the spouse or other family members to spend so-called "family income" on family assets or needs against the wishes of the income recipient.

As an indicator of societal income disparities, or as an indicator of access to income of individual family members, family income as a variable is not particularly useful (Eichler, 1980).

Miscategorizations are problematic in as far as they draw misleading boundaries around phenomena which would better be classified according to different criteria. Within the sociology of families, one consequence of prevalent miscategorizations is an ensuing misidentification of what constitutes "problem families."

Misidentification of "Problem Families"

There is a general agreement within the literature that so-called one-parent families experience special problems. Although Schlesinger (1979:vi) argues that this group of families should not be viewed as a "problem" and that "It would be a disaster if we should seem to endorse any notion that the one-parent family is an oddity, that it presents a special problem per se, or that members of one-parent families constitute a group to be looked down upon," he identifies problems which these families normally have, namely prejudice on the part of landlords and employers, loneliness, social isolation, and the absence of adult male models for boys in fatherless homes (ibid.).

In spite of Schlesinger's disclaimer, there seems to be near unanimity that one-parent families *are* problem families, or at least are families which have special problems which need special attention. This suggests that families are perceived by the public (and by writers, policy makers, etc.) as problematic according to pre-established categories which are based on a monolithic conception of the family according to which any *visible* incongruity between the various dimensions of familial interaction is defined as problematic while other incongruities which are less easily visible or invisible (e.g., parental neglect by one parent in an "intact" family, sexual abuse of a family member) are defined as non-existent and therefore non-problematic.

Instead of using organizational criteria for identifying problem families, one could identify any family in which the physical, mental, economic, and educational well-being of all members is not safeguarded as a family with a problem. Such problems can be generated (a) extrinsic to the family system, (b) intrinsic to the family system through negative interaction patterns, and (c) intrinsic to the family system through idiosyncratic problems of individual family members. For instance, poverty is an awesome problem for all families and all individuals affected, irrespective of other factors. Poor families are, therefore, families with a problem (usually extrinsically generated), no matter what their organizational structure is. While it is true that a very high proportion of sole support mothers live in poor families, it is nevertheless also true that the numerically largest group of poor women are wives in husband-wife families (National Council of Welfare, 1979:4, Table 1). Other extrinsically generated problems include families which suffer from racial, ethnic, religious, language, or any other discrimination which is based on ascriptive criteria.

Problems which are generated within the family itself through negative interaction patterns include all types of physical, emotional, or sexual abuse of any family member, economic exploitation within a family, or the authoritarian denial of basic human rights (e.g., the right of association with people of one's choice) for any family member. Idiosyncratic problems of individual family members, finally, may include a mental or physical handicap, drug dependency (including dependency of housewives on psychotropic drugs, cf. Cooperstock, 1976), conflict of any family member with law enforcement agencies, and others. To the degree that other family members have close ties with members who have idiosyncratic problems, the entire family is affected. For instance, one hyperactive child will alter the family situation for every other member. So will the presence of a mentally retarded member, the prison sentence of a member, and so on.

By contrast, any family in which the physical, mental, economic, and educational well-being of all members is safeguarded should not be regarded as a problem family, no matter how unconventional its organizational structure may be. For instance, the exclusion of one violent family member may be a precondition to that group becoming a family without major problems. Using such a definition of problem versus non-problem family would include many more families than are presently identified as problem families (including some with sterling qualities) and would exclude some families which are currently seen as problematic.

We have seen that the monolithic model of the family which still predominates within the social sciences leads to an unwarranted assumption of congruence. This assumption generates a bias in the data collection process which, in turn, leads to an underestimation of the incidence of non-congruence and an inappropriate categorization system, which leads to a misdefinition as to what constitutes problem families. Altogether, this means that questions which are vitally important for an understanding of the structures, functions, and dynamics of different types of families in contemporary societies have been largely ignored. In this book, some (but not all) of these questions will be posed. It will often not be possible to answer the questions fully because in many cases the information is simply not available due to the still prevailing bias in the data collection process that stems from adherence to a monolithic model of the family.

Conclusion: The Epitomy of the Monolithic Approach to Families — The "Death of the Family" Argument

We started with the observation that in a period of rapid social, technological, and economic change, we cannot reasonably expect that the one institution in which the majority of people spend the major portion of their lives — the family — remain unchanged. Many of the changes affecting families that have taken place have included changes that are generally viewed in a negative manner, namely a rapid increase in the divorce rate, an increase in the number of one-parent households, and an increase in the rate of births to unwed mothers. Concern about these developments as well as the re-emergence of a small number of alternative family forms such as communes or group marriages,[20] has led to anxious questions about the continued viability of "the family." Sussman (1978) for instance, asks "The Family Today — Is It an Endangered Species?" To researchers who pose this question, the answer is usually no; the reason being remarriage.

Veevers, in discussing the question of the death of the family, calls it "the great exaggeration" and concludes:

> By and large, the Canadian family is demonstrated to be a viable and a dominant social institution, and to have remained so over the past decade. The changes that have occurred are not so much replacing the Canadian family with an alternative form as they are modifying certain aspects of the existing structure. In considering the family in terms of its future or lack of it, the gradual trends involved do not lend support to the hypothesis of its imminent demise.[21]

This line of argument hinges on identifying "the" family with a particular structure, such that changes in this structure can be perceived as a threat to the family's continued survival. The "death of the family" argument can therefore be comprehended as a result of an interaction between the monolithic and conservative biasses (the latter will be discussed in Chapter 2). A reaffirmation of the continued viability of the family follows only from downplaying the importance of the changes that have in fact occurred.

If we free ourselves from the monolithic notion that families have a particular structure and instead operate on the assumption that the structure of families is (and always has been) fluid, there is no reason to concern ourselves with the thought of the "death of the family." At the same time, there is also no need to downplay the importance of the changes that have already taken place and that continue to occur. Never before have we lived in a society in which a very substantial portion of children live in households with one parent (and potentially that parent's new spouse) while the other parent lives in a different household. This is truly a *new* phenomenon, as yet uncharted in its social implications. This does not mean that family disruption is a new phenomenon — it emphatically is not — but the reasons have shifted from death to divorce, thus changing its consequences.

Likewise, we have never before lived in a society in which the majority of wives earn an income independent from their husbands. Never before have so many marriages ended in divorce and have so many newlyweds been previously married (and a second marriage cannot be assumed to be the same as a first marriage).

In short, then, families are currently in a process of transition that can be expected to continue for another generation since many of these changes at present involve the middle aged, and patterns of familial interactions for the young are still in the process of emerging. These changes are touching the very basis of our definitions of self and others. We have neither fully understood what the changes are, nor have we sufficiently tried to describe and analyze them and to try to look at some of their implications for individual members of families and policy makers. Working towards an understanding of some of the contemporary changes seems to be the most appropriate response to the situation.

Notes

1. George Peter Murdock, *Social Structure* (New York: Macmillan, 1949), p. 1.
2. From *The Family: Its Structure and Functions*, 2nd ed. by Rose Laub Coser © 1974 reprinted by permission of St. Martin's Press, Incorporated, p. xvi.
3. William N. Stephens, *The Family in Cross Cultural Perspective* (New York: Holt, Rinehart and Winston, 1963), p. 5. For instance, Nett (1979: 60) draws on this definition.
4. Ibid., p. 4.
5. For a discussion of some of the difficulties attached to this concept, see onward.
6. A short discussion of sexual interaction between marriage partners follows.
7. Jean E. Veevers, *The Family in Canada*, 1971 Census of Canada, Vol. 5, Part 3, Catalogue 99–725, bulletin 5.3–3 (Ottawa: Minister of Supply and Services, 1977), p. 3.
8. This section of the chapter relies on ideas developed in a previous publication. See Eichler, 1981.
9. In Eichler, 1981 the legal dimension was included.
10. It should be noted that only structural variations are considered here. There are

several other factors that influence interaction in each of the dimensions specified that have been excluded from consideration, such as volitional factors: a couple may *wish* to reside together, but circumstances (the economic situation, a prison term) may make this impossible, or they way *wish* to have children together, but one or both of them is/are sterile, etc. Here, we are only concerned with outcomes.

11. I have chosen the term "dimensional" rather than "interactional" in order to distinguish this approach from the interactional approach as outlined, for example, by Schvaneveldt (1981).
12. This survey was performed by Linda Yanz while she worked as my research assistant.
13. The selection criteria were the following: the book had to be a text (not edited) and had to have been published or republished in the 1970s. It had to have an index and a table of contents. In order to locate suitable texts, the stacks in the Robarts Library in Toronto were searched. In addition, the book review sections of the *Journal of Marriage and the Family* for 1973–1979 inclusive were screened and possible texts were noted. If they were available in the Robarts Library and met the other criteria, they were added to the list. The list thus generated consisted of Aldous, 1978; Blood, 1972; Eshelman, 1974; Folkman and Clatworthy, 1972; Kantor and Lehr, 1975; Kenkel, 1973; Klemer, 1970; Lee, 1977; Leslie, 1976; Martinson, 1970; Reiss, 1980; Rice, 1979; Rodgers, 1973; Schulz, 1972; Schulz and Rogers, 1975; Weil, 1971; Winch, 1971; Yorburg, 1973.
14. It is indicative of the general approach to this issue that physical violence among family members can be discussed under the heading of conflict *resolution*. For the wife or child who is being beaten the beating is hardly a resolution of a conflict — it *is* the problem.
15. In all fairness, however, it must be noted that the studies cited by Reiss were not available at the time when Blood wrote his book.
16. The words checked in both the table of contents and the index were: abuse, aggression, battering, beating, child beating, wife beating, and violence. In addition, all sections referring to "problems" or "crises" were checked to see whether any of them mentioned any form of familial violence.
17. Bane (1979:280) has noted that the marital disruption in the earlier cohorts is probably underestimated, due to the nature of the sampling design.
18. The interviews were conducted with children who had experienced marital disruption during the preceding twelve-month period.
19. Out of a total of thirty cases.
20. It should be noted that North America has a long and healthy tradition of alternative family forms, including the Hutterites and Mennonites.
21. From *The Family in Canada*, Census 1971, Volume 5, Part 3, catalogue number 99–725, Bulletin 5.3–3. Reproduced by permission of the Minister of Supply and Services Canada.

References

Ahrons, Constance R., "Joint Custody in the Postdivorce Family," *Journal of Divorce*, Vol. 3, No. 3, 1980, pp. 189–205.

Aldous, Joan, *Family Careers: Developmental Change in Families*. New York: John Wiley and Sons, 1978.

Ball, Donald W., "The 'Family' as a Sociological Problem: Conceptualization of the Taken-for-Granted as Prologue to Social Problems Analysis," in Arlene and Jerome H. Skolnik (eds.) *Intimacy, Family and Society*. Boston: Little, Brown and Co., 1974, pp. 25–40.

Bane, Mary Jo, "Marital Disruption and the Lives of Children," in George Levinger and Oliver C. Moles (eds.) *Divorce and Separation: Context, Causes, and Consequences*. New York: Basic Books, 1979, pp. 276–286.

Blood, Robert O., *The Family*. New York: The Free Press, 1972.

CCH Canadian Ltd., *Canadian Family Law Guide*, Vol. 1, Don Mills, 1981.

Cloutier, J.E. and A.M.M. Smith, *The Evaluation of an Alternative Unemployment Insurance Plan*. Ottawa: Economic Council of Canada, 1980.

Cohen, Gaynor, "Absentee Husbands in Spiralist Families," *Journal of Marriage and the Family*, Vol. 39, No. 3, 1977, pp. 595–604.

Cooperstock, Ruth, "Psychotropic Drug Use among Women," *Canadian Medical Association Journal*, Vol. 115, 1976, pp. 760–763.

Coser, Rose Laub, *The Family: Its Structure and Functions*. New York: St. Martin's Press, 2nd ed., 1974.

Dominic, Katherine Tasios and Benjamin Schlesinger, "Weekend Fathers: Family Shadows," *Journal of Divorce*, Vol. 3, 1980, pp. 241–247.

Duberman, Lucile, *Marriage and Other Alternatives*. New York: Praeger, 2nd ed., 1977.

Eichler, Margrit, "'Family Income' — A Critique of the Concept," *Status of Women News*, Vol. 6, No. 2, 1980, pp. 20, 21, 24.

Eichler, Margrit, "The Inadequacy of the Monolithic Model of the Family," *Canadian Journal of Sociology*, Vol. 6, No. 3, 1981, pp. 367–388.

Eshelman, J. Ross, *The Family: An Introduction*. Boston: Allyn and Bacon, 1974, and 2nd ed., 1978.

Folkman, Jerome D. and Nancy M. Clatworthy, *Marriage Has Many Faces*. Columbus, OH: Charles E. Merrill Publishing Co., 1972.

Gagné, Gilles, "La Division Intra-Familial des Revenus," unpublished paper. Hull: Université du Québec, 1980.

Gross, Harriet Engel. "Dual-Career Couples Who Live Apart: Two Types", *Journal of Marriage and the Family*, Vol. 42, 1980, pp. 567–576.

Huddart, Carol Mahood, "Property Division on Marriage Breakdown in the Common Law Provinces," in Audrey Doerr and Micheline Carrier (eds.) *Women and the Constitution in Canada*, Canadian Advisory Council on the Status of Women, Ottawa: Minister of Supply and Services Canada, 1981, pp. 94–112.

Jacobson, Doris S., "The Impact of Marital Separation/Divorce on Children: I. Parent-Child Separation and Child Adjustment," *Journal of Divorce*, Vol. 1, No. 4, 1978, pp. 341–360.

Kantor, David and William Lehr, *Inside the Family. Toward a Theory of Family Process*. San Francisco: Jossey-Bass Publishers, 1975.

Kenkel, William K., *The Family in Perspective*. Santa Monica: Goodyear Publishers, 3rd ed., 1973.

Kincaid, Patricia, *The Omitted Reality: Husband-Wife Violence in Ontario and Policy Implications for Education*. Unpublished Ed.D. thesis, University of Toronto, Dept. of Educational Theory (O.I.S.E.), 1981.

Kirschner, Betty Frankle and Laurel Richardson Walum, "Two-Location Families: Married Singles," *Alternative Lifestyles*, Vol. 1, No. 4, 1978, pp. 513–525.

Klemer, Richard H., *Marriage and Family Relationships*. New York: Harper and Row, 1970.

Lasch, Christopher, *Haven in a Heartless World: The Family Besieged*. New York: Basic Books, 1977.

Leslie, Gerald R., *The Family in Social Context*. New York: Oxford University Press, 1967 and 3rd ed., 1976.

Levitin, Teresa E., "Children of Divorce: An Introduction," *Journal of Social Issues*, Vol. 35, No. 4, 1979, pp. 1–25.

Martinson, Floyd Mansfield, *Family in Society.* New York: Dodd, Mead and Co., 1970.
McFarlane, Kee, "Sexual Abuse of Children," in Jane Roberts Chapman and Margaret Gates (eds.), *The Victimization of Women.* Beverly Hills: Sage Publications, 1978, pp. 81–110.
McLeod, Linda, *Wife Battering in Canada: The Vicious Circle,* prepared for the Canadian Advisory Council on the Status of Women. Ottawa: Minister of Supply and Services Canada, 1980.
Meissner, Martin et al., "No Exit for Wives: Sexual Division of Labour and the Cumulation of Household Demands," *Canadian Review of Sociology and Anthropology,* Vol. 12, No. 4, Part I, 1975, pp. 424–439.
Murdock, George Peter, *Social Structure.* New York: Macmillan, 1949.
National Council of Welfare, *Women and Poverty.* Ottawa: National Council of Welfare, 1979.
Nett, Emily M., "Marriage and the Family: Organization and Interaction," in G.N. Ramu (ed.) *Courtship, Marriage and the Family in Canada.* Toronto: Macmillan of Canada, 1979, pp. 59–77.
Ngai, Suk Yin Agnes, "Long-Distance Commuting as a Solution to Geographical Limitation to Career Choices of Two-Career Families," unpublished M.Sc. thesis, M.I.T., 1974.
Ontario. Family Law Reform Act, 1978.
Ontario. Ministry of Community and Social Services, *Report of the Task Force on Child Abuse.* Toronto: Ministry of Community and Social Services, 1978.
Ontario. Provincial Secretary of Social Development, *The Family as a Focus for Social Policy.* Toronto: Secretary for Social Development, 1979.
Reiss, Ira, *Family Systems in America.* New York: Holt, Rinehart and Winston, 3rd ed., 1980.
Report of the Committee on the Operation of the Abortion Law, Ottawa: Minister of Supply and Services, 1977.
Report of the Standing Senate Committee on Health, Welfare and Science, *Child at Risk.* Ottawa: Minister of Supply and Services Canada, 1980.
Rice, David G., *Dual Career Marriage: Conflict and Treatment.* New York: The Free Press, 1979.
Rodgers, Roy H., *Family Interaction and Transaction: The Developmental Approach.* Englewood Cliffs, NJ: Prentice Hall, 1973.
Schlesinger, Benjamin (ed.), *One in Ten: The Single Parent in Canada.* Toronto: University of Toronto Guidance Centre, 1979.
Schulz, David, *The Changing Family: Its Function and Future.* Englewood Cliffs, NJ: Prentice-Hall, 1972.
Schulz, David A. and Stanley Rogers, *Marriage, the Family and Personal Fulfillment.* Englewood Cliffs, NJ: Prentice-Hall, 1975.
Schvaneveldt, Jay D., "The Interactional Framework in the Study of the Family," in F. Ivan Nye and Felix M. Berardo (eds.), *Emerging Conceptual Frameworks in Family Analysis.* New York: Praeger, 1981, pp. 97–129.
Steinmetz, Susanne K. and Murray A. Straus (eds.), *Violence in the Family.* New York: Dodd, Mead and Co., 1974.
Stephens, William N., *The Family in Cross Cultural Perspective.* New York: Holt, Rinehart and Winston, 1963.
Sussman, Marvin B., "The Family Today: Is It an Endangered Species?" *Children Today,* Vol. 7, No. 2, 1978, pp. 32–37, 45.
U.S. Department of Commerce, Bureau of the Census, *Divorce, Child Custody and Child Support* (Current Population Reports Special Studies Series, p. 23, No. 84). Washington: Bureau of the Census, Population Division, 1979.

Vanier Institute of the Family, *A Statement on Contemporary Familial Lifestyles*. Ottawa: Vanier Institute of the Family, 1977.

Van Stolk, Mary, "The Battered and Abused Child," in S. Parvez Wakil (ed.), *Marriage, Family and Society: Canadian Perspectives*. Toronto: Butterworth, 1975, pp. 213–222.

Veevers, Jean E., *The Family in Canada*, 1971 Census of Canada, Vol. 5, Part 3, (Catalogue 99–725, bulletin 5.3–3). Ottawa: Minister of Supply and Services, 1977.

Veevers, Jean E., "Voluntary Childlessness: A Review of Issues and Evidence," *Marriage and Family Review*, Vol. 2, No. 2, 1979, pp. 1, 3–26.

Weil, Mildred W., *Marriage, the Family and Society: Towards a Sociology of Marriage and the Family*. Danville: The Interstate Printers and Publishers, 1971.

Weiss, Robert S., "Growing Up a Little Faster: The Experience of Growing Up in a Single-Parent Household," *Journal of Social Issues*, Vol. 35, No. 4, 1979, pp. 97–111.

Winch, Robert F., *The Modern Family*. New York: Holt, Rinehart and Winston, 3rd ed., 1971.

Yorburg, Betty, *The Changing Family*. New York: Columbia University Press, 1973.

CHAPTER 2

Beyond the Conservative Bias in Family Literature

Introduction

In the preceding chapter several dimensions of familial interaction were identified, and it was argued that each of them may vary independently. The assumption that high interaction in one dimension results in high interaction in all other dimensions was identified as constituting a monolithic approach to the family. A consequence of adhering to a monolithic model of the family is a conservative bias. While there are other important biasses that will be considered later — namely a sexist and a microstructural bias — the link between the monolithic bias and the conservative bias is particularly close. We have already identified two of the consequences of using a monolithic model of the family which are also characteristic of a conservative bias: namely, ignoring, to a large degree, recent changes that have taken place in Canadian families and that have fundamentally altered the structure and functions of families (as will here be argued), and, secondly, painting a rosy image of families that largely ignores the ugly aspects of familial interactions, such as abuse, violence, and neglect. A third bias that has so far not been touched on, is the pervasive tendency to treat children as if they were merely passive members of familial systems, if they are considered at all and not simply ignored.

A conservative bias in the literature is here defined, then, as being displayed in three tendencies: (1) a tendency to regard as ephemeral recent changes affecting families that in fact constitute dramatic and fundamental changes in the structure of families and the way in which they function; (2) a tendency to either completely ignore or see as atypical deviations the ugly aspects of familial interactions such as intrafamilial violence and neglect; and (3) a tendency to either ignore children altogether, or to see them merely as objects to be acted upon, rather than as active participants in family life.

In the following, we will consider ways of overcoming this bias. The greatest emphasis will be placed on the major historical changes that have taken place in families.

Major Historical Changes Concerning Families

In the past few decades, some major historical changes have occurred (and are still in the process of occurring). The most important ones are the following four: (a) drastic changes in demographic patterns, specifically greatly reduced fertility and greatly increased longevity; (b) the industrialization of housework; (c) increased labor force participation of women; and (d) a dramatic increase in the rate of divorce.

In subsequent chapters, specific aspects of these changes will be discussed in detail. The effects of reduced fertility on childrearing patterns will be discussed in Chapter 8, the process of industrialization of housework and the organization of housework will be discussed in detail in Chapter 5, the effects of labour force participation of wives will be discussed in Chapter 6, the effects of labour force participation of mothers in Chapter 8, and the effects of divorce on spousal and parental roles will be discussed in Chapter 7. Here, the intent is to provide the broad outlines of the changes that have occurred, to place them into an international perspective, to discuss their overall significance, and to attempt some guesses towards their interconnections.

Changes in Demographic Patterns

The two most important demographic changes that concern us here are increased longevity and drastically reduced fertility. Both phenomena are world-wide trends, although taking place at very different levels depending on whether we are dealing with a developed or a developing country. For families, increased longevity and decreased fertility have a multitude of consequences. Some of these are briefly discussed here.

Increased Longevity

As stated, an increase in life expectancy is a world-wide phenomenon. In fact, there is not a single country in the world in which the number of years that a person born in that country could expect to live at the point of his or her birth did not increase between 1960 and 1978. However, the absolute difference in life expectancy is still enormous between developed and developing countries. Canada, as a highly industrialized country, has a high life expectancy which is similar to that of the Scandinavian and Western European countries, Australia and New Zealand, the U.S.A., and Japan (World Bank, 1980:150–151, t. 21).

By contrast, most developing countries have a very low life expectancy. To take only those countries with the lowest life expectancy: people born in 1978 in Ethiopia and the Arab Republic of Yemen could expect to live 39 years; those born in the same year in Bhutan and

Angola could expect to live 41 years; and those born in 1978 in the People's Republic of Lao, in Mali, in Upper Volta, Niger, Afghanistan, Mauritania, and Senegal could expect to live 42 years (World Bank, 1980:150, t. 21).

In Canada, the life expectancy for a male at birth was 69.6 years in 1976, and has been estimated to reach 70.2 years for a male at birth in 1986. For a female, life expectancy at birth in Canada was 76.9 years, and is expected to reach 78.3 years by 1986 (Canada: Statistics Canada, 1979a:21, t. 3). To compare these figures, for a male born in Canada in 1931, the life expectancy at birth was 60 years, and for a female born in that year, the life expectancy was 62.1 years. In other words, between 1931 and 1986, males will, on average, have added an estimated 10.2 years to their lives, and women will have added an estimated 16.2 years.

Increased longevity has quite different implications for old women, old men, and their middle-aged adult daughters and sons (provided they have any). As we have just seen, in general, women outlive men by about seven or eight years. One of the consequences of this simple fact is that the vast majority of men die as married men, while the vast majority of women die as widows. This is so not only because of the different life expectancies, but because the already uneven balance in years is exacerbated by a tendency of men to marry women younger than themselves, and, by implication, of women to marry men older than themselves. The effects of these two factors — longer life expectancy of women and older age of males at marriage — produce quite marked differences in marital status of older men and women. For instance, of all men aged 65 to 69 in Canada in 1976, 82.3 percent were still married, and only 7.1 percent were widowed (the rest were either never married — 9 percent — or divorced — 1.6 percent) as compared to 56 percent of the women of the same age who were still married, and with 32.7 percent of them being widowed (as well as 9.8 percent never married and 1.1 percent divorced). While this is already a very great differential, this difference in marital status by sex becomes ever more marked the higher the age range considered. When we consider only men age 80 and over, the so called "old-old," who tend to be most in need of care, we find that over half of them were still married at that age (53.2 percent) in 1976, while only 14.5 percent of the women of the same age were still married (Fletcher and Stone, 1981, t. 3.3).

In plain words, this means that the majority of men can expect to be cared for in their old age by their (younger) wives, while the women, when they reach that same age, can only rarely expect to be looked after by their husbands. It seems that this problem could only be redressed if people were to drastically change their marrying habits, with women marrying men who are approximately eight years younger than themselves, and, by implication, with men marrying women older than themselves. Were there such a change, we could expect a gradual evening out of the widowhood ratios. So far, however, there is no evidence of such a reversal of behaviour. In 1977, the average age of a never previously married bride in Canada was 22.8 years, and of a never previously married bridegroom, 25.1 years (Statistics Canada, 1979c:6, t. 3). We can therefore expect that the likelihood of women becoming widows will continue to be much greater than the likelihood of men becoming widowers.

If our economic system were different, the situation would not give quite as much reason for concern. However, unfortunately, Canada's pension system is quite inadequate, and particularly so for women. Not only do women receive significantly lower pensions than do men if they have an individual pension entitlement, (see Chapter 10 for some figures), but unfortunately many women do not have any individual pension entitlements when their husbands die, other than the universal old age pensions that government pays. As a consequence, the *majority* — 66 percent — of all widows over the age of 65 in 1975 were poor; that is, they lived at a level below the official poverty standards (National Council of Welfare, 1979:31).

Not only do people live longer *on average,* but a greater proportion of people than before live to a very old age, reaching over 80 and even over 90 years. Seen from the perspective of their adult children, their parents' longevity may be a mixed blessing. Normally, one assumes that people do not wish for their parents to die, of course. On the other hand, we are now, for the first time, confronted with a phenomenon that has never existed to the same degree before, in which people who are themselves elderly, and possibly grandparents, still have their own parents alive who most likely require care. Women around 65 years of age may thus find themselves in a demographic squeeze, in which they are expected to look after their own mother, and possibly father, or their in-laws, at a time when they probably expected to be free of the obligation of looking after other people (with the exception of looking after their husbands) (cf. Shanas, 1980). Since it seems to be the women who are doing the caring, rather than the men, a very long-lived parent may thus place a great burden on a woman who is herself no longer young. Today, older people tend to live neither with their children nor in institutions. In 1976, only 10 percent of the women aged 65 and older lived in collective dwellings and only 4 percent were inmates of institutions (Fletcher and Stone, 1982:37).

One immediate consequence of a generally higher life expectancy is that people are married for more years than they used to be, and as Ambert has pointed out, this must be seen as one factor contributing to divorce:

> The fact that people live longer means that they go through more stages of life than in the past. Life cycles used to consist of childhood and

> adulthood only; now they include young adulthood, middle age, the retirement years, and senior citizen status. Because of the diversity of personal and social situations inherent in these various stages, individuals' needs vary accordingly. Consequently, marital needs may also change so that a partner who was just right for one stage may not be so for the next one. Moreover, an increased life-span means a different philosophy of life; one which must come to terms with the realization that one may have much time left to spend in retirement with a person one may no longer love or even like.[1]

Lastly, increased longevity has implications for grandparental relationships. Theoretically, there should now be more grandparents around than there ever were before, and these same grandparents should have fewer grandchildren between them than ever before, because of the strong demographic trend towards fewer children per woman. The implications of this situation are totally unexplored. It is possible that each grandchild will receive more attention from his or her grandparents, simply because there are fewer grandchildren to share their attention. Another compounding factor for grandparental relationships is divorce. The relations between grandparents and their grandchild(ren) in cases in which their child does not have custody of their grandchild(ren) is virtually unresearched. In case of remarriage, one might hypothesize that parents of adult remarried children might be more disposed towards accepting children brought by the adult child's spouse into the marriage as their grandchildren if they have no grandchildren of their own or if they can maintain only sporadic contact with them. However, these are only speculations. Obviously, here is another fruitful and highly important area of research that has been greatly neglected so far.

Decreased Fertility

Again, we are dealing with a world-wide trend, although the trend is not quite as clear as the trend towards higher life expectancies. There are a few countries in which the birth rate did increase between 1960 and 1978; namely the People's Democratic Republic of Lao, Tanzania, Senegal, Zimbabwe, Kuwait, and Czechoslovakia. In a few other countries, it remained stable during this time period; namely in Mozambique, Rwanda, Afghanistan, the Central African Republic, Lesotho, Uganda, Kenya, Liberia, the Ivory Coast, Ireland, Israel, Saudi Arabia, and Hungary (World Bank, 1980:144–145, t.18).

Ireland is the only highly industrialized country in which the birthrate remained stable. It is also a country in which the sale of contraceptives is illegal except to *bona fide* married couples upon a prescription filled out by a physician (Irish Republic, 1980). All other highly industrialized countries experienced a rapid decline in fertility, as can be seen from Table 2.1.

TABLE 2.1

Changes in Fertility Rates from 1960 to 1979 in Selected Industrialized Countries

Country	Crude Birth Rate per 1000 Population 1960	1979	Percentage Change in Crude Birth Rate 1960–1979	Total Fertility Rate 1979
Ireland	22	21	− 1.9	3.3
Italy	18	14	−27.0	2.0
New Zealand	26	18	−31.0	2.2
United Kingdom	17	12	−29.1	1.8
Finland	19	14	−26.6	1.7
Austria	18	12	−32.0	1.7
Japan	18	15	−17.6	1.8
Australia	22	17	−24.8	2.1
France	18	14	−23.1	1.9
Netherlands	21	13	−38.9	1.6
Belgium	17	13	−25.1	1.8
Canada	27	17	−36.9	1.9
Norway	18	13	−24.9	1.9
Federal Republic of Germany	17	10	−40.2	1.5
United States	24	17	−29.8	1.9
Denmark	17	13	−24.9	1.8
Sweden	15	12	−20.0	1.7
Switzerland	18	12	−34.8	1.6

Source: World Bank: World Development Report, 1981, (New York: Oxford University Press, 1981), t. 18, pp. 168–169. Reprinted by permission.

Note: Countries are listed in ascending order of income per capita.

Crude birth rate = the number of live births per thousand population in a year.

Total fertility rate = the number of children that would be born per woman, if she were to live to the end of her childbearing years and bear children at each age in accord with prevailing age-specific fertility rates.

World-wide, there is a clear relationship between poverty and fertility, with poorer people in general having more children, and richer people having fewer children.

In Canada, fertility is at an all-time low. So far, it has dropped more or less steadily since the 1960s, although one would expect that this trend would in the near future either level off or even modestly reverse itself. The drop in fertility has not meant, so far, that fewer women have children, but that each woman has on average fewer children than before. Whereas in 1960 about 3.9 children were the norm, by 1980 this had decreased to about 1.7 children per woman. This can be seen in Table 2.2 by looking at the total fertility rate.

TABLE 2.2

Age-specific Fertility Rates, Canada 1960–1980

Year	Fertility rates per 1000 women, by age groups							Total fertility rate	Gross reproduction rate	General fertility rate
	15–19	20–24	25–29	30–34	35–39	40–44	45–49			
1960	59.8	233.5	224.4	146.2	84.2	28.5	2.4	3,895	1.893	114.1
1961	58.2	233.6	219.2	144.9	81.1	28.5	2.4	3,840	1.868	111.5
1962	55.0	231.6	214.6	143.1	77.1	27.6	2.1	3,756	1.830	108.3
1963	53.1	226.0	210.6	140.3	75.8	25.9	2.1	3,669	1.788	105.3
1964	50.2	212.8	203.1	134.9	72.0	25.1	2.1	3,502	1.702	100.2
1965	49.3	188.6	181.9	119.4	65.9	22.0	2.0	3,145	1.529	90.3
1966	48.2	169.1	163.5	103.3	57.5	19.1	1.7	2,812	1.369	81.5
1967	45.2	161.4	152.6	91.8	50.9	15.9	1.5	2,597	1.267	76.1
1968	43.0	152.6	148.7	86.3	44.8	13.8	1.4	2,453	1.190	72.9
1969	42.2	147.7	149.8	85.0	42.6	12.5	1.1	2,405	1.170	72.3
1970	42.8	143.3	147.2	81.8	39.0	11.3	0.9	2,331	1.132	71.2
1971	40.1	134.4	142.0	77.3	33.6	9.4	0.6	2,187	1.060	67.7
1972	38.5	119.8	137.1	72.1	28.9	7.8	0.6	2,024	0.982	63.4
1973	37.2	117.7	131.6	67.1	25.7	6.4	0.4	1,931	0.937	61.5
1974	35.3	113.1	131.1	66.6	23.0	5.5	0.4	1,875	0.911	60.6
1975	35.3	112.7	131.2	64.4	21.6	4.8	0.4	1,852	0.902	61.2
1976	33.4	110.3	129.9	65.6	21.1	4.3	0.3	1,825	0.887	60.3
1977	32.0	108.0	129.8	67.1	20.5	3.6	0.3	1,806	0.876	59.4
1978	29.7	103.1	128.1	67.1	19.5	3.6	0.3	1,757	0.857	58.0
1979	27.9	101.8	130.8	69.1	19.5	3.4	0.2	1,764	0.856	58.2
1980	27.6	100.1	129.4	69.3	19.4	3.1	0.2	1,746	0.849	57.9

Source: Statistics Canada, Catalogue 84–204, 1977, Table 6, p. 19, 1978, Table 4, pp. 6–7; 1979, Table 5, pp. 7–8; 1980, Table 5, p. 8.

Note: *Total fertility rate* = sum of female age-specific fertility rates multiplied by five; *Gross reproduction rate* = average number of live daughters that would be born to a hypothetical female birth cohort if subjected to current age-specific fertility rates, and assuming that mortality before age 50 is zero; *General Fertility Rate* = birth rate per 1000 women 15–49.

As we can see from the table, fertility rates in each age group have declined drastically. The implications of this trend, singly and in conjunction with the increase in life expectancy, are enormous.

For example, it means that there are, on average, fewer children per household. This suggests that there should be more space for each inhabitant of a household (e.g., a greater likelihood that each child will have a separate room) with more privacy (and possibly more isolation) and overall more material comfort. Since children are expensive for their parents, fewer children per family means that these children are likely to have more possessions, such as toys, hockey equipment, ice skates, roller skates, clothes, than if there were more children. Obviously, this will depend to a large degree on the overall socio-economic position of the family; nevertheless, fewer children should mean more access to material things even for poorer families, since we are comparing in the latter case poorer families with one or two children against poorer families with three or more children.

The greatest effect of the decline in fertility, however, is probably that which it has on women. For a mother, fewer children mean a shorter timespan devoted to childbearing, and, more importantly, fewer years devoted to childrearing, provided the spacing of children is rather close. This must certainly be seen as one factor influencing the increased labour force participation of mothers. While it is unclear what sort of causal relationship exists between labour force participation of mothers and fertility, there is a negative correlation between fertility and labour force status of the mother. One might hypothesize that there is an interactive relationship of the following nature: if a woman wishes to have both a paying job and at least one child, she will limit her childbearing to one or two children, in order to make it easier for her to combine childrearing with paid work. If that were the case, the relationship between labour force status of the mother and the number of children she has should gradually weaken over time as the labour force participation of wives becomes the norm. There is some slight evidence that this may be happening (Ciuriak and Sims, 1980).

For the children, a fertility rate which has, for all intents and purposes, been halved within one generation, means that more of them grow up with only one sibling or none at all. (This is ignoring the complication that because of divorce and remarriage, they may now more frequently have half-siblings rather than full siblings.) It stands to reason that interaction in families in which there are three to four children will be quite different from interaction in families in which there are only one or two children. Unfortunately, this is an aspect of family interaction that is rarely studied, possibly because we tend not to look at matters from the perspective of children at all, and because we seem to assign a vastly greater importance to parent-child relationships than to sibling relationships. But even in the absence of empirical studies, we can consider some of the relevant factors. Where there are fewer people in a group, it is easier to accommodate the needs and desires of each individual member. Fewer siblings probably means less sharing between siblings, and probably also less taking of responsibility for younger siblings, possibly less sibling rivalry, and possibly more attention for each child from the parents, or possibly less: more attention because there are fewer children; less attention because it is conceivable that parents can now get involved in so many other things that the one or two children who are around actually receive less attention than if there were more of them.

However, one thing seems fairly clear: fewer children per family are likely to contribute to a trend towards increasing age homogeneity. In a family of four children, each spaced two years apart, the age differential between the youngest and the oldest would be six years. For young children, six years is an appreciable age difference. If there are two children, equally spaced two years apart, the age difference is only two years. Children who grow up with siblings who are some years older and/or younger than themselves therefore interact on a day-to-day basis with children of different ages. In addition, they are also likely to have some contact with their siblings' same-aged friends, thus being exposed to even more children of different ages. Where there are only two (or one), this non-formal interaction with children of a whole range of ages can be expected to be greatly curtailed. This will probably mean that children who are already very much segregated according to age in most organized settings will also move largely in an age homogeneous setting within their homes (ignoring the adults for a moment). This would tend to further increase reliance of children on their peers rather than on older siblings. Provided this were found to be so, it would probably be useful to start thinking about ways in which children can be exposed to those older and younger than themselves, preferably on a daily basis, since a lot of learning can take place between age heterogeneous children, both for the younger and for the older ones.

The Combined Effects of Reduced Fertility and Increased Longevity

The combined effects of increased longevity and decreased fertility are resulting in a rapid aging of our society. In 1966, 50 percent of all Canadians were under 25.4 years old. By 1976, the median age had increased to 27.8 years, and it is estimated that by 2001 it will have reached nearly 36 years. This will mean that, "At the turn of the century, the most numerous generations are those who are entering the second half of their working life" (Statistics Canada, 1979a:41). So far, and until 1991, young people of working age have been numerically dominant in Canada.

We are therefore dealing with a very fundamental change in the age composition of our population, one of the ramifications of which can already be discerned. Economically, it means that a greater proportion of the population will draw pensions than ever before, unless we drastically revise our retirement practices. Politically, older people will become an ever more important constituency, because they will represent an even greater share of the vote. It is to be expected that increased political pressure on the part of older people will translate itself into a greater proportion of monies from the social envelope spent on programmes, projects, and needs of older people.

In and of itself, this could be a very positive development, of course. There is no doubt that as a society, Canada needs to treat its elderly better than it has done so far. However, we have also entered into a period of economic restraint, with high inflation and high unemployment, and great economic pressures. There is an overall tendency to try to curb government expenditures. It is to be feared that cuts will be made where the constituency affected is least powerful. One political constituency which, due to the demographic changes noted, is comparatively getting weaker are children who cannot even politically speak for themselves, but require their parents (or other people) to act as their political spokespersons. It is already the case that, inadequate as the old age pensions are, they are nevertheless vastly *more* adequate than the monies that families on family benefits receive (predominantly so-called welfare mothers) (See Table 6.6 for some comparative figures.). It is a sad commentary on the organization of a rich society like Canada, when it does not adequately provide for its youngest citizens. The future consequences of neglecting to provide for our young could possibly disrupt the entire society. After all, it is the younger ones who have to produce the goods from which pensions are paid.

One effect of the reduced fertility which we have already encountered is a decline in enrolment in educational institutions which in turn has led to a lack of employment opportunities for teachers at the primary and secondary levels of education. (The current squeeze on universities is not due to declining enrolment, since more mature students are being attracted to universities, but to government cutbacks and resulting financial problems for postsecondary educational institutions.) At the primary and secondary levels of education, the decline in enrolment has sometimes translated itself into a loss of teaching jobs for some competent, qualified teachers. Since teachers tend to be retained on the basis of seniority, this means that very highly educated, young teachers are likely to not find or to lose a job, in favour of older, and often less well qualified, staff. We are therefore dealing with a shrinking system which maintains an aging staff who have little incentive to upgrade their qualifications because there is only minimal financial remuneration for doing so (i.e., few opportunities for promotion). There is a real danger that the quality of education our children receive will decline for this reason.

The problem is compounded by the manner in which education is financed in Canada. The major sources of finances are provincial grants and property taxes. Where there is per capita funding, declining enrolment means reduced government funding. Property taxes, which date back to the Common Schools Act of 1850, were an innovative and appropriate method of financing public education at the time, but create serious problems today.[2]

Since homeowners tend to be older, and are often people who themselves no longer have children in school, it means that our public education system is largely financed by those people who not only do not have a vested interest in the educational system, but whose interests may be in direct conflict. We have already noted that the older population is often poor, since our pension system is by-and-large inadequate. Using property taxes for financing public education therefore puts the burden unevenly on a population of whom many are in fact under financial constraint. It also makes educational expenditures highly visible and therefore vulnerable. Everybody who pays taxes pays for military expenditures, for instance, but since there is no special designation for this purpose on the tax bills, most people are not aware just what proportion of their personal taxes is allocated for that purpose, nor are there public protests when military expenditures are raised, because it is unclear to people where exactly the monies will come from. Singling out public education by keeping it highly visible is likely to work against maintaining the quality of education currently in existence. Should the quality of the public educational system decline, richer parents are likely to send their children to private schools, thus raising the costs associated with having children, which might lead to a further decline in fertility.

So far, we have looked at only one of the fundamental changes which are currently occurring in Canada and which are affecting families. Demographic changes have been widely discussed and many people are aware that they are taking place. The next change, however, is one which has escaped the notice of most people, although in one way or another it is affecting every one of us: namely the industrialization of housework.

The Industrialization of Housework

The early socialist writers of the 19th century were the first who argued that the socialization of housework was an indispensable precondition for equalizing the positions of women and men. Since that time, housework has gone through changes that are comparable to those through which the money economy has gone, yet the positions of women and men in highly industrialized societies are by no stretch of the imagination equal. Women still do most of the housework,[3] and hours spent on housework have not decreased in spite of the vast array of technology that has been introduced into households and which has drastically reformed the character of the work that is being performed within households.

In the early thinking on this subject, socialization of housework was usually identified with industrialization of housework, both referring to a process whereby housework would be largely externalized, thereby cease to be *house*work, and instead become a public service. An example of the externalization of household tasks is the food industry, such as when family members eat in restaurants, cafeterias, or fast food outlets, instead of eating food at home that has been prepared by a homemaker.

What has in fact happened, however, over the past hundred years is not the socialization of housework, but its industrialization *without* an attendant socialization. Industrialization of housework is characterized by two features: first, a high level of technology within individual households (e.g., electric stoves, refrigerators, washing machines, oil heaters, etc.); and second, the production of all household goods and services on the money market, such that all services and goods previously produced within households become available for purchase. (Chapter 5 will be devoted entirely to the topic of housework, and the process of industrialization will be discussed in detail at that point.) Since, however, these goods and services are privately produced, and privately purchased and consumed, housework has been industrialized, but not socialized.

The second major trend that has occurred during the past hundred years is that while housework, meaning all aspects of housekeeping, has been industrialized, childcare (which is often subsumed under the label housework) has *not* been socialized, and today requires more time and more attention than in earlier times.

In previous times, an individual who wanted the same standard of living as the single adult can experience today with respect to shelter, food, and clothing would have either to spend almost all of his or her time trying to maintain that standard, or else have somebody who did so instead, such as a wife or servant. In fact, average household size in Canada has decreased consistently over time. In 1976 it was 3.1 persons per household (down from 3.5 persons in 1971 — a rather significant decline for such a short period of time) (Davids, 1980:179). At the same time, we can note a sharp increase in the number of single persons keeping a household alone. ". . . it is reasonable to say that the single lifestyle has 'caught-on' in Canada very substantially during the early part of this decade, so that living alone or in non-couple arrangements is considerably more common than it has been, although it is still far from likely to replace the husband-wife household as the model reality" (Davids, 1980:182).

The industrialization of housework must be seen as a major factor in facilitating the entrance of women into the labour market. It is now possible to combine paid work with housework, although only with difficulties, and when there are children in need of care, only with replacement for childcare services during time away from the home. We will consider this fundamental change next.

Increased Labour Force Participation of Women

Women have always worked, and a proportion of wives have always worked outside their own homes. However, a large-scale participation of wives and mothers in the paid labour force is a relatively new phenomenon. It is one that is found in all highly industrialized countries. If we look at Table 2.3 we find that the female activity rate in

TABLE 2.3

Percent Economically Active Population, by Sex, Selected Countries

Country	Year	Total Activity Rate	Male Activity Rate	Female Activity Rate
Canada	1978	46.7	57.6	35.6
U.S.A.	1979	47.7	57.4	38.5
Japan	1979	48.2	60.1	36.6
Denmark	1979	51.3	58.5	44.3
Finland	1979	48.5	54.0	43.4
France	1979	43.1	54.2	32.3
Federal Republic of Germany	1979	44.4	57.8	32.1
Iceland	1979	51.5	59.6	43.3
Ireland	1977	35.0	50.8	19.0
Italy	1979	39.4	54.3	25.4
Netherlands	1979	37.4	52.9	22.1
Norway	1978	46.5	56.1	37.0
Switzerland	1979	47.2	63.2	32.0
Sweden	1978	50.9	57.1	44.7
United Kingdom	1978	47.1	59.4	35.4

Source: International Labour Organization, 1980 Year Book of Labour Statistics, pp. 18–29.

Canada in 1978 was comparable to that of the United States, Japan, France, the Federal Republic of Germany, Norway, Switzerland, and the United Kingdom.

Female labour force participation rates can be understood as being due partially to a shift in the structure of the labour market in highly industrialized countries which pulls women into the paid labour force, and partially to a reaction of women to the industrialization of housework which pushes them into the labour market. Since the beginning of this century, the labour force participation of women in Canada has been increasing steadily, as can be seen from Table 2.4.

In 1979, for the first time, the *majority* of wives of working age (age 20--64) in Canada were actively involved in the labour force (51.3 percent) (see Table 6.2). This is an unprecedented shift in the economic

TABLE 2.4

Labour Force Participation Rates for Women and Men Over 15 Years, Canada, 1911–1980

Year	% Men	% Women
1911	89.7	16.2
1921	88.7	17.6
1931	87.5	19.7
1941*	85.8	20.7
1951	83.8	24.1
1961	77.7	29.5
1966	79.8	35.4
1967	79.3	36.5
1968	78.6	37.1
1969	78.3	38.0
1970	77.8	38.3
1971	77.3	39.4
1972	77.5	40.2
1973	78.2	41.9
1974	78.7	43.0
1975	78.4	44.4
1976	77.6	45.2
1977	77.6	46.0
1978	77.9	47.8
1979	78.4	48.9
1980	78.3	50.3

Sources: Statistics Canada, 1911–1961: 1961 Census of Canada, Vol. III (Part 1) Labour Force, t. 1, pp. 1–2; 1966–80: Historical Labour Statistics, 1980, Catalogue, 71–201, p. 153, D767420+p. 158, D767552.

*Includes persons on Active Service on June 2, 1941.

structure of Canadian families from a breadwinner family to a two-earner family. There are many strains attached to this shift since it involves a fundamental reorganization of familial structures.

When wives work for pay, a complete restructuring of the household necessarily ensues. From the limited evidence available, it seems that this restructuring is mostly and sometimes exclusively carried out by the wives rather than by husbands and wives together. (The effect on children is even less explored, and will be discussed in detail in Chapter 8.) So far, for instance, there is no evidence that husbands do a larger share of housework when their wives work for pay than when their wives are housewives (Meissner et al., 1975 and Clark and Harvey, 1976. For international sources to the same effect, see Bose, 1979). This means, of course, that wives working for pay usually carry a double burden — holding down a job plus doing the major share (or even all) of the housework. Nevertheless, there continue to be more women looking for jobs than there are jobs available. One reason for seeking paid labour is, of course, financial. However, sufficient numbers of wives who have husbands earning a large enough salary to support the entire family are either holding a job or looking for one so that this cannot be the only explanation.

To the degree that housework became industrialized, husbands became potentially less dependent on their wives for their survival and comfort (see Eichler, 1981). I say potentially, because wives continued to render those services and produce those goods that they used to, but as these goods and services became available for purchase, husbands (and other household members who depended on the labour of the homemaker for their food, shelter, maintenance, and comfort) could substitute commercial products if the homegrown variety were not available for some reason. This past century, then, showed a gradual increase in the dependence of homemaker wives on breadwinner husbands, with a concomitant gradual decrease in the dependence of the breadwinner husband on the homemaker wife. The dependency, in other words, became increasingly lopsided.

One direct effect of paid labour for wives is that they cease to be totally economically dependent on their husbands. Once a wife takes a paying job, the old pattern abruptly shifts. Even if the husband's job is given precedence over that of his wife by both spouses, and even if she earns about half of what he earns (both of which are highly likely) the wife is no longer asymmetrically dependent on the husband for economic goods as she is without a paying job. This will affect not only familial interactions, but also her self-esteem.

Ironically, it is only with the increased labour force participation of women and the feminist movement that the value of housework has started to be appreciated. As housework is no longer performed on a full-time basis by the majority of Canadian wives — in other words, as there is a *partial* withdrawal of previously automatically rendered services — their value is starting to become recognized. This is perhaps best displayed in the recent changes in provincial family laws, many of which recognize the wife's contributions to a marriage through *housework* which were previously considered valueless. The first of these changes was incorporated into the Ontario Family Law Reform Act of 1978 (see Chapter 9 for a discussion of these changes). Other provinces made changes subsequent to this one; in other words, we are dealing again with a very recent phenomenon.

For children, a mother with a paying job means in the vast majority of cases that they will be cared for outside of their own home for substantial portions of their waking time, provided they are small enough to need constant supervision. This is not only a radical change in the way we bring up our children, but also changes the socialization pattern. No longer is the mother the only, or even the most important, socializer of the child, but this task is now often shared with virtual strangers. This fact has not yet penetrated the consciousness of theorists who continue to ignore the role of babysitters and day care staff as socializers of small children, and fail to even comment on the fact that this is now a very common pattern. For instance, Elkin and Handel (1978:41) suggest that "the relationship with the mother is virtually all the social life an infant has and therefore presents his or her first expectation of the social world." This ignores not only the possible presence of siblings, but when an infant experiences any form of day care — and increasing numbers of them do — this statement is obviously no longer applicable.

For a husband, a wife's labour force participation means that his claims for personal services are increasingly difficult to justify since they were premised on the breadwinning function of the husband. Data from a recent Canadian survey[4] suggest that the majority of people, when asked, endorse the notion that a married couple in which both spouses are working and where there are children, should divide housework equally between husband and wife. This must not be confused with current reality which shows no such equal division of labour, but as an indication of a shift in norms it is of great significance.

Lastly, where a marriage is experiencing difficulties, particularly if the wife finds the situation unsatisfying, an independent income will make it easier for her to contemplate, and eventually sue for divorce. In this sense, one might expect that increased labour force participation of wives might possibly have contributed to the recent drastic increase in the number and rate of divorces. However, in families with higher incomes, there tend to be fewer divorces. Since wives who earn money increase the overall amount of money available within a household, wives' labour force participation may stabilize marriages and prevent divorce in cases where it would have been likely to take place without this additional income. Statistically, it is likely that these two opposite effects may cancel each other out. Indeed, the U.S. evidence on the effect of wives' labour force participation on marital disruption is contradictory, as would be expected if two opposite effects are simultaneously at work (Moore and Hefferth, 1979:29). In individual marriages, however, labour force participation of the wife may determine whether a marriage will end in divorce or will be maintained. Over the long haul, greater financial independence of wives should lead to better quality marriages, marriages which are maintained because of mutual love and pleasure derived from them, rather than because of economic dependency of one spouse on the other.

Increased Numbers and Rates of Divorce

Like the other trends so far considered, a high divorce rate is a phenomenon that is typical of most highly industrialized countries, as can be seen from Table 2.5. Italy, with its traditional Catholic orientation, presents an obvious exception to an otherwise very high overall divorce rate.[5]

TABLE 2.5

Comparative Divorce Rates for Some Selected Countries

Country	Year	Divorces per 1,000 Marriages
Australia	1977	430.6
Belgium	1979	206.2
Canada	1979	316.7
Denmark	1978	454.5
Federal Republic of Germany	1978	98.9*
Finland	1978	348.4
France	1978	208.5
Italy	1978	30.9
Netherlands	1978	249.8
Norway	1979	263.7
Sweden	1978	540.5
Switzerland	1978	326.8
United Kingdom	1978	345.1
United States	1979	505.9
U.S.S.R.	1978	326.5

Source: Statistics Canada, Vital Statistics, Vol. II, Marriages and Divorces, 1980, Catalogue 84–205, t. 21, p. 32. Reprinted by permission of Statistics Canada.

*See note 5.

In Canada, the divorce rate has increased with almost breathtaking speed, but as can be seen from Table 2.5, there are countries with a considerably higher divorce rate, especially Australia, Denmark, Sweden, and the United States. This is important to keep in mind when we try to explain the increased tendency to divorce. Obviously we are dealing with a phenomenon that is not confined to Canada and therefore cannot be explained with factors found only in this country.

Within the last ten years, the divorce rate in Canada has almost doubled, and if we take a longer time perspective, the increase is even more marked, as can be seen from Table 2.6. The sudden jump in divorces between 1968 and 1969 is due to the enactment of the federal Divorce Act of 1968. It provided Canada with its first uniform divorce code, and instituted significant changes, especially by increasing legal

TABLE 2.6

Divorces and Divorce Rates in Canada 1960 to 1980

Year	Number of Divorces	Rate per 100,000 Population
1960	6,980	39.1
1961	6,563	36.0
1962	6,768	36.4
1963	7,686	40.6
1964	8,623	44.7
1965	8,974	45.7
1966	10,239	51.2
1967	11,165	54.8
1968	11,343	54.8
1969	26,093	124.2
1970	29,775	139.8
1971	29,685	137.6
1972	32,389	148.4
1973	36,704	166.1
1974	45,019	200.6
1975	50,611	222.0
1976	54,207	235.8
1977	55,370	237.7
1978	57,155	243.4
1979	59,474	251.3
1980	62,019	259.1

Sources: Statistics Canada, Vital Statistics, Vol. II — Marriages and Divorces, 1979, Catalogue 84–205, table 11, and 1980, table 11, 1982, table 10.

reasons for divorce. The change was especially marked for Quebec and Newfoundland, which switched from a parliamentary to a judiciary system for divorce (Abernathy and Arcus, 1977:412).

In discussing divorce rates prior and subsequent to the change in the federal divorce law, Pike notes that "the incidence of divorce is a very poor guide to the actual rate of marriage breakdown in the society. Indeed, in order to ascertain the level of marriage breakdown at any one point in time, we would have to add the number of judicial separations, migratory divorces, and desertions to the number of divorces granted through the Canadian courts" (Pike, 1975:124). McVey and Robinson (1981:361) recently computed that if we add the separated population to the divorced population to arrive at a "dissolution index" this provides us with estimates of marital disruption which are at least one and a half times greater than estimates based upon the incidence of divorce alone.

One would expect that one of the major functions of the new divorce law would be to make divorce accessible to those in marriages which had already broken down. However, permanent desertions and separations rather than divorces continue to exist for some people. For instance, Peters (1976:344) has noted that, contrary to trends in other countries, provinces with a low average family income in 1973 did not have a comparatively speaking high divorce rate. Ontario, Quebec, Alberta, and British Columbia had relatively high incomes, but nevertheless their divorce rates were comparatively moderate or high. Peters explains this unusual finding by suggesting that this does *not* mean that the usual positive relationship between low income and marital dissolution does not hold in Canada. Instead, he suggests, it probably means that couples with little or no income separate rather than divorce (Peters, 1976:344).

The Divorce Act, as presently constituted, has been identified as a compromise between the wholly restrictive law of the 19th century and the move to unilateral divorce. The "1968 Act is aimed as much at saving marriages as making divorce painless" (Veitch, 1979:304). Where allegations which are cited as grounds for divorce are not contested "(as in 90 percent of the divorce cases) the petitions are granted routinely. When there is some attempt by a spouse, for whatever reason, to reply to the accusations by denial or counter-allegation, the clash between the aim of protecting the institution of marriage and the goal of making divorce as painless as possible becomes evident. The courts in those contested cases tend toward restrictive interpretations of the legislative grounds for divorce, even in situations where it is pellucid that the marriage is dead" (Veitch, 1979:300).

This statement is confirmed by a recent study which involved 427 Quebec residents, 229 of whom were late divorced (meaning they had ended marriages which had lasted for at least twenty years) and 198 of whom were long-term married. Of the late divorced respondents, 75 percent reported long-term marital unhappiness. "It was clear that regardless of the federal divorce law, marital breakdown was occurring and separation would result. The law simply made it easier and perhaps less painful for the spouses legally to leave each other — emotionally they had done so many months prior to the final decrees" (Deckert and Langelier, 1978:387–388).

Nor does an increase in divorce rates — even one as dramatic as the one we are currently witnessing — necessarily imply that marriages are unhappier than they used to be. There is, by now, a fair amount of evidence that suggests that unhappy marriages are not necessarily unstable, and that happy marriages are not necessarily stable (Albrecht and Kunz, 1980:325).

What may have happened, however, is that expectations as to what are tolerable levels of discord and unhappiness have changed. One prevalent explanatory framework for divorce is social exchange theory, which has as its main variables costs and rewards:

> The cost-reward framework implies that the decision to divorce will be made only after it is determined that the alternative to sustaining a marital relationship is either more rewarding or less costly than the decision to remain with the relationship. It implies the ability on the part of the individual actor to compare the outcomes of his or her own marital relationship with some internal standard as well as with other options that are available or that are made available in the actor's environment. Such comparisons are highly dependent upon individual *sui generis* judgement of reward and cost.[6]

In applying this framework to a large-scale American study, Albrecht and Kunz (1980:333) found that "personal unhappiness was perceived as more important than the availability of alternative financial support or involvement with some other person. Present costs, then, seem more important than alternative rewards."

Deckert and Langelier (1978:387), in their study of late divorces in Quebec, found that "the primary legal cause for the divorce was adultery. The primary 'real' cause was 'multiple causes' which, when broken down into the five top-ranking variables, were adultery, sexual problems, in-law problems, alcoholism, and mental cruelty, in that order."

Ambert has tried to identify reasons for the continuing increase in the divorce rate which she has separated into societal and personal causes. As societal causes, she lists the following:

> the individualist and hedonist mentality of the technological era; a general climate of liberalism; a reduction of religious influence and a greater acceptance of divorce in certain religions; a secularized view of marriage;

> the relaxation of divorce laws; the increased independence of individuals and a lessening of family pressures; more numerous alternatives for both sexes; social and geographic mobility; greater emancipation of women; a relative lack of psychological emancipation in men; increased longevity; the sub-cultural effect (pockets of high or low divorce rates); a surfeit of alternatives and choices that are offered to individuals, and poverty.[7]

Under personal variables that contribute to divorce she mentions youthful marriages and premarital pregnancies, brief acquaintance of the couple before marriage, unhappiness in parental marriages, dissimilarity of background of spouses, mixed-faith and non-religious marriages, and disapproval of the union by family and friends. She further mentions as personal variables which contribute towards likelihood of divorce alcoholism, mental problems, total career immersion, failure in communication, sexual problems, adultery, children in first marriages and in remarriages, emotional immaturity of one or both spouses, mental and physical cruelty, and unrealistic expectations on the part of one or both of the spouses (Ambert, 1980:74–75).

Overall, then, we are dealing with a complex phenomenon that has certainly more than just one cause, especially since we are dealing with a phenomenon that is occurring in many industrialized countries, not just in Canada. Divorce is so very important for two reasons: first, where it involves children, it functions as one pathway to the establishment of one-parent households and/or remarriage families; secondly, whether or not children are involved, and whether or not a couple actually divorce, the very prevalence of divorce has fundamentally changed the meaning and structure of marriage, by making it a more volitional union. We will briefly discuss each of these aspects of divorce.

While one-parent households which are due to divorce and remarriage families are, in some ways, very different from each other, they do share one important feature: in both of them there is a discrepancy between parental and spousal roles. The biological parents are high in interaction with each other in the procreative dimension, but low in the residential, sexual, and most likely in the emotional and economic dimensions, and they may or may not be high in interaction in the socialization dimension. The children concerned have two living parents, and they are probably emotionally connected with both of them.

While the ultimate impact of divorce on children is unclear — Longfellow, in the most thorough review of the relevant literature to date has concluded that "findings to date are equivocal; they do not permit assertions that divorce has any single, broad-reaching impact on children" (Longfellow, 1979:287) — one datum is very clear: the majority of children desire continuing contact with both their parents, and divorce is perceived as less dramatic by them when they have freedom of access to the noncustodial parent. In one recent U.S. study, which interviewed 92 children, ranging in age from 9 to 28, whose parents had divorced in the ten years prior to the investigation, "56 stated that their choice would have been to have free access to the noncustodial parent, 12 expressed preference for regulated access, nine expressed the desire to see the noncustodial parent only occasionally, and four were reluctant to see this parent at all. Most of the children indicated that continued contact with the noncustodial parent was important to them; 33 percent of the sample considered that they had not had as much contact as they would have liked with this parent.[8]

What is particularly problematic, then, in divorced families is how the access of the noncustodial parent (usually the father) to the children is regulated. This is an area in which we have, collectively speaking, no widespread prior experience, because we have never before had such numbers of parents and children involved in divorce. This question will be explored further in subsequent chapters.

It seems obvious that divorce is important when it has happened within a particular family, especially when children are involved. It may seem less obvious that the increase in the divorce rate is also highly significant for those families in which divorce has not yet happened, and indeed, even for those families where it never will happen.

Until recently, it could be legitimately said that in a sociological sense "marriage is not a voluntary union" (LaRossa, 1977:123). In a situation in which over 90 percent of all people eventually marry, and only a small percentage divorce, there is considerable social pressure towards being married. However, in the seventies the divorce rate rose to an unparalleled level. There was a public divorce (rather than a discreetly handled *de facto* separation without attending publicity) within the royal family of Britain, and the Prime Minister of Canada publicly separated. With such examples, divorce and separation have indeed reached the highest social circles, and this has contributed to making it more socially acceptable. Conversely, only because divorce and separation were already widespread at the time was it possible for these people to divorce and separate, otherwise the public pressure might have made that impossible.

The effect of very widespread divorce, then, is to make marriage more of a volitional union. It is no longer unthinkable that people divorce, and by now the likelihood is very great that practically everybody personally knows someone — in his or her family, among friends, or at least among acquaintances — who has at some point gone through a divorce. When a marriage turns sour today, divorce will come to mind as a possible solution to the problem. Indeed, people may have to ask themselves, if they happen to live in a high divorce environment, why they desire to maintain their marriages.

At this point in time, the majority of marriages are still maintained until the death of one of the spouses. For the near future (at least to the end of the eighties) one would expect the divorce rate in Canada to continue to climb, or at a minimum, not to decline, primarily because those factors which have been identified as contributing to it are not likely to vanish within that time period. In addition, the emergence of marriage as a *voluntary* union means that people's preformed expectations of marriage will have to change. For instance, in the previously cited study involving late divorces in Quebec, the researchers found that late divorce was more likely to occur in a traditional type of marriage "with defined sex roles" than in a companionship type of marriage with "interchangeable sex roles and emphasis on the affective aspects of the relationship" (Deckert and Langelier, 1978:381, 382, 384). Of those who eventually divorced, 80 percent had a traditional type of marriage, whereas 60 percent of the married controls reported a companionate type of marriage (Deckert and Langelier, 1978:389).

In the end effect, then, we must see an increase in the divorce rate as a great revolutionizer of marriage, even for those marriages which persist.

Interaction of the Various Changes

We have identified and briefly discussed four major historical changes which have been taking place in families: a drastic shift in demographic patterns (namely increased longevity and reduced fertility); the industrialization of housework; greatly increased labor force participation of women; and a dramatic increase in the rate of divorce. All of these changes are characteristic of all highly industrialized countries. We are therefore not dealing with changes which only affect Canadian families, but families in most of the developed Western world, although each country has its own variations, and there are still significant differences in the degree to which the trends manifest themselves. While each of the historical changes has its own causes, the various changes also interact with each other.

Chronologically speaking, a gradual industrialization of housework was the first by-product of an overall industrialization process that has been going on throughout this century. Industrialization brought an improved standard of living, both at the individual and at the collective level. This, coupled with advances in medical science, new drugs, more efficient food production and distribution (for the Western world only), and a better social insurance legislation (even in countries in which social insurance is particularly poorly developed, such as the United States), eventually translated itself into increased life expectancies. Fertility started to drop only after the baby boom following the Second World War, but in general we can observe a worldwide connection between poverty and high fertility, and high income and low fertility. The industrialization of housework facilitated the mass entry of women into the paid labour force which in turn increased the independence of women (although it has not resulted in social equality of the sexes as yet). Improved female independence must be seen as one contributing factor to the increase in divorce, although in no simple manner: it is not true that wives who earn money are more likely to divorce than housewives; indeed, there is some evidence to the contrary. But female labour force participation does mean that unhappy wives are more likely to consider divorce and to actually sue for divorce than previously. (The majority of divorces are initiated by wives rather than husbands.)

This, in turn, must be seen as a great turning point for marriages: we are now at a point where marriage starts to be a truly voluntary union. Since this involves a monumental shift, it is only reasonable to expect that such change is accompanied by a considerable amount of personal and social anguish. Further, the change from an involuntary to a voluntary union has only begun, and is by no means complete. Indeed, it can be expected that it will take at least another generation until the process will be completed. Until that time, we are likely to continue to have a high divorce rate, with all its attending consequences.

So far, we have looked at only one of the ways in which a conservative bias in the literature could be overcome, namely the recognition of those changes that have occurred as central in an attempt to comprehend what is currently happening to and within families. However, there are two other ways in which a conservative bias manifests itself: in the tendency to ignore the ugly aspects of familial relationships, and in the tendency to treat children only as passive members of families.

A monolithic model of the family is very much an idealized model of the family, and a conservative bias in viewing families is a consequence of using a monolithic model of the family. Until we see families in both their positive and their negative aspects, we will totally fail to grasp their reality as it is experienced by millions of people all over the world.

The Ugly Aspects of Familial Interactions

Until about the beginning of the seventies, family violence was one of the best kept secrets. Even today, we do not have a single representative study of family violence in Canada which would allow us to deduce its prevalence. The first American study which used a representative sample of couples living together found that 28 percent of the couples in the study experienced at least one violent incident during the history of their marriage. However, the author concludes that because of various factors which would lead to underreporting of incidences of violence in marriage, "the true incidence for violence in a marriage is probably closer to *50 or 60 percent of all couples* than it is to the 28 percent who were willing to describe violent acts in a mass interview survey" (Straus, 1980:31, emphasis in the original).

If we take together all forms of violence that can take place within a familial setting, such as wife battering, husband battering, child battering, sibling battering, parent battering, sexual molestation on the part not just of parents and siblings but also of stepparents and other relatives such as uncles, grandfathers, and others, an estimate of 50 to 60 percent of Canadian families experiencing some form of familial violence may not be too high. One problem with estimates of that sort, however, exists in the fact that the definitions of what is seen as violence vary greatly (cf. Kincaid, 1981, chapter 3). Nevertheless, we are not dealing with an isolated type of phenomenon. The editors of one of the most recent comprehensive American books on family violence conclude:

> . . . the family is the predominant setting for every form of physical violence from slaps to torture and murder. In fact, some form of physical violence in the life cycle of family members is so likely that it can be said to be almost universal. . . . If this is indeed the case, then violence is as typical of family relationships as is love.[9]

Although violence between family members is not a special focus of this book, this aspect, more than any other, helps to illuminate the paradoxical nature of familial relationships. It is not *in spite of* the fact that family members are supposed to love each other, but *because of it* that we find such a high degree of violence between them. Hotaling and Straus (1980) list eleven factors which explain why families are particularly prone to violence, and each of them is at the same time either a precondition or a consequence of intimacy. The eleven factors they list are (with some adaptations) the following:

1. *Time at Risk.* An elementary factor accounting for the high incidence of violence is that so many hours of the day are spent interacting with other family members. However, although this factor is important, the ratio of intrafamily violence to violence experienced outside the family far exceeds the ratio of time spent in the family to time spent outside. Comparing the family with

another group in which large amounts of time are spent, such as a work group, provides a concrete example that far more is involved than "time at risk."

2. *Range of Activities and Interests.* Most non-familial interactions are focussed on a specific purpose or issue; family interactions cover a vast range of activities. In practical terms, this means more "events" take place over which a dispute or a failure to meet expectations can occur.
3. *Intensity of Involvement.* Not only is there a wider range of possibilities for disputes or dissatisfactions, but, in addition, the degree of injury felt in such instances is likely to be much greater than if the same issue were to arise in relation to someone outside the family, due to the deeper involvement of the various participants.
4. *Infringing Activities.* Many family activities have a "zero sum" aspect. Conflict arises from such decisions as whether to play Bach or Mendelssohn on the family stereo, whether to go to a movie or bowling, or how to line up for the bathroom. Less obvious, but equally important, is the infringement of one's personal space or self-image of the life style and habits of others in the family, such as those who leave things around versus those who put everything away, or those who eat quickly and those who like leisurely meals.
5. *Right to Influence.* Membership in a family carries with it an implicit right to influence the behavior of others. Consequently, the dissatisfaction over undesirable or impinging activities of others is further exacerbated by attempts to change the behavior of the other.
6. *Age and Sex Discrepancies.* The difference in age and sex of family members (especially during the childrearing years), coupled with the existence of generational and sex differences in culture and outlook, make the family an arena of culture conflict. This conflict is expressed in such phrases as "the battle of the sexes" and "the generation gap."
7. *Ascribed Roles.* Compounding the problems of age and sex differences, family statuses and roles are assigned, to a considerable extent, on the basis of biological characteristics rather than on the basis of competence and interest. A male-dominated family has especially high conflict potential when it exists in a society with an egalitarian ideology. However, even without such an ideological inconsistency, the conflict potential is high, because inevitably not all husbands can fulfill the culturally prescribed leadership roles, and, one can add, inevitably not all wives can be expected to be competent and enthusiastic housekeepers.
8. *Family Privacy.* The conjugal family system of urban-industrial

societies makes the dampening effects of the presence of third parties in husband-wife arguments and disputes less likely.

9. *Involuntary Membership.* Birth relationships are obviously involuntary, and under-age children cannot themselves terminate such relationships. In addition, conjugal relationships also have some non-voluntary aspects. Economic, legal, and emotional constraints often make leaving the family impractical or impossible, although this aspect more than any of the others is changing, at least for the conjugal partners, with the high increase in divorce rates and recent legal changes in some of the provincial legislations concerning matrimonial property.
10. *High Level of Stress.* Paradoxically, in light of the previous paragraph, nuclear family relationships are unstable. For one, dyadic relationships have a built-in instability. In addition, the nuclear family continually undergoes major changes in structure because of processes inherent in the family life cycle — the birth of children, maturation of children, aging, and retirement, all of which have a crisis-like nature. Combined with the huge emotional investment typical of family relationships this means that the family is likely to be the locus of more, and more serious stresses than other groups. And although greater availability of divorce serves to modify the involuntary membership aspect of familial relationships, at the same time it too must be recognized as a stressor in its own right.
11. *Extensive Knowledge of Social Biographies.* Because of the intimacy of familial relationships, spouses and parents usually have an in-depth knowledge of each other's social histories — their abilities and short-comings, their strengths and vulnerabilities, their likes and dislikes. Such information can be used to support and enhance each other's identities, as well as to damage the identity of the other spouse, or of the child (and sometimes of the parent).[10]

This list of factors contributing to violence within families demonstrates the paradoxical nature of family relationships: the very factors that make intimacy between family members possible also make violence between family members likely. In the emotional, as well as in all other dimensions of familial relationships, intensity of interaction ranges from one extreme to the other.

So far, we have considered two ways in which a conservative bias manifests itself: in a tendency to see fundamental recent changes as ephemeral (if they are considered at all), and a tendency to ignore the ugly aspects of familial relationships. The third major aspect of a conservative bias is a tendency to treat children as passive members of families.

Children as Participants in Families

Families are, in the conservative image, seen as centring around children. Indeed, children are to such a degree seen as the raison d'être for families that childless couples are often not even called families, but simply childless couples. Even so, there are very few studies that focus on children *themselves,* although there are studies which assess the impact of various events, such as divorce, on children by asking adults associated with them (usually the mother) about this impact. For instance, Longfellow (1979:299), on reviewing the impact of divorce on children, has noted "the lack of systematic studies on children's reactions *at the very time of divorce*" (emphasized in the original).

In the vast majority of family studies, children are, at best, seen as individuals who have to be cared for, who need to be socialized, but not as people who may have divergent viewpoints of what is happening within a particular family, or as people who themselves may exert an influence on the nature of familial relationships. Overall, then, the child's perspective is ignored, and children are seen as passive members being acted upon by their parents, not as active participants who themselves exert an influence on the adults they are dealing with as well as on their siblings.

La Perriere (1980:84), for instance, has noted that in the mental health profession, students either learn about children or they learn about adults, and that this same split is displayed by the researchers. "The child who is studied in isolation appears to be totally governed by an inner clock that times his/her growth and unfolding. Most normative studies of infant development use this approach. They study affect, reactivity, intelligence, and motor skills, without noting the interpersonal and social context of the process."

In quite a different context, Veevers has noted that "In examining the parent-child relationship, social scientists have been so preoccupied with the impact that parents have upon the lives of their children that they have virtually precluded consideration of the reciprocal impact that children have upon the lives of their parents" (Veevers, 1979:6).

Troyer makes a passionate plea to his readers to recognize the differential importance of a marital break-up for the children involved; he argues that the children have a right to feel angry, shocked, and frightened by what's happening around them, and to them:

> Why shouldn't they? They've invested their whole lives, not just a few adult years, in that family unit. It's *theirs.* So they damn well should feel disappointed and, yes, angry.
>
> Once more, *children are not witnesses to divorce; they are participants.*
>
> That line should be engraved on the consciousness of every divorcing parent, nailed to the wall of every divorce lawyer, judge, social counsellor.[11]

When researchers are concerned about children, they tend to ask their mothers or other adults about the effect of particular events on children, rather than asking and/or observing the children themselves. Levitin (1979:18), in discussing this point, suggests that although parents may in general have more information about their children than other respondents, "they are hardly unbiassed reporters of that information, and, when under stress themselves, they may be particularly unreliable . . . the frequently automatic, often uncritical, and sometimes inappropriate reliance on this type of data is problematic."

In effect then, we know almost nothing about how children perceive their families and how they experience particular events while they happen. Fulton (1979:133), when interviewing 560 divorced American parents, found that in 12 percent of the cases for custodial wives and 27 percent of the cases for custodial husbands, one or more of the children had moved back and forth between parents or had changed custodians at least once. "This post-divorce mobility of children is an issue that has received almost no attention in the divorce literature: it has not been documented or described; its effects are unknown."

In the same context, Kargman (1979) argues that children need a child advocate in divorce cases. A court appointed child advocate (guardian *at litem*) herself, she discusses some case histories. "Parents when they separate their joint residence are no longer solely qualified to make residence decisions for their children. They have vested interests in their own comfort, which may be in conflict with the best interests of the children" (Kargman, 1979:87). As an example she cites the custom of parents with joint custody who make their children spend one-half of a week with each parent. "Perhaps if the children had their own counsel, the children would stay in their own home and the parents would alternate their residence" (Kargman, 1979:87).

Arrangements, then, may look very different depending on whether we consider them from the perspective of the adults involved or of the children involved. For instance, parents, in forbidding their children contact with specific other children, may simply wish to protect them from company that they consider undesirable, while for the children this may mean the destruction of an incipient or ongoing friendship, and a denial of the right to choose their own companions.

Children also are likely to have a strong independent effect on the quality of the lives of their parents. While some children undoubtedly bring happiness, love, purpose, and meaning into the lives of their parents, others may also bring unhappiness. There is some limited evidence that children have a corrosive effect on marriages, counter to the current stereotype. Renne, in examining a large-scale sample of urban married American couples found that "children reduce marital satisfaction, just as they seem to have a negative effect on the physical health and psychological well-being of parents in the younger age groups. In the later stages of marriage, also, the difference between *former* parents and those still involved in childrearing is striking. Former parents married 30 years or more were three times as likely to be happily married as active parents, although they were less positive about their marriages than couples who had never had children."[12]

These findings are partially confirmed by Booth and White who found in interviewing 1364 married persons that preschoolers put a strain on a marital relationship. "For both men and women, those with preschoolers in the home were twice as likely to have considered divorce within the last two years as were those with either none or older children. In fact, households with teenagers were somewhat less likely to be considering divorce than those without teenagers. These data suggest that, while the presence of preschoolers may deter separation and divorce, it does not keep people from thinking about it. Rather the stresses and demands of very young children may increase the frequency with which their parents consider divorce."[13]

On the other hand, children may be the greatest joy for their parents. In either case, they must be seen as active participants in families who exert a powerful influence on how a family functions. Although it is customarily the parents who will decide where a family will reside, what religion a child will be brought up in (if any), how a house will be furnished, where and how vacations are spent, nevertheless children exert a powerful influence in structuring the parents', and particularly their mothers', lives. Clearly, this is one more aspect of familial relationships and structures which has been greatly neglected and which should be intensively studied in order to gain a more balanced picture.

Summary

In this chapter, we have looked at three ways in which a conservative bias manifests itself in the literature: namely, a tendency to see fundamental changes as merely ephemeral, a tendency to ignore the ugly aspects of familial interactions, and a tendency to see children only as passive members of families. In order to overcome the prevailing conservative bias, then, we need to first recognize the changes that have been identified — increased longevity and decreased fertility, the industrialization of housework, increased labour force participation of women, and increased divorce rates — as fundamental, and, indeed, revolutionary changes, and secondly we need to integrate them into our overall approach to families. For instance, we cannot treat the issue of childcare as if the vast majority of children were still being brought up in their homes by their housewife mother when for the *majority* of children such is no longer the case. We cannot consider marriage necessarily as a lifelong union when for a very substantial number of people it is not. We cannot assume that children live with both their parents during their entire childhood when a very significant group (and possibly as many as half of them) do not share a household with both their parents (see Chapter 7).

Third, we must recognize and acknowledge that families incorporate the most brutal and exploitative relationships as well as the most loving and caring ones. Lastly, we must recognize that children are active participants in families, with their own perceptions, which may be significantly different from those of their parents. They are also people who have their own interests, which may in some cases conflict with the interests of their parents. Certainly, and whether for better or for worse, it is a substantially different experience to participate within the same family as an adult or as a child.

Of all the tasks, taking the perspective of children will be the hardest to do, since there is literally no research to draw upon. For the time being, we may have to content ourselves with simply raising the issue, rather than trying to provide the answers.

Notes

1. From *Divorce in Canada* by Anne-Marie Ambert reprinted by permission of Academic Press Canada, 1980.
2. The last two paragraphs are based on some work done by Wendy Wyles on the issue in question.
3. This statement will be discussed further in Chapter 3.
4. The POW Canada Study. See appendix 1 for a short description of the study.
5. It is here assumed that the comparatively low divorce rate of the Federal Republic of Germany is due to some printing or computational error. For 1976, the divorce rate for the FRG was reported as 296 per 1000 marriages; see Statistics Canada, Vital Statistics, Vol. II, Marriages and Divorces, Catalogue 84–205, 1979, p. 32, t. 21. A real drop from 296 down to 98.9 within a year would be unprecedented and seems unlikely.
6. Stan L. Albrecht and Phillip R. Kunz, "The Decision to Divorce: A Social Exchange Perspective," *Journal of Divorce,* Vol. 3, No. 4 (1980):321–322.
7. From *Divorce in Canada* by Anne-Marie Ambert reprinted by permission of Academic Press Canada, 1980.
8. Rhona Rosen, "Some Crucial Issues Concerning Children of Divorce," *Journal of Divorce,* Vol. 3, No. 1 (1979):22–23.
9. "Culture, Social Organization, and Irony in the Study of Family Violence." From *The Social Causes of Husband-Wife Violence* by Gerald T. Hotaling and Murray A. Straus reprinted by permission of University of Minnesota Press, 1980, p. 4.
10. Adapted from ibid., pp. 15–18.
11. Warner Troyer, *Divorced Kids: A Candid and Compassionate Look at their Needs* (Toronto: Clarke, Irwin and Co., 1979), p. 41.
12. Karen S. Renne, "Childlessness, Health, and Marital Satisfaction," *Social Biology,* Vol. 23, No. 3 (1976):195.

13. Alan Booth and Lynn White, "Thinking About Divorce," *Journal of Marriage and the Family*, Vol. 42, No. 3 (1980):610. Copyright 1980 by the National Council on Family Relations. Reprinted by permission.

References

Abernathy, Thomas Jr. and Margaret Arcus, "The Law and Divorce in Canada," *The Family Co-ordinator*, Vol. 22, 1977, pp. 409–413.

Albrecht, Stan L. and Phillip R. Kunz, "The Decision to Divorce: A Social Exchange Perspective," *Journal of Divorce*, Vol. 3, No. 4, 1980, pp. 319–337.

Ambert, Anne-Marie, *Divorce in Canada*. Don Mills: Academic Press Canada, 1980.

Booth, Alan and Lynn White, "Thinking About Divorce," *Journal of Marriage and the Family*, Vol. 42, No. 3, 1980, pp. 605–616.

Bose, Christine, "Technology and Changes in the Division of Labor in the American Home," *Women's Studies International Quarterly*, Vol. 2, No. 3, 1979, pp. 295–304.

Canada. Statistics Canada, *1961 Census of Canada*, Vol. III, Part I, Labour Force. Ottawa: Minister of Trade and Commerce, 1965.

Canada. Statistics Canada, *Historical Labour Force Statistics 1980*. (Catalogue 71–201). Ottawa: Minister of Supply and Services, 1981.

Canada. Statistics Canada, *Population Projections for Canada and the Provinces, 1976–2001*. Ottawa: Statistics Canada, 1979a.

Canada. Statistics Canada, *Vital Statistics, Vol. I, Birth, 1977*. (Catalogue 84–204 annual). Ottawa: Treasury Board, 1979b.

Canada. Statistics Canada, *Vital Statistics, Vol. II, Marriages and Divorces, 1977*. (Catalogue 84–205 annual). Ottawa: Treasury Board, 1979c.

Canada. Statistics Canada, *Vital Statistics, Vol. I, Births and Deaths, 1978*. (Catalogue 84–204 annual). Ottawa: Minister of Supply and Services, 1980.

Canada. Statistics Canada, *Vital Statistics, Vol. I, Births and Deaths, 1979*. (Catalogue 84–204). Ottawa: Minister of Supply and Services, 1981.

Canada. Statistics Canada, *Vital Statistics, Vol. I, Births and Deaths, 1980*. Ottawa: Minister of Supply and Services, 1982.

Canada. Statistics Canada, *Vital Statistics, Vol. II, Marriages and Divorces, 1978*. (Catalogue 84–205 annual). Ottawa: Minister of Supply and Services, 1980.

Canada. Statistics Canada, *Vital Statistics, Vol. II, Marriages and Divorces, 1979*. (Catalogue 84–205). Ottawa: Minister of Supply and Services, 1981.

Canada. Statistics Canada, *Vital Statistics, Vol. II, Marriages and Divorces, 1980*. Ottawa: Minister of Supply and Services, 1982.

Ciuriak, Dan and Harvey Sims, *Participation Rates and Labour Force Growth in Canada*. (Series of papers on medium and long-term economic issues.) Ottawa: Department of Finance, 1980.

Clark, Susan and Andrew S. Harvey, "The Sexual Division of Labour: The Use of Time," *Atlantis*, Vol. 2, No. 1, 1976, pp. 46–66.

Davids, Leo, "Family Change in Canada, 1971–1976," *Journal of Marriage and the Family*, Vol. 42, No. 1, 1980, pp. 177–183.

Deckert, Pamela and Régis Langelier, "The Late-Divorce Phenomenon: The Causes and Impact of Ending 20-Year-Old or Longer Marriages," *Journal of Divorce*, Vol. 1, No. 4, 1978, pp. 381–390.

Eichler, Margrit, "Power, Dependency, Love and the Sexual Division of Labour. A Critique of the Decision-Making Approach to Family Power and an Alternative Approach. With an Appendix: On Washing My Dirty Linen in Public," *Women's Studies International Quarterly*, Vol. 4, No. 2, 1981, pp. 201–219.

Elkin, Frederick and Gerald Handel, *The Child and Society: The Process of Socialization.* New York: Random House, 3rd ed., 1978.

Fletcher, Susan and Leroy O. Stone, *The Living Arrangements of Canada's Older Women.* Statistics Canada Catalogue 86–503. Ottawa: Minister of Supply and Services, 1982.

Fulton, Julie A., "Parental Reports of Children's Post-Divorce Adjustment," *Journal of Social Issues,* Vol. 35, No. 4, 1979, pp. 126–139.

Hotaling, Gerald T. and Murray A. Straus, "Culture, Social Organization, and Irony in the Study of Family Violence," in Murray A. Straus and Gerald T. Hotaling (eds.), *The Social Causes of Husband-Wife Violence.* Minneapolis: University of Minnesota Press, 1980, pp. 3–22.

International Labour Organization, *1980 Yearbook of Labour Statistics.* Geneva: International Labour Office, 1980.

"Irish Republic makes legal birth control for marrieds," *Globe and Mail,* 1980 11 01, p. 12.

Kargman, Marie Witkin, "A Court Appointed Child Advocate (Guardian At Litem) Reports on Her Role in Contested Child Custody Cases and Looks to the Future," *Journal of Divorce,* Vol. 3, No. 1, 1979, pp. 77–90.

Kincaid, Patricia J., *The Omitted Reality: Husband-Wife Violence in Ontario and Policy Implications for Education,* Unpublished Ed.D. thesis, University of Toronto, Department of Educational Theory, O.I.S.E., 1981.

LaPerriere, Kitty, "On Children, Adults, and Families: The Critical Transition from Couple to Parents," in John K. Pearce and Leonard J. Friedman (eds.), *Family Therapy.* New York: Grune and Stratton, 1980, pp. 81–92.

LaRossa, Ralph, *Conflict and Power in Marriage: Expecting the First Child.* (Vol. 50 Sage Library of Social Research). Beverly Hills: Sage Publications, 1977.

Levitin, Teresa E., "Children of Divorce: An Introduction," *Journal of Social Issues,* Vol. 35, No. 4., 1979, pp. 1–25.

Longfellow, Cynthia, "Divorce in Context: Its Impact on Children," in George Levinger and Oliver C. Moles (eds.), *Divorce and Separation: Context, Causes and Consequences.* New York: Basic Books, 1979, pp. 287–306.

McVey, Wayne W. Jr. and Barrie W. Robinson, "Separation in Canada: New Insights Concerning Marital Dissolution," *Canadian Journal of Sociology,* Vol. 6, No. 3, 1981, pp. 353–366.

Meissner, Martin et al., "No Exit for Wives: Sexual Division of Labour and the Cumulation of Household Demands," *Canadian Review of Sociology and Anthropology,* Vol. 12, No. 4, Part I, 1975, pp. 424–439.

Moore, Kristin A. and Sandra L. Hofferth, "Effects of Women's Employment on Marriage: Formation, Stability and Roles," *Marriage and the Family Review,* Vol. 2, No. 2, 1979, pp. 1, 27–36.

National Council of Welfare, *Women and Poverty.* Ottawa: National Council of Welfare, 1979.

Peters, John F., "Divorce in Canada: A Demographic Profile," *Journal of Comparative Studies,* Vol. 7, No. 2, 1976, pp. 335–349.

Pike, R., "Legal Access and the Incidence of Divorce in Canada: A Socio-historical Analysis," *Canadian Review of Sociology and Anthropology,* Vol. 12, No. 2, 1975, pp. 115–133.

Renne, Karen S., "Childlessness, Health, and Marital Satisfaction," *Social Biology,* Vol. 23, No. 3, 1976, pp. 183–197.

Rosen, Rhona, "Some Crucial Issues Concerning Children of Divorce," *Journal of Divorce,* Vol. 3, No. 1, 1979, pp. 19–25.

Shanas, Ethel, "Older People and Their Families: The New Pioneers," *Journal of Marriage and the Family,* Vol. 42, No. 1, 1980, pp. 9–15.

Straus, Murray A., "Wife-Beating: How Common and Why?" in Murray A. Straus and Gerald T. Hotaling (eds.), *The Social Causes of Husband-Wife Violence.* Minneapolis: University of Minnesota Press, 1980, pp. 23–36.

Troyer, Warner, *Divorced Kids: A Candid and Compassionate Look at their Needs.* Toronto: Clarke, Irwin and Co., 1979.

Veevers, J.E., "Voluntary Childlessness: A Review of Issues and Evidence," *Marriage and Family Review,* vol. 2, No. 2, 1979, pp. 1+3–26.

Veitch, Edward, "Divorce Under the Divorce Act of Canada, 1968–1978," *Journal of Divorce,* Vol. 2, No. 3, 1979, pp. 295–312.

World Bank, *World Development Report, 1980.* New York: Oxford University Press, 1980.

World Bank, *World Development Report, 1981.* New York: Oxford University Press, 1982.

CHAPTER 3

Beyond the Sexist Bias in Family Literature

Introduction

Sexism can be defined as the socially structured expectation that people perform certain social roles and not others simply on the basis of their sex. For instance, if it is expected that a man be wholly responsible for the economic well-being of his wife and children simply because he is a man, this is a sexist expectation. Conversely, if a woman is expected to do all or the major part of the housework simply because she is a woman, this is likewise a sexist expectation. This definition of sexism is a very broad one which uses the criterion of the double standard — differential evaluation on the basis of sex of identical behaviours, norms, and practices — and is thereby more comprehensive as well as more easily employable than other definitions (see Eichler, 1980).

Within the family literature, sexism manifests itself primarily in two assumptions which are both very commonly made. The first assumption is that there is a natural functional differentiation on the basis of sex within families. The second assumption — which clashes directly with the first — is that there is only one reality for family members; in other words, that living within a given family unit results in a shared experience in which events or circumstances have the same effects on, and are perceived in the same way by, the various family members.

The two assumptions have two methodological consequences. Out of the assumption that there is a natural differentiation on the basis of sex comes the habit of researchers to ask different questions of the sexes. If one asks different questions, one gets different answers. The previously made assumption that the sexes do, indeed, have different functions is thereby seen to be confirmed.

Deriving from the assumption that family members share one reality is the methodological practice to ask only one family member — usually the wife/mother — about how a family functions, how the people within it feel, think, experience life, what they do. The answers are then *not* interpreted as the *perceptions* of the respondent about her (his) spouse's or children's experiences, thoughts, acts, feelings, but are treated as if they were fact.[1]

This is a rather extraordinary practice to engage in. Our entire sampling theory in the social sciences is based on the notion that people in different life circumstances — people of different ages, sexes, occupations, etc. — will perceive things differently. We therefore tend to control carefully for these variables, except when we study families, where it is suddenly assumed that one respondent can speak authoritatively for somebody else. Since there is also the first assumption, according to which there is a natural functional differentiation between the sexes which must therefore automatically result in very different experiences for women and men within the *same* family, the two assumptions are obviously contradictory. Nevertheless, they have happily co-existed for many decades. In this chapter, we will examine both assumptions, and some manifestations and implications of the ensuing methodological practices in detail.

Functional Differentiation Within Families

The most basic manifestation of an assumption of a natural differentiation of functions within families according to sex can be found in the equation whereby men are identified with work, and women and children with the family and home, which by definition is understood as a place of non-work, a place for leisure. A more sophisticated but related notion is that within families, wives and mothers function as the expressive leaders, while husbands and fathers function as the instrumental leaders.[2]

It is, of course, undoubtedly the case that in most families there is some task differentiation along sex lines. To identify this differentiation along expressive/instrumental lines, however, is problematic because first, it treats instrumentality-expressivity as two mutually exclusive dichotomous traits, rather than as two independently varying continua, and, second, it misinterprets the nature of the work of women, and possibly the emotional involvement of men in both their paid work and their families (see Eichler, 1980:39–45).

Nevertheless, time budget studies have confirmed time and again that women do, in fact, do most of the housework and are much more involved in childcare, and that men do tend to earn more (or all) of the money that is eventually spent on behalf of family members (for instance, on the house or apartment in which the family lives, on groceries, clothes, etc.). This is demonstrated by labour force participation rates which are still considerably higher for husbands/fathers than for wives/mothers, and by income differentials, which show that overall men's income is almost double that of women. The point is, however, that there is nothing *natural* about such differentiation, as demonstrated most plausibly by the fact that some of these things are changing at the present time, and can be expected to change even more in the future. We exaggerate the *degree* to which tasks, feelings, and interactions are differentiated if we assume, *a priori*, that they are (and possibly that they should be) so differentiated. Another point is that because a division of labour, as just described, used to be the societal norm, there is no reason to expect that it will continue to be the norm. Women may, in fact, still be doing most of the housework, but how many women still believe that they *should* be doing the major part of all housework, especially if they hold down a paying job themselves? As a matter of fact, how many men still believe that?

There are two major criticisms, then, that must be directed towards the assumption of a natural task differentiation between the sexes: first, an assumption of a *natural* differentiation leads to an overestimation of *actual* functional differentiation, and blinds us to changes that have occurred and can be expected to continue to occur in the future. Second, actual differentiation should not be equated with normative agreement with such a situation. It is possible that in the family interaction realm normative changes have developed more quickly than behavioural changes within the last decade. Should it be possible to demonstrate a large-scale discrepancy between norms and behaviours, we can expect some changes in this area, such that the one or the other is adjusted to reduce the discrepancy. Whether the norms or the behaviour will change will, in that case, depend largely on the overall context within which specific discrepancies occur.

The overestimation of functional differentiation becomes possible through the methodological practice of asking different questions of the sexes. In the following, we will examine in detail one example of how such overestimation may take place, by focussing on the work/family conflict for "working" mothers.

An Example of the Effects of Asking Different Questions of the Sexes

A very traditional question in sociological research is a question concerning the perceived conflict between work and family duties for mothers. The data that follow are taken from a recent Canadian survey, the POW Project.[3] In this survey, respondents were asked to agree or disagree with the following statement:

> If a married woman has to stay away from home for long periods of time in order to have a career, she had better give up the career.

The distribution of responses on the part of blue collar men and women, white collar men and women, male and female teachers, and male and female decision-makers (for a definition, see Appendix 1) was as seen in Table 3.1.

TABLE 3.1

Career/Family Conflict for Married Women

Women should give up careers	Blue Collar Workers				White Collar Workers				Teachers				Decision-Makers			
	Men		Women		Men		Women		Men		Women		Men		Women	
	%	n	%	n	%	n	%	n	%	n	%	n	%	n	%	n
Agree	59.4	57	64.5	60	56	56	34.6	34	30.2	29	22.2	22	33.5	49	13.1	19
Disagree	40.6	39	35.5	33	44	44	65.3	64	69.8	67	77.7	77	66.3	97	86.9	127
Total	100	96	100	93	100	100	99.9	98	100	96	99.9	99	99.8	146	100	146

Source: Previously unpublished data for POW Project.

As we can see from Table 3.1, agreement that women should give up their careers is substantial, although it varied greatly by socio-economic status. Of the blue collar workers, 59 percent of the males and 65 percent of the females thought that women should give up their careers if they took them away for long periods of time from their families. Of the white collar workers, 56 percent of the males and 35 percent of the females thought so as well, as did 30 percent of the male teachers, 22 percent of the female teachers, and 34 percent of the male decision-makers, compared to a low of 13 percent of the female decision-makers.

A conclusion one can reasonably draw on the basis of these data is that blue collar workers, both male and female, are more conservative in terms of sex role expectations than members of the other occupational categories, and that female blue collar workers are slightly more conservative than male blue collar workers. With increasing socio-economic status, both males and females become more liberal in their attitudes. With the exception of blue collar workers, women within each occupational category are more liberal in their sex role expectations than men. Overall, resistance to career involvement of married women is quite considerable, except in the case of the female decision-makers.

These findings are not inconsistent with those found in another Canadian survey. In this survey, respondents were told

> Mothers with pre-school age children are often restricted in their freedom to seek a job. Here is a card with two statements. Which one would you say you are most in agreement with, *assuming that there is no financial necessity for the mother to have a job.*

They were then handed a card with the following two statements:

> Do you feel that mothers with pre-school age children should stay at home and spend full-time with their children?
>
> OR
>
> Do you think that mothers with pre-school age children should be freed of the necessity of looking after their children if they choose to take a job?[4]

Of all the respondents (over 1000), 73 percent chose in December 1974 the statement that women should stay at home, and 75 percent chose this statement in December 1975. When the responses are broken down by sex and age, it turns out that women are more likely than men to think that women should be freed of the responsibility of looking after the children, and men and women under 35 are more likely to think so than men and women over 35. Finally, with increasing education, respondents are more likely to think that women should be freed of the responsibility, and people in professional/managerial occupations are more likely to think so than people in sales, clerical jobs, skilled labour and unskilled labour occupations (Decision Marketing Research, 1976:50–54).

The generally higher agreement in comparison with the POW data that women should stay at home can be attributed to the explicit and emphasized statement that there is no financial necessity for the mother to have a job. Overall, it is reasonable to conclude that there is as yet a high degree of resistance in Canada towards labour force participation of mothers of young children.

The problem with this type of conclusion is, of course, that it is based on one-sided and therefore biassed data. Childcare is defined exclusively as the responsibility of the mother, and the father's responsibility is totally ignored. We are making a conclusion about *sex* roles by asking only about women, without also asking about men.

In the POW survey, a corresponding question for men was, in fact, posed. It read as follows:

> If a married man has to stay away from home for long periods of time in order to have a career, he had better give up the career.

The responses to this statement are summarized in Table 3.2. Looking at the responses to this question changes dramatically our interpretation of the responses to the first question. Of the blue collar workers, 34 percent of the males and 49 percent of the females agree with the statement that men should give up their careers if they have to stay away too long from their homes, as do 44 percent of the male white collar workers, 24 percent of the female white collar workers, 19 percent of the male teachers, 23 percent of the female teachers, 25 percent of the male decision-makers, and 13 percent of the female decision-makers. Now can we truly still conclude that a majority of the blue collar workers is very traditional in their sex role attitudes, and furthermore that female blue collar workers are the most conservative of the lot? It now seems that a substantial portion of the agreement with the statement that in the case of a career/family conflict married women should give up their careers was *not* an expression of a conservative attitude with respect to sex roles, but instead an expression of how career involvement is valued in comparison to family involvement for all people, men as well as women.

In order to pursue this question further, the responses to the two questions were cross-tabulated, thus giving us information on how many respondents who agreed that married women should give up their careers also agree that married men should give up their careers, etc. The results of this operation are summarized in Table 3.3

For each category of respondents, the first cell gives the percentage of respondents who think that both the man and the woman should

TABLE 3.2

Career/Family Conflict for Married Men

Men should give up careers	Blue Collar Workers				White Collar Workers				Teachers				Decision-Makers			
	Men		Women		Men		Women		Men		Women		Men		Women	
	%	n	%	n	%	n	%	n	%	n	%	n	%	n	%	n
Agree	34.4	33	48.9	46	44	44	23.7	23	18.6	18	23	23	25.2	37	13	19
Disagree	65.7	63	51	48	56	56	76.3	74	81.5	79	77	77	74.8	110	87	127
Total	100.1	96	99.9	94	100	100	100	97	100.1	97	100	100	100	147	100	146

Source: Previously unpublished data from POW Project.

TABLE 3.3

Percent Double Standard re Family/Career Conflict*

	Blue Collar Men		Blue Collar Women		White Collar Men		White Collar Women		Male Teachers		Female Teachers		Male Decision-Makers		Female Decision-Makers	
	agree	dis-agree	agree	dis-agree	agree	dis-agree	agree	dis-agree	agree	dis-agree	agree	dis-agree	agree	dis-agree	agree	dis-agree
for women: agree	[1] 30	[2] 29	37	19	37	19	20	14	18	13	18	4	24	10	9	4
for men: disagree	[3] 4	[4] 37	7	37	7	37	4	62	1	68	5	73	1	65	4	83
**Double Standard Score	25		12		12		10		12		−1		9		0	

*all percentages have been rounded.

**Cell 2 − cell 3.

Source: Previously unpublished data from POW Project.

give up their careers if it takes them away from home too much. The second cell gives the percentage of those who think the woman should give up her career, but the man should not. This cell manifests a double standard with respect to women's family responsibility. The third cell gives the percentage of those who think a man should give up his career, but who do not think that the woman should do so. This group therefore manifests a reverse double standard with respect to men's family responsibility. The fourth cell, finally, shows those who think that neither the man nor the woman should give up the career. If we subtract cell 3 from cell 2, we get a composite measure of the degree of a double standard with respect to women's family responsibilities vis à vis her career. The last row in Table 3.3 gives the double standard score for each category of respondent.

The picture that emerges is very substantially different from that which was found in Table 3.1. When considering only a statement concerning a potential career/family conflict for women, female blue collar workers seemed to be the most conservative group. When putting the attitude in the context of a potential career/family conflict for men, female blue collar workers display attitudes similar to those of male and female white collar workers, and male teachers. Blue collar men now seem to be the most conservative group. However, while before 59 percent of them seemed to hold a traditional sex role attitude, now it becomes apparent that this can be rightfully said about only 25 percent; in other words, less than half the previously identified proportion. Large as the error is in this case, it is even greater for the other categories of respondents. Blue collar women, especially, drop from a proportion of 65 percent being traditional to 12 percent traditional, white collar men from 56 percent down to 12 percent, white collar women from 35 percent down to 10 percent, male teachers from 30 percent to 12 percent, female teachers from 22 percent to less than zero (one teacher more adhered to a reverse double standard than there were teachers who endorsed a double standard for women), male decision-makers from 34 percent to 9 percent, and female decision-makers from 13 percent to zero.

The magnitude of the error due to the simple fact that a question was addressed only with reference to one of the sexes suggests that we can no longer accept at face value any study that is based on one-sided questions asked of one sex only if it draws references with respect to both of them.

Nevertheless, this is so much the habit that we have virtually ignored the father role of men, and have assumed that women who are married and/or have children and a job necessarily have a role conflict, but that men who are in an identical situation do not. In the following, we will briefly consider both of these issues.

Men as Fathers

In a recent review of the literature on fathering, Fein (1978:127) described as a new and *emergent* perspective "the notion that men are psychologically able to participate in a full range of parenting behaviours, and furthermore that it may be good both for parents and children if men take active roles in childcare and childrearing." The *ability* of fathers to parent, then, is not even taken for granted; it is something that has just recently been discovered by researchers. Fein provides an illustrative example of the degree to which people even nowadays fail to consider fathers as parents:

> Describing the debate about family policy in the United States... Kenneth Keniston, comments on widespread concerns that maternal employment has resulted in inadequate care for many children. While noting that research has not supported a linkage between maternal employment and negative child outcomes (such as failure to thrive in infancy or criminality in adulthood), and arguing that children have a right to be nurtured, Keniston, amazingly, does not once mention fathers as a part of the solution to these problems... In ignoring almost one-half of potential child-carers (men), Keniston may be seen as writing from the traditional perspective on fathering. The exclusion of fathers in a consideration of the needs of children and families would appear to underscore the need for a new perspective.[5]

The fact that families with divorced and unmarried mothers are called one-parent families is also indicative of the degree to which fathers are ignored. Because they are not married to the mother of their children, they are treated as if they were non-parents. Since we do not ask about the fathering activities of fathers, we treat them as if they did not exist. While it may be true that many fathers do not engage much in parenting activities, those few studies that have actually tried to find information on this issue demonstrate that a blanket statement that men do not act as fathers is untrue, even in cases in which they do not live with their children.

There is now some research evidence from the United States that unwed fathers are by no means as unconcerned and uninterested in the child they fathered and the women they inseminated as has been assumed for so long. Pannor et al. (1978:333), for instance, found that in general birth fathers were concerned about the mother and the child in cases in which the child was eventually relinquished for adoption.

More importantly, Fürstenberg and Talvitie (1980) report from a longitudinal American study involving the male partners, most of whom were black, of 323 unmarried teenage childbearers, ranging from the time of pregnancy until the time when their first child had reached the age of five. Although the data are somewhat tentative, having been collected initially for a different purpose, and being based mostly on retroactive information derived principally from the mothers, the results are nevertheless fascinating.

By the final interview (age of the child five years), nearly half the couples had married, but of those married 51 percent had since broken up. This meant that about one father in five (21 percent) was residing with his child after delivery. Looking only at those situations in which the father had never married the mother of his child, about 50 percent maintained contact with their children, as compared to 59 percent of those fathers who had at some time been married to the mother but had since left. Where a father-child relationship existed, its quality was consistently rated very high by the mother. About 35 percent of the fathers provided some support to the family among those never married to the mother and among those at one time but no longer married to her.

The relationship between father and child depended heavily on whether the mother married another man: when the mother remained unmarried, 62 percent of the fathers continued to see their children, at least occasionally, as compared to only 9 percent when a surrogate father was living at home.

This suggests that a study of residence alone does not suffice to adequately judge the father-child relationship. As Fürstenberg and Talvitie argue:

> Little is known about the sexual dynamics of premarital dyads resulting in preganancy or the male's involvement in the resolution of pregnancy when conception occurs.
>
> Once the child is born, the father drops even further from sight. If, as is usually the case, the couple elects not to marry, it is more or less assumed that the father absents himself from the family altogether . . . . To substantiate this belief, researchers typically rely on marriage statistics or data on household composition. As we . . . show in this article, these measures do not reveal the role that males actually assume in child-rearing. Marriage figures and patterns of coresidence are at best an incomplete indication of the father's collaboration, for they do not show his participation in the day-to-day activities of the family at any given point in time or how such participation may vary over the child's lifespan.[6]

This demonstrates once more that relationships within the various dimensions of familial interactions can vary independently.

A complement to the notion that men do not act as fathers is the widespread concern with the dual role of women who are workers and mothers/wives. While it is undoubtedly true that in the majority of cases women who have paying jobs carry the major or the entire burden of the household as well as of childcare, and that they therefore experience role conflict between their work roles and their family roles, it is also true that few researchers try to explore whether men may also experience role conflicts between their work and family roles.

The Dual Role of Men, or, Why Sexist Science Fails to Understand Men

A recent article states explicitly what is still the predominant view on this subject, namely that "the role requirements of having a career and being a good father are not contradictory" (Darley, 1976:95).

This is, as yet, the consensus within the pertinent literature, with some exceptions. The classic book which for the first time explored fully "women's two roles" and which became, by focussing attention on this topic, a predecessor to much of the later literature, for one, had a much more sophisticated understanding of the intertwinings of the work and family roles of women and men. Myrdal and Klein wrote:

> We nowadays consider that the relation between husband and wife should be that of a partnership and this is the only pattern consistent with our democratic ideology. But the unholy alliance between an accepted ideal of partnership, on the one hand, and the persistence of the outward forms of the patriarchal family pattern, on the other hand, has led to many frictions and has put the contemporary marriage relationship under a heavy strain. This state of tension will only be overcome when between husband and wife there is a more equitable distribution of work and leisure, a common level of interests, and a joint share of responsibilities for home and family.[7]

And further along, the authors state explicitly, "Making husbands, and fathers, full partners in the affairs of their families, instead of mere *'visiteurs du soir,'* seems to us so much to be desired that, with a general shortening of working time in mind, we think the full-time employment of married women preferable to their doing part-time work" (Myrdal and Klein, 1968, 2nd ed.: 192).

Since that time, however, there has been a plethora of works which are concerned with the "dual" role of women, but which tend to downplay or ignore a potential conflict between work and home for men. A recent review of the literature examined all issues of 1975 to 1978 inclusive of the following journals: *The Journal of Marriage and the Family, The Journal of Social Issues, The Family Coordinator, The Journal of Comparative Family Studies*, the *American Journal of Sociology*, and *American Sociological Review*, and the *Canadian Review of Sociology and Anthropology*. The review found a total of eleven articles concerned with dual roles, plus two articles on dual-career couples. Of the eleven articles on dual roles, ten concerned the dual role of women, and only one considered the relation between work and family for males (Clark, Nye and Gecas, 1978).[8]

To cite just a few examples of a rich and varied literature, the dual roles of women[9] have been documented and/or commented upon for Canada (e.g., Armstrong and Armstrong, 1978; Nett, 1979; Lupri and Mills, forthcoming; Symons, forthcoming), Western Europe in general (Tomeh, 1975), Eastern European Socialist countries in general (Horna, 1977), Poland (Lobodzinska, 1977), Czechoslovakia (Horna, 1978), Italy (Balbo, 1978), Austria (Szinovacz, 1977), Mexico (Brinkerhoff, 1979), India (Ross, 1977), Kenya (Mutiso, 1978), and the U.S., for blacks as well as whites (Tomeh, 1975; Harrison and Minor, 1978), for married as well as cohabiting couples (Stafford, Backman and Dibona, 1977).

The problem we are dealing with, then, is generally seen as important. Nevertheless, to assume that while women experience family/work conflicts of a great magnitude men do not is unwarranted. It derives from the methodological fault, previously commented upon, of asking different questions of the sexes. By concentrating on the work/family conflicts for women — imporant as that is — we have neglected to study in a similarly intensive manner the work/family conflicts of men. This perpetuates, in a more subtle manner, the old identification of women with the family and men with paid work.

There is, by now, some limited evidence that men also experience work/family conflicts. A recent nationwide American study, for instance, asked working adults of both sexes how important their family, marriage, or children was in making the decision about "The hours you work, for example, overtime, full or part time, or day or night;

TABLE 3.4

Family/Work Interactions for Working Women and Men, U.S.A., 1980

	Percent stating that family, marriage or children were very or somewhat important in making decisions concerning:	
	Working Men	**Working Women**
Hours Worked	55	71
Commuting Distance	69	78
Accepting Promotion	63	73
On-the-Job Travel	72	77
Relocation of Family	80	85

Source: General Mills, Inc., *The General Mills American Family Report, 1980–81*, Minneapolis, 1981: p. 39, t. 27.

How far you commute to work; Accepting a promotion requiring greater responsibility and longer hours; How much on-the-job travel you'll accept; Transferring and relocating your family" (General Mills, 1981:39, t. 27). The results are intriguing. Women indicated on each item a higher degree of consideration given to their family than did men, but the differences between working women and men was comparatively small, and there was a substantial indication that men do consider their families when making such decisions.
Even in the case of the *least* consideration given to the family, a *majority* of men said that their family was very or somewhat important in making the decision they eventually did make. Of course, consideration is, as yet, not evidence of conflict, although it strongly suggests that decisions of men concerning their work are, in general, at a minimum influenced by their familial situation.

The POW Project provides us with some recent Canadian data on potential conflict between work and family roles for men. Among other things, respondents were asked a hypothetical question about a possible promotion in various situations of conflict. One of the situations included a work/family conflict. The question read as follows:

> Imagine you were offered the following possibilities at your place of work. Would you accept them or not?
>
> > Move to a higher level position even though it will make difficulties for your family?

The responses are summarized in Table 3.5.

TABLE 3.5

Accepting a Promotion That Would Entail Family Difficulties

	Women		Men	
	% Yes	% No	% Yes	% No
Blue Collar Workers (n = 100 females, 100 males)	5.4	94.6	13.3	86.7
White Collar Workers (n = 100 females, 100 males)	11.1	80.9	13.1	86.9
Teachers (n = 100 females, 100 males)	16.3	83.7	14.3	85.7
Decision-Makers (n = 150 females, 150 males)	48.6	51.4	28.8	71.2

Source: Previously unpublished data from POW Project.

There is no statistically significant difference by sex for the likelihood to accept the promotion for the blue collar workers, white collar workers, or teachers. In the case of decision-makers, there is a statistically significant association between sex and likelihood to accept a promotion ($\alpha = 0.05, x = 10.6$), with the women decision-makers indicating greater willingness to accept family difficulties than man. The most important finding, however, is the generally low willingness to accept a promotion under the condition stated.

To probe what workers consider to be problems for their families would be an obvious next step. Nevertheless, even if the meanings assigned to what constitutes a difficulty varies drastically by sex, it is interesting to note that men are aware of family/work conflicts within their own roles and that there are situations in which they are obviously willing to give precedence to the family role.

When researchers have bothered to ask about work/family conflict for men they have usually found some. Young and Willmott (1975:117), for instance, asked the working wives and married men of their large-scale British sample "whether they felt 'that the demands of your work interfere at all with the demands of your home and family.'" Of those working full-time 31 percent of the wives and 38 percent of the husbands, as compared to 17 percent of wives working part-time said that there were such conflicts.

Rapoport and Rapoport (1977), when studying and re-studying British dual career families, explored systematically the interrelationships between work and family life for both women and men and found a considerable amount of strains as well as gains deriving from a dual-career pattern for both the husbands and the wives.

The important point, then, is a methodological as well as a substantive one: substantively, there is sufficient evidence of family/work conflicts for men to make any broad statements as to the absence of such conflicts untenable; methodologically, we will only start to better understand the *nature* of these conflicts for men once we cease the sexist practice of asking women and men different questions. Of course we will find evidence for a dual role conflict for "working wives" (or a triple role conflict for "working wives and mothers," depending on author) if we ask about it. And of course we will not find such conflicts for men if we fail to ask them about it. Such one-sided questioning gives us at best a one-sided picture. Or worse, when authors fail to ask the same questions of both sexes because they assume that there is some natural differentiation of tasks between the sexes, they will greatly exaggerate the degree of differentiation by failing to observe indications of levelling of existing differences. We will turn to this question next.

Indications of Levelling of Differences between the Sexes

As far as family sociology is concerned, the greatest and most important difference between the sexes is in the identification of women with the family and housework and of men with paid labour. We have already seen that women are, in increasing numbers, participating in the paid labour force. This suggests that the behaviour of the women has changed. This is, of course, very true. What has received less attention, however, is that the behaviour of men has also changed somewhat (far less drastically, it is true) during this century with respect to labour force participation. This point is made by Hesselbarth (1978:8–10) for the United States, and it is also valid for Canada. If we plot the data concerning labour force participation of women and men contained in Table 2.4 on a chart to make the information visually more accessible, it becomes obvious that the great narrowing of the gap between male and female labour force participation is mostly due to an increase in female labour force participation, but also partially caused by a drop in male labour force participation.

The narrowing of the gap is even more impressive if we apply some more controls with respect to age. Chart 3.1 is based on information concerning all women and men over 15 years of age. This includes many people still in school, and a fair contingent of women who would probably like to have a job, but due to the combined effects of age and sex discrimination cannot find one. If we look, therefore, at men and women 20 to 24 years of age and at men and women 25 to 54 years of age, we get a more accurate impression of the sex differences in labour force participation that can be expected to be relevant for the future.

In the youngest age cohort, women and men of 20 to 24 years of age, the difference in labour force participation between the sexes was only around 13 percent in 1980. For the age cohort of men and women of 25 to 54 years of age, the difference in labour force participation rates between women and men declined from 59.6 percent in 1966 to 34.7 percent in 1980 — a really dramatic change considering it happened within only fourteen years.

As far as the greatest and most important sex difference concerning family and work is concerned, then, we still find a marked sex difference, but it is declining rapidly due to the greatly increased influx of women into the labour market and the slight decline of male labour force participation.[10]

A correlate to work in the paid labour force is, of course, unpaid work in the household. Even with extreme streamlining of tasks, there remains a substantial amount of housework to be done. Unfortunately, studies do not provide much evidence that men are partici-

CHART 3.1

Labour Force Participation Rates for Women and Men Over 15 Years, Canada, 1911–1980

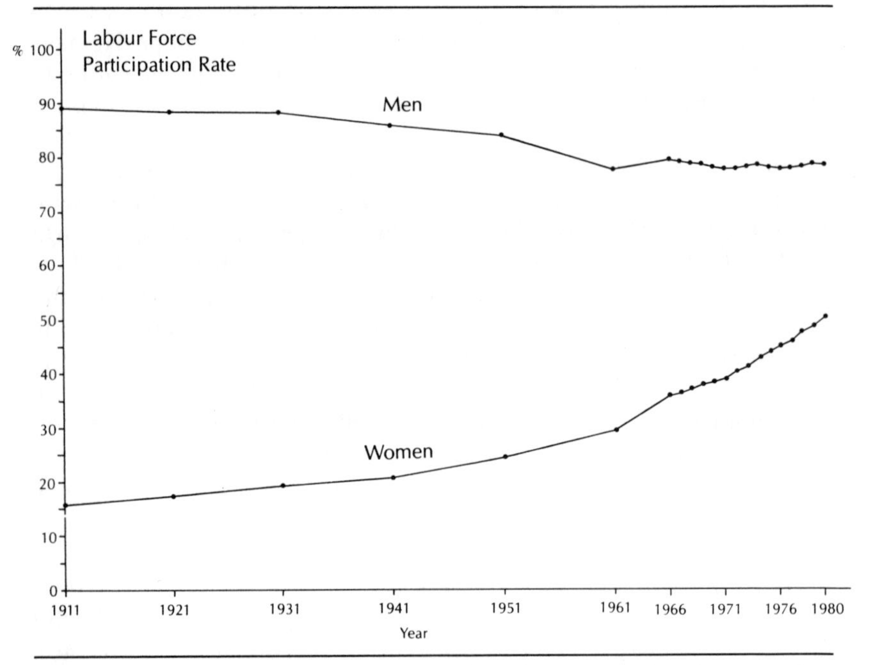

Sources: Statistics Canada, 1961 Census of Canada, Vol. III (Part 1) Labour Force, t. 1, for 1911–61; for 1966–79: Catalogue 71–201, Historical Labour Force Statistics, p. 151 and 156.
Note: Figures for 1941 include persons on Active Service on June 2, 1941.

pating to a comparable degree in household tasks as women are participating in paid work. To put this into a world-wide perspective, it has recently been calculated, by taking women's unpaid labour into account, that women today perform 66 percent of all the labour in the world while receiving only 10 percent of the total of all salaries and owning only 1 percent of all property (As, 1981:105). In this sense, the concern with the dual roles of women is still well founded.

On the other hand, the influx of women into the labour force has been recent and extremely rapid, while patterns concerning the division of labour in the household have been established for a long time. The fact that there is as yet little evidence of male participation in household work is, therefore, not necessarily an indication that male participation in the household will not substantially increase in the future. One indication that there may be future changes in the division of labour in the household are changes in the normative expectation as to who *should* do household tasks.

TABLE 3.6

Labour Force Participation Rates for Women and Men 20–24 Years, Canada, 1970–1980

Year	Men	Women
1970	82.7	60.7
1971	82.8	62.3
1972	83.4	62.8
1973	84.6	64.8
1974	85.5	65.4
1975	85.0	67.0
1976	85.1	67.4
1977	85.2	68.9
1978	85.8	70.3
1979	86.4	71.3
1980	86.2	73.0

Source: Statistics Canada, Historical Labour Force Statistics, 1980, Catalogue 71–201, pp. 154 and 159.

TABLE 3.7

Labour Force Participation Rates for Women and Men 25–54 Years, Canada, 1966–1980

Year	Men	Women
1966	96.5	36.9
1967	96.2	38.5
1968	95.7	39.3
1969	95.6	40.6
1970	95.3	41.9
1971	95.2	43.1
1972	95.0	44.6
1973	95.3	46.4
1974	95.4	48.0
1975	94.8	50.5
1976	94.8	52.1
1977	94.6	53.6
1978	95.0	56.6
1979	95.1	57.8
1980	94.8	60.1

Source: Statistics Canada, Historical Labour Force Statistics, 1980, Catalogue 71–201, pp. 155 and 160.

CHART 3.2

Labour Force Participation Rates for Women and Men, 20–24 and 25–54 Years, Canada, 1966–80

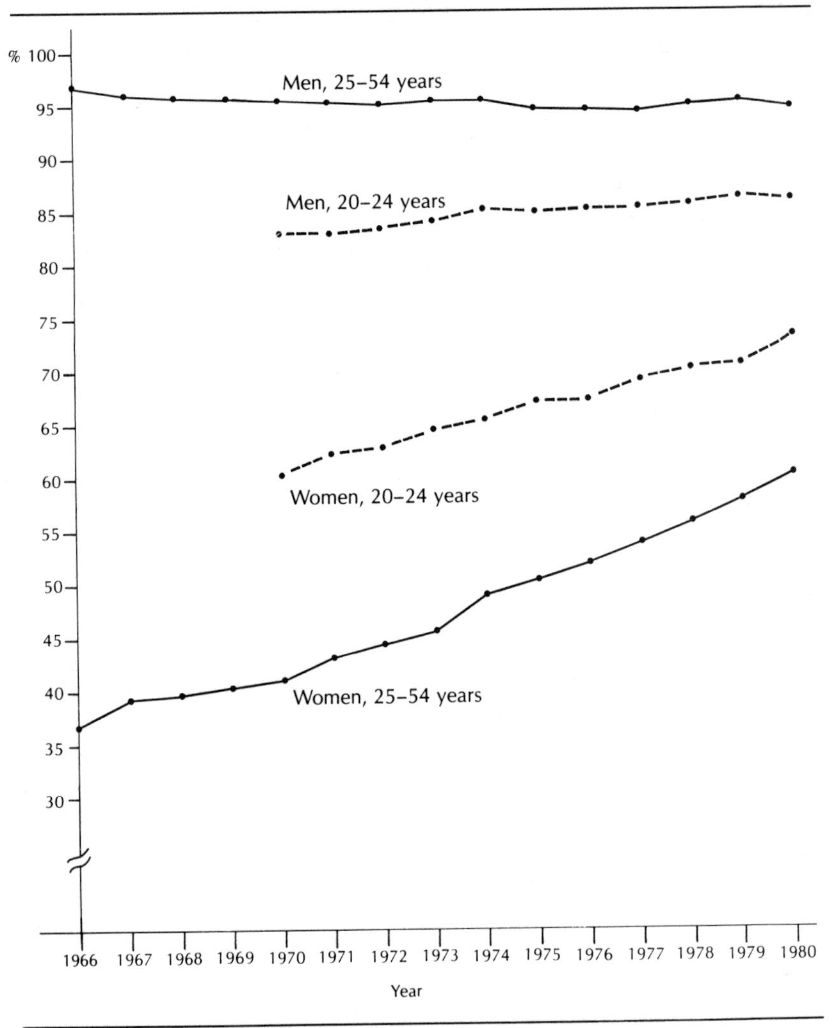

Source: Statistics Canada 1980, Historical Labour Force Statistics, Catalogue 71–204, pp. 152 and 157–178.

Where there is a situation in which a husband is solely responsible for the economic well-being of his family and a wife is responsible for the household, there is some justification in arguing that the major household jobs should be performed by the woman alone, since this constitutes her contribution to the family. Where, however, a wife and a husband both earn money, there is no reason why they should not also share the housework. The time of both of them is equally scarce, and it is blatantly unjust to expect one person to carry the entire or major portion of what may amount to an additional job.

This type of thinking seems to be making some inroads. In the POW Project respondents were asked:

> If two people are married and both have jobs and they have children who do you think:
>
> —should cook the family's meals?
> —should do the dishes?
> —should do the everyday family shopping?
> —should do the laundry?
> —should usually clean the house?
> —should look after the children?

The response options were *husband always, husband more than wife, husband and wife equally, wife more than husband, wife always.* This question is somewhat problematic in that it allows only for husband/wife participation in housechores, thereby excluding third party participation (e.g., children, domestic personnel, relatives) and in that it lists only those activities which traditionally have been assigned to women, rather than also some of the tasks that traditionally have been assigned to men (e.g., repair jobs, car maintenance, etc.), as well as by failing to specify that both jobs are full-time. Nevertheless, it does give us some suggestions about current normative thinking, which, of course, must not be confused with how housework is actually being done at present.

Looking at the responses by occupational category, we find the distribution in Table 3.8.

It is clear from Table 3.8 that the majority of respondents think that the majority of tasks should be performed by husband and wife equally (and in a few cases by the husband more or always).[11] A notable exception concerns the laundry. Among both male and female blue collar workers and male white collar workers a majority think that this task should be performed more often or always by the wife. Overall, however, the agreement with the non-traditional stance of sharing household labours is very pronounced.

Of course, this normative agreement is not yet translated into actual behaviour on the part of many people. This pattern was found by the previously cited nation-wide study of Canadians concerning women's roles (Decision Marketing Research Ltd., 1976:88–89). When respondents were asked who is at present involved in various household tasks, and who should be involved in them, the discrepancy between actual involvement and normative views was very pronounced. With respect to helping children with homework, 30 percent indicated either

TABLE 3.8

Normative Division of Household Labour

	Blue Collar Workers Men (n=100)		Blue Collar Workers Women (n=100)		White Collar Workers Men (n=100)		White Collar Workers Women (n=100)		Teachers Men (n=100)		Teachers Women (n=100)		Decision–Makers Men (n=150)		Decision–Makers Women (n=150)	
	% non-trad.	% trad.	% non-trad.	% trad.	% non-trad.	% trad.	% non-trad.	% trad.	% non-trad.	% trad.	% non-trad.	% trad.	% non-trad.	% trad.	% non-trad.	% trad.
Meals	61.1	38.9	58.3	41.7	45.3	54.5	62	38	73.4	26.6	75.5	24.5	69.1	31	78.3	21.6
Dishes	72.4	27.7	81.1	19	81.7	18.4	88.9	11.1	89.3	10.6	89.7	10.3	89.3	10.7	94.1	5.9
Shopping	75	25	66	34	75.5	24.5	72	28	87.2	12.8	80.6	19.4	82.1	17.8	85.7	14.3
Laundry	32.3	67.8	36.6	63.5	44.9	55.1	50	50	65.6	34.4	79.4	20.6	70.7	29.3	80.5	19.6
Cleaning	48.9	51.1	62.8	37.3	65.3	34.7	69.7	30.3	79.8	20.2	89.7	10.3	80.6	19.4	86.5	13.6
Children	80.9	19.1	84.4	15.5	79.4	20.6	87	13	91.3	8.6	96.9	3.1	82	17.9	91.7	8.3

Note: *Non-traditional responses include:* husband always, husband more than wife, husband and wife equally. *Traditional responses include:* wife more than huband, wife always. Figures do not always add to 100 due to rounding error.

Source: Previously unpublished data from POW Project.

that both husband and wife or the entire family was involved in that activity in 1976, versus 81 percent who thought that it should be a joint or family activity. With respect to taking the children shopping for clothes, the actual joint or family involvement was 18 percent; the normative agreement with joint or family responsibility was 46 percent. With respect to reprimanding the childen, the respective figures were 49 percent as compared to 87 percent; with respect to decorating a room, 39 percent versus 68 percent; with respect to painting woodwork outside the home 18 percent as compared to 37 percent; doing major food shopping 30 percent versus 46 percent, looking after the family budget 45 percent versus 74 percent; and lastly, doing the dishes, 31 percent of actual joint or family responsibility versus 66 percent of normative commitment to equality.

We are therefore dealing with a discrepancy between what people think they should do and what they actually do, and/or what their spouses think they should do and what they do. At a minimum, we can state with certainty that it is no longer accepted as unquestionably appropriate that the wife does the lion's share (the lioness' share?) of housework, if she holds down a paying job. One can perhaps cautiously interpret this discrepancy as a harbinger of social change and expect some modest changes towards increased involvement of men in household tasks within the next ten years, for two reasons: first, with increasingly long-term rather than short-term labour force participation of wives, husbands' lack of household participation becomes increasingly unjustifiable; second, with increasing divorce rates, there will be more re-negotiating of family roles, both in remarriage families as well as in first marriages, and most people will become aware of a variety of possible family styles because more people will be involved in non-traditional families with less sex stereotyped interaction patterns.

Complete sharing of household tasks, for a majority of couples is, however, only likely to occur when the generation of youth growing up in the 1980s form their own families. Unfortunately, there is no indication that parents are asking their children to participate to the limit of their capacities in household tasks. This is not a question which has received much research attention, and one is therefore reduced to trying to form a picture on the basis of impressions rather than on the basis of solid data. For as long as parents expect more household work of their girls than of their boys (Propper, 1979:165), and for as long as the mass media and the education system support a sexist division of labour within the home and in society, the young couples of tomorrow will have to repeat the struggles of their parents' generation.

By the same token, studies which show great conservatism on the part of adolescents or young adults with respect to sex roles must be considered with a grain of salt. There is a pervasive notion in the literature, stemming from a particular orientation within psychology that the major part of our learning is completed by the age of six, or possibly at a later stage of childhood. While undoubtedly the young years are very important for social learning, one must not forget that a lot of learning also occurs in the adult years, and as a reaction to growing into particular types of situations. For instance, adults are socialized into their work roles at their place of work.

Likewise, just as it is reasonable to expect that people will change their orientation by virtue of being within a particular job, we can expect them to change their orientation by virtue of forming their own families. With both spouses working for pay (as is highly likely to happen) new modes of internal divisions of labour are also likely to emerge.

So far, we have been dealing only with one manifestation of sexism within the family literature, namely the assumption that there is a natural division of labour between the sexes which is supported by the methodological practice of asking different questions of the sexes, thereby failing to notice the degree and manner in which things change.

The second major expression of sexism within the family literature is the assumption that living within the same family is a comparable experience for wives and husbands, and males and females in general. The same point made with respect to sex could be made with respect to age, of course. The fiction that family experiences are similar or identical for all family members is buttressed by the methodological practice of asking one family member to respond on behalf of herself (sometimes himself) as well as the other family members. When researchers take the trouble to investigate the same matters from the perspective of the various family members, they usually find rather large differences in how the same situation or event looks from the perspective of the various family members. We will turn to this question next.

The Separate Realities of Husbands and Wives, Women and Men

It may seem paradoxical to argue within one and the same book, and indeed within the same chapter, that the functional differentiation between the sexes has been somewhat overestimated due to sexist methodology and assumptions, but that the separate realities of husbands and wives, and women and men in general have been largely ignored also because of sexist assumptions and methodological practices. However, the two types of problems, although they go in opposite directions, are in fact mutually supportive. *Because* we have assumed that there is a natural functional differentiation between spouses we have not bothered to ask individuals to what extent these assumptions are true, thus misrepresenting the actual degree and nature of sexual differentiation. *Because* we assume that family members share one reality we often find it sufficient to ask only one family member about family circumstances thereby greatly underrepresenting the complexity of actual familial situations and relationships. Because we ask, in general, one-sided questions of only one member of an entire familial unit, we can maintain both fictions.

The first person to systematically elaborate the concept of "his" and "her" marriage was Jessie Bernard (1973). By bringing together existing evidence from the United States in a new manner, she demonstrated that, in general, marriage is good for men. Married men live longer and are happier and healthier than unmarried men. Married women, by contrast, are more likely to suffer from feelings of depression, to be unhappy, and generally be bothered by pains and ailments in various parts of the body than unmarried women. Bernard explains these findings by the objectively and subjectively different conditions of marriage for women and men (Bernard, 1973:16–58).

Since Bernard's book was published, more evidence of both subjective and objective differences, not only concerning the overall effect of marriage but also the effect of divorce and other family-related issues, has emerged. In the following, we will look at some of the existing evidence as well as at two case studies which exemplify both the subjective and the objective differences within marriage and divorce for women and men.

Objective Differences

The classic case of objective differences for women and men joined together in marriage exists in the case of breadwinner marriages, in which the husband goes every day to work and the wife stays at home, managing the household and childen, where present. We will briefly consider one case study from the Atypical Families Project.[12]

At the time of the interview (1978), Cheryl and Vincent Thompson had been married for about six years. They were both from a somewhat socially and economically depressed background. In 1972, Vincent came from Newfoundland to Toronto to find a job, and when he had found one, Cheryl came to join him. They married soon after. They had one son, Jason, four years old, and Cheryl was pregnant with the second (and last, as she says) child. Cheryl was a housewife, and Vincent manager of a firm that produced safety devices, a position to which he had to work his way up, having started as "low person on the pole."

They lived in one of those older and bigger Toronto houses, which was originally built for one family only, but which is now inhabited by several parties. The Thompsons lived on the ground floor and rented the second and third floor, which proved to be highly inconvenient for them, since there was no way to partition these two floors off or to provide separate entrances. This meant that everybody who lived in the house, or who came visiting one of the tenants, entered through the main front door. There was only one bell which Cheryl answered for the entire house. For the Thompsons to reach their bathroom in the basement, or to go from the living and dining room to the kitchen, meant that they had to cross the public hallway, through which at any moment one of the tenants or one of their guests might have walked. The living situation proved to be so difficult, indeed, that at the time of the interview the house had been put up for sale. The Thompsons have since sold the house and moved to an apartment.

When asked about her relationship with Vincent, Cheryl said:

Cheryl: You know, we get along. Our relationship is pretty good, you know, and he works a lot. Sometimes I'm alone quite a bit and I get very aggravated at that. He works a lot. I'm home all day with Jason and then I've got no one to talk to. I get cranky when he's not home and then when he does come home I'm so tired from the whole day that I don't feel like talking anymore, and sometimes he likes to talk about his work, you know. It's not that I am not interested in it — it's just that I don't know what his work is about. Like I know some of it, but not all of it, you know. We get along pretty well. We have our arguments off and on, but I think it's healthy to have your arguments. Because if you're married and you don't have any arguments, you know, it's just like he's walking in the door and you're going out. You're not communicating. You're not sitting down and talking it out and even if you are arguing, it's better that way to get it all out of your system. We argue, sure, like everybody else.

M.E.: What do you argue about?

Cheryl: Sometimes we argue about me because I do some silly things at times, you know.

M.E.: Like what sort of things?

Cheryl: Complaining about him working. Like not coming home earlier. Because he's had to do a couple of courses at work which demand a lot of his time and then I get very cranky and agitated because he's not home and I have to sit home alone and that just aggravates me no end. And then, when I call him up and tell him to come home, and he says, well, I have to work, and I'll say, can't you come home once in a while to see your wife and your son. What I am married to is your work. So he'll come home and then we'll start an argument about work.

M.E.: What time does he often come home or normally come home?

Cheryl: He normally comes home around 7:00, but basically now he's been coming home around 9:00 or 10:00 because he has to get this work done.

M.E.: How often has this been going on that he comes pretty late?

Cheryl: Let's see — for about a few months now. I guess five or six months. You see, it's a course he has to do and it's a lot of work. Like where he works it demands a lot of his time. I'm just starting to get used to the idea, you know.

M.E.: If Vincent comes home pretty late, does he see Jason at all?

Cheryl: No, if Jason's asleep, no.

M.E.: Like for a couple of months he actually had very little contact with Jason, then?

Cheryl: That's right.

M.E.: How about weekends?

Cheryl: Weekends, no, he's usually home. He's usually home and he spends a lot of time with Jason and me. You know, he sort of makes up for the lost time during the week, you know. Him and Jason play and they pal around, which is good. He makes up for it.

Vincent, when asked, describes a very similar picture.

M.E.: I was wondering how much time you yourself spend at home, because you have a lot of work to do?

Vincent: Well, let me put it to you this way. In the past, very little time. Not enough, okay. Mainly, because the company was growing so fast and they needed me, okay. And I was willing to work it, because there is a future there, and right now, it is tapering off.

M.E.: When did that start to taper off?

Vincent: In the last few months. Now that we've grown into a new plant and things are getting — like I've organized things better. It's getting to the stage where now I can leave at 5:00 or 6:00 as opposed to 8:00 and 9:00.

M.E.: So, what used to be your pattern and what is your pattern now? Before it tapered off, that's a couple of months ago. What would be a typical week then and what would it be now?

Vincent: A typical week, I would leave the house at 6:30 and I would get home maybe at 10:00. That was a typical week.

M.E.: That's Monday to Friday?

Vincent: Monday to Friday. And sometimes Saturday I would work from 8:00 in the morning at the company until 2:00 in the afternoon.

M.E.: Wow. And what would it be like now?

Vincent: Now it's more — I leave the house at the same hours because I start work at 8:00. I have to open the plant up. You see, I hold the keys. I leave around 5:00. I get home — it's very frustrating — I get home late. It annoys me, because I get stuck in the buses or something ridiculous happens. I've been trying so hard to get home, and it seems, the harder I try, the worse off I get.

M.E.: So when do you actually come home?

Vincent: I get home around 6:00, 6:30, 7:00.

M.E.: So then, for instance, you would see now, in this new pattern, you would see Jason in the evening but you wouldn't see him in the mornings?

Vincent: Right.

M.E.: And you would see him on weekends and things?

Vincent: Right. And this is what I want. I feel it is important. I should be around to play with him. I mean, my father was around when I needed him so, and I learned a lot from my father.

Cheryl and Vincent describe pretty much the same situation. There is not much discrepancy in their subjective appreciation of actual circumstances. But objectively, their circumstances are maximally different. Cheryl stays home the entire day. She suffers from a variety of allergies and back problems, and describes herself as a very shy person who does not easily make friends and who, indeed, does not have a single close personal friend in the city in which she lives. She is basically together with her four-year-old son during his entire waking time, without any adult company. She does not even go out to do the shopping by herself; she and Vincent go together on weekends to shop. She has no family here besides her husband and son (they all live in Newfoundland) and is not involved in anything but her household matters.

By contrast, Vincent spends almost all his waking hours either at his company or getting to and from it. (When their house was finally sold they took an apartment closer to his place of work, thus presumably cutting down on transportation time for Vincent.) He interacts all day long with other adults, and is tired when he comes home. He cares deeply for his family, and considers it his duty to carry life insurance, insurance for their furniture, and generally to provide for them. When asked about the importance of his family for him, Vincent said that it was important for him to have a wife like Cheryl and a son like Jason, who are there when he comes home.

Vincent: I find it important. And somebody to look after. To know that I am looking after them. I don't know if I could be the type of person where the wife could work and the man couldn't. I don't think I could live that situation. I have to be the one that is going out there making the money, looking after the family.

M.E.: Would it make any difference if you both went out to work?

Vincent: It wouldn't make any difference if Cheryl went to work. She would have the money herself. I would not, unless it was absolutely necessary, consider it part of the family money, in the sense, I would still, it would be my obligation to pay all the bills, etc. I would feel that whatever money she made would be hers to decide what to do with as opposed to mine. What she did with it then is again her own business.

The daily activities, the number and types of contacts with other people, the sense of purpose of life, the relationship with their son, the amount of time actually lived in the house, the approach to money, the involvement in household activities are maximally different for Cheryl and Vincent, and both would agree that this was so. The effect of Vincent's late work ensures a continuing upward career for him, but means very lonely days for her. The effect of the same event — the company's spurt of growth — has opposing consequences for the two. For Vincent, it broadens his responsibilities. He takes a course to improve his skills. For her, it means that she is without intermission responsible for their small son, and it results in a contracting of her social horizon, since she does not know how to go out on her own (with a young child and pregnant with the second) and develop her own social contacts.

This was not so before Vincent and Cheryl got married. Before their marriage, Cheryl took a waitressing course through Manpower, and worked for a short time after coming to Toronto. She quit her job after only two months because she had become pregnant and very sickly. Up to the time she quit her job, her life and Vincent's life were quite similar, but they started to diverge sharply after she stayed at home and even more so after Jason was born. This is a rather typical pattern (see La Rossa and La Rossa, 1981).

Both agree that with respect to Jason she is the "disciplinarian" and he is the "softie," so that even when Vincent is interacting with his son, he is interacting in a different manner from Cheryl. Objectively, then, the circumstances of Cheryl and Vincent are extremely different, although they are part of the same family unit.

Their circumstances were different in one other area as well. During the interview, Cheryl related that she had been raped at eighteen, had become pregnant as a result, and had given the child that she eventually gave birth to to an aunt of hers in Europe who could not have any children and wanted to adopt the child. This happened before she had met Vincent. Since I had neglected to ask her whether Vincent knew of this, but deduced from one comment Vincent made during the interview that he might not be aware of this circumstance, I did not feel free to bring it up in the discussion with him, and hence there is no comment from his side about the fact that Cheryl already had two children while he had one, and they were both expecting one more.

Vincent and Cheryl are just one example of how the same marriage may constitute a very different experience for the two marital partners. For him, being married and having a child or children constitutes his proclaimed reason for working hard at his paying job, while for her it means giving up a paying job.

Even when a wife continues to hold a paying job, the objective realities for husband and wife may nevertheless also be very different, due to the fact that the division of labour in the household tends to be very unequally distributed, with the wife doing most of the family-related work.

Just as the same marriage is likely to be different for the husband and wife within it, so divorce is a different experience for the divorcing spouses. Albrecht (1980) systematically examined the differences in the divorce experience of U.S. women and men. He found that overall the most important difference was that there was an immediate and dramatic downward economic mobility for women, while for men this change was much less important, and in fact, more of them experienced upward economic mobility than experienced downward economic mobility (Albrecht, 1980:67).

It is interesting to note that in spite of the wide divergence in the economic situation of divorced women and men, there was no significant difference in the proportion of women and men rating the post-divorce situation as much better than the pre-divorce situation, suggesting that the economic tradeoffs are worth it for women in terms of psychological gains made.

Canadian evidence is of a less systematic but similar nature. Baker (1980) looked at the consequences of divorce in an exploratory study involving 150 separated and divorced people in Toronto (53 men and 97 women). Respondents were identified through snowballing. She found that, in general, men were less likely to have money problems than women, and more likely to have opposite sex lovers and friends shortly after separation, while women were less likely to have lovers, and more likely to confide in same sex friends; in other words, both men and women were likely to fall back on female friends rather than on male friends. Women predominantly had custody of children, but men seemed to worry about their children to a considerable degree. The sheer fact of sole custody is an extremely important differentiating factor for divorced women and men, of course, resulting in different lifestyles, obligations, problems, and gratifications.

So far, we have been considering some of the objective differences in circumstances of wives and husbands, and divorced women and men. Just as important as the objective differences are subjective differences in the experience of being married, or divorcing, or having a child, etc. In the following, we will look at some manifestations of subjective differences.

Subjective Differences

Subjective differences manifest themselves primarily in discrepant responses to the same question (which may or may not reflect objective differences) and in differential experiences and evaluations of familial situations or events.

In a recent Canadian study, Brinkerhoff and Lupri (1981) compared the congruency of responses of husbands and wives with respect to who makes decisions about what within a couple. While the decision-making approach to conjugal power is a highly problematic method for assessing conjugal power (see Eichler, 1981), a focus on incongruencies in responses sheds some very interesting light on the different perceptions of wives and husbands concerning supposedly the *same* events. Brinkerhoff and Lupri (1981, t. 5) found that out of a total of fourteen decisions, the congruence in responses of husbands and wives exceeded 60 percent for only four of the decisions. Where there were incongruencies, the wife either reported herself as more or less powerful than her husband reported her to be, or the husband reported himself as more or less powerful than the wife reported him to be. With respect to four of the decisions, indeed, the discrepant perceptions as to who actually made the relevant decision exceeded the amount of agreement as to who made the decision. Looking only at those decisions with respect to which there was *least* agreement as to who made them, only 16.3 percent of respondents provided the interviewer with the same assessment as to who decided which job the respondent should take. Both spouses tended to see each other as more influential in this matter than they saw themselves to be. With respect to the spouse changing jobs, the congruence was 32.7 percent (meaning that 67.3 percent of the respondents disagreed as to who made that decision); with respect to money spent on food, 45.8 percent agreed as to who made that decision (meaning 54.2 percent disagreed); and with respect to the doctor called, 49.7 agreed (51.3 percent disagreed). Congruency for the rest of the decisions was between 40 and 50 percent.

This denotes a very high degree of discrepancy in perceptions as to who makes decisions, and underlines once more the need to ask both spouses separately about the same matters in order to get a full picture.

Lupri and Frideres (1981), using the same sample of Calgary couples, looked at marital happiness by sex, and found consistent differences between the expression of happiness with the marriage on the part of husbands and wives. Interestingly, they found that in their sample husbands were less contented with their marriages than were wives (the opposite of what is usually reported in the literature). They also found that the wives' employment had a positive effect on both the husbands' and wives' marital satisfaction, but the effect was much greater for husbands than for wives. While only 38 percent of husbands with wives who were not working outside the home reported that they were very satisfied or very happy with their marriages, 50 percent of those husbands whose wives worked for pay reported themselves to be very satisified or very happy. The corresponding figure for housewives was 48 percent and for wives working full-time 53 percent.

Other studies have documented similar discrepancies in the perceptions of wives and husbands with respect to a large range of issues. When Fulton (1979) interviewed 560 divorced U.S. parents, a distinct "his" and "her" perception of the marriage emerged. While only 6 percent of the divorced wives said the marriage was happy for them most of the time, 19 percent of the husbands stated that they were nearly always happy in the marriage. Correspondingly, the wives saw a higher degree of conflict and described arguments as violent significantly more often than did husbands. With respect to parenting contributions of both spouses during the marriage, both husbands and wives reported that the wife assumed the larger role in childrearing, but "The wives were far more likely than the husbands to say that they did each task alone or with very little help from their spouse, whereas the husbands suggested that they did more in terms of childrearing than would seem possible, given the wives' replies" (Fulton, 1979:130). Overall, "Husbands were more satisfied with themselves (81 percent) than were the wives (73 percent), but more of the wives (72 percent) were critical of their ex-spouses than were the husbands (55 percent)" (Fulton, 1979:130).

Similarly, Albrecht and Kunz (1980:325–336) found in a representative sample of 500 ever-divorced Americans that 84 percent of the females as compared to 74 percent of the male respondents reported that their marriage had failed to live up to their expectations for it.

On the issue of sexual satisfaction within marriage, Deckert and Langelier (1978), in examining the causes and impact of late divorces (after at least twenty years of marriage) of 299 late divorced Quebec residents and a control group of long-term married people, found that

> 63% of the late-divorced males reported that they had been sexually dissatisfied during their marriage, with 32% stating that sexual problems were the real reason for the divorce. Sexual dissatisfaction was reported by 75% of the divorced females, but only 3% felt that sexual problems

> were the real cause of the divorce. The married males reported a high percentage of sexual satisfaction (93.2%), whereas the corresponding females reported less sexual satisfaction (78.6%).[13]

Finally, Felton, Brown, Lehmann, and Liberatos (1980:246), in examining the function of sex-role attitudes as a coping resource to ameliorate the distress of marital disruption for an American sample, found that non-traditonal sex-role attitudes functioned as a coping resource for women, but not for men, although they are associated with decreased distress for men as well as women.

To provide one last illustration of subjective differences with respect to shared events among husbands and wives we will briefly consider one more case of the Atypical Families Project. This case involves a man, Robert Green, who divorced his first wife (Dorothea) and subsequently remarried. He had two children with his first wife, both of whom were adopted as infants. He has no children with his second wife, Kelly. All people concerned are from an upper-middle class background. I interviewed (separately) Robert Green, his second wife, Kelly Green, and his eldest son, Richard Green, then thirteen years of age.[14]

In this case, as in most others, there were several very clear expressions that the same event, arrangement, or relationship was experienced very differently by the different participants. Robert met Kelly about six months after he had separated from Dorothea. His son, Richard, saw Kelly (incorrectly) as the reason for his parents' divorce. Two or three months after they had met, Robert and Kelly started to live together. Robert got a Mexican divorce. Robert and Kelly married abroad, but the marriage was not legally recognized in Canada. Dorothea agreed to a divorce three years later, and Robert and Kelly celebrated a Canadian marriage almost immediately following Robert's Canadian divorce. When I asked Robert whether the Canadian marriage made any difference to them, he answered:

> Robert: None. It was just a ceremony. We didn't have a honeymoon or anything. I think it made Kelly's parents feel a lot stronger about me that I made the final commitment. So maybe it improved things with regards to her parents. Maybe it made us feel a little more secure, but I don't think it affected us very much.

By contrast, when I asked Kelly whether the Canadian marriage (by a Rabbi) made a difference, she responded:

> Kelly: Not because it was by a Rabbi but because it was a legal marriage — yes, it made a tremendous difference. It made a difference in our relationship, but part of it was also because he got his divorce. Yea, I think there was a tremendous difference, because I really felt he always felt his family was still his ex-wife and kids. I wasn't his family yet. He said I was imagining it, but the difference afterwards was tremendous, it really was.

M.E.: How did it show itself?

Kelly: Well, I just felt like he was more committed to me. I was his family. Whereas before, they were his family. He would feel guilty doing things for me. He wanted to spend every weekend with his kids. He would take them to hockey and it would be every weekend, and it was like they were his family. He used to say I was imagining this. It was a very real thing in my life.

The differential interpretation of the same event — marriage which is legal in Canada — is obvious from the comments. Another, equally marked difference shows itself with respect to the relationship of Kelly with Robert's two children, especially with his eldest son, Richard, whom Kelly describes as "a totally obnoxious child." While Richard considers Kelly as one of his special friends, lists her as a member of his family, considers her as somebody to whom he can turn for advice, Kelly does not consider Richard as part of her family, considers her contact with him as full of tensions, and sees him as conflict-producing for the relationship between herself and her husband. (This is in accord with the literature on remarriage which has identified children of previous marriages as a major source of stress for the new marriages. See Messinger, 1976:196.) To take a concrete example, there is the question of constant and uncontrolled access by the boy to her home. Kelly describes the issue as follows:

Kelly: . . . the eldest one wanted a key and my husband and I had a big fight about it. I said that it is my home and I don't feel like him being able to walk in at any time and my husband felt this was terrible. This was his son, and his son had a right to have a key to his house. How would I feel if my parents said that to me? And I had no argument other than the fact that I don't feel comfortable with his having a key. And he doesn't have one right now.

By contrast, Robert does not mention the issue of a key at all when asked about his own and Kelly's relationship to his children. He has noted that the relationship between Kelly and his eldest son was quite bad in the beginning, but considers it greatly improved at present. Kelly does not. According to Robert:

Robert: So, if anything, now I am closer to both boys than I have ever been. And Kelly has enhanced the situation a lot in the last year, too. I think she has done a lot on purpose. She knew why she was wrong and we know why the older boy had these feelings and could understand them — and things have improved a lot.

In fact, Kelly seems to have more contact with Richard than does Robert, since Richard occasionally drops in on Kelly during his lunch hour (without telling his own mother who would disapprove), and since he and his brother often have to wait for their father at his house when he wants to take them some place. Robert, then, sees the relationship between Kelly and Richard as smoother than does Kelly. Richard, likewise, experiences less conflict with his father's wife than she does with him.

This case provides some illustration of the different perceptions of the same situation on the part of different members of a family. It also demonstrates that the distinction between subjective and objective differences is a fluid one. While it is a useful heuristic distinction to make, subjective differences may be due to objective differences, as in the case of the relationship between Kelly and Robert's children, where both objective and subjective realities vary for Robert and Kelly.

On the other hand, subjective differences may increase objective differences, as in the case of Cheryl and Vincent. Cheryl's social isolation, for instance, is compounded by the fact that she considers herself a shy and retiring person who cannot make contacts on her own with other people. Even though she labours under great restrictions due to the unmitigated and constant responsibility for a very active four-year-old, given a somewhat different personality she might be able to establish some contact with neighbours, or with her tenants, which goes beyond exchanging the time of day. By doing this, one aspect of the objective differences in her and Vincent's situation — her total lack of adult company as against his constant interacting with other adults — might be somewhat lessened.

Summary

In this chapter, we have looked at two ways in which a sexist bias manifests itself in family literature, namely through an assumption that there is a natural functional differentiation on the basis of sex within families, and an assumption that living within the same family unit results in comparable experiences for all family members. Both assumptions are supported by two methodological practices which in turn are themselves derived from the two assumptions, namely the practices of asking different questions of the sexes and asking only one family member a question in order to find out information about all members of a particular family.

The two assumptions and methodological practices pervade large segments of the family literature. Often the bias that is introduced through them is of a subtle rather than of an obvious nature. The examples that we have been looking at so far have not been particularly blatant examples of sexism. There are, of course, many instances of a sexist bias which are much more blatant. A recent example, for instance, is a study which asks itself "Do Adolescents Believe the Employment of Wives is a Threat to Marital Relationships?" This question is addressed by analyzing the responses to the following five items:

1. A husband should feel like a failure if his wife works.
2. A husband should feel like a failure if his wife earns more than he does.
3. A working wife is likely to be less of a companion to her husband.
4. A working wife is likely to neglect her husband.
5. A working wife is likely to become too independent.[15]

This is a much more blantant example of sexist research. The questions are premised on the notion of a natural differentiation of tasks on the basis of sex which results in one-sidedness — there are no corresponding items, for instance, that state that a wife should feel like a failure if her husband works, or if he earns more money than she does, that a working husband is likely to be less of a companion to his wife, is likely to neglect her, and to become too independent. There is also no possibility of finding out if a husband feels like a failure if his wife does *not* work. Beyond that, there is no possibility of a positive outcome of a wife's working for pay; in other words, the questions allow only for half of a possible continuum of responses. All questions are phrased in negative terms. The most a respondent can do is to reject the negativism, but there is no possibility of expressing a positive reaction to a wife's holding a paid job. This could, of course, be easily achieved by phrasing the questions differently. For instance, if the intent of a question is to explore the relationship between perceived companionship within a marriage and working status, a non-sexist way of addressing this issue could be "A couple in which both spouses have paying jobs is likely to share more (less, the same amount of) companionship than a couple in which only one spouse has a paying job."

Another reason why the above example is sexist which has not been touched upon so far is that the wife's job is seen only in relation to her husband, not to herself. Ostensibly, the intent of the article, as expressed in the title, is to see whether adolescents perceive a wife's employment as a threat to a marital *relationship,* but in fact, the questions address themselves to the reaction of the *husband* only. What if the wife's job had a positive effect on her but a negative effect on the husband? (As we have seen above, there are Canadian data which suggest that the wife's job increases the husband's marital happiness significantly, but we are here concerned with the phrasing of the question.) Whose definition of the effect on relationships would prevail? The fact that male and female respondents were asked to respond to the statements does not alter the fact that they were both asked to respond in terms of the effect on the husband only.

Another sexist assumption underlying the above set of questions is that female dependency is seen as a positive aspect of marital relationships, and female independence is seen as a threat. Presumably, the corresponding assumption that a man is independent by virtue of having a job is not seen as a threat to the marital relationship. The questions, as posed, are therefore sexist in a way that goes beyond the two types of sexist assumptions and methodological practices that have been considered.

We have focussed the discussion on particularly salient aspects of sexism in the family literature, such as the neglect of the parenting role of fathers, the neglect of examining the work/family linkages for working husbands not just from the perspective of a job intruding on the family, but also of the family intruding on the job (dual roles of working husbands), the failure of the literature to focus on changes and the thereby resulting overestimation of actual degrees and types of differentiation, the neglect of systematically exploring the different subjective and objective realities of women and men living in the same families, and others.

However, sexist biasses pervade the entire literature and go beyond these points. For instance, in the literature on alcoholism, there is a tendency to blame the wife of an alcoholic husband but not to blame the husband of an alcoholic wife. In two recent reviews of the pertinent literature, sexist biasses were pointed out. Steinglass (1979:13) has noted "The intense interest in identifying personality factors associated with wives of alcoholic men has not been paralleled by a similar level of interest in husbands of alcoholic women." And McCormack (1980) has demonstrated that the drinking of women has been studied as a private problem while the drinking of men has been studied as a public problem.

As a last example, one of the areas in which we find sexist attitudes displayed particularly often is the area of sexuality, especially teenage sexuality. In a review of the literature on illegitimate births to adolescents, the author identifies a sexist bias as one of the problems in the literature:

> It is blatantly sexist to assume, as much of the social and psychological research and clinical literature does, that nonmarital pregnancy and childbearing is a peculiarly female problem. Although it is the young woman who becomes pregnant, her male partner shares equally in creating this condition.
>
> This sexist bias is further reflected in much of the research about illegitimacy (not to mention nonmarital sex, contraception, and abortion). Only a few investigators have studied the causes of unmarried fatherhood . . . . These studies of unmarried fathers are characterized by extremely small and seriously inadequate samples. It is frequently said

> that it is much more difficult to reach adolescent males than females in studies of sexual behaviour. One reason for this difficulty is the conviction that this is true.[16]

Sexism in family studies, then, goes beyond the two manifestations focussed on in this chapter. Nevertheless, they can be identified as the *most important* manifestations of sexism in the family literature.

If we wish to go beyond a sexist bias in family studies, we need to avoid all forms of sexist thinking. This includes using non-sexist language and concepts, considering the perspective of both women and men, as well as not making an assumption about a natural differentiation of tasks between the sexes. Instead, we need to explore the current differentiation that does exist by examining each issue with respect to its applicability for and effects on both sexes. This means that we must avoid asking different questions of the sexes and must start asking the same questions of both of them. Maybe it is true that a husband feels like a failure if his wife earns more money than he does, and maybe it is also true that a wife feels like a failure if her husband earns more than she does. Better yet, we could explore the effects of salary differentials on marital relationships in general, and what the reasons are that enable some couples to cope better with them than others.

We must also cease to assume that one person within a family can speak for another. This means more cumbersome and more costly research. If we ask both husband and wife about their marital relationship, or all family members, including children, about general family matters, we need to study the incongruities, and we will end up with much less clear-cut data than we get if we only examine one version as to what is happening within a family. But maybe those more cumbersome data will provide us with more useful information. Real life is never very clear-cut and unambiguous, either.

For reasons of practicality and economy, it can be expected that many researchers will continue to ask only one person in a family about family matters. At the least, in such a case, we must interpret the responses as only one person's perceptions, and not confuse them with reality. Even very simple, straightforward looking questions may result in complex answers if we ask them of more than one person. When I asked Cheryl how many children she had, she said two and expecting another. When I asked Vincent, he said one and expecting another. It was a first marriage for both of them, and only one child was living with them. Both responses were correct; they reflected the fact that the number of children was not identical for the two spouses. This type of probing will be increasingly important in the future, with more and more divorces and remarriages, and more and more discrepancy between spousal and parental roles. Once we drop the prevailing sexist bias, along with the monolithic, conservative, and micro-structural biasses, family literature might start to reflect some of the complexity, intensiveness, importance, and internal and external contradictions inherent in family relationships.

Notes

1. This practice has been severely criticized by Safilios-Rothschild (1970) and others, and since that time, there has been an increasing awareness that it is necessary to investigate husbands and wives separately if we wish to learn about both of them. Some of the literature which is aware of the problem inherent in asking only one family member will be cited in this chapter. However, the practice of treating respondents' statements about their spouses' or children's behaviours and feelings as if they constituted an accurate representation of these behaviours and feelings persists to this day.
2. It is interesting to note that children are seen only as the beneficiaries of the instrumental/expressive activities of their parents in this approach. They seem to perform neither expressive nor instrumental functions themselves.
3. See appendix 1 for a description of the POW Project.
4. From *Women in Canada*, 2nd ed. Prepared for International Women's Year Secretariat Privy Council Office, released by the Office of the Co-ordinator, Status of Women, Ottawa, © 1976, p. 213. Reprinted by permission of Status of Women Canada.
5. From "Research on Fathering: Social Policy and an Emergent Perspective" which appeared in *Journal of Social Issues*, Vol. 34, No. 1 © 1978 reprinted by permission of Journal of Social Issues, p. 113.
6. Frank F. Fürstenberg, Jr. and Kathy Gordon Talvitie, "Children's Names and Paternal Claims: Bonds between Unmarried Fathers and their Children," *Journal of Family Issues*, Vol. 1, No. 1 (1980):32.
7. From *Women's Two Roles: Home and Work*, 2nd ed. by Alva Myrdal and Viola Klein © 1968 reprinted by permission of Routledge & Kegan Paul Ltd. and Humanities Press Inc., Atlantic Highlands, NJ 07716
8. This literature review is contained in an unpublished paper by Hanneke van Leeuwen, written for the Advanced Research Seminar on Education and the Sociology of Women and Gender Relations, taught by M. Eichler, in the winter of 1979.
9. Occasionally the discussion is conducted in terms of the *triple* rather than dual roles of women, depending on whether the breakdown is conceptualized as one of work/family, or as one of paid labour/wife role/mother role. The following references are in no way intended to provide an overview of the literature, but merely to suggest the vastness and diversity of the literature by citing some recent examples.
10. The male decline in labour force participation levelled off in the sixties. It is not reflected in Tables 3.6 and 3.7, which are restricted to a more recent time period.
11. This statement is based on the uncollapsed data; it cannot be deduced from Table 3.8.
12. The Atypical Families Project is briefly described in appendix 2. The Thompsons were selected for the project not because of some structural or compositional atypicality, but simply by virtue of the fact that they had tenants living within the same house, from whom the Thompson household was only imperfectly separated, due to the architecture of the house.
13. Pamela Deckert and Régis Langelier, "The Late-Divorce Phenomenon: the Causes and Impact of Ending 20-Year-Old or Longer Marriages," *Journal of Divorce*, Vol. 1, No. 4 (1978):387.

14. The first wife and the younger son were not available for an interview.
15. Karl King, Thomas J. Abernathy, Jr., and Ann H. Chapman, "Do Adolescents Believe the Employment of Wives is a Threat to Marital Relationships?" *The Family Coordinator,* Vol. 27, No. 3 (1978):232.
16. "Illegitimate Births to Adolescents: An Overview of Social and Psychological Research." From *Marriage & Family Review,* Vol. 2, No. 4, by Catherine S. Chilman reprinted by permission of The Haworth Press, Inc., 1979, p. 5.

References

Albrecht, Stan L., "Reactions and Adjustments to Divorce: Differences in the Experiences of Males and Females," *Family Relations,* Vol. 29, No. 1, 1980, pp. 59–68.

Albrecht, Stan L. and Phillip R. Kunz, "The Decision to Divorce: A Social Exchange Perspective," *Journal of Divorce,* Vol. 3, No. 4, 1980, pp. 319–337.

Armstrong, Pat and Hugh Armstrong, *The Double Ghetto: Canadian Women and their Segregated Work.* Toronto: McClelland and Stewart, 1978.

As, Berit, "A Five-Dimensional Model for Change: Contradictions and Feminist Consciousness," *Women's Studies International Quarterly* (special issue on Women in Futures Research, ed. by Margrit Eichler and Hilda Scott), Vol. 4, No. 1, 1981, pp. 101–114.

Baker, Maureen, *Support Networks and Marriage Dissolution* (Final Report of Project Funded by Connaught Foundation, University of Toronto, 1979–80), 1980.

Balbo, Laura, "Emerging Family and Work Role Patterns in Italian Society: Women and Social Change," unpublished paper delivered at the International Sociological Association Meetings, in Uppsala, Sweden, 1978.

Bernard, Jessie, *The Future of Marriage.* New York: Bantam Books, 1973.

Brinkerhoff, Merlin B., "Structural Factors that Affect Married Women's Work Status: A Comparative Analysis of Canada and Mexico," unpublished paper delivered at Pacific Sociological Association Meetings, Anaheim, California, 1979.

Brinkerhoff, Merlin B. and Eugen Lupri, "Conjugal Power and Family Relationships: Some Theoretical and Methodological Issues," in K. Ishwaran (ed.), *The Canadian Family.* Toronto: Gage Publishing Limited, 1983.

Canada. Statistics Canada. *Historical Labour Force Statistics 1980.* Catalogue 71–201. Ottawa: Minister of Supply and Services, 1981.

Chilman, Catherine S., "Illegitimate Births to Adolescents: An Overview of Social and Psychological Research," *Marriage and Family Review,* Vol. 2, No. 4, 1979, pp. 1, 3–11.

Clark, Robert A., F. Ivan Nye and Victor Gecas, "Husbands' Work Involvement and Marital Role Performance," *Journal of Marriage and the Family,* Vol. 40, No. 1, 1978, pp. 9–21.

Darley, Susan A., "Big Time Careers for the Little Woman: A Dual-Role Dilemma," *Journal of Social Issues,* Vol. 32, No. 3, 1976, pp. 85–98.

Decision Marketing Research Ltd., *Women in Canada* (Prepared for International Women's Year Secretariat Privy Council Office, released by Office of the Co-ordinator, Status of Women). Ottawa: 2nd ed., 1976.

Deckert, Pamela and Régis Langelier, "The Late-Divorce Phenomenon: The Causes and Impact of Ending 20-Year-Old or Longer Marriages," *Journal of Divorce,* Vol. 1, No. 4, 1978, pp. 381–390.

Eichler, Margrit, *The Double Standard: A Feminist Critique of Feminist Social Science.* London: Croom Helm; New York: St. Martin's Press, 1980.

Eichler, Margrit, "Power, Dependency, Love and the Sexual Division of Labour: A Critique of the Decision-Making Approach to Family Power and an Alternative Approach. With an Appendix: On Washing My Dirty Linen in Public," *Women's Studies International Quarterly,* Vol. 4, No. 2, 1981, pp. 201–219.

Fein, Robert A., "Research on Fathering: Social Policy and an Emergent Perspective," *Journal of Social Issues*, Vol. 34, No. 1, 1978, pp. 122–135.

Felton, Barbara J., Prudence Brown, Stanley Lehmann, Penny Liberatos, "The Coping Function of Sex-Role Attitudes during Marital Disruption," *Journal of Health and Social Behavior*, Vol. 21, No. 3, pp. 240–248.

Fulton, Julie A., "Parental Reports of Children's Post-Divorce Adjustment," *Journal of Social Issues*, Vol. 35, No. 4, 1979, pp. 129–139.

Fürstenberg, Frank F. Jr. and Kathy Gordon Talvitie, "Children's Names and Paternal Claims: Bonds between Unmarried Fathers and their Children," *Journal of Family Issues*, Vol. 1, No. 1, 1980, pp. 31–57.

General Mills, Inc., *The General Mills American Family Report, 1980–81. Families at Work: Strengths and Strains*. Minneapolis: General Mills, 1981.

Harrison, Algea Othella and Joanne Holbert Minor, "Interrole Conflict, Coping Strategies, and Satisfaction Among Black Working Wives," *Journal of Marriage and the Family*, Vol. 40, No. 4, 1978, pp. 799–805.

Hesselbart, Susan, "Some Underemphasized Issues About Men, Women, and Work," paper given at the American Sociological Association Meetings in San Francisco, 1978.

Horna, Jarmila L.A., "Women in East European Socialist Countries," in Patricia Marchak (ed.), *The Working Sexes: Symposium Papers on the Effects of Sex on Women at Work*. Vancouver: Institute of Industrial Relations, University of British Columbia, 1977, pp. 137–150.

Horna, Jarmila L.A., "Current Literature on the Position and Roles of Women in Czechoslovakia," *Canadian Slavonic Papers*, Vol. 20, No. 1, 1978, pp. 78–90.

King, Karl, Thomas J. Abernathy, Jr., and Ann H. Chapman, "Do Adolescents Believe the Employment of Wives is a Threat to Marital Relationships?", *The Family Coordinator*, Vol. 27, No. 3, 1978, pp. 231–235.

LaRossa, Ralph and Maureen Mulligan LaRossa, *Transition to Parenthood: How Infants Change Families* (Vol. 119 Sage Library of Social Research). Beverly Hills: Sage Publications, 1981.

Lobodzinska, Barbara, "Married Women's Gainful Employment and Housework in Contemporary Poland," *Journal of Marriage and the Family*, Vol. 39, No. 2, 1977, pp. 405–415.

Lupri, Eugen and James Frideres, "The Quality of Marriage and the Passage of Time: Marital Satisfaction over the Family Life Cycle," *Canadian Journal of Sociology*, Vol. 6, No. 3, 1981, pp. 283–305.

Lupri, Eugen and Donald L. Mills, "The Changing Roles of Canadian Women in Family and Work: An Overview," in Eugen Lupri (ed.), *The Changing Positions of Women in Family and Society: A Cross-National Comparison*. Leiden: E.J. Brill, 1982, pp. 8–32.

McCormack, Thelma, "Drinkers, Drys and Drunks: Women and Alcohol Consumption in Popular Culture and Ideology," unpublished paper presented at the York University of Toronto Women's Research Colloquia, 1980.

Messinger, Lillian, "Remarriage Between Divorced People with Children from Previous Marriages: A Proposal for Preparation for Remarriage," *Journal of Marriage and Family Counselling*, 1976, Vol. 2, No. 2, pp. 193–200.

Mutiso, Roberta M., "Career-Role/Family-Role Conflict among Women Agricultural Extension Officers in Kenya," unpublished paper delivered at the International Sociological Association Meetings in Uppsala, Sweden, 1978.

Myrdal, Alva and Viola Klein, *Women's Two Roles: Home and Work*. London: Routledge and Kegan Paul, 2nd ed., 1968.

Nett, Emily M., "Marriage and the Family: Organization and Interaction," in G.N. Ramu (ed.), *Courtship, Marriage and the Family in Canada*. Toronto: Macmillan of Canada, 1979, pp. 59–77.

Pannor, Reuben, Annette Baran, and Arthur D. Sorosky, "Birth Parents Who Relinquished Babies for Adoption Revisited," *Family Process*, Vol. 17, No. 3, 1978, pp. 329–337.

Pleck, Joseph H., "The Work-Family Role System," *Social Problems*, Vol. 24, No. 4, 1977, pp. 417–427.

Propper, Alice, "The Relationship of Maternal Employment and Sex to Adolescents' Parental Relationships," in K. Ishwaran (ed.), *Childhood and Adolescence in Canada*. Toronto: McGraw-Hill Ryerson, 1979, pp. 161–176.

Rapoport, Rhona and Robert Rapoport, *Dual-Career Families Re-examined: New Integrations of Work and Family*. New York: Harper Colophon Books, 1977.

Ross, Aileen D., "Some Comments on the Home Roles of Businesswomen in India, Australia, and Canada," *Journal of Comparative Family Studies*, Vol. 8, No. 3, 1977, pp. 327–340.

Safilios-Rothschild, Constantia, "Family Sociology or Wives' Family Sociology? A Cross-Cultural Examination of Decision-Making," *Journal of Marriage and the Family*, May 1969, pp. 290–301.

Stafford, Rebecca, Elain Backman and Pamela Dibona, "The Division of Labour among Cohabiting and Married Couples," *Journal of Marriage and the Family*, Vol. 39, No. 1, 1977, pp. 43–57.

Steinglass, Peter, "Alcoholism and the Family: A Review," *Marriage and Family Review*, Vol. 2, No. 4, 1979, pp. 1, 12–19.

Symons, Gladys L., "Egalitarianism in Marriage? Graduate Education and the Sexual Division of Labour in the Canadian Family," in Eugen Lupri (ed.), *The Changing Positions of Women in Family and Society: A Cross-National Comparison*. Leiden: E.J. Brill, 1982.

Szinovacz, Maximilliane E., "Role Allocation, Family Structure and Female Employment," *Journal of Marriage and the Family*, Vol. 39, No. 4, 1977, pp. 781–791.

Tomeh, Aida K., *The Family and Sex Roles*. Toronto: Holt, Rinehart and Winston, 1975.

Van Leeuwen, Hanneke, "Dual Roles for Women and Men?" Unpublished paper. Toronto: The Ontario Institute for Studies in Education, 1979.

Young, Michael and Peter Willmott, *The Symmetrical Family: A Study of Work and Leisure in the London Region*. Harmondsworth: Penguin, 1975.

CHAPTER 4

Beyond the Microstructural Bias in Family Literature

Introduction

So far we have looked at three prevailing biasses in family literature: a monolithic bias, a conservative bias, and a sexist bias. These three biasses support each other in a very direct manner. The conservative bias can be understood as a direct consequence of the monolithic bias, while the sexist bias is an integral aspect of the monolithic and the conservative biasses and vice versa. The situation is somewhat different with respect to the microstructural bias. The relationship between this bias and the other three biasses is an indirect rather than a direct one, since there may be a microstructural bias whether or not any of the other three biasses obtain. Conversely, family literature which is oriented towards macroanalysis may still be monolithic, conservative, and sexist.

The microstructural bias is here defined as the tendency within family literature to concentrate attention on the internal workings of families, on psychological rather than sociological variables, and the tendency to treat families as self-contained units within which behaviours and attitudes can be explained by reference to other internal variables. This state of affairs has been described as follows: "Viewed as a semi-autonomous system of interacting personalities, the structure of family relations and interaction had been conceptualized as a theater of action only tangentially related to the society at large in a truly dynamic sense" (Ismael, 1979:108)[1].

There is, of course, at least one tradition within sociology that does place families within a societal context; namely, that part of a functional analysis which examines the functions families perform for society. There is less of an emphasis on trying to understand how societal changes affect families, although there are, of course, some notable exceptions (such as Goode, 1963; Boulding, 1979; Allen, 1979).

The microstructural bias, then, can be seen as a *disproportionate* emphasis on psychological variables and a concomitant comparative neglect of macrostructural variables, one of which (but not the only one) is social policy. Criticizing the microstructural bias does not imply that studies which focus on psychological variables are useless or unimportant. (Quite a number of them have been drawn upon in the writing of this book.) The critique maintains that the prevailing *balance* is inappropriate, and that misinterpretations may take place if macro variables are being largely ignored. Conversely, stratification and mobility studies as well as policy analysis suffer from the opposite problem: by ignoring studies of familial interactions, and worse, relying on untested assumptions about how families work and are structured, they largely fail to explain what they set out to explain.

Traditional Macrostructural Analysis: Societal Functions of Families

Two functions of families are particularly relevant in this context: the social placement function of families and the economic co-operation and mutual support function of families. In the following, we will discuss the lack of integration of these functions with the family literature.

The Social Placement Function of Families

Sociologists and anthropologists have long argued that one of the major functions of marriage is to socially place children. In highly industrialized societies, however, this function has been eroded, although by no means eliminated. Smelser argues that the shift that has occurred in this area can be understood as a shift from a family's capacity to *guarantee* the status of its offspring to one in which families merely function to increase the *probability* (above chance) of continuing to transmit their status to their children via three types of mechanisms: by shaping the motivational and affective lives of their young children; by expending resources for socialization by agencies other than the family (e.g., schools); and by differentially utilizing influence (Smelser, 1981:34–36).

The *outcome* and the *process* of social placement of children are usually seen as the domains of stratification and mobility studies, respectively. Stratification studies describe the system of inequality which exists at given times in societies, while social mobility studies describe the process whereby people find their place in a given system of inequality. To the degree, therefore, that families are actually successful in placing their children, we are dealing with a system of ascribed inequality, while to the degree that the children's social place is independent from that of their parents', we have moved away from an ascribed system of stratification. The erosion of the placement function of families may therefore be seen as a positive factor in society, in as far as it indicates a democratization of access to different positions in society.

The erosion of the placement function of families is complemented by the erosion of the legal authority of the husband/father over his wife and children. Under common law, a married woman and her children once had no separate legal existence from that of the husband/father. This is no longer the case in Canada for the wives, whose legal capacities are now comparable to those of their husbands. However, children are still to a high degree legally as well as economically and socially dependent on their parents.

The way stratification studies have traditionally translated the placement function of families into stratification terms was by equating the socio-economic status of all family members with that of the male breadwinner. However, due to the recent changes within families, models based on this approach are hopelessly outdated. New models of stratification have not yet been sufficiently elaborated to provide a comprehensive framework for analysis, and the consequence is that stratification must be seen to be ill-understood in contemporary highly industrialized societies.

We have shifted from a situation in which the breadwinner family was the modal type of family for husband-wife families to one in which the two-earner family has become the norm for husband-wife families. However, we understand poorly, to date, in what manner the socio-economic position of husbands and wives interact, or how the lifestyles of the children as well as of the adults are affected by the jobs of both spouses. We do know that the husband's occupational prestige has an impact on the wife's status if she is a housewife (for Canadian data, see Eichler, 1977; for American data, Bose, 1973), but we have a poor understanding of how the wife's occupational prestige may affect the husband's social standing when she has a paying job, and vice versa (see Delphy, 1981).

A child's likelihood for occupational success, if he is male, has so far been largely explained in terms of his father's socio-economc position. Social mobility studies therefore typically compare the social placement of sons with that of their fathers. For female children social placement has been largely accounted for in terms of homogamy: studies focussed on comparing the social position of their hubands with those of their fathers. The hypothesis was that young women were likely to marry young men who would eventually reach a socio-economic status which would be similar to that of their fathers.

Now, with the majority of wives/mothers in the labour force, and their female children highly likely to be permanent members of the labour force themselves, this type of approach to social mobility is obviously outdated and inappropriate. On the other hand, mobility patterns themselves are in flux: it is as yet unclear what exactly the patterns of influence from both parents to children of both sexes with respect to social placement are, since a situation in which the majority of children have mothers with paying jobs is a very recent phenomenon.

Another issue which severely muddies the understanding of the social placement of families and which to my knowledge has received no attention to date in this context is the prevalence of divorce. When parents with children divorce, two things happen in the majority of cases: the mother receives custody of the children, and mother and children sink into instant poverty (see Chapter 7). In such a case, what happens to the socio-economic placement of the children? Will it follow that of the father, or that of the mother? What happens if the mother remarries? Are the children socially placed through the stepfather? their mother? their absentee father? a combination of two of them? a combination of all three of them? So far, there are no studies which look specifially at the social mobility of children of divorced marriages and of remarriages, which would answer these questions.

Overall, then, we can note that the social placement function of families has been eroded, but not eliminated. For instance, the physical health of children is partially determined by the financial situation in the home in which they are growing up. This certainly holds for the negative case (poverty is bad for the physical and mental health of young and old people; see National Council of Welfare, 1975) but it does not necessarily hold for the opposite case (a generally affluent home can still produce physically and/or mentally unhealthy children). Occupational aspirations still seem to be partially determined by the occupations of the parents, although we do not know to what degree and in which manner under the complicating circumstances just outlined. Educational achievement of children still seems to be partially determined by the education of their parents, although universal free education has slightly opened the door to gifted children who are from uneducated backgrounds who would have been previously excluded from any extended education.

The major task now is to accept the changes which have occurred within families as necessitating a basic rethinking as to how stratification and social mobility studies should be approached.

We will now look at the other major macro-sociological function that families play for society; namely, economic co-operation and mutual support of family members.

The Support Function of Families

Economic co-operation between family members is so much a part of our understanding of families that it has been integrated into many definitions of the family (see Chapter 1). However, economic co-operation is not *per se* a macro-sociological function. The economic exchange patterns of family members become important for society at large when families are supposed to support their own members. It is the support function of families rather than economic co-operation which is particularly important in this context, but the one cannot be understood without the other.

Having stated that family members co-operate economically, most sociologists and other social scientists writing about families proceed to ignore economic co-operation between family members. It is generally postulated, not studied.

Economic co-operation can be of two types: the exchange of monies, and the exchange of services or goods. Until very recently, this latter type of exchange was largely ignored. It is only since feminist scholars have focussed attention on housework that there has been an incipient understanding emerging that rendering services and producing goods can actually be understood as one form of economic exchange. This issue will be dealt with at length in the next chapter.

The other form of economic co-operation which involves the exchange and actual spending of monies between family members, has not even been studied to the very modest degree to which the economic non-monetary exchanges have received attention. Indeed, there is practically no literature which concerns itself with the manner in which monies are actually spent *within* the family unit. Economists tend to regard income which accrues to a member of a particular family unit as family income, although this does not correspond to legal and actual reality. When there is income from more than one source or to more than one family member, typically this income is aggregated and the sum total is regarded as family income. Therefore, when in a husband-wife couple the husband has a job and the wife also takes a paying job, the two incomes are added together and considered — by economists — as family income, irrespective of who makes decisions about it, whether it is, indeed, spent for family purposes or not (conceivably, a spouse may utilize all his or her income for only personal purposes). On one of the most important functions of the family, then, neither family studies nor economic studies can enlighten us about actual behaviours, because family studies bracket economic issues, (having before, however, asserted their importance) and economic studies treat the family as a unit rather than as an interactive system of individuals.

As far as the support function of families is concerned, there is widespread consensus that families not only do support their own, but *should* do so. What is often overlooked is that there tends to be a direct opposition between the notion of the family as a support system and social security programmes: to the degree that the proper locus of support for an individual is seen to lie within that individual's family, the individual becomes *disentitled* from public support.

Just as the placement function of families has been eroded, but not eliminated, so has the support function. Social security programmes such as Unemployment Insurance, Old Age Security, the Canada/Quebec Pension Plan, etc. provides income that was previously provided only through families, if at all.

To put this into positive terms, to the degree that we make social security programmes available to individuals, we guarantee, as a society, some income security to individuals. Conversely, to the degree that we let eligibility to social security programmes be determined by family status, we disentitle individuals from access to social support on the basis of their family status. This disentitlement is usually justified by reference to the support function of "the family" — and with the pious wish that the state (or government) must not usurp the functions of the family. This encapsules nicely the basic paradox which underlies any social security policy that is geared towards families rather than individuals: in the name of protecting "the family" people are disentitled from public support on the basis of their family status. Family-oriented transfer programmes therefore usually discriminate against people on the basis of their family status. This paradoxical relationship between family-oriented social security programmes and their effects on families will be explored in one of the subsequent sections. Before addressing this issue, however, it is useful to see the erosion of both major societal functions of families in relation to each other.

The Relationship between the Erosion of the Support and Placement Functions of Families

Glendon has drawn a direct connection between changes in family law and changes in employment law.

> We have left a time when one's position in society was fixed by one's family, not for the reign of contract, but for a situation in which one's status is fixed by one's occupation or lack thereof. The relationships which, unlike marriage and contract, are relatively hard to enter and leave today are the preferred sorts of new property — good jobs with good fringe benefits.[2]

Jobs and entitlements are seen as the major form of "new property," while the "new family" is characterized by increasing fluidity, detachability, and interchangeability of family relationships. We can observe the concomitant decline of the family as a property-regulating institution with the rise of jobs as the most important form of property. This shift in the nature of property, then, has brought about a shift in the nature of marriage, which in turn has reduced the importance of the family as a status determinant and as a support institution. This process is most visibly being played out before our eyes at the present time with respect to wives, who are moving from a position of derived status via their husbands' jobs to a position of independent status via their own jobs.

In terms of intrafamilial relationships, this trend towards a "new property" and a "new family" which is characteristic of all highly industrialized countries (Glendon, 1981) has resulted in two highly evolved processes and one incipient process: (a) the gradual emancipation of wives from their husbands' control, (b) the gradual emancipation of adult children from their parents and *vice versa*; and (c) the incipient emancipation of dependent children from their parents' control.

None of these three processes is completed, but the first and second are quite advanced. While husbands and wives owe each other mutual support, this support obligation now tends to cease with or soon after divorce. Legally, wives are now on an equal footing with their husbands, although in practical terms, they may still be under their husband's control such as when they do not earn incomes (still true for a very large minority of couples). The prevailing economic discrimination against women ensures that in most cases the wife is the economically weaker partner in a marriage. Some social policies, notably social welfare, are still premised on the notion of female dependency on males (see Chapter 10).

By contrast, in the case of adult children and their parents, although there is a mutual support obligation, nevertheless our social policies tend to be based on the notion of mutual independence. For instance, an adult becomes elegible for welfare even if his or her parents are quite rich or if his or her adult child(ren) are quite rich, provided they do not share a household together. In both instances we can note a discrepancy between legal and transfer policies, but they go in opposite directions.

As far as the emancipation of dependent children from their parents is concerned, this is a process which has barely started. There is some modest popular concern with children's rights, and the state does remove children from their parents' control when there is evidence of abuse, but by and large parents still have an extremely high degree of control over their children.

Overall then, the erosion of the support and placement functions of families can both be seen as consequences of an overall shift in the society of the manner in which wealth is acquired and distributed for the majority of people — from inherited wealth to wealth acquired through one's job. This shift has resulted in an international tightening of legal prescriptions concerning access to and exit from jobs, and to a legal loosening of exit from marriages. The ensuing increase in divorce has, in turn, resulted in a fundamentally changed conglomeration of different family types. This necessitates a reconsideration of policies geared towards families.

Family Policy as a Field of Study

Kamerman and Kahn have drawn a distinction between an *explicit* family policy, and an implicit family policy. An explicit family policy includes:

> (a) specific programs and policies designated to achieve specified, explicit goals regarding the family; (b) programs and policies which deliberately do things to and for the family, but for which there are no agreed upon over-all goals regarding the family,

while an implicit family policy is composed of

> governmental actions and policies not specifically or primarily addressed to the family, but which have indirect consequences.[3]

The authors classify Canada, along with the United Kingdom, Israel, and the United States, as a country which does not have an explicit family policy and where, furthermore, the notion of such a policy is rejected (Kamerman and Kahn, 1978:viii).

Along with the absence of any coherent positive family policy in Canada, "Canadian social policy shows much more evidence of the influence of assumptions about the family, and latent consequences for the family, than deliberate planning for the family" (Armitage, 1978:399).

Since the late 1970s, there has been a marked revival of interest in family policy in Europe as well as in North America. This can be explained as a reaction to the changes which have been taking place within families which, together, have created a situation in which existing policies are no longer adequate for meeting the needs of a large proportion of families. To take just one obvious example: when a large proportion or the majority of mothers take on paid labour, their children must be cared for in alternative ways. The recent changes, then, have made visible the fact that there always has been an *implicit* family policy. By being out-of-step with current reality, the current situation brings the existence of assumptions about families which underlie our policies to the level of consciousness. As long as there is a reasonable fit between assumptions about families on which policies are based and the majority of actual families, chances are that most people will not be aware that there is such a thing as an implicit family policy, simply because the issue is non-problematic.

Today, however, the issue has become problematized. This is reflected in a modest increase in the literature about family policy. However, there is no consensus as to what "family policy" is or should be, or, indeed, what the concept is or should denote. There have been some attempts to clarify the concept (see, for example, Nye and McDonald, 1979; Dumon and Aldous, 1979; Tallman, 1979; or Zimmerman, 1979), but there is no agreement as to what goals should be aimed for. There is some concern that family policy must be geared towards the existing multiplicity of family types, rather than towards one type of family (see, especially, Feldman, 1979; Rice, 1977; and Moroney, 1979). However, it was partially around this issue of the multiplicity of family types that the American 1980 White House Conference on Families turned, according to some observers, into a debacle (for a strong critique, see Steiner, 1981; for a summary of the recommendations, see Dale, 1981). Not everybody agrees that policies should favor *all* types of families.

In Canada, there is not a single comprehensive treatment of Canada's family policy. In 1977, the Canadian Council on Social Development ran a conference on family policy, the proceedings of which were eventually published (Canadian Council on Social Development, 1977), but it neither aspired to be nor is a comprehensive look at Canada's policies which are relevant to families. There has been some work done on individual aspects of family-oriented policies, such as the Mothers' Allowances (Hepworth, 1980), on the effects of social security programmes on women (Kitchen, 1980; and Finley, 1980), and on other issues (Abernathy, 1979; Armitage, 1978; Hepworth, 1979). There is also a very useful comprehensive treatment of the overall social security programmes in Canada which is highly relevant but not specifically geared towards the effects on families (Guest, 1980).

Overall, then, there is not a single comprehensive treatment of Canada's social policies in print which are of particular importance to families. Since many of the relevant policies are under provincial jurisdiction, it is very difficult and time-consuming to find out what policies exist across the country.[4] Nor is there a common framework that would allow us to evaluate different policies as to their positive or negative effect on families. Moving towards developing such a framework, rather than providing an overview of the existing policies is one of the goals of this book.

Family Policy vs. Policies for Families

There is, as Hepworth (1979a:1) has pointed out, "an assumption that family policy is a Good Thing." This need by no means be the case. Explicit family policy may mean state intervention in the most intimate relationships between people. For instance, laws regulating (or prohibiting) the sale and distribution of contraceptives can be one aspect of an explicit family policy, as can be laws that prohibit abortion, and/or impose abortion in other cases, or that provide penalties or incentives if people exceed or fail to reach the officially designated desired number of children.

Family policy, if it is geared towards the protection and fostering of a particular type of family, thereby almost by necessity works to the detriment of other types of families which do not happen to conform to the prescribed structure. Laws and policies concerning illegitimate children provide a case in point. Laws making distinctions between legitimate and illegitimate children tend to be justified by the rationale that such distinctions are necessary to protect the claims of the legitimate children against those of illegitimate children who could potentially absorb resources that would otherwise be available to the legitimate children. This makes some sense if seen from the perspective of the so-called legitimate family. However, what about the illegitimate children and their mothers? Do they not also constitute a family? Is not an illegitimate child of a man as much his child as a legitimate child? Should children be penalized on the basis of their parents' relationship or lack of it? It is, of course, just such considerations which led to the abolition of the legal category of "illegitimate" children in Ontario, New Brunswick, and Quebec. A family policy is unlikely to serve all families if it is premised on a particular image as to what should characterize a family.

To take another example, once policy makers start defining eligibility criteria on the basis of structural features of a family, certain types of families will fail to become eligible for support simply because they are *not* missing a certain member. For instance, a policy designed to help mothers with dependent children who live in one-parent households, fails to serve husband-wife families with dependent children although the financial or other needs of the latter family may be identical to those of the former family. The explicit intention *not* to help certain types of families was well expressed by the Saskatchewan Commissioner on Child Welfare when he stated in his 1930/31 Annual Report:

> ... we, like all child caring agencies working up to the approved standards, avoid falling into the error of trying to assist children in their own homes or relieving parents of their responsibility for sentimental reasons. We must be hard-headed as to why we do it.[5]

In cases in which structural prerequisites supersede considerations of need, family policy must be seen not only as a tool for what it is ostensibly meant to do — namely to support families in need of support — but also as a tool for social control which imposes moral and behavioural standards upon people. (This process is well described for historical France by Donzelot, 1979.)

Chances are, then, that "family policy" is as much of a "Bad Thing" as it is a "Good Thing." It is likely to be a bad thing when it is geared towards one particular type of family. On the other hand, we desperately need to support our families, all of them. In the latter case, it would be more appropriate to speak of policies for families rather than of family policy. This terminology will henceforth be used to indicate whether a particular policy is actually beneficial for families or not. Failure to take a policy approach that incorporates all types of families, results in discrimination against certain types of families, often those which are considered to be most desirable by many policy makers; that is, families which consist of a husband, wife, and dependent children. This paradoxical aspect of family policy will be examined in the next section.

The Paradox of the Familism-Individualism Flip-Flop

The prevailing wisdom behind our existing medley of policies and programmes which at present make up Canada's family policy seems to be that public support systems must not usurp the support function of the family. It is assumed that transferring funds to so-called intact families would sap their initiative and start them on a destructive cycle of dependency. Existing programmes and services are, therefore, typically geared towards families, which, according to some organizational criterion, are considered to be in need of special help (e.g., mother-led one-parent households) or towards individuals who are bereft of family. The irony in this type of policy approach is that it tends to have the opposite effect of what it was intended to have.

We will consider a few concrete examples as to how policies geared towards people on the basis of their family status can work against the entire family.

> Emily Van Geffen and her paraplegic husband, Matt, 27, have been married only since September, now she's afraid she may have to get a legal separation and let the province take care of her husband in a $120-a-day chronic care hospital.

> She wants to provide the extensive daily care that Van Geffen needs in their Cityhome apartment and to work three days a week at nursing.
>
> But if she earned $600 a month at part-time nursing — she's a registered nursing assistant — her husband's $536 a month disabled allowance would be cut to $136 monthly. If she worked full-time it would be cut off completely.[6]

Ontario calculates the need of a disabled person on the basis of family income rather than individual income. A spouse is allowed the first $150 of earnings without any reduction in the allowance; then 50 percent of the next $100. The irony of the situation is that if the couple separates, Emily Van Geffen's husband will cost the province of Ontario either $120 a day in a chronic care hospital or $220 a day in an active care hospital bed (McNenly, 1981).

In another similar case, a couple had to actually separate to be able to survive financially.

> A couple from nearby Constance Bay have filed for a legal separation of their three-year marriage because the terminally-ill husband will be denied his veteran's pension if the marriage continues.
>
> John Brown, 52, who served 14 months in the Korean War, was told by the Veterans' Affairs Department that he is not eligible for his $365-a-month pension as long as his wife works.
>
> His wife, Shirley Brown, 47, says she cannot afford to quit her $14,000-a-year job as a Government clerk, but is worried because her husband cannot take care of himself.
>
> "It's all very cruel," Mrs. Brown said. "I thought we could get an annulment and live common law, but they told us no. If we legally separate, he gets the money and he would have enough to live. But we haven't been able to figure out how to provide care for him."
>
> Mr. Brown, a heavy-equipment operator, was forced to quit his job in 1977 because of poor health.[7]

Yet a third case involves a paraplegic and his wheel-chair-bound fiancée. Raymond Maver, 37, paraplegic, was told that he would lose his $151 provincial welfare cheque as well as his free prescription drug privileges if he married his fiancée, Miss Jowell, who earned $9100 annually as a girl Friday for the Anglican Church. Mr. Maver's only other income was a $135-a-month federal pension, but his wife's salary would have been too high to qualify him for the provincial welfare payment in case of a marriage (Ferry, 1979).

All three cases cited so far involve handicapped people, which reflects in a particularly poignant manner the paradoxical effect of social security programmes which assume that families *should* be able to support their members, irrespective of whether they actually *can* do so. But the paradoxical relationship obtains in all cases. In a recent court decision, for instance, a Hamilton County Court judge jailed a bus driver and his wife for defrauding the Regional Municipality of Hamilton-Wentworth of $5500 over fourteen months. "A jury found the couple guilty of fraud last month, determining that they had been living together while Mrs. Nash claimed benefits as a single mother" (Welfare fraud, 1981).

It is worthwhile to consider this reasoning carefully. There was no doubt that the couple needed the money badly — they were described to be in a "pitiful state" — but because the welfare legislation is geared towards a particular category of family — in this case single mothers — other types of families which are in identical situations as far as their needs are concerned are excluded from access to these funds. Had Mrs. Nash been living without her husband, she would have been entitled to exactly what she did receive.

This last example exemplifies the manner in which social policies which identify recipients by some organizational family criterion in fact discriminate against families in an identical situation of need but of a different structure (in this case, one-parent households as compared to two-parent households). The impetus behind earmarking financial support was certainly to provide financial help where it was most needed, but the criterion adopted to identify that need was *not* the issue the monies are meant to address — namely financial need — but financial need coupled with a particular type of family structure; in other words, a proxy variable was attached to the real criterion. The effect of this is that such policies discriminate against certain types of families, and may, in extreme cases, generate the problem the consequences of which the policies were designed to alleviate.

The cases cited are not specific instances which are atypical, but logical consequences of adopting family status as a relevant criterion for eligibility to public monies. This becomes obvious when considering tax, which affects every single citizen in one way or the other. As a reader in a letter to the editor of *The Citizen* pointed out in 1980, the Income Tax Act penalizes a married couple over a common-law couple (although the opposite is true if the wife does not hold a paying job). If both spouses have a paying job, neither can deduct the marriage partner. However, in the case of a common-law couple, the partner with the higher income could deduct their child for the "equivalent to married" exemption, which in 1980 was an extra $800 refund at the lowest marginal tax rate.

> As I see it, parents who chose to have and raise children out of wedlock profit $15,000-$20,000 for remaining unmarried, while the chilren (sic) are dependent. Additionally, household income can be as high as $36,000 annually before the $200 "child tax credit" is reduced. For married couples, the figure is half that.[8]

This issue will be taken up again in more detail in Chapter 10. It has been introduced here merely to make the point that the mechanisms which penalize family members *because* they belong to some type of family are an issue which applies whenever family status is made a criterion for eligibility to public funds rather than an issue which is only relevant in a few marginal cases. The examples cited which involved handicapped recipients make the case particularly clearly, but the issue is one which transcends certain categories of people and affects everybody.

To put the issue into general terms: programmes earmarking funds or services for people on the basis of their family status will result (a) in the discrimination of some people in the same objective circumstances who do not meet the organizational criterion specified (e.g., marital status), and will (b) in some cases where circumstances are sufficiently tight, result in the creation of the problem the consequences of which the programme was set up to alleviate.

Policies, then, that are justified in the name of "the family" may actually work against some families. In order to recognize which policies are beneficial or detrimental to what types of families, we need a set of criteria for evaluating policies or programmes which are geared to families.

Criteria for Evaluating Policies or Programmes for Families

The criteria for policy analysis elaborated in the following are derived from the insights gained through critiquing the monolithic, conservative, and sexist biasses. They constitute a translation of the main criticisms into policy terms. From the recognition of the current coexistence of a multiplicity of family types derives the criterion (1) that every policy analysis should ask what type of family is served by a particular programme or policy, and what type of family is, by implication, not served. From the recognition that families are experienced differentially by their various members derives the criterion (2) that every policy analysis should ask what the differential effects of any given policy or programme are for every individual family member. In the following each criterion will be elaborated.[9]

Criterion of Applicability to Multiplicity of Family Types

Families are differentiated along many lines. They vary in terms of composition, religion, ethnic background, place of residence, socioeconomic status, etc. All of these differences are important, but for policy purposes, one difference is of particular importance: whether a family is a breadwinner family or a two-earner family. The reason this difference is of particular importance is twofold: on the one hand, we have just witnessed a shift in which the breadwinner family ceased to be the modal family and the two-earner family became the modal family instead. Since this is a very recent phenomenon, it can be expected that many policies are still oriented towards the breadwinner type of family. On the other hand, depending on whether one wishes to support the breadwinner type of family or the two-earner type of family, the policy consequences are exactly opposite. Clarifying the relationship of policies and programmes to these two basic types of families is, therefore, of particular importance.

In the *breadwinner family,* the husband/father is the economic provider for the entire family. The wife ceases her involvement in the labour market at marriage or, at the latest, upon the birth of her first child, in order to become a full-time homemaker. Henceforth, being a wife and/or mother is her full-time occupation. She is thus economically dependent on her husband, who is the breadwinner for the family. This implies a rather strict division of labour: the wife is responsible for childcare and housework, and the husband is responsible for the economic well-being of the family. By implication, the husband is *not* responsible for childcare and housework, and the wife is *not* responsible for either her own economic well-being, or that of her children or husband. The economic dependency of the wife extends beyonds his death or divorce: the family must be provided for through his means (e.g., through life insurance, survivor's benefits) even after his death, or after divorce (e.g., through maintenance, pension splitting).

Policies oriented towards this type of family will display the following features: giving primacy to the economic needs of breadwinners over those of other labour force participants; facilitating the homemaker functions of wives and mothers; compensating for the economic functions of the husband/father in the case of divorce, death, desertion, or incapacity of the breadwinner; and compensating for the homemaker functions of the wife/mother in the case of death, desertion, or incapacity of the wife/mother. By implication, there will be no entitlements to compensation if economic contributions of wives/mothers cease or are interrupted, or if childcare or housekeeping contributions of husbands/fathers cease or are interrupted.

The situation is markedly different for two-earner families. In the *two-earner family,* every adult is considered responsible for his or her own economic well-being. The wife continues to remain involved in the labour market even after the birth of her child(ren). Responsibility for the economic well-being of the child(ren), and for childcare in general, is shared equally between the father and the mother, and society shares a part of the responsibility. The parental economic responsibility ceases as children reach adulthood. Consequently, when grown children continue to need care (as is the case, for instance, with handicapped adults), primary responsibility for providing this care lies with society (not with the parents) or with a potential marital partner. In other words, there is no assumption of economic dependency except in the case of dependent children and adults in need of care, and the responsibilities of husbands and wives and fathers and mothers are presumed to be equal in all spheres of activity.

Policies oriented towards this type of family will display the following features: equal treatment of every labour force participant; assurance of equality of women with men in the economy; enablement of equality of men with women in the family; the recognition that society shares a part of the responsibility for the children's care and welfare irrespective of the structure and composition of a particular family unit; and the facilitation of the combination of involvement in the economy and in the family for husbands and wives, mothers and fathers.

Policies which are oriented towards the breadwinner type of family treat the family as the smallest economic and administrative unit, while policies which are oriented towards the two-earner type of family, treat the individual as the smallest economic and administrative unit. Breadwinner types of families and policies oriented towards them are based on the notion of sex differentiation, while two-earner types of families and policies oriented towards them are based on the notion of sex equality.

At present, there are more two-earner families than breadwinner families. However, the numerical difference is slight, and it can be assumed that we will continue to have a mix of these two types of families for at least another generation. It is likely that many families will shift from the one type to another. In addition, there are, at present, a substantial number of one-parent households, which have some features from both types of families. In other words, it is highly likely that we will continue to live in a society where different families conform to different economic patterns. This being the case, it is highly important that any policy analysis clarify whether a particular policy or programme serves a breadwinner type of family, a two-earner type of family, neither, or both.

The other major change that has been taking place in families is an increasing discrepancy between parental and marital roles. Policies tend to be based on the assumption that a family consists of a father, mother, and children, all of whom share the same household. In Chapter 7 this issue is examined in detail, and it is estimated that approximately 50 percent of all Canadian families exhibit some form of discrepancy between spousal and parental roles, either because the household contains a child who does not live with both his or her biological father and mother, (or either of them) or because the household contains an adult who does not live with any or all of his (occasionally her) children.

The most obvious, and in our context most relevant, discrepancy exists when we are dealing with one-parent households, most of which have become one-parent households not because of death of one parent but because of divorce, separation, or births to unmarried women. The second major way in which the criterion of applicability to a multiplicity of family types needs to be applied consists of systematically examining what effects a given policy or programme has for one-parent households and husband-wife families, and whether it is positive, negative, or neutral towards one or both of them.

The second criterion shifts the types of concerns addressed in the first criterion to the level of intrafamilial differentiation.

Criterion of Differential Effects of Policies and Programmes for Individual Family Members

In the chapter addressed to overcoming the sexist bias (Chapter 3), we have seen that one cannot make any assumption that the experience of women and men within the same familial unit is identical or even comparable. In the chapter addressed to overcoming the conservative bias (Chapter 2), we briefly touched on the prevailing agist bias. There are systematic differences in the experience of living within the same family along sex and age lines. In the subsequent chapters, this theme is developed further; here, a short example will suffice to show the applicability of this very fundamental observation to policy analysis.

Divorce has maximally different implications for the women, men, and children involved. Mothers tend to receive custody of their children and also tend to become instantly poor; lower income often entails having to move from their accustomed social and physical environments to different (and less desirable) locations. This tends to be true regardless of whether or not the woman had a paying job before the divorce, due to the prevailing wage differentials between women and men and the low (if any) child support payments from fathers.

Fathers, by contrast, tend to lose control over their children, and to have only severely restricted access to them, but they are unlikely to be economically as negatively affected as the wives.

Children tend to lose daily contact with one parent, but may gain life in a less conflict-ridden environment. Children also have to suffer the consequences of divorce without having had, as a rule, any say as to whether there should or should not be a divorce — a fact which is likely to produce profound feelings of powerlessness and anomie.

Divorce, then, is a fundamentally different experience for those who participate in it according to age and sex. This is the case with just about all other familial experiences, and means in policy terms that any policy analysis should systematically assess the potential differential impact of any policy or programme on the various family members.

For instance, the Child Tax Credit, which is paid to the mother, declines as the family's (usually the husband's) income rises. Therefore, a positive economic effect on one spouse has a negative economic effect on the other.[10] Or, a policy of restricting access to subsidized day care spaces to children from one-parent households may have a positive effect on a huband (presuming that he wishes his wife to be a housewife) but a negative effect on the wife (presuming she wishes to take on a paying job and cannot do so for lack of adequate day care).

Indeed, it is possible that there may be a conflict of interests between various family members concerning some issue. For instance, in Canada, welfare cheques for a husband-wife family are made out to the husband on behalf of the entire family. If it so happens that the father/husband is irresponsible (e.g., a heavy drinker) the fact that he controls the money clearly constitutes a conflict of interests with all other family members. (Of course, even if he does not drink, one cheque to which she has access only through her husband's signature is clearly not in the interest of the wife.) If the available amount of money was split into two portions and each sent as a separate cheque to the husband and to the wife, at least each of them would control half of it.

One must also recognize that there are situations in which parents may not be able to recognize and/or act in the best interests of their children. To stay within the example of divorce, in the best of all possible solutions the parents would have mutually agreed to practise joint custody and would have been legally assigned such. (This, of course, is extremely rare!) In such a situation, it is typical that the child(ren) involved move(s) in some type of pattern from the residence of one parent to that of the other. This is, however, quite likely to be highly inconvenient for the child. Another alternative would be for the child to stay put in the main residence and for the parents to alternate living in that residence. This, of course, would probably be highly inconvenient for the parents. Even in this type of almost ideal situation, then, there is a conflict of interest between parents and child(ren) — whose convenience will be sacrificed?

In terms of policy analysis, recognizing the multiplicity of family types and the diversity of familial experiences means that every policy or programme must be assessed with respect to its applicability and potential differential implications for — as a minimum — breadwinner and two-earner families and one-parent and two-parent households.[11] At least as important, if not more so, the assessment of every policy or programme in terms of its applicability and potential differential implications for every individual family member: mother/wife, father/husband, and child (separately for boys and girls). A *minimal criterion* for deciding that a policy or programme qualifies as "good" for "the family" would be that it can be demonstrated to have beneficial effects on at least one family member and no detrimental effects on any other. Preferably, it should have beneficial effects on more than one family member, but such a criterion may not always be feasible or appropriate. Clearly, however, one cannot call any policy or programme "good" if it has demonstrably negative effects on at least one family member.

So far, we have identified problems in family policy as a field of study, and problems in actual policies (the familism-individualism flip-flop). We have also identified criteria for policy evaluation which are derived from theoretical insights concerning the co-existence of a multiplicity of family types and diversity of familial experiences for members of the same family. These problems are not only problems in the context in which they have so far been dealt with, but represent real problems for policy development, since they invoke ostensibly opposite principles for policy development.[12] In the following, we will address the issue as to how to overcome the real problems of creating equitable policies given the diversity of family types and the diversity of policy effects on individual family members. Before doing so, however, it is necessary to reflect on the concept of equity in social policies.

Equity in Social Policies

There are two conceptions of equity in social policies: horizontal equity (equal treatment of those in equal circumstances) and vertical equity (reducing income disparities) (cf. Bergeron, 1979:48). Generally, there tends to be agreement among policy makers as well as policy analysts that social policies should preferably be equitable, in both senses of the word. However, the definition of equity is neither as simple nor as clear as it once appeared to be. In the following, we will briefly discuss both types of equity.

Horizontal Equity

Most analysts define horizontal equity as equity between family units, rather than between individuals. Depending on whether we wish to argue for horizontal equity between families or between individuals, we may come up with two *opposite* conclusions, using identical rationales but different reference units.

An example will make this clearer. Different countries use different approaches to taxation. As far as income tax in concerned, there are two very distinct approaches to taxation: individual taxation or family taxation (with some in-between measures also in existence). In individual taxation a person is taxed on his or her income irrespective of family status. In family taxation, the incomes of both spouses are added together, and the tax rate of the couple is determined by the *total* income of the couple. Where there is a progressive tax structure, in general taxes are higher for a family when family or joint taxation is used, than when individual taxation is used. Internationally there seems to be a trend towards individual taxation (Organization for Economic Co-operation and Development, 1977:15–18), but there are still a number of countries which use family taxation. Canada has a system of individual taxation, with the exception of determining eligibility for the refundable child tax credit, while the U.S. has a system of family taxation.

Both types of taxation systems are defended in terms of horizontal equity. If we have a couple in which the husband earns $20 000 and the wife earns $12 000, their combined income is $32 000. If we argue for equity in terms of *family* income, the argument is that a family with $32 000 income should pay the same amount of taxes, irrespective of whether this income is generated by one or two earners. Correspondingly, it is argued that they should have the same access to tax concessions (deductions, exemptions, etc.) (cf. Salyzyn, 1980). In that case, we end up with some system of joint taxation. If we argue for equity in terms of individual income, the argument is that married persons earning $20 000 or $12 000, respectively, should pay the same amount of taxes as if they were single. Taxing them at a higher rate amounts to a "tax on marriage" (Schnepper, 1978). Taking this thought somewhat further, there are different ways in which a family tax is levied. However, overall it is the spouse with the lower income (usually the wife) who will pay particularly high taxes, since the first dollar earned by the wife will be taxed at the same marginal tax rate as the last dollar earned by the husband (Dulude, 1979:9). Most wives who earn income will therefore be personally more disadvantaged than husbands who earn income.

Canada, as noted, has a system of individual taxation. However, with respect to transfer payments we have a mixed system, with some transfers being made on an individual basis and others, notably social welfare,[13] on a family basis.

Since for increasing numbers of people membership in a *particular* marital unit is no longer a lifelong affair, defining horizontal equity in terms of family units rather than in terms of individuals seems no longer appropriate. If we define equity in terms of family units, we may disentitle or disadvantage a substantial proportion of people who will bear the consequences of such disadvantage not only during marriage, but particularly after a marriage has ended (through death or divorce) and they are, once more, in an administrative sense, single persons.

Several other considerations are of relevance in this context. To argue that a two-earner couple should face the same tax liability as a single individual or a breadwinner couple in which the man earns as much as the two-earner couple, is to value the work of the so-called secondary earner, who is almost always the wife, as nothing. If eighty hours of work are performed, most analysts would agree that this would be worth double the amount of money as forty hours of work. In the case of a two-earner family, however, eighty hours of work are suddenly equated in value with forty hours. In addition, there are just about always expenses attached to a family in which both husband and wife earn money, most particularly when there are children in need of care and supervision. The same analysts who argue for family taxation do not rush forward in great numbers to argue for tax transfers that would absorb the costs of childcare and possibly of other expenses attached to having both spouses out of the house during the work week. As one analyst who is aware of this issue has put it:

> Child day care is one area where policy-makers and politicians have failed abysmally to recognize a major social change that has occurred, and that is unlikely to be reversed. Most politicians are now wise enough not to say that a woman's place is in the home; they are not wise enough to recognize that there are social consequences which require recognition and remedy.[14]

Arguing for family taxation, then, argues that the work of the wife *in the house as well as out of the house* is of no value.

Another problem that arises when arguing for equity on the basis of family units rather than individuals, is that married couples face a greater tax liability than common-law couples. Kirshna (1980) who argues for family taxation (in the name of horizontal equity!) acknowledges the problem but suggests that it is an acceptable cost to pay for a generally more equitable system:

> True, if one ignores the issue of common-law spouses completely, one is left with a tax system that has a built-in bias against marriage; to that extent, the tax system is not neutral. Ignoring the issue may, however, be justified by arguing that the number of people who live in common-law relationships is, relatively speaking, a miniscule portion of the total taxpaying population and that the price of a perfectly neutral solution is too high.[15]

This statement puts forward the familism-individualism flip-flop rather nicely. Besides, Kirshna may be wrong in stating that only a miniscule proportion of taxpayers would be involved. In Sweden, it has been estimated that 15 to 16 percent of all cohabiting relationships involve couples cohabiting without marriage (Trost, 1980:18). Since 1965, there has been a marked drop in marriages which is matched by a corresponding increase in cohabitation arrangements. In Canadian terms, this would mean that 15–16 percent of all marriages in Sweden are currently common-law marriages. In the United States, which has a system of family taxation, 4 percent of all households involved experimental families or cohabiting couples in 1975 (Ramey, 1978:1). While Canadian figures are probably quite a bit lower, a recent study from B.C. found that an astounding 64 percent of their married respondents stated that they had cohabited prior to marriage (Watson, 1981:9). While all of these couples eventually married, it is not impossible to imagine that if the taxation system were to start to seriously discriminate against married people, that a substantial portion of cohabitants might be very reluctant to participate in a legal marriage, even after a very long period of cohabitation.

So far, we have dealt primarily with horizontal equity in taxation. While this is an extremely important policy instrument, other social policies are also important. If it is inequitable to tax people on a family basis, it is also inequitable to disadvantage people on the basis of their marital status in other types of social programmes. Those social programmes which define eligibility on the basis of family income discriminate against married people in comparison with unmarried people. This is the case with the Guaranteed Income Supplement, for example, where two adults married to each other receive less money than they would if they were not married. The solution is, of course, to raise benefits for a married couple to the level of benefits for two singles, and to separate eligibility requirements totally from marital status and the income of the spouse. In effect, this would transform our system of social programmes into a system of various universal programmes (of which we already have some components in place, such as the Family Allowance, Old Age Security, etc.). Before we discuss fully the issue of selective versus universal programmes and the attendant issues of costs and financing, we must briefly consider the issue of vertical equity.

Vertical Equity

Usually, a social programme is considered equitable if it provides higher benefits to poorer people, and lower or no benefits to richer people. Higher benefits to poorer people can be achieved by paying poorer people high benefits, or, alternatively, by paying all recipients the same but taxing the benefit progressively, such that the poorest pay least tax on it and the richest most. One benefit that is always regressive is tax expenditures. All tax deductions always give more money to higher income people and less money to lower income people. An example provided by Maslove (1981:238) in Table 4.1 will make this clear. He utilizes the charitable deduction to make his point, but the same mechanism works for all other tax exemptions or deductions.

In 1978, the average personal income tax expenditures in Canada for tax filers with an income of less than $1000 was $286, for tax filers with an income of $5000–10 000, $306, and for tax filers with an income of over $50 000 it was $12 611((Maslove, 1981:240).

In principle, then, all preferential tax treatments are always regressive, and therefore extremely inequitable. The more money a person has, the more he/she will gain from an exemption. If there is a concern about vertical equitability, then, in principle, all personal tax exemptions and deductions should be abolished and replaced with universal tax credits. Tax credits, if they are taxable, are progressive. Every person receives the same amount, but since higher income earners have to pay a higher tax on the same amount, they in effect receive a lower — and occasionally no — net benefit.

Progressivity is not a criterion that can meaningfully be applied to *all* social programmes: since Unemployment Insurance and the C/QPP are based on prior contributions they are not progressive. Family Allowance is mildly progressive since it is taxed. The Refundable Child Tax Credit is a special case, since it is progressive on a family income basis, but may very well be regressive for women to whom it is paid (the higher the husband's income, the less money she gets, if she has low or no income herself). Old Age Security and the Guaranteed Income Supplement would be progressive if there was no exemption for the first $1000 of pension income. Health care and public education,

TABLE 4.1

Example of Regressivity of Tax Deduction

Your income is	You pay	Government Pays	Total
Under $1 000	$100	$ 0	$100
$7 500–8 000	$ 74	$26	$100
$12 000–12 500	$ 73	$27	$100
$24 000–25 000	$ 60	$40	$100
over $200 000	$ 48	$52	$100

Source: Maslove, 1981, p. 238.

finally, can be considered as progressive since they give services that most poor families could probably otherwise not afford, even though the rich may derive the greatest benefits from both programmes.

Overall, then, in the Canadian social security system progressive and regressive elements are mixed. This is reflected in the fact that over the last ten years the income gap between rich and poor has not been narrowed. A discussion of regressivity and progressivity cannot be meaningfully conducted without touching on the issues of universal versus selective programmes.

Universal vs. Selective Programmes

There is a widespread belief that selective programmes are more desirable and efficient than universal programmes in that they channel money to the poor without paying out vast sums to the rich. Unfortunately, this is accepted as true by many analysts, as well as by large portions of the public. Selective programmes, therefore, are often seen as politically more feasible, since they seem ostensibly less costly. In a period of economic restraint, selective programmes therefore seem highly attractive (cf. Kesselman, 1980:154). Unfortunately, considering selective programmes as more progressive (or more "target efficient," as economists would say) is based on a misperception which in turn derives from the habit of ignoring the interaction between the direct transfer programme and the tax structure. Kesselman provides a simple example which illustrates the point:

> Imagine an economy with one rich person and one poor person. For now, assume that the programs do not influence individual behaviour. Suppose that the government decided to increase the poor person's income by $1,000. The government could tax the rich person by $1,000 and transfer this sum to the poor person. Alternatively, the government could tax the rich person by $2,000 and transfer $1,000 to each person. The former programme would be called selective, the latter programme universal.[16]

Of course, matters are not quite that simple. However, the whole debate is largely based on a misunderstanding. The major difference between selective and universal programmes is that "Selectivity imposes income tests before benefit payments are received. Even though both programme types may use tax recovery devices, selective programmes typically impose much higher total marginal tax rates at the bottom of the income scale" (Kesselman, 1980:157). In effect, then, selective programmes may be more regressive than universal programmes! (See also Mendelson, 1980; Shifrin, 1980; Kesselman and Garfinkel, 1978; Garfinkel, forthcoming.) The supposed greater cost of universal programmes is therefore highly deceptive, since net costs depend on what proportion of any particular transfer programme is recouped through taxes.

We can now return to the question as to how to create equitable policies which are truly policies *for* (rather than against) families given the types of problems that have been outlined.

Principles for Equitable Policies for Families

One of the major problems discussed for developing equitable policies for families is the current co-existence of breadwinner and two-earner families which, respectively, presuppose economic dependence of the wife on the husband versus equal economic responsibility for both spouses. Another major problem is how to avoid the familism-individualism flip-flop; that is, how to avoid policies which are ostensibly meant to be beneficial for families, actually turning out to be detrimental to at least some types of families. A third major problem is how to ensure that policies (due to their differential effects on individual family members) do not have a detrimental effect on any one family member. And lastly, equitable policies must obviously be equitable both in a horizontal and in a vertical sense.

To be able to develop policy principles which overcome these problems, it is necessary to introduce two new thoughts. First, we are obviously in a transitional stage as far as family structures are concerned. The change has been extraordinarily rapid in the past decade, and more changes can be expected. That being the case, we need to distinguish between short-term and long-term policies, to allow us to make short-term adjustments to problems which are due to the fact that we *are* in a transitional period. Specifically, although as a society we seem to be moving towards the two-earner type of family, there are some families which will not make this change, for a number of reasons, such as that the wife's age is restricting her from finding employment. With this changeover from one type of family to the other, the homemaker function of the wife in breadwinner families (or of any spouse at home) has become problematic for social policy development. If we develop or maintain policies which transfer benefits to families which follow the breadwinner model, we may be subsidizing a type of family which keeps one of its adult members as a dependent. On the other hand, if we fail to subsidize such families, we may (a) penalize wives for having fulfilled their homemaker functions in a time in which there was virtually no alternative to doing so, and (b) push such families into poverty. This is where the distinction between short-range and long-range policies becomes useful.

Although for the long range our policies must be grounded in the notion of sex equality, for the short range policies must also protect the interests of those people who started their families in times when sex differentiation rather than sex equality was the norm. This can be achieved through supplementary provisions which make up for historically grounded differences between the sexes, *without permanently enshrining such provisions based on differences.*

The other necessary ingredient in solving the contradictory policy requirements which ensue from the co-existence of the breadwinner and two-earner types of families is to distinguish between the various functions which are performed by housewives according to whether they are socially useful or only privately useful.[17] Looking at housework in this manner, it becomes obvious that whenever housewives look after dependent children or dependent adults they are performing socially useful work, since if they failed to do so, society would take over the care of these dependent children or adults. Whenever housewives perform services for adults (or for themselves) which are useful only for adults who are, in principle, physically and mentally able to take care of themselves, they perform labour that is privately useful, but it is not socially useful (society does *not* replace the services of a wife it it merely means inconvenience for a husband, for instance).

Socially useful and necessary services should be regarded as such and should therefore receive the normal benefits that are attached to socially useful work, while privately useful work is of use only to one or some individuals, who, if they desire to receive such services, should be fully responsible for paying for them.

Lastly, both men and women have children. This being the case, it seems equitable that the responsibilities of both fathers and mothers for childcare should be identical, rather than differentiated.

With these considerations in mind, we can now formulate principles which, if jointly applied to social policies, would result in equitable policies for all families and for all their members. They are the following five principles:(1) Principle of Individual Equality; (2) Principle of Shared Societal Responsibility for Dependants; (3) Principle of Eliminating Structural Disadvantages for Women; (4) Principle of Adherence to a "Grandmother Clause"; (5) Principle of Universality and Progressivity.

In the following, each principle will be briefly discussed.

Principle of Individual Equality

The principle of individual equality implies that everybody should be administratively treated as an individual, rather than as a family member. This is one of the major ways in which to avoid the familism-individualism flip-flop, since it means that there could be no discrimination on the basis of sex, marital status, or family status in general. This would imply that eligibility to all social benefits be determined on the basis of individual status and individual income only, and, correspondingly, that nobody could be disentitled from any social benefit on the basis of family status. Social programmes currently in place which are geared to couples would need to be restructured to serve individuals, thus raising the benefits that a couple would receive. This would allow all individuals who wish to pool their benefits by living together to do so without discrimination, interference, or lowering of benefits.

Treating people administratively as individuals allows them to socially live in families without financial or other penalties. However, this principle becomes problematic when applied to current welfare regulations, since it would entitle wives (or husbands) of wealthy spouses to welfare payments. This issue can only be addressed in conjunction with the second principle, and the question will be picked up again after the second principle has been elaborated upon.

Principle of Shared Societal Responsibility for Dependants

There are distinct categories of dependents: dependent children and adults in need of care. While daycare is a responsibility that is shared between parents and society, care for adults who need partial or total care for reasons of accident, sickness, old age, or mental or physical handicaps must be seen as a societal responsibility. This implies four subprinciples which will be discussed in turn.

Principle of childcare as a joint societal/parental responsibility. While parents have a responsibility to care for their children, this responsibility must be shared by society irrespective of the family structure within which children are being raised. To a very limited degree this principle is already accepted as manifested in the Family Allowances, and in free public education and almost free medical services. Caring for one's own children is already seen to be of social value in the case of single mothers who are eligible for Family Benefits, but it is at present less likely to be seen as a social service when it is done by fathers or by married women. This obviously discriminates against married mothers and fathers.

Principle of recognizing childbirth as a societal contribution. If children constitute part of the wealth of a society, then clearly, giving birth must be recognized as a societal contribution. Women should therefore not be economically or socially disadvantaged for giving birth.

Principle of equality of parental responsibilities of fathers and mothers. Since both women and men have children, their rights and obligations towards these children should be identical, including in the case of adoptive parents, except where benefits are differentiated due to medical reasons related to maternity. Parental involvement of fathers should be actively encouraged by all relevant policies.

Principle of care for adults in need of care as a societal responsibility. To the degree that an adult person needs care for reasons of accident, sickness, old age, or mental or physical handicap, the costs associated with such care should be understood as a societal responsibility. Where an adult is able to look after his or her own affairs, but needs care for physical reasons (such as a quadriplegic), any care allowances should be paid directly to the person in need of care, in order to enable him or her to purchase the necessary care. Where an adult is mentally handicapped to the degree that he or she needs a legal guardian, any care allowances should be disbursed by the guardian. In order to avoid the familism-individualism flip-flop, relatives rendering care should be eligible to act as paid caregivers.

The first and second principle together solve the thorny issue of how to deal with the co-existence of breadwinner and two-earner families. The question has been converted from one of the economic style of a family to the question: who profits from the labour of the spouse at home? Only the other spouse who is mentally and physically fit to look after himself/herself? If so, and if one wishes to have a spouse at home for the sake of convenience, that is the joint privilege of the spouses, but it should not be paid for by society. No benefits should therefore be transferred to a family with a dependent spouse provided both spouses are mentally and physically fit, (and provided none of the conditions dealt with in the subsequent principles applies). If, on the other hand, a spouse stays at home either to care for dependent children or to care for adults who for physical or mental reasons need care, this means that this person is rendering a social service, rather than only a private service, and therefore social benefits should accrue to this person.

This means that in principle, for reasons of sex equality (to which Canada, as a country, has committed itself many times) the two-earner model of the family should be used to guide our policies, except when an adult stays at home because there is a person who needs full-time care.

The next two principles recognize explicitly that the consequences of the changes that have recently occurred within families affect different people differentially, according to age and other variables. They therefore constitute principles which are meant to be operative in the short term, while principles 1 and 2 as well as 5 are meant to be operative in the short term as well as in the long term. In addition they are written with respect to women, rather than with respect to both sexes, since in the vast majority of cases only women would be affected. Where, however, men were in a comparable situation, they should of course also be applied to men.

Principle of Eliminating Structural Disadvantages for Women

If we are moving towards equality of responsibilities of husbands and wives, and fathers and mothers, it must be recognized that equality of responsibilities is only fair if there is equality of opportunities for women and men. This is, at present, not the case. Therefore, policies need to be designed such that they eliminate the structural disadvantages of women, and, where necessary, positive policies should be created for an interim period to correct historical imbalances. This implies the following three subprinciples.

Principle of avoiding disparate impact because of structural disadvantages for women. Where eligibility criteria for entitlements to social benefits are such that for reasons of structural disadvantages women are less likely to qualify for such benefits, eligibility criteria should be so formulated that women qualify in comparable proportions and to comparable degrees. For instance, women constitute the bulk of part-time workers, yet part-time workers tend not to have any of the fringe benefits that full-time workers have. Women who care for dependent children or adults are currently not eligible to participate in the Canada/Quebec Pension Plan, for example. This situation could be remedied by making this benefit available on a pro-rated basis.

Principle of supplementary benefits in the case of historically determined disadvantages for women. Where, for historical reasons, new benefit programmes would not address the needs of all women, due to historically determined structural disadvantages of certain groups of women, supplementary plans should be devised to serve their needs in an equivalent manner. For instance, one interesting proposal suggested the institution of a "negative mortgage" plan for the elderly, which would allow them to increase their income by receiving negative mortgage payments *from* a financial institution for their house. However, while widowers and elderly men tend to own their homes, there are a substantial number of widows who live in a house which belongs to the estate of their deceased husband. Such widows would not be able to participate in a negative mortgage plan, and other plans would have to be developed to assist them.

Creation of specific policies to overcome structural disadvantages for women. In order to overcome structural disadvantages for women, positive policies need to be created that aim to remove such disadvantages. For instance, when a housewife has been out of the labour force for many years, she may need access to a special re-entry programme in order to be able to eventually participate as an equal in the labour market. Such programmes, however, should be so designed that they discontinue automatically as the structural disadvantages are overcome.

Principle of Adherence to a "Grandmother Clause"

Where a benefit that currently exists alleviates the situation of structurally disadvantaged women, such benefit should not be removed unless the group that has been singled out can no longer be regarded as disadvantaged, or unless the benefit has previously or will simultaneously be replaced by another benefit at least as high as the benefit to be eliminated. For instance, the spouse's allowance discriminates against single women aged 60-65 on the basis of their marital status. However, it is addressed towards extremely needy people. Rather than eliminate it (in the name of principle 1), therefore, it would be better to extend it to all people in a similar situation.

Principle of Universality and Progressivity

In order to be truly equitable, all policies and programmes should be equitable in vertical and horizontal terms. This implies that all benefits should be progressively taxed — on an individual basis! — with the exception of child-related benefits which should be attributed, for taxation purposes, 50 percent to the mother and 50 percent to the father, unless special circumstances prevail (e.g., only one parent has custody). This principle also suggests that wives might be eligible to receive benefits that they would not be eligible to receive if family income was taken into account. Since higher benefits imply higher costs, such costs would have to be financed via an increase in the progressivity of the income tax. This would mean that in middle to higher income categories, the absolute income coming to a husband and wife might be the same as before, but it would be distributed differently, with the higher income earner paying higher taxes, and the lower income earner receiving higher benefits.

Conclusion

In this chapter, we have been looking at the microstructural bias within family literature which manifests itself by a disproportionate emphasis on psychological rather than sociological variables and a concomitant comparative neglect of macrostructural variables. Nevertheless, there is at least one strong tradition of macrostructural analysis in the family literature: namely that part of the literature which concerns itself with the placement and social support functions of families. However, a closer reflection showed that while these functions are postulated in the family literature, they are studied outside it, with the consequence that the relevant literatures (stratification and mobility studies and social policy analysis) have largely failed to incorporate within them the recent changes that have been taking place within families. Stratification and mobility models which fail to deal with two-earner families and with the effects of divorce for social mobility are largely irrelevant nowadays. Likewise, social policy analysis which fails to take into account the co-existence of a multiplicity of family types and the potential diversity of policy effects for individual family members may end up doing as much (or more) harm than good for those selfsame families that they are supposed to serve, and in the name of which they are being justified.

This paradoxical situation has been termed the familism-individualism flip-flop. In order to recognize its existence and operation, several criteria for evaluating policies or programmes were proposed. Following this, equity in social policies was discussed and principles for developing equitable policies for families were suggested.

The greatest dilemma in developing equitable policies for families are, first, how to avoid the familism-individualism flip-flop. Ironically, in order to serve families as *social* units best, and to avoid discrimination against certain types of families, it is necessary to treat people *administratively* as individuals so that they can live together *socially* in families. This statement applies only to transfer programmes, however. In policies which do not involve monies (e.g., immigration policies), it may make sense to treat people as family members rather than as individuals.

The second dilemma is how to deal at a policy level with homemakers. Here, two strategies were suggested: on the one hand, separating the socially useful work from the privately useful work that housewives perform, and on the other recognizing that for historical reasons, short-term policies are necessary to eventually eliminate the prevailing sex inequalities or at least alleviate their consequences. We are, therefore, no longer dealing with a categorization — for policy purposes — of families into two-earner and breadwinner families, but instead with a categorization which divides homemakers into those who perform socially useful work — for which the state should pay — and those which perform privately useful work — for which the individual recipients should pay.

This conceptualization overcomes the otherwise insurmountable problem of how to devise policies which recognize the social value of the work that is done by housewives without institutionalizing the dependency of wives.

Notes

1. Ismael identifies the problem very well, although I do not agree with her cure for it.
2. Mary Anne Glendon, "The New Marriage and the New Property." From *Marriage and Cohabitation in Contemporary Societies*, ed. J.M. Eekelaar and S.N. Katz reprinted by permission of Butterworth & Co. (Canada) Ltd.
3. Sheila B. Kamerman and Alfred J. Kahn, eds., *Family Policy, Government and Families in Fourteen Countries* (New York: Columbia University Press, 1978), p. 3.
4. During 1980–1981 I gave a number of public lectures on selected issues of social policies. In general, I found that the majority of people with whom I spoke (and the majority of them were very well educated indeed) did not even know the major social security programmes that are currently in existence.
5. Philip H. Hepworth, "Family Policy in Canada: Some Theoretical Considerations and a Practical Application" (Unpublished paper, 1979).
6. Pat McNenly, "Paraplegic and wife find love expensive," *Toronto Star*, 1981 02 21, p. A13. Reprinted with permission — *The Toronto Star.*
7. "Wife to go to let vet get pension," *Globe and Mail*, Toronto, 1980 08 15, p. 3. Reprinted by permission of the *The Canadian Press.*
8. Scott MacMartin, "Better unmarried," *The Citizen*, Ottawa, 1980 10 21, editorial page.
9. The following and subsequent sections constitute a fusion of thoughts previously expressed in three other papers: Eichler, 1979; Status of Women, 1980; and Eichler, 1981.
10. See Chapter 10 for a full discussion of this issue.
11. The latter is really a shorthand expression for a more complicated issue: namely, the assessment of policies for families in which there is congruency between parental and spousal roles and those in which there is incongruency. Phrased in these terms, it becomes obvious that there are other issues, such as the thorny issue of the relationship of a parent's spouse to her (or his) children when the other parent is alive and to some degree involved with the children. The whole issue of discrepancies between parental and spousal roles is discussed in Chapter 7.
12. See the previous discussion of the policy consequences of a breadwinner vs. a two-earner type of family.
13. See Chapter 10 for a summary of the main transfer programmes and their unit of administration.
14. Philip H. Hepworth, "The Child and Social Policy in Canada" (Unpublished paper, 1979b).
15. Vern Kirshna, "Selectivity in Tax-Transfer Programs and the Tax-Unit Problem," *Canadian Taxation*, Vol. 2, No. 3 (1980):166.
16. Jonathan R. Kesselman, "Pitfalls of Selectivity in Income Security Programs," *Canadian Taxation*, Vol. 2, No. 3 (1980):156.
17. The nature of housework is discussed in detail in Chapter 5.

References

Abernathy, Thomas J., Jr., "Selected Aspects of Canadian Family Policy: Their Formulation, Implementation and Effects," *International Journal of Sociology for the Family*, Vol. 9, No. 2, 1979, pp. 209–219.

Allen, Catherine M., "Defining the Family for Post-Industrial Public Policy," in David Pearce Snyder (ed.), *The Family in Post-Industrial America. Some Fundamental Perceptions for Public Policy Development.* (AAAS Selected Symposium 32). Boulder, CO: Westview Press for the American Association for the Advancement of Science, 1979, pp. 21–36.

Armitage, Andrew, "Canada," in Sheila B. Kamerman and Alfred J. Kahn (eds.), *Family Policy. Government and Families in Fourteen Countries.* New York: Columbia University Press, 1978, pp. 367–399.

Bergeron, Michel, *Social Spending in Canada. Trends and Options.* Ottawa: Canadian Council on Social Development, 1979.

Bose, Christine E., *Jobs and Gender. Sex and Occupational Prestige.* Baltimore: Center for Metropolitan Planning and Research, The Johns Hopkins University, 1973.

Boulding, Kenneth E., "The Market and the Budget in Perspective: The Economics of Human Relationships in the Household and in the Society," in David Pearce Snyder (ed.), *The Family in Post-Industrial America. Some Fundamental Perceptions for Public Policy Development.* (AAAS Selected Symposium 32). Boulder, CO: Westview Press, for the American Association for the Advancement of Science, 1979, pp. 5–20.

Canadian Council on Social Development. *Proceedings. Conference on Family Policy,* Ottawa, April 24-26, 1977.

Dale, Emily Dunn, "The White House Conference on the Family: Some Observations," unpublished paper presented at the American Sociological Association Meeting, Toronto, 1981.

Delphy, Christine, "Women in Stratification Studies," in Helen Roberts (ed.), *Doing Feminist Research.* London: Routledge and Kegan Paul, 1981, pp. 114–128.

Donzelot, Jacques, *The Policing of Families.* New York: Pantheon Books, 1979.

Dulude, Louise, "Joint Taxation of Spouses — a Feminist View," *Canadian Taxation,* Vol. 1, No. 4, 1979, pp. 8–12.

Dumon, Wilfried and Joan Aldous, "European and United States Political Contexts for Family Policy Research," *Journal of Marriage and the Family,* Vol. 41, No. 3, 1979, pp. 497–505.

Eichler, Margrit, with the assistance of Neil Guppy and Janet Siltanen, "The Prestige of the Occupation Housewife," in Patricia Marchak (ed.), *The Working Sexes.* Vancouver: Institute for Industrial Relations, University of British Columbia, 1977, pp. 151–175.

Eichler, Margrit, "Towards a Policy for Families in Canada." Paper prepared for Status of Women Canada. Ottawa: Status of Women Canada, 1979.

Eichler, Margrit, "Groundrules for Analysis." Unpublished paper. Toronto: O.I.S.E., 1981.

Feldman, Harold, "Why We Need a Family Policy," *Journal of Marriage and the Family,* Vol. 41, No. 3, 1979, pp. 453–455.

Ferry, Jon, "Disabled pair say Ontario is ruining marriage plans," *Globe and Mail,* 1979 07 06, p. 12.

Finlay, Peter C., "A Note on Social Policy Analysis in Canadian Schools of Social Work: Women and Social Policy," Social Policy and Administration Network, *SPAN Newsletter,* Issue #4, June 1980, pp. 18–28.

Garfinkel, Irwin, "Overview," unpublished paper.

Glendon, Mary Ann, "The New Marriage and the New Property," in John M. Eekelaar and Sanford N. Katz (eds.), *Marriage and Cohabitation in Contemporary Societies. Areas of Legal, Social and Ethical Change.* Toronto: Butterworths, 1980, pp. 59–70.

Glendon, Mary Ann, *The New Family and the New Property.* Toronto: Butterworths, 1981.

Goode, William J. *World Revolution and Family Patterns.* New York: The Free Press, 1963.

Guest, Dennis. *The Emergence of Social Security in Canada.* Vancouver: University of British Columbia Press, 1980.

Hepworth, Philip H., "Family Policy in Canada: Some Theoretical Considerations and a Practical Application." Unpublished paper, 1979a.

Hepworth, Philip H., "The Child and Social Policy in Canada." Unpublished paper, 1979b.

Hepworth, Philip H., "Family Policy in Canada: The Case of Mothers' Allowances." Social Policy and Administration Network, *SPAN Newsletter*, Issue #4, June 1980, pp. 29–54.

Ismael, Jacqueline S., "The Family and Social Change: A Historical (sic) Research and the Historical Alternative," *Journal of Comparative Family Studies*, Vol. 10, No. 9, 1979, pp. 107–117.

Kamerman, Sheila B. and Alfred J. Kahn (eds.), *Family Policy, Government and Families in Fourteen Countries*. New York: Columbia University Press, 1978.

Kesselman, Jonathan R., "Pitfalls of Selectivity in Income Security Programs." *Canadian Taxation*, Vol. 2, No. 3, 1980, pp. 154–163.

Kesselman, Jonathan R. and Irwin Garfinkel, "Professor Friedman, Meet Lady Rhys-Williams: NIT vs. CIT," *Journal of Public Economics*, Vol. 10, 1978, pp. 179–216.

Kirshna, Vern, "Selectivity in Tax-Transfer Programs and the Tax Unit Problem," *Canadian Taxation*, Vol. 2, No. 3, 1980, pp. 164–166.

Kitchen, Brigitte, "Women and the Social Security System in Canada," *Atlantis*, Vol. 5, No. 2, 1980, pp. 89–99.

MacMartin, Scott, "Better unmarried," *The Citizen*, 1980 10 21, Editorial page.

Maslove, Allan M., "Tax Expenditures, Tax Credits and Equity," in G. Bruce Doern (ed.), *How Ottawa Spends Your Tax Dollars. Federal Priorities 1981*. Toronto: James Lorimer & Co., 1981, pp. 232–254.

McNenly, Pat, "Paraplegic and wife find love expensive," *Toronto Star*, 1981 02 21, p. A13.

Mendelson, Michael, "The Selectivity Mistake," *Canadian Taxation*, Vol. 2, No. 3, 1980, pp. 167–169.

Moroney, R.M., "The Issue of Family Policy: Do we Know Enough to Take Action?" *Journal of Marriage and the Family*, Vol. 41, No. 3, 1979, p. 461–467.

National Council of Welfare, *Poor Kids*. (A Report of the National Council of Welfare on Children in Poverty in Canada.) Ottawa: National Council of Welfare, 1975.

Nye, F. Ivan and Gerald W. McDonald, "Family Policy Research: Emergent Models and Some Theoretical Issues," *Journal of Marriage and the Family*, Vol. 41, No. 3, 1979, pp. 473–485.

Organization for Economic Co-operation and Development, *The Treatment of Family Units in OECD Member Countries under Tax and Transfer Systems* (A Report by the Committee on Fiscal Affairs). Paris: OECD, 1977.

Ramey, James, "Experimental Family Forms — The Family of the Future," *Marriage and Family Review*, Vol. 1, No. 1, 1978, pp. 1, 3–9.

Rice, Robert M., *American Family Policy. Content and Context*. New York: Family Service Association of America, 1977.

Rice, Robert M., "Exploring American Family Policy," *Marriage and Family Review*, Vol. 2, No. 3, 1979, pp. 1+3–11.

Salyzyn, Vladimir, "Savings, Labour Supply and Tax Equity," *Canadian Taxation*, Vol. 2, No. 3, 1980, pp. 142–148.

Schnepper, Jeff A., "A Tax on Marriage," *Intellect*, Vol. 106, No. 2395, 1978, p. 381.

Shifrin, Leonard, "The Meaninglessness of the Selectivity versus Universality Debate," *Canadian Taxation*, Vol. 2, No. 3, 1980, pp. 170–171.

Smelser, Neil J., "Contemporary Social and Economic Developments and the Functional Capacities of the Family," paper written for The Educational Role of the Family Project of the Organization for Economic Co-operation and Development and the Centre for Educational Research and Innovation, (CERI/ERF/81.03) Paris, 1981.

Status of Women Canada, General Principles for Evaluation and Development of Policies Based on Sex Equality. Ottawa: Status of Women Canada, 1980.

Steiner, Gilbert Y., *The Futility of Family Policy.* Washington: The Brookings Institution, 1981.

Tallman, Irving, "Implementation of a National Family Policy: The Role of the Social Scientist," *Journal of Marriage and the Family,* Vol. 41, No. 3, 1979, pp. 469–472.

Trost, Jan "Cohabitation Without Marriage in Sweden," in John M. Eekelaar and Sanford N. Katz (eds.), *Marriage and Cohabitation in Contemporary Societies. Areas of Legal, Social and Ethical Change.* Toronto: Butterworths, 1980, pp. 16–22.

Watson, Roy E. L., "The Effects of Premarital Cohabitation on Subsequent Marital Adjustment," unpublished paper given at the Canadian Sociology and Anthropology Meetings in Halifax, 1981.

"Welfare fraud of $5,500 jails husband, wife," *Globe and Mail,* 1981 10 16, p. 9.

"Wife to go to let vet get pension," *Globe and Mail,* 1980 08 15, p. 3.

Zimmerman, Shirley L., "Policy, Social Policy, and Family Policy; Concepts, Concerns, and Analytic Tools," *Journal of Marriage and the Family,* Vol. 41, No. 3, 1979, pp. 487–495.

CHAPTER 5

Changing Patterns in Household Management

Introduction

Work, the division of labour, and all other processes that are associated with the production and exchange of goods and services are preeminently the domain of economics. Economics has been defined as the social science "that deals with the ways in which men and societies seek to satisfy their material needs and desires, since the means at their disposal do not permit them to do so completely" (Rees, 1968: 472). The unwitting sexism of the term "men and societies" is probably unconscious but not inappropriate: models of economic man are literally models of economic man and not of economic woman (see Cohen, 1981). *One* of the ways in which this exclusion of women is achieved is through the frequent treatment of the family (or the household) as the smallest analytic unit. This has as a consequence that the type of division of labour which is internationally and cross-culturally the most pervasive one can be considered insignificant: namely the division of labour *within* families or households, which is largely a division of labour on the basis of sex. In other words, exchanges of goods and services as well as of monies within households or families are considered largely irrelevant to economic analysis. (There are, of course, some noteworthy exceptions. See, for instance, Boulding, 1979; or Galbraith, 1975.) If, for instance, a wife renders services to her husband and children and in exchange receives goods (e.g., shelter, money to buy food for her family and herself, etc.) this is typically not seen as an economically relevant exchange, since it is occurring *within* the unit, rather than *between* different units.

It is only quite recently that some researchers have become aware that restricting the analysis to that sector of the economy which is typically the topic of economic analysis — namely the institutionalized, formal sector of the money economy — not only disregards the basis on which this economy is built, but also distorts the real nature of economic exchanges. As a consequence, there have been some attempts to conceptualize both the money economy and the non-money economy, of which labour performed in households is a part, as an integrated system. Robertson (1978:53) has devised a useful figure on the interrelations between the formal and informal economies (see Figure 5.1).

The formal or institutionalized part of the economy is largely identical with the money economy. It comprises all work performed formally in the labour market for money, and the goods and services generated by this activity, as well as their exchange for money. It also includes the formal transfer of monies from people and institutions to governments (via taxes) and from government to people and institutions (via government transfer payments).

The informal, non-institutionalized part of the economy comprises all unpaid and voluntary work, performed for oneself or others, as well as gifts of goods and services, barter transactions, and cash gifts between people. It includes, as a very major part, all household work done by family members for each other. By contrast, if a household employs a housekeeper who is paid a regular salary, this is part of the formal economy. It is therefore not the nature of the work performed that makes it belong to one part of the economy or the other, but rather the circumstances under which the work is performed.

There are some activities which hover at the dividing line of the two types of economies. One example of such an intermediate type of economic activity would be babysitting on a regular basis in an unlicensed neighbourhood household — at present probably the predominant form of day care in Canada. This type of work is normally paid for by the parents of the children who are being taken care of, but the amounts of money are very small, and the money so earned is typically unreported in the income tax, and therefore not incorporated in the Gross National Product (GNP) or treated as an important aspect of the labour market. When income is not declared, the worker is not entitled to most of the normal benefits enjoyed by most of the workers in the formal economy, such as unemployment insurance, eligibility to participate in the Canada/Quebec Pension Plan, subsidized health insurance, legal holidays, and the like.

Restricting our attention to housework alone (which ignores other aspects of the non-formal economy such as unpaid labour performed for voluntary organizations), the value produced through this type of economic activity is by no means negligible. In fact, empirical estimates of the value of housework performed within private households usually place it at one third of the GNP (see Hawrylyshyn, 1976:129. A later article by Adler and Hawrylyshyn (1978) estimates the value of housework done in Canada at 40 percent of the GNP.) In other words, our Gross National Product would probably increase by about one third or more were we to include the value of the labour which is performed within households.

FIGURE 5.1
The Dual Economy

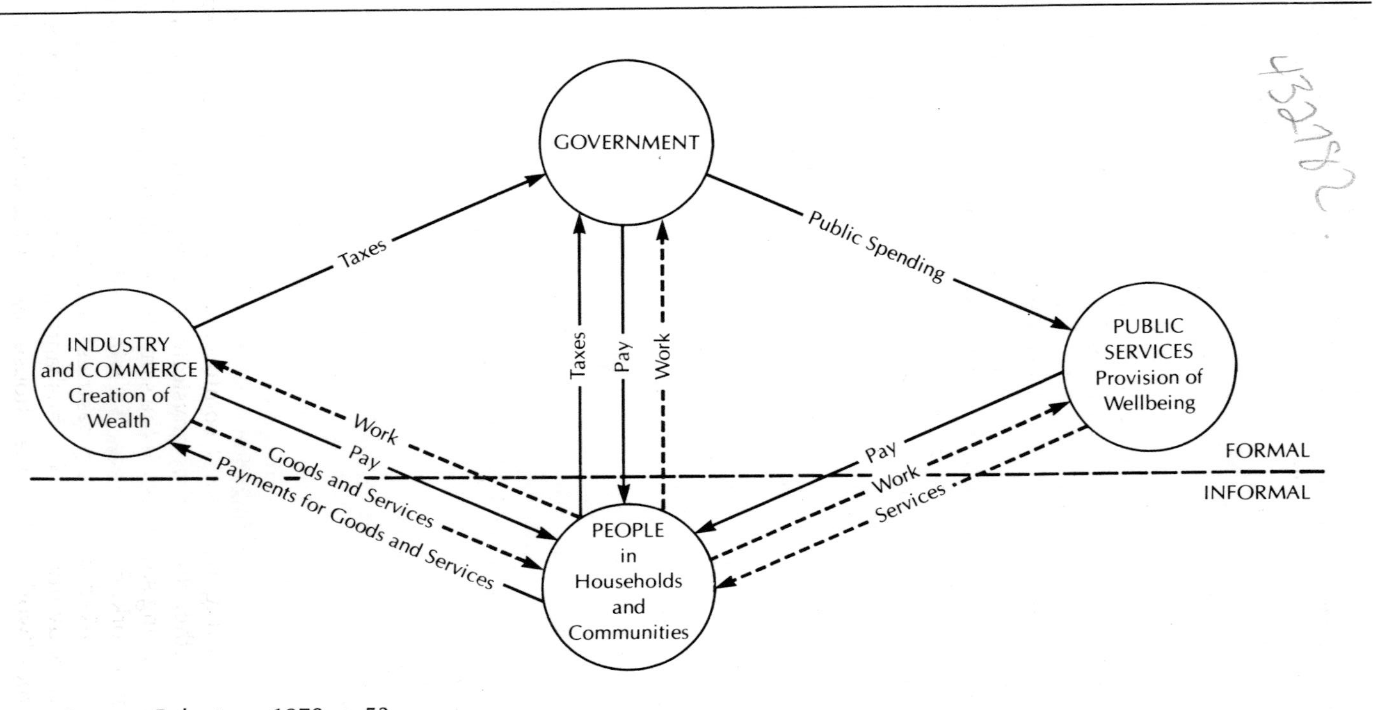

Source: Robertson, 1978, p. 53.

In this chapter we will consider the unpaid work done in households, explore how it has changed over time, and reflect on the significance of these changes for family life in general. In the next chapter, we will deal with the formal aspect of the economy and how it interacts with family life, as well as with the interaction between the unpaid work within households and the paid work performed in the labour market.

A Word on Terminology: Housework and Housewives[1]

Considering its pervasive importance, housework (as well as housewives) has received very scant attention from the social sciences. There are a few empirical studies (for instance, Gavron, 1966; Lopata, 1971; Oakley, 1974; Eichler, 1977; Stephenson, 1977; Berk and Berk, 1979; and Luxton, 1980; and a good summary of the literature up to 1977 can be found in Proulx, 1978), and a number of theoretical considerations (e.g., Benston, 1969; Eichler, 1973; Glazer-Malbin, 1976; Smith, 1977; Malos, 1977; Fox, 1980; Hartmann, 1981; Delphy, 1981), but by and large housework (and housewives) is excluded from consideration. An effect of the lack of attention addressed to the issue of housework is that there is no generally shared understanding as to its nature, importance, and meaning. This lack of shared understanding is, among other things, expressed in conceptual inexactness and a lack of clear definitions. We will therefore briefly discuss the meaning of the terms housework and housewife.

The term *housewife,* to attempt a definition, refers to a sexual status (female); a marital status (married); a particular type of economic relationship (economic dependence of the wife on the husband, and the receipt of goods such as shelter, food, and clothes in exchange for personal services); often, but not always, parental status (mother); and the tasks associated with that parental status (mothering); as well as a type of work (consisting primarily of housekeeping and personal service functions).

Housework, in turn, refers to all unpaid labour performed by a housewife for the maintenance of the household (including maintenance of a garden or yard, where applicable) and the work expended on ensuring the personal comfort of household members, irrespective of whether this work is physically done in the house or outside of it (e.g., going shopping). If the same work is done for pay it ceases to be housework. For instance, if a wife starts a small-scale service selling home-baked bread and pastries, or takes in typing for money for somebody other than the husband or another family member, it becomes "work" rather than housework. If the same work is done for pay in somebody else's household (such as the work that a "cleaning lady'' does) it also counts as ''work.'' If the same type of work is done without pay for somebody who is not attached to the household or the family (e.g., caring for an aged unrelated person a couple of times a week in that person's home) it also is not housework, it is voluntary labour. Lastly, all those functions performed within a household by people other than a housewife that are done without pay for oneself or a person attached to the same household, or that simply contribute to the maintenance of the household (such as a child cleaning up his or her room, a husband cooking dinner, etc.) also constitute housework.

To attempt a definition, then, housework refers to unpaid work performed by a household or family member for another household or family member or for oneself, and includes maintenance and personal service functions.

Obviously, neither ''housework'' nor ''housewife'' are clearly delimited concepts nor are they parallel to each other. It is this very lack of conceptual clarity which goes a long distance in explaining the often contradictory statements made about housework in the relevant literature as well as the lack of focus on real changes that have taken place with respect to household management within this century.

The most important precondition for being able to discuss housework and the changes it has undergone during this century in a meaningful manner is the analytical separation of the major functions which are ordinarily referred to when housework is discussed. At a minimum, we can distinguish between three major functions: *housekeeping* functions, which comprise everything that is done to maintain the living space (inside as well as outside) as well as cooking and its attendant tasks (such as shopping, washing the dishes, storing food, etc.); *childcare,* which includes looking after the physical, mental, and emotional well-being of dependent children; and *personal services* to adults (such as a husband or wife, adult children, other adult household members). Personal services would include personal maintenance work such as doing the laundry for an adult who is mentally and physically fit to do so himself or herself; rendering emotional support such as listening to problems, by stroking, etc.; organizational work such as reminding others of dates and duties, making appointments and reservations, entertaining (*provided it is done for the sake of the other person* rather than for one's own sake), etc. Separating the three major functions analytically is useful in that it allows discussion to focus on one function at a time, yet it must be recognized that there is a considerable amount of overlap between the functions.

In the following, we will consider some of the changes that have taken place in household management; in particular, the suggestions that housework (in its housekeeping functions) has been industrialized, that childcare has been professionalized, and that notions concerning personal services are currently in a state of flux.

The Industrialization of Housework

Industrialization, in the strict sense of the term, refers to "the extensive use of inanimate sources of power in the production of economic goods and services" (Moore, 1968:263). Housework, in its housekeeping functions, has become progressively more industrialized on a world-wide level. The process has taken place (and is still occurring) at varying speeds and in different ways in all industrialized nations, and to a much lesser degree in less developed nations. The speed with which housework has become or continues to become industrialized varies not only by society, but also by regions within a country as well as by urban-rural differences and differences in strata. The upper strata in comparatively well-to-do urban regions are likely to experience the industrialization of housework first. To illustrate just how great a change has occurred with respect to housework in the past six centuries, an example will be useful.

The Ontario Science Centre in Toronto had a marvellous display in one of its halls which made the point succinctly. It was a model of a castle with many little figures engaged in a large variety of activities. A mellow voice recounted what was being done in different parts of the castle which lit up, along with their occupants, as they were being discussed. The narrative was as follows:

> Six centuries ago the well-to-do were few. To be sure, the well-to-do lived graciously. Helpers, servants, serfs, minions, and courtiers, such were the status symbols of the time.
>
> Six centuries ago the well-to-do entertained lavishly. A 'soiree': The Lord, his Lady, sundry courtiers and hangers-on. To serve this chic gathering takes many clever fingers, sturdy arms and strong backs, guards to keep the peace — lest the party turn rowdy — servants to bring the fare [to the] musicians, and a jester to amuse the dining company.
>
> Six centuries ago much toil went on behind the scenes. In the kitchen a company of servants, cooks, scullions, water-boy, spit guard, oven attendant.
>
> Six centuries ago it took several men to bathe one Lord, draw water, heat water, haul hot water, haul away used water, set the canopy against the ever-present draughts and carry the Lord's clothing.
>
> Six centuries ago it took one monk to set in writing the thoughts of one Lord and often read the books the Lord could not read.
>
> Six centuries ago it took a spinner, a weaver, and a carder to keep the Lord and his family in daily clothing and Sunday finery.
>
> Six centuries ago it took two blacksmiths and one stable hand to tend to the Lord's horses — his only means of transportation.
>
> Six centuries later the stove, the refrigerator, the sink, the toaster, the mixer, the blender and the shredder, the newspaper and the paperback,

> the transistor radio and the colour TV, the slide projector and the tape recorder, the car, the out-board motor, the snowmobile, the bus, the truck, the train, the plane, the textile mill, the department store, the supermarket, the washer, the dryer and the electric iron, the electric heater, the oil furnace, the gas furnace, the telephone, the light bulb, the clock and the air conditioner [are] the silent servants which make almost every home a castle.
>
> Fact is that in terms of working time alone the average Canadian household through access to modern sources of energy has the equivalent of 330 servants — each working a 12-hour day — at its constant disposal.[2]

This example provides a good illustration of a time when housework was completely non-industrialized. Going forward in time four to five centuries, to frontier Canada, it might seem at first glance that there had been no development in this area whatsoever. Descriptions of early settlers' lives show us people fashioning the necessities of life often without any mechanical aids to speak of, including in the construction of their shelter. The following, for instance, is a description of the method used by one settler to construct and hang the door in his hand-built log house:

> A man and his wife, with two children, moved into the Township of Ops, into a dense forest, eight miles from the nearest settler. For months he chopped away at the forest trees, all alone, and succeeded at length in making a clearing in the forest, and erecting a log house for himself and his family. The logs were peeled and notched at the ends, and laid up squarely, each tier making the house the diameter of a log higher. A hole was cut through for a doorway, and another for a window. To form a door he split some thin slabs from a straight-grained cedar and pinned them with wooden pins to cross slats.
>
> The most ingenious parts of the construction, however, were the hinges. Iron hinges he had not, and could not get. With the auger he bored a hole through the end of a square piece of wood, and sharpening the other with his axe he then bored a hole into one of the logs of the house, constituting in part a door-jamb, and drove the piece of wood into this hole. This formed the top part of the hinge, and the bottom part was fashioned in exactly the same way. Now to the door, in like manner, he fastened two pegs of wood with holes bored through their ends. Placing the ends of the hinges above one another they presented the four ends with holes leading through them, the one above the other. Next he made a long pin with his handy jack-knife, leaving a run at one end of it, and making it long enough to reach from the top to the lower hinge. Through the holes at the ends of the hinge this long pin was placed, and thus the door was hung.[3]

The work generated due to the lack of as simple an implement as a set of iron hinges is vividly described. Similarly, the wives in the bush initially often had to cope without the most basic of tools of their trade, such as a good oven for baking, yeast, soap, candles, clothing, etc., unless they made them. Catherine Parr Traill, in writing a guide to settlers in Canada which was originally published in 1855 admonishes the females who were about to emigrate to Canada:

> Let them remember that all practical knowledge is highly valuable in the land to which they are going. An acquaintance with the homely art of baking and making bread, which most servants and small housekeepers know how to practise, but which many young females that live in large towns and cities where the baker supplied the bread to the family, do not, is necessary to be acquired.
>
> Cooking, curing meat, making butter and cheese, knitting, dressmaking and tailoring — for most of the country people here make the everyday clothing of their husbands, brothers, or sons — are good to be learned.[4]

Nevertheless, this same book also gives advice on what to bring along from the old country to the new one, on prices for purchasing goods that are available in the cities and towns, and suggestions on what to purchase and what to produce oneself. As Nett (1981:244) notes, "the economic self-sufficiency of family households in the past has undoubtedly been exaggerated. The employment of paid servants in the households of New France, 1651-1663 . . . indicates at least incipient consumption features in the earliest settler families. Furthermore, the more privileged European immigrant families in Upper Canada, in their journal accounts, reveal the family as consumer (Moodie, 1962). Backwoods families purchased furniture, some cloth, staple food, and perhaps in greatest quantity, alcohol. Consumption, of course, is essential in urban life; often ignored in the picture of the past is that not all families in Quebec were *habitants*, and not all in Ontario were 'backwoods' or wilderness families."

There was, then, a century ago already an incipient industrialization of housework in the sense that there was specialization of functions (butchers, bakers, tailors, etc., from whom people could buy ready-made products) in the cities. There were machines which were employed in the production of these goods — spinning looms, mechanical mills for grinding flour, etc. However, access to the products of this incipient industrialization of housework was extremely uneven, and, in the case of very isolated settlers, almost non-existent. Nevertheless, the settlers came from cultures in which this process had already started, and therefore it was reproduced extremely rapidly in North America. Traill describes the amount of change that occurred within one generation:

> The emigrants of the present day can hardly now meet with the trials and hardships that were the lot of those who came to the Province

> twenty years ago, and these last infinitely less than those who preceded them at a still earlier period.
>
> When I listen, as I often do, to the experience of the old settlers of forty or fifty years standing, at a time when the backwoodsman shared the almost unbroken wilderness with the unchristianized Indian, the wolf, and the bear; when his seed-corn had to be carried a distance of thirty miles upon his shoulders, and his family were dependent upon the game and fish that he brought home till the time of the harvest; when there were no mills to grind his flour save the little handmill, which kept the children busy to obtain enough coarse flour to make bread from day to day; when no sabbath-bell was ever heard to mark the holy day; and all was lonely, wild and savage around him. Then my own first trials seemed to sink into utter insignificance, and I was almost ashamed to think how severely they had been felt . . .
>
> These old settlers and their children have seen the whole face of the country changed. They have seen the forest disappear before the axe of the industrious emigrant; they have seen towns and villages spring up where the bear and the wolf had their lair. They have seen the white-sailed vessel and the steamer plough those lakes and rivers where the solitary Indian silently glided over their lonely waters in his frail canoe. They have seen highways opened out through impenetrable swamps where human foot however adventurous had never trod. The busy mill-wheels have dashed where only the foaming rocks broke the onward flow of the forest stream . . .
>
> In the long-settled portions of the Province a traveller may almost imagine that he is in England; there are no stumps to disfigure the fields, and but very few of the old log-houses remaining; these have for the most part given place to neat painted frame, brick or stone cottages, surrounded with orchards, cornfields and pastures.[5]

Today in Canada the industrialization of housework is just about completed. The speed with which it has been implemented (and in a few isolated places the process is still occurring) has varied with respect to regional, urban-rural, and class differences, but this refers merely to a difference in the speed of implementation, not in the substance of the process.[6] During this century, two processes have taken place: technology has invaded households on a large scale and goods and services previously produced within households are now available for purchase on the market place. We will briefly consider the outcome of both processes.

The Effect of Technology on Housework

Just about all Canadian households nowadays own some major appliances which include a gas or electric stove, a refrigerator, hot and cold running water, and a gas, oil, or electric heating system. The vast majority of households have many more appliances, such as electric vacuum cleaners, toasters, blenders or mixers, washing machines, dryers, freezers, electric sewing machines, radios, TVs and so on. Table 5.1 displays some of the household equipment owned in Canadian households over a period of just over thirty years.

The single most important change for household management is the almost universal accessibility to energy sources such as electricity, oil, and/or gas. Prior to the use of such sources of energy people were dependent on fires for heating, cooking, heating water, washing, and light (the fire was needed to light candles). The amount of work

TABLE 5.1

Percentages of Canadian households surveyed that had certain household equipment, 1948–1981 *

Item	1948	1953	1958	1963	1968	1975	1981
Hot and cold running water	—	62.57	73.50	84.86	90.97	96.73	98.54
Gas or electric stove	48.49†	62.73	76.66	87.24	94.03	98.33	99.13§
Mechanical refrigerator	29.26‡	66.33‡	86.24‡	94.20	97.44	99.25	99.43
Home freezer	—	2.22	8.17	17.66	29.16	41.83	52.86
Electric washing machine	59.21	76.38	84.28	86.81	83.57	76.86	76.68
Vacuum cleaner	32.02	48.01	60.94	72.45	—	86.54	90.90
Electric sewing machine	—	23.43	36.30	49.03	—	65.43	66.25
Gas or electric clothes dryer	—	—	—	21.60	36.79	51.62	63.86
Automatic dishwasher	—	—	—	2.08	5.08	15.20	31.18

*Does not include households in the Yukon, Northwest Territories or on Indian reservations.

†Includes piped and bottled gas and oil or kerosene.

‡Includes both gas and electric refrigerators. The number of gas refrigerators, however, dwindled rapidly, so that their exclusion from the statistics after 1958 probably makes little difference.

§Includes all stoves.

— No statistics available.

Source: 1948–1968 figures adapted from Report of the Royal Commission, 1970: 34 (table 3). For 1975 and 1981 data, see Statistics Canada, catalogue 64–202.

that these energy sources have saved is perhaps best displayed by reflecting on the work involved in lighting fires. In the early days, fires were lit by means of the flint and tinder-box:

> When fire was so difficult to obtain people were very careful not to let their fires go out, and it was no uncommon sight to see persons going a mile or two through the snow to their nearest neighbour's to get a few coals to start the fire on a cold winter's morning. It was the custom to cover up the bed of coals with ashes at night before retiring, so that there would be some left with which to start the fire in the morning, all that was necessary being to add kindling wood and blow the embers into a flame with the hand bellows . . .
>
> When matches were first introduced they were not, as now, tipped with phosphorus, but were simply pieces of stick dipped in melted sulphur. These sulphur sticks, or matches, as they were called, were lighted by placing them in contact with live coals or the flame of a candle . . .
>
> The tinder-box was a tin box with a tight-fitting cover, used for making and preserving the tinder, which was made by holding finely-cut cotton or linen rags over the uncovered box, setting them on fire and, after they were all in a blaze, allowing them to drop into the box beneath, then replacing the cover and smothering the fire. The charred remains formed the tinder. To get a light all that was necessary was to strike the flint and steel together over the opened box, so that the sparks would fall into it and ignite the tinder, after which it was touched with a sulphur stick and the fire applied to the kindling-wood in the fire-place. This was the English way.[7]

The implications of the household appliances listed in Table 5.1, then, are staggering as far as the nature of housework is concerned. Automatic washing machines, for example, have completely changed one of the most arduous, physically strenuous, and time-consuming work processes into one which is comparatively easy. In this context, it is somewhat puzzling to see that electric washing machines constitute the only major appliance which shows a retrogressive trend. This should probably not be interpreted to mean that people use fewer electric washing machines today than before, but merely that they have access to washing machines that are not privately owned but are situated either in a communal laundry room in an apartment building or in a laundromat.

In addition, new materials make the storage and cleaning of clothes much easier than before. Ready-made clothes make mending and darning a less relevant occupation, and special fabrics can make ironing entirely unnecessary for those who wish to avoid it.

A comparable process has taken place with food production. Since virtually all Canadian households now have refrigerators, families can shop for food weekly rather than daily. Milk can be kept for days in the refrigerator without spoiling. Frozen and ready-to-serve foods have reduced the necessary labour for preparation of foods to a minimum. Prepared baby foods are accepted staples in households with babies. Breads are available everywhere, as are preserves of all types. Fresh vegetables are available on a year-round basis due to massive importation from southern areas (which is only possible with a highly developed transportation system, another aspect of industrialization) and large-scale production of vegetables in greenhouses out of their natural seasons. The result is that the preparation of vegetables and fruits in the summer for use in the winter has become superfluous. Where canning and preserving are still done, this constitutes the personal preference of individuals, rather than necessity.

Cleaning the living space has also become a vastly different task. Modern floor coverings, cleaning agents, and cleaning machines have made a physically demanding and tiring job much easier.

With all these changes, one would expect that housekeeping would become a negligible occupation. That, however, is not the case. Hareven (1976:201) notes that "housework . . . remained nonmodern, despite all the technological innovations. One of the deepest misconceptions about the impact of technology on women's work is the myth that it released time." Indeed, time budget studies show that there is no negative correlation between increased household technology and time spent on housework. Before turning to this puzzle, we will consider the other aspect of the industrialization of housework, namely the availability on the market of all goods and services originally produced within individual households.

The Replaceability of Household-produced Goods and Services through Purchase on the Market

We noted previously that the industrialization of housework has two components: the large-scale invasion of technology into the household as well as the availability for purchase of all goods and services produced within households. Goods and services that used to be produced predominantly or exclusively within households may be available for purchase in one of two forms or in both of them: either by having them brought into households where they are consumed, or by consuming them outside of the household. Food is a case in point. Most households buy ready-made bread rather than baking their own bread on a regular basis. Other ready-made foods can also be brought into households; for example, pizzas, chicken, hamburgers, Chinese food. Alternatively, household members can take their meals outside their own homes in cafeterias, restaurants, and fast food places. And of course people continue to prepare and consume their meals at home.

Cleaning of living space can be bought by hiring "cleaning ladies," housekeepers, services from professional cleaning agencies, or homemaker services. Clothes can be cleaned by dry cleaners; clean diapers can be purchased through diaper delivery services. Repair people can be hired when home maintenance chores become necessary.

Childcare can be purchased through babysitters, day care centres, nannies, by sending children to camps, etc.

A whole range of personal services are available for purchase. Amusements are offered in many forms, through the mass media (particularly television), in the home as well as outside of the home, in the form of movies, concerts, plays, museums, sports events, parades, amusement parks, etc. Entertaining can now be done as well outside the home in restaurants. Some restaurants and fast food chains offer packaged parties, such as birthday parties for children, including treats for the guests, birthday cakes, and the like.

Psychiatrists and psychoanalysts may play the role of a friend or spouse by listening to a person's troubles, and vacations can be bought as ready-made packages with human company included.

Even sex, if one wishes to consider that a personal service rather than a mutual gratification, can be purchased in a variety of forms, as can companionship, in the form of escort services. Indeed, it is hard to think of anything that can be produced as a service or good in the home that is not also available for purchase on the market.

With all these changes, one might reasonably expect that housework has dwindled to the point where it only takes a marginal amount of time per day. This, however, is by no means the case. While time budget studies are difficult to interpret with respect to the sorting out of different types of activities performed, they do demonstrate unambiguously that the average amount of time spent on housework has *not* decreased over the past few decades while this process of industrialization of housework has been taking place (see Vanek, 1973; Meissner et al., 1975; Clark and Harvey, 1976). How is this possible?

For one, availability on the market does not imply accessibility for everybody. If goods are available for purchase but so expensive that many people cannot afford to buy them, then for those people who cannot afford them, housework has only been partially industrialized. Others might want not to purchase these goods and services: individual preferences may lead to the home production of some goods (e.g., many women and some men bake or sew their own clothes). The point is merely that they are available for purchase. Some production activities may be experienced as enjoyable (for instance, some people enjoy cooking, gardening, or childcare). Home-produced goods may be considered superior in terms of quality (parents tend to think that only they are capable of the best childcaring).

Whether or not household goods are home produced or purchased, their consumption and/or maintenance still takes time and effort. If food has been brought into the house, dishes may still have to be washed (even a dishwasher has to be loaded and unloaded). At a minimum, garbage has to be put into bags and put on the curb. A hobbyist may spend an enormous amount of time tinkering with a car. Yet nobody would dispute that cars are specialized products of a highly industrialized society. The same argument applies to goods which were previously produced within individual households.

In addition, housekeeping standards seem to have gone up (see, for example, Cowan, 1974:249). In some frontier households, laundry was done only four times per year! Today, doing the laundry at least once per week seems to be the norm.

A second factor is of a different nature. We have previously distinguished between three major functions of housework: housekeeping, childcare, and personal services. The first aspect of the industrialization of housework, the large-scale invasion of technology into the household, affects only one of these functions, namely housekeeping. By their nature, childcare and personal services cannot be highly technologized. We have argued that these functions can be purchased on the market, but price puts high quality childcare and personal services out of reach for vast numbers of people. In addition, if all childcare and personal service functions were bought on the market rather than performed by family members for each other, could we still say that the people involved constituted a family? Substitutability through purchase is therefore limited in terms of price and ideological notions concerning families.

With respect to the latter two functions of housework, two contradictory trends can be noted: on the one hand, it *is* possible to purchase childcare as well as a large array of personal services. In this sense, then, even these two functions have been industrialized. On the other hand, while the *necessary* housekeeping functions have been reduced and downgraded in importance (meaning that the *voluntary* aspects may not have been reduced or may even have expanded), the childcare function has been upgraded in importance, and the personal service function is currently in a process of change. In the following we will briefly consider the latter two aspects of housework.

The Professionalization of Childcare

One of the reasons why the amount of housework performed has not diminished over time in spite of the great increase in household technology seems to be that the childcare function has been upgraded (cf. Vaneck, 1973 and Slater, 1970).

Gauger and Walker (1980) found that in the United States there was no statistically significant difference in the total amount of time that female homemakers spent on housework between the period of 1967 and 1977. "However, there were some differences in specific activities: time used for care of family members increased, while time used for washing dishes and laundry decreased" (Gauger and Walker, 1980:1).

Another American study which made a limited comparison on time spent on housework in 1965 and 1976 found that hours of work and time spent commuting to work declined slightly for men with a corresponding slight increase in housework (and for unmarried men, in watching television). Women during the same time span decreased their housework time slightly, but baby and child care time remained largely unchanged for both women and men (Stafford and Duncan, 1977:41). However, time budget data do not give any information on the quality and imputed importance of work performed. We will therefore turn to the child development literature for an indication of the reconceptualization of childcare, and particularly the emphasis on mothering that emerged during the past half century.

In the 1950s, childcare manuals based on the work done previously by theorists such as Freud, Piaget, Gesell, Spitz, Bowlby, and others began to encourage mothers to become more attentive to their children's cognitive growth. "Whatever increased time mothers might have gained from washing machines and prepackaged foods was directed to higher standards of cleanliness and attending to the scholastic achievement of their children" (Ramkhalawansingh, 1978).

The task was defined as one in which mothers became responsible for ensuring the success of their children by providing the right type of emotional, intellectual, social, and physical environment for them. One of the most outspoken recent supporters arguing this point is Burton White, Director of Harvard University's preschool project, who also occasionally travels to Canada to give talks on the subject.

White's approach has been characterized as follows by one of his critics:

> White contends that psychologists like himself hold the key to equalizing opportunity in our society; social reform is less a matter of providing the poor with new economic resources than of teaching poverty mothers scientific child-rearing methods. Viewing American family life in near total isolation from the rest of society, he holds mothers wholly responsible for the intellectual development and competence of their children. Children who fail in school do so mainly because of their mothers' prior neglect. Almost needless to add, White's work is incredibly de-

> manding and anxiety producing for women. White judges women as shortsighted and overly self-involved if they fail to see that child rearing is the most challenging and fulfilling social role possible. No rational woman, in his view, would sacrifice the privilege and joy of child rearing for alternative sources of employment or pleasure, or shirk her responsibilities by relying primarily on day care during the child's early years. In White's work, despite the scientific jargon, one sees a clear parallel to the nineteenth century "cult of domesticity," which placed women on pedestals as objects of reverence so long as they confined their energies to domestic pursuits. Under the sponsorship of experts like Burton White — whom I have singled out only because of his direct influence and continuing role in federal programs — parent education not only tends to blame the victim; it places an inordinate share of the blame on women alone.[8]

The term "professionalization of childcare" therefore refers to the introduction of professional standards for child development techniques for *mothers,* rather than on the development of professional care in non-family settings. It is interesting to note that in the child development literature, overall the role of the father is seen as fairly negligible. It is likewise interesting to note that the child development techniques recommended for use to mothers tend to be developed in institutional, non-family settings, by professionals for whom concern with childcare is a job with limited hours of work and holidays, rather than a twenty-four hour responsibility.

The concerted advice to mothers has created a cultural environment in which expectations concerning childcare are very high, and without providing concomitant services and facilities which would aid in meeting such high standards. Services are typically available only either on a private basis (and therefore only to those who can afford some extras) or on a public basis if the family has been defined as in need. Although much of the advice given may be sound in an abstract sense, it is likely to increase stress for mothers as it results in performance standards which are very high without a support structure that would aid in meeting such standards.

A more useful approach would be to develop services which would be available to all parents (female and male, of one-parent or two-parent households, and irrespective of economic status). In addition, and just as importantly, it is a fairly recent phenomenon that a majority of Canadian children are receiving some care on an ongoing basis from people other than their mothers. This care is at present still predominantly rendered in a *non-professional manner,* by untrained people in non-supervised settings (see Chapter 8 for a discussion of contemporary childcare patterns). It is this aspect of childcare which is in urgent need of upgrading, and where increased professionalization would likely be beneficial rather than stress-provoking.

Changing Notions Concerning Personal Services

One of the important functions of housework is the rendering of personal services. These are primarily services rendered by a wife to her husband and by a mother to her children; in other words, services which are rendered by the woman in the family to the other family members. Indeed, this is partially what is meant by the term "wifely duties," or the "wife role," as well as what is implied in the "mother role."

Personal services may cover a large range of activities of very different kinds. They may include physical maintenance functions (e.g., keeping clothes in order, buying shirts, pants, underwear, etc. for a spouse or child or other household member), emotional support functions (listening sympathetically to work- or school-related problems or other problems, bolstering the other person up, creating an environment which is generally morally and emotionally sustaining and supportive, etc.), social support functions (maintaining contact with friends and kin, not only for one's own sake and in one's own name, but also *on behalf* of the other persons, buying and sending presents which are given in the name of the couple or the family, entertaining not just for one's own sake but also on behalf of the other, making excuses for the other, etc.).

The classical wife role would be that of the wife of the organization man who was described so trenchantly by Whyte (1956) a generation ago. She would accept, not only without demur but with delight, that her ability to entertain the boss and his wife has an impact on the career chances of her husband. Such an understanding of a marriage in which the wife participates vicariously in her husband's job by a full range of background activities as "supporter, comforter, backstage manager, home maintainer, and main rearer of children" (Papanek, 1973:853) has been termed the "two-person career." In the extreme case of a highly visible man, such as for instance a very prominent politician, his wife may become a "public wife" (Gillespie, 1976).

Personal services may all be offered and accepted in the name of love and may never be perceived as work or even as services by the parties involved. However, when wives take full-time jobs two things are likely to happen: both the wives and the husbands are likely to start realizing that the wife did render personal services to her husband, and she will find it impossible to continue to render such services at the previous level, and maybe desire some services in return for those she does continue to render.

In a couple in which two people have paying jobs surely the ideal situation would be a balanced exchange of services between the two partners (and, to the degree possible, between parents and children). This is, of course, a radically different notion of spousal rights and obligations than the majority of people were raised with. In addition, there should be a critical examination of the question of eliminating altogether functions which on closer inspection are found to be unprofitable. For instance, certain social relations may not be enjoyable to anybody involved, and it may not be useful to maintain certain social customs such as excessive present giving or excessive Christmas card sending.

At present, there seems to be pervasive confusion as to what are appropriate behaviours for husbands and wives. Ross (1980:112) has noted that "Marriage has been saddled with unprecedented ideological burdens. It has become the framework for couple relationships based on perfect mutuality, intimacy, sexual ecstacy, and mutual growth. Most marriages fail to fit this prescription." Beyond that, many middle-aged people and possibly many younger people as well were raised with a set of behaviour norms which are no longer appropriate for them. Many of these women and men will have grown up in a breadwinner family, in which the mother-wife stayed at home and was responsible for all aspects of housework. However, this type of division of labour is both dysfunctional and unjust for a two-earner family. On the other hand, breadwinner families continue to constitute a very significant minority of contemporary families. Two basically incompatible sets of norms therefore co-exist for different couples and sometimes for the same couple at different points in time. This requires considerable flexibility. Above all, however, it constitutes a considerable amount of strain for *both* types of families. It is no longer clear what being a good husband or a good wife means, there are conflicting notions as to who should do what aspect of the housework, and what a legitimate request for a spousal service is.

True symmetry in spousal relations is so rare that empirical studies which utilize any type of random sample usually do not turn up any couples who are truly symmetrical in their role allocation, even though the majority of wives are now in the labour force.

Recognizing this problem, a small-scale American study utilized a strategic sampling technique which eventually produced thirty-one couples who employed fully developed role-sharing. This was defined as the sharing by husband and wife of the traditionally segregated roles, namely the breadwinner role, the domestic role, the handyman role, the kinship role, the childcare role, and the major/minor decision-making roles.

> Specialization within any of these roles (e.g. husband cooks, wife launders) would be compatible with role-sharing, as long as specific tasks are not assigned to a spouse *on the basis of sex* (i.e. because they are deemed more appropriate for someone of his/her gender) and as long as the over-all responsibility for the duties of *each* role is evenly shared.[9]

Asked about their motives for engaging in role-sharing, "the vast majority of couples said they became pessimistic about traditional marriage after trying a traditional pattern in their marriage in its early years" (the couples had on the average been married for six years) (Haas, 1980:291). Couples listed as benefits greater opportunities for both spouses to develop their abilities and pursue their personal interests without being limited by traditional role expectations. It provided relief from the stress and overwork resulting from having primary responsibility for a broad area of family life, especially eliminating the overload dilemmas faced by women with a job when they remain responsible for housework and childcare. It also unburdened the husband from the provider role, with its attendant stress and anxiety. It gave greater independence to each spouse: for the wife, it avoided economic dependence; for the husband, it avoided dependence on getting domestic chores done. It reduced resentment and conflict resulting from asymmetrical power of the husband, and brought greater intimacy between the spouses, partially because joint decision-making required more communication. It also fostered closeness due to more similarity in the situations of husbands and wives, and led to their doing more things together, which in turn further enhanced closeness. Lastly, it led to improvement in parent-child relations, and greater financial security.

Problems included, in order of their frequency:

> disinclination to do non-traditional tasks, discrepancies in housekeeping standards, wife's reluctance to delegate domestic responsibility, and lack of non-traditional skills.[10]

Another type of conflict involved conflict between jobs and family responsibilities.

> This was reported by over half of the total sample, by husbands a little more often than wives (in contrast to typical dual-career couples, where the wife usually reports job-family conflicts). Most of those individuals reporting job-family conflicts mentioned that their jobs interfered with family responsibilities in various ways: housework didn't get done, they lacked energy and patience to interact well with their children, or they did not have enough leisure to spend with their families. About one-third of those reporting conflicts mentioned that family duties interfered with their job performance: they had to cut down on over-time and work, had trouble doing job-related work at home, had to rearrange their schedules when children became ill, or had little time to attend job-related meetings in the evenings and on weekends.[11]

Nevertheless, the author observed that "Many of the role-sharers in the study were noticeably productive in their fields, so perhaps a role-sharing lifestyle contains some compensations that allow an individual to do well at a career . . ." (Haas, 1980:296).

Small-scale studies of this nature do not portray a picture that is at all typical of current role allocations among spouses in two-job families, but they are important because they suggest that in a few cases a pattern that seems more appropriate for a two-job family is already in existence, thus providing hope that such patterns will eventually become more widespread. The simple fact that the majority of wives now have paying jobs has fundamentally shifted the nature of marriage, parenthood, the family as a whole, and a social structure which was built around the notion that a wife is somebody who renders personal services to her husband, without having the right to expect in return the rendering of reciprocal services from her husband.

The Effects of the Industrialization of Housework and the Professionalization of Childcare on Women, Men, and Children

We have briefly considered three processes: the industrialization of housework, the professionalization of childcare, and changing notions concerning personal services. Of these, the last one is the least developed, and the first one is the most important.

The most important effect of the industrialization of housework is a very basic devaluation of the housekeeping functions that traditionally used to be performed by the housewife. In other words, housewives have become replaceable in their housekeeping functions. This is partially reflected in the increasing number of one-person households (Davids, 1980). (This increase is, of course, also due to other factors. The point is that an increasing number of people do survive in one-person households.)

While this devaluation of the housekeeping function of housework has taken place, the childcare function has *not* decreased in importance and possibly it has increased. Due to declining fertility, decreased infant mortality, and close spacing of births, children are now highly likely to grow up in a family with only one other sibling who is very close in age. This spacing is likely to place a great burden on the mother who has to cope with a newborn infant exactly at a time when her toddler needs more supervision than ever, due to his or her newly found mobility. In the reverse, the care for the newborn may so preoccupy the mother that she does not, in fact, have sufficient time or energy for her slightly older child. "Close spacing between children may also have stimulated far more sibling rivalry than existed in the past: the birth of a sibling may be felt far more keenly as a displacement when a child is between one and four years of age than it is when the child is older" (Rossi, 1977:23).

One rather jolting finding within sociological research is that children apparently impose a strain on marriages. Renne (1970:66) in a large-scale study found that people currently engaged in raising children were more likely to be dissatisfied with their marriage than people who had never had children or whose children had left home, regardless of race, age, or income level.

In a further study on this question, she discovered, by focussing particularly on childless couples, that they were not only happier, but that those in the younger age groups were healthier as well than couples with children. After a careful analysis considering a number of variables, she concluded:

> . . . the most obvious explanation is that children reduce marital satisfaction, just as they seem to have a negative effect on the physical health and psychological well-being of parents in the younger age groups. In the later stages of marriage, also, the difference between *former* parents and those still involved in childrearing is striking. Former parents married thirty years or more were three times as likely to be happily married as active parents, although they were less positive about their marriages than couples who had never had children.
>
> The implication, of course, is that children impose a strain on marriage.[12]

The relationship held true regardless of labour force participation of the wife (Renne, 1976:196). Renne suggests that the phenomenon of unhappiness which tends to accompany active parenting is probably a social rather than a biological phenomenon, since former parents show less evidence of strain than active parents.

Since we have no comparable data for earlier times, it is not possible to state that parents nowadays are more likely to be unhappy raising their children than parents were one or two generations ago. Nevertheless, it is possible to identify some factors which are different in childrearing today and which make it reasonable to assume that the strain involved in raising children has increased.

One is the role of the mass media, which monopolizes a large share of the children's time. This issue will be discussed in more detail in Chapter 8. Briefly, the values propounded by the mass media are likely to be at a variance with what most parents would consider useful and desirable values. It seems therefore a likely hypothesis that this creates a strain which did not exist to this degree when children were less exposed to mass media in general, but particularly to television.

Also, children are dependent for a longer time due to longer schooling, later entry into the labour market, and a lack of jobs for youths.

Third, there are fewer adults within households than there were before. On the one hand, this may remove one source of potential strain. On the other hand, it is likely to intensify the relationships between children and parents, due to the simple fact that children are unlikely to interact on a daily basis within the household with adults other than their parents. There are also fewer children, and although this too may in one sense lead to reduced strain, again it is likely to lead to intensified relationships between children and parents and siblings. Intense relationships are implicitly more explosive than less intense relationships.

If we add to this, finally, increased demands which are put on parents with respect to the education of their children due to the professionalization of childcare, it seems reasonable to hypothesize that there are new strains on parents and therefore also on their children.

With respect to the industrialization of housework, one of the net effects is that the husband is less dependent on the housekeeping services of his wife, for the simple reason that these services are easier to replace. The husband does not profit *directly* from the increased effort which the mother may be putting into childcare, but only *indirectly* to the degree that he identifies himself with the children's well-being and agrees with the mother's educational methods and aims (see Eichler, 1981).

Meanwhile, the increased labour force participation of wives, which must at least partially be seen as a reaction to the industrialization of housework, requires a new set of spousal roles, particularly with respect to personal services, which is likely to be different from the one that both spouses were socialized into. This must be seen as a further source of strain.

Conclusion

Overall, then, we can conclude that the housekeeping functions of housework have become industrialized, while childcare standards have become professionalized. Notions concerning personal services are at present in flux.

Housework constitutes an important, although often ignored aspect of our economy. At the macro level, the formal economy and the informal economy are intertwined such that changes in the one will have ramifications for the other. At the micro level, the same holds true. The industrialization of housework can, in this sense, be seen as contributing to the increasing labour force participation of women. In the next chapter, we will explore some of the consequences of this phenomenon.

Notes

1. This section is based on ideas first developed in Eichler, forthcoming.
2. The text is adapted from a transcript of the narration, provided by courtesy of the Ontario Science Centre. Reprinted by permission.

3. From *Pioneer Days in Upper Canada* by Edwin C. Guillet (Toronto: University of Toronto Press, 1975), pp. 7–8.
4. From *The Canadian Settlers Guide* by Catherine Parr Traill used by permission of The Canadian Publishers, McClelland and Stewart Limited, Toronto, 1969, p. 2.
5. From *The Canadian Settlers Guide* by Catherine Parr Traill used by permission of The Canadian Publishers, McClelland and Stewart Limited, Toronto, 1969, pp. 16–17.
6. For a description of the cultural lag experienced by some immigrant women with respect to the industrialization of housework, see Ng and Ramirez (1981).
7. "Canuck," A., *Pen Pictures of Early Pioneer Life in Upper Canada* (Toronto: William Briggs, 1905).
8. Steven Schlossman, "The Parent Education Game: The Politics of Child Psychology in the 1970s," *Teachers' College Record*, Vol. 79, No. 4 (May 1978):795–796.
9. Linda Haas, "Role-Sharing Couples: A Study of Egalitarian Marriages," *Family Relations*, Vol. 29, No. 3 (1980):290 (emphasis in the original).
10. Ibid., p. 293.
11. Ibid., pp. 295–296.
12. From *Social Biology*, Vol. 23, No. 3, by Karen S. Renne (c) 1976 reprinted by permission of Social Biology, p. 195.

References

Adler, Hans J. and Oli Hawrylyshyn, "Estimates of the Value of Household Work, Canada, 1961 and 1971," *The Review of Income and Wealth*, Series 24, #4, December 1978, pp. 333–355.

Beck, Joan, *How to Raise a Brighter Child: The Case for Early Learning*. New York: Trident Press, 1967.

Benston, Margaret, "The Political Economy of Women's Liberation," *Monthly Review*, September 1969, pp. 13–27.

Berk, Richard A. and Sarah Fenstermaker Berk, *Labor and Leisure at Home: Content and Organization of the Household Day* (Volume 87, Sage Library of Social Research). Beverly Hills: Sage Publications, 1979.

Boulding, Kenneth E., "The Market and the Budget in Perspective: The Economics of Human Relationships in the Household and in the Society," in David Pearce Snyder (ed.), *The Family in Post-Industrial America: Some Fundamental Perceptions for Public Policy Development* (AAAS Selected Symposium 32). Boulder, CO: Westview Press, 1979, pp. 5–20.

Canada, Statistics Canada. *Household Facilities and Equipment, May 1981*. Ottawa: Minister of Supply and Services, 1982. Catalogue 64–202.

"Canuck," A. *Pen Pictures of Early Pioneer Life in Upper Canada*. Toronto: William Briggs, 1905.

Clark, Susan and Andrew S. Harvey, "The Sexual Division of Labour: The Use of Time," *Atlantis*, Vol. 2, No. 1, 1976, pp. 46–66.

Cohen, Marjorie, "The Problem of Studying 'Economic Man'" paper presented at the Learned Societies Conference, interdisciplinary session on the Politics of Feminism, Halifax, May 1981.

Cowan, Ruth Schwartz, "A Case Study of Technological and Social Change: The Washing Machine and the Working Wife," in Mary Hartman and Louise W. Banner (eds.), *Clio's Consciousness Raised: New Perspectives on the History of Women*. New York: Harper and Row, 1974, pp. 245–253.

Davids, Leo, "Family Change in Canada, 1971–1976," *Journal of Marriage and the Family*, Vol. 42, No. 1, 1980, pp. 177–183.

Delphy, Christine, "Women in Stratification Studies," in Helen Roberts (ed.), *Doing Feminist Research*. London: Routledge and Kegan Paul, 1981, pp. 114–128.

Eichler, Margrit, "Women as Personal Dependents: A Critique of Theories of the Stratification of the Sexes and an Alternative Approach," in Marylee Stephenson (ed.), *Women in Canada*. Toronto: New Press, 1973, pp. 38–55.

Eichler, Margrit, with the assistance of Neil Guppy and Janet Siltanen, "The Prestige of the Occupation Housewife," in Patricia Marchak (ed.), *The Working Sexes*. Vancouver: Institute for Industrial Relations, University of British Columbia, 1977, pp. 151–175.

Eichler, Margrit, "Power Dependency, Love and the Sexual Division of Labor. A Critique of the Decision-Making Approach to Family Power and an Alternative Approach with an Appendix: On Washing My Dirty Linen in Public," *Women's Studies International Quarterly*, Vol. 4, No. 2, 1981, pp. 201–219.

Eichler, Margrit, "The Industrialization of Housework," in Eugen Lupri (ed.), *The Changing Positions of Women in Family and Society*. Leiden: Brill, 1982.

Fox, Bonnie (ed.), *Hidden in the Household: Women's Domestic Labour under Capitalism*. Toronto: Women's Educational Press, 1980.

Galbraith, John Kenneth, *Economics and the Public Purpose*. Ontario: Signet Books, 1975.

Gauger, William H. and Kathryn E. Walker, *The Dollar Value of Household Work*. Ithaca, NY: Cornell University, 1980.

Gavron, Hannah, *The Captive Wife*. London: Routledge and Kegan Paul, 1966.

Gillespie, Joanna B., "The Phenomenon of the Public Wife," paper presented at the American Sociological Meetings, New York, 1976.

Glazer-Malbin, Nona, "Housework," *Signs*, Vol. 1, No. 4, 1976, pp. 905–922.

Guillet, Edwin C., *Pioneer Days in Upper Canada*. Toronto: University of Toronto Press, 1975.

Haas, Linda, "Role-Sharing Couples: A Study of Egalitarian Marriages," *Family Relations*, Vol. 29, No. 3, 1980, pp. 289–296.

Hareven, Tamara K., "Modernization and Family History: Perspectives on Social Change," *Signs*, Vol. 2, No. 1, 1976, pp. 190–206.

Hartmann, Heidi I., "The Family as the Locus of Gender, Class, and Political Struggle: The Example of Housework," *Signs*, Vol. 6, No. 3, 1981, pp. 366–394.

Hawrylyshyn, Oli, "The Value of Household Services: A Survey of Empirical Estimates," *Review of Income and Wealth*, Sept. 1976. pp. 101–131.

Lopata, Helena Z., *Occupation: Housewife*. New York: Oxford University Press, 1971.

Luxton, Meg, *More than a Labour of Love*. Toronto: Women's Educational Press, 1980.

Malos, Ellen, "Housework and the Politics of Women's Liberation," *Socialist Review*, Vol. 8, No. 1, 1977, pp. 41–70.

Meissner, Martin et al., "No Exit for Wives: Sexual Division of Labour and the Cumulation of Household Demands," *Canadian Review of Sociology and Anthropology*, Vol. 13, No. 4, Part I, 1975, pp. 424–439.

Moodie, Susanna, *Roughing it in the Bush, or Forest Life in Canada*. Toronto: McClelland and Stewart, 1962.

Moore, Wilbert E., "Industrialization II: Social Aspects: *International Encyclopedia of the Social Sciences*, Vol. 7. New York: Macmillan and Co. and the Free Press, 1968, pp. 263–270.

Nett, Emily, "Canadian Families in Social-Historical Perspective," *Canadian Journal of Sociology*, Vol. 6, No. 3, 1981, pp. 239–260.

Ng, Roxana and Judith Ramirez, *Immigrant Housewives in Canada*. Toronto: The Immigrant Women's Centre, 1981.

Oakley, Ann, *The Sociology of Housework*. New York: Random House, 1974.

Papanek, Hanna, "Men, Women, and Work: Reflections on the Two-Person Career," *American Journal of Sociology*, Vol. 78, No. 4, 1973, pp. 852–872.

Proulx, Monique, *Five Million Women: A Study of the Canadian Housewife.* Ottawa: Advisory Council on the Status of Women, 1978.

Ramkhalawansingh, Ceta, "Children and Infants as Objects of Affection — The Development of the Importance of Cognitive Skills for Infants and Children," unpublished paper submitted for a reading course to M. Eichler, September 1978, p. 18.

Rees, Albert, "Economics," in *International Encyclopedia of the Social Sciences.* New York: Macmillan Co. and the Free Press, 1968, Vol. 4, pp. 472-485.

Renne, Karen S., "Correlates of Dissatisfaction in Marriage," *Journal of Marriage and the Family,* Vol. 32, No. 1, 1970, pp. 54–67.

Renne, Karen S., "Childlessness, Health, and Marital Satisfaction," *Social Biology,* Vol. 23, No. 3, 1976, pp. 183–197.

Robertson, James, *The Sane Society: Signposts to a Self-Fulfilling Future.* London: Villiers Publications, 1978.

Ross, Ellen, "'The Love Crisis': Couples Advice Books of the Late 1970s," *Signs,* Vol. 6, No. 1, 1980, pp. 109–122.

Rossi, Alice S., "A Biosocial Perspective on Parenting," *Daedalus,* 106, 1977, pp. 1–31.

Schlossman, Steven, "The Parent Education Game: The Politics of Child Psychology in the 1970s," *Teachers College Record,* Vol. 79, No. 4, 1978, pp. 788–808.

Slater, Philip, *The Pursuit of Loneliness.* Boston: Beacon Press, 1970.

Smith, Dorothy E., "Women, the Family and Corporate Capitalism," in Marylee Stephenson (ed.), *Women in Canada,* 2nd ed. Don Mills: General Publishers, 1977, pp. 17–48.

Stafford, Frank and Greg Duncan, "The Use of Time and Technology by Households in the United States," unpublished paper. Ann Arbor: Dept. of Economics, University of Michigan, 1977.

Stephenson, Marylee, "Housewives in Women's Liberation: Social Change as Role-Making," in Marylee Stephenson (ed.), *Women in Canada,* 2nd ed. Don Mills: General Publishers, 1977, pp. 109–125.

Traill, Catherine Parr, *The Canadian Settler's Guide.* Toronto: McClelland and Stewart, 1969.

Vanek, Joan, *Keeping Busy: Time Spent in Housework, United States, 1920–1970,* unpublished Ph.D. dissertation, University of Michigan, 1973.

Waerness, Kari, "The Invisible Welfare State: Women's Work at Home," *Acta Sociologica,* 1978 Supplement, pp. 193-207.

Whyte, William H., Jr., *The Organization Man.* Garden City, NY: Doubleday Anchor Books, 1956.

CHAPTER 6

Patterns of Income Generation and Their Effects on Families

Introduction

In this chapter we will be primarily concerned with the formal or institutionalized sector of the economy, which is largely synonymous with the money economy.

Income can be generated in a variety of ways. The different types of income include wage and salary income, income from self-employment, investment income, pension income, and government transfer payments (see Horner and McLeod, 1975:7). In addition, in special cases there may be income which one ex-spouse receives from the other ex-spouse or a non-resident co-parent.

Typically, private incomes which are derived from wages, salaries, self-employment, or investments are acquired on an individual basis, the widespread use of the concept of "family income" notwithstanding. *Some* transfer payments, by contrast, are made on the basis of an assessment of *family* income, although they are typically paid to one individual of this family unit. This is the case, for instance, with welfare, the Guaranteed Income Supplement, the Child Tax Credit. Irrespective of who is the official recipient of an income, it may be used for the benefit of varying numbers of people, depending on the circumstances.

For the purposes of this chapter, it is useful to distinguish between different types of income generation and income disposition. We will here distinguish between *private incomes* (e.g., wages, salaries, investment income) and *government transfers* (such as Old Age Security, welfare, the Child Tax Credit, Unemployment Insurance, worker's compensation, etc.).[1] In addition, we can distinguish between households by the number of income recipients within a household and by the number of household members. Once a typology of income generation units has been created, we can then systematically discuss the consequences of different types of income generation for women, men, children, and families. Such a systematic approach will also allow us to trace historic shifts in income generation patterns, and to dis-

FIGURE 6.1
Types of Income Generation Units

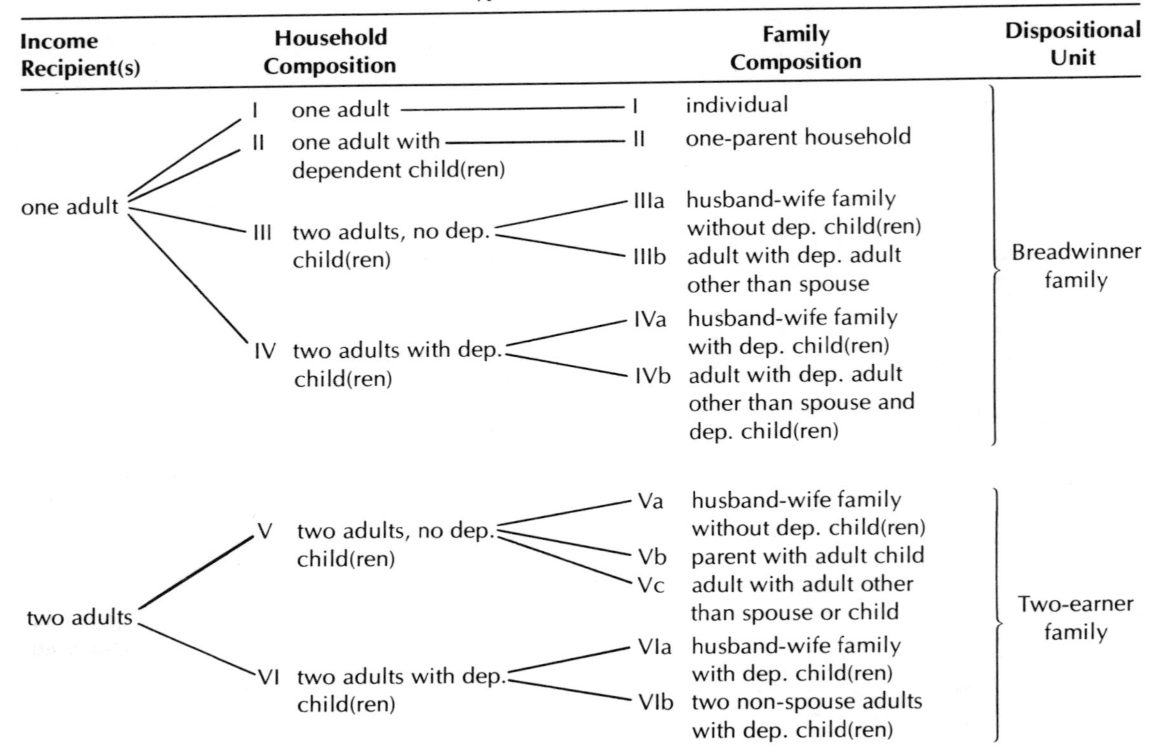

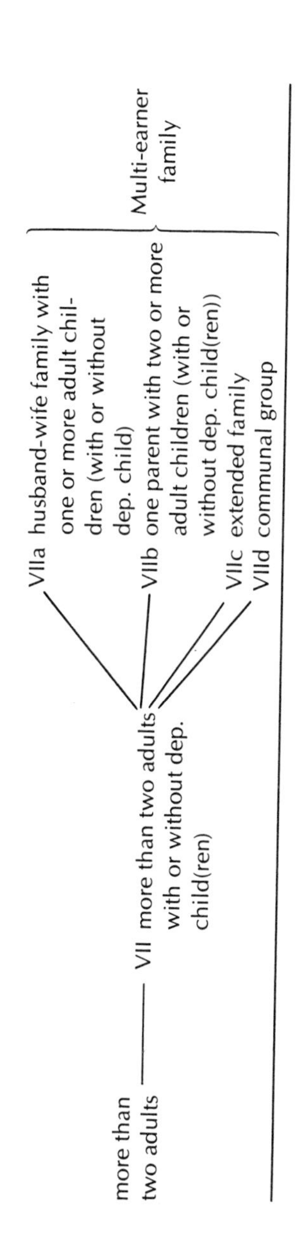
more than
two adults
VII more than two adults
with or without dep.
child(ren)
VIIa husband-wife family with
one or more adult chil-
dren (with or without
dep. child)
VIIb one parent with two or more
adult children (with or
without dep. child(ren))
VIIc extended family
VIId communal group
Multi-earner
family

cuss reasons for them. Finally, it allows us to discuss how private incomes and government transfers intersect, and the effects of such intersections.

Types of Income Generation Patterns

If we distinguish households by the number of income recipients, as well as by household and family composition, we arrive at a classification system in which we can distinguish between breadwinner families, two-earner families, and multi-earner families, each with various subtypes. The possible types are represented in Figure 6.1.

Clearly, some of the types are numerically more common and therefore more important for our analysis than others. Among the various types of breadwinner families, II (a one-parent household), IIIa and IVa (a husband-wife family without and with dependent child(ren), respectively) are the most important types. Among the two-earner families, Va and VIa (a husband-wife family without and with dependent children, respectively) are the most important ones. For purposes of the analysis here, we will largely ignore all types of multi-earner families, since numerically they comprise only a small proportion of all households.

It must be noted that families will be assigned to one type or the other on the basis of their *major* income source. In fact, a large proportion of families is likely to have some supplementary income which would alter the classification if taken into account. For instance, in the case of the majority of families of the type IVa (a husband-wife family with dependent children) the husband will be the breadwinner but the wife will receive the Child Tax Credit.

Further, there are some marginal cases which do not fit into the schema as presented. For instance, the case of an adult in a breadwinner or two-earner type of family who has to make regular and substantial payments to another household (e.g., his children who live with his ex-wife), would constitute a type of income distribution pattern which is not adequately reflected in Figure 6.1.

Finally, the income generation units, as represented, do not specify the source of income. The schema could be further refined (but would in the process become unmanageable) by specifying the source of income. In lieu of doing this, we will first consider the difference between breadwinner and two-earner families in terms of private income, and with a focus on salaries and wages, and subsequently repeat the analysis with respect to government transfer payments. Since transfer payments are often dependent upon other sources of income (or the lack thereof), the interactions between the two types of income, private income and government transfer payments, will also be explored.

Private Income

The most important historical change that we can note is a gradual shift from the breadwinner type of family to the two-earner type of family as the modal family type in Canada. This shift is not completed but is still in progress, resulting in the co-existence of different types of families and an overall rather confused picture. This general shift is, of course, due to the greatly increased labour force participation of wives.[2] In the following, we will explore to what degree and why wives are now participating in the labour force. The consequences of this important shift in income generation patterns will be considered later.

Shift from the Breadwinner Family to the Two-Earner Family

Women in general and wives specifically have, of course, always worked, including participation in many activities that generated money; that is, their participation has been historically not only in the informal sector of the economy. However, such participation has often taken the form of working in the family business or farm or taking in boarders and has therefore not been statistically counted as work. The major change that we can observe in the past few decades is that more and more wives have become officially attached to the labour force, and are therefore being counted (and considered) as working, which is symbolized by the fact that they receive a payment in their own names.

We saw in Table 2.4 that the labour force participation of all women increased from 16.2 percent in 1911 to 50.3 percent in 1980. However, these figures include many single, widowed, and divorced women, and they can therefore not be taken as representative of the shift in labour force participation that has taken place for married women. To document the shift from a breadwinner to a two-earner type of family, we need to consider the labour force participation of wives, rather than of all women, over time. If we do this, the increase in the labour force participation of wives turns out to be much more dramatic than the overall increase in the labour force participation of women, as reflected in Table 6.1.

While in 1931 the labour force participation for all women was 19.7 percent (Table 2.4), the labour force participation rate for *wives* was only 3.5 percent. By contrast, in 1979, 48.9 percent (Table 2.4) of all women and 47.4 percent of all wives were in the labour force. These figures, however, include some women who are too young or too old to be likely to be in the labour force. In order to get a more accurate image of how many wives of working age are actually participating in the labour market, we need therefore apply an age criterion. If we

TABLE 6.1

Female Participation Rates by Marital Status, Canada, Selected Years, 1931–81

Year*	Married %	Single %	Other %
1931	3.5	43.8	21.3
1941	4.5	47.2	17.3
1951	11.2	58.3	19.3
1961	22.0	54.1	22.9
1971	37.0	53.5	26.5
1975	41.6	59.2	31.3
1976	42.9	58.8	31.5
1977	44.2	59.0	32.2
1978	46.3	60.5	33.5
1979	47.4	61.8	34.9
1980	48.9	63.3	34.8
1981	50.5	64.6	35.1

*Statistics from 1931 Census are for females 10 years and over; 1941, 1951, 14 years and over; 1961, 1971 and all other years 15 years and over.

Source: Swan, 1980, p. 10, t.2; for 1980 and 1981, Statistics Canada, Catalogue 71–001.

compare cohorts at one point in time it allows us, together with considering the trends over time, to assess contemporary trends more accurately. Table 6.2 therefore provides labour force participation rates of women by age and marital status. Participation rates of men are included for comparative purposes.

As can be seen from Table 6.2, slightly more than half of all wives in the normal "working age" (20–64) participated in the labour force in 1979. Of the wives aged 25 to 34 — that is, those wives who are most likely not only to have young children but also to be actively involved in rearing them — fully 55.3 percent were in the labour force in 1979.

Looking at the other columns in Table 6.2, we find that labour force participation declines for single, widowed, divorced, or separated women the older they are, but rises slightly for married women in the 35 to 44 years category, to decline thereafter. This probably means that there are still some women who dropped out of the labour force with the birth of the first child and returned after the last child had reached a certain age — old enough to either attend a day care centre, kindergarten, public school, or the like.

Overall, however, the correspondence between higher labour force participation and younger age suggests that we are dealing with a change in behaviour that is particularly marked for the younger cohort. We can therefore expect a continuing rise in the labour force

TABLE 6.2

Participation Rates of Women and Men, by Marital Status and Age Group, Canada, 1979

Age Groups	Single		Married		Other*		Total	
	% Women	% Men	% Women	% Men	% Women	% Men	% Women	% Men
20–24 years	79.9	82.7	63.8	94.2	65.4	89.4	71.3	86.4
25–34 years	86.6	90.1	55.3	97.2	70.2	94.0	60.4	95.7
35–44 years	82.5	86.3	56.7	97.4	69.0	91.1	59.4	96.3
45–54 years	73.3	74.5	48.7	94.6	63.9	85.0	52.1	92.7
55–64 years	59.5	57.6	28.9	79.1	42.9	64.7	34.0	76.5
20–64 years	80.0	83.3	51.3	93.4	59.1	83.4	56.3	90.8

*widowed, divorced or separated

Source: From *Women in the Labour Force 1978–1979*. Part I Participation, Women's Bureau, Labour Canada, 1980, p. 71, t.25. Reprinted by permission of Labour Canada, Women's Bureau.

participation of wives in the future, since, as the younger cohorts age they are likely to maintain their high levels of labour force attachment while the young women entering working age are likely to work for pay in high proportions as well. Eventually, the labour force attachment of married women may approach that of married men.

There is no doubt, then, that while it was highly likely for a wife *not* to be in the labour force not so long ago (in 1961, 22 percent of all wives were in the labour force, meaning that 78 percent were *not* in the labour force — see Table 6.1) we have now reached a stage where the majority of wives *are* in the labour force (see Table 6.2). This is a historic change indeed, which greatly alters family interactions (see *Changing Dependence of Women*, 1978). Before we consider some of the *consequences* of this historic shift, we will briefly consider some of the *reasons*.

Reasons for the Increased Labour Force Participation of Wives

If people want to have jobs but there are none to be had, they will not be employed. The primary factor for the increased labour force participation of wives, therefore, must be seen in changes in the national economy which resulted in a disproportionate growth in the service sector which has traditionally been more likely than other sectors to employ women. At the same time, when jobs are available, people must be willing to take them. In the following, we will look at some of the motives that may have induced wives to enter (or remain in) the paid labour force.

The most common interpretation for the increased labour force participation of women in general and wives specifically is economic need. And, indeed, for many women this must be seen to be the overriding cause. All women who are not married — that is, who are single, divorced, separated, or widowed — generally need to earn their living. However, in the case of married women, the situation is somewhat more complex.

In many cases, the husband's income is simply so low that the family would live on his income alone at or below the poverty line. The National Council of Welfare has calculated that in 1975, 9 percent of all Canadian families were poor.[3] If wives did not have paying jobs, the percentage of poor families would have been higher by 51 percent to encompass a total of 14 percent of all Canadian families (National Council of Welfare, 1979:21).

When economic need is discussed at this income level, there is no question that it constitutes a sufficient explanation for wives' labour force participation. However, the picture gets more complicated as income levels rise.

The usual argument put forward is that there tends to be a straight correlation between husband's income and wife's labour force participation: the lower the husband's income, the more likely the wife is to be in the labour force (e.g., National Council of Welfare, 1979:22; Connelly, 1978:70, 107). The case for economic need as the explanation for wives' labour force participation has been made forcefully by Connelly (1978) and elaborated by Fox and Fox (1981):

> It would appear, then, that as the standard of living in Canada rises, married women whose husbands earn low incomes must work outside the home to maintain their relative standard of living. That is, married women don't work in order to close the gap between rich and poor families. Rather, they work to prevent the difference from increasing. To stay at home and try to stretch their husband's wage is no longer a viable alternative. To maintain what is now considered a reasonable standard of living, families must purchase a growing number of goods and services which are rapidly becoming indispensable. For their families to be in a financial position to purchase them, many wives must work outside the home. . . . In other words, married women are 'free' to work because of the creation of necessities which in fact determine their need to work.[4]

However, a more recent analysis failed to find a consistent pattern between family income less wife's income and the wife's labour force participation. While it is possible that in the past there was a direct correlation between husband's income and wife's labour force participation, by 1977 this association had loosened considerably. As Table 6.3 shows, there is no cohort in which there is a straight correlation between family income and wife's labour force participation.

Using correlational data is, of course, only one way of approaching the question of economic need. Another method is to ask whether, objectively speaking, the economic needs of families increased during the time in which the labour force participation of wives increased.

Comparing family income over time will not help us gain this information, because in many cases family income consists of the income of more than one earner. We therefore need to look at individual incomes over time, taking into account the effect of inflation. This is done by using constant dollars, which take 1971 as the base year. Using constant dollars, it becomes clear from Table 6.4 that *individual* incomes went up rather than down between 1965 and 1980, while at the same time the labour force participation of wives increased considerably (Table 6.1).

As Table 6.4 shows, the proportion of low-income individuals, computed in stable dollars, decreased considerably during 1965 and 1980. While in 1965 about 43 percent of all individuals had an income of less than $3000, this proportion had shrunk to about 36 percent in 1980,

TABLE 6.3

Participation Rates of Wives, Cross-Classified by their Age and by Family Income Less Wives' Wage and Salary Income, Canada, 1977 (1)

	Age of Wife				
Family Income less Wives' Wage and Salary Income	**15–24**	**25–34**	**35–44**	**45–64**	**Total 15–64**
	Participation Rates				
4,000 and under	61	60	49	34	46
4,000–7,999	55	52	46	29	41
8,000–11,999	66	58	56	34	52
12,000–15,999	61	56	55	37	52
16,000–19,999	54	54	51	42	50
20,000 and over	44	47	53	39	45
All income classes	58	53	53	37	48

(1) The participation rates are for the survey reference week of April 1978, classified by incomes registered in 1977. The definition of the family used here is the Census family.

Source: From *Participation Rate and Labour Force Growth in Canada* by Dan Ciuriak and Harvey Sims (c) 1980 reprinted by permission of Department of Finance, p. 70.

still representing a great number of poor people, but nevertheless showing an improvement in the financial situation of individuals.

The problem with the term "economic need" is, of course, that it is a very flexible term which has both an objective and a subjective side to it. Up to a level (where exactly to draw the dividing line is a matter of dispute) economic need is absolute; above that level, wherever the line may have been drawn, it becomes increasingly a subjective need. Luxton provides an empirical example of just how flexible the criterion of "economic need" is. By interviewing forty women in Flin Flon, Manitoba, twenty of whom were from a working class background and twenty from a middle class background, she found that "all the women maintained that their main reason for taking on paid work was because 'we need the money':"

> In one case, the wage earning husband was injured at work, and was therefore transferred to another job with lower pay rates. The result was an immediate drop in income. This household had been carrying substantial debts — a mortgage on the house and outstanding payments for their car. They also incurred heavy medical bills as a result of the injury. In contrast, another middle class household was deeply in debt because in one year they bought a new and larger house, a cabin in the country, skidoos so they could use the cabin in the winter and a trip to Europe 'as an education for the children'. In both cases, the women took on paid employment to pay off their household debts but obviously they were doing so under very different circumstances.[5]

TABLE 6.4

Percentage Distribution of Individuals by Income Groups in Constant (1971) Dollars for 1965 and 1980

	1965	Cumulative %	1980	Cumulative %
Under $1,500	28.4	28.4	17.9	17.9
$ 1,500–$2,999	14.3	42.7	18.2	36.1
3,000– 4,999	20.4	63.1	16.1	52.2
5,000– 6,999	17.5	80.6	12.9	65.1
7,000– 9,999	12.7	93.3	15.8	80.9
10,000–14,999	5.0	98.3	13.6	94.5
15 and over	1.8	100.1	5.5	100.0

Source: Statistics Canada, Income Distributions by Size in Canada, 1980. Catalogue 13–207, t. 34 p. 65. Reprinted by permission of Statistics Canada.

In the late seventies and early eighties, economic need has taken on yet another meaning. With double digit inflation and record high mortgage rates, families who wish to maintain the living quarters they have been used to may experience money problems of a kind they may not have had before. Besides, with unemployment affecting about a tenth of the population (not counting the discouraged workers who no longer look for a job because they assume that they will not find one and who are therefore not included in the official unemployment statistics), there may be a very strongly felt need to have a second income in the family, as insurance against a possible lay-off or job loss.

Where these conditions prevail, economic need is a satisfactory explanation for the increased labour force participation of wives. But two other factors are also important: the divorce rate and the satisfactions derived from having a paying job, as compared to being a housewife.

Since divorce rates have increased dramatically (see Chapter 2) women may *individually* experience economic need in spite of the fact that their husbands may have adequate incomes. A woman may wish to have a paying job in anticipation of a possible divorce, or simply as a safeguard (or to avoid a divorce because of excessive dependency on the husband's income).

One important contributing factor to the increase in the labour force participation of wives must surely be the industrialization of housework. It has devalued the contributions housewives make to their families and to society, with the exception of childcare. It has also led to a continuing social isolation of housewives; there are few structural aspects to housework that lead to consistent prolonged interactions with other adults. For as long as wives who had paying jobs were a minority, they had to justify their having jobs. By now, the situation is reversed: as the majority of wives have paying jobs and continue to be married and have families, housewives are increasingly on the defensive. An increase in the labour force participation of wives is also likely to further contribute to social isolation of housewives for the simple reason that there are fewer of them with whom to interact during the working day.

The reasons why women want to work at paying jobs should be no different than those for men. Yet how many researchers try to explain the phenomenon of "working husbands" in cases in which a husband has a wife with a well-paying job? It is generally understood that having a paying job confers feelings of status, satisfaction, self-fulfillment, prestige, and a measure of economic independence. If these are factors that weigh heavily for men, why should they not weigh heavily for women?

Indeed, there is a fair amount of evidence that women want to have jobs simply in order to have jobs. For instance, in the POW Project, respondents were asked "Would you start working or continue working if you did not need the money?" A majority of both male and female respondents answered that they would start or continue working even in the implied absence of economic need, as displayed in Table 6.5.

What is, however, surprising is that within each occupational category, with the exception of blue collar workers, the women were *more* likely to say that they would start or continue working than the men. When looking at the responses of housewives, of which there were two types — housewives I who were married to working class men, and housewives II who were married to professional and managerial men — we find that 57 percent of the housewives married to working class men and 77 percent of the housewives married to professional and managerial men would like to start working even if they did not need the money. Indeed, when asked what type of work they thought they would do five years from then, 63.9 percent of the housewives I and 55 percent of the housewives II thought they would have jobs by that time.[6]

Findings concerning a high level of interest of married women in paid work is supported by other research. The Bureau of Advertising of the American Newspapers Association asked those women of a national (American) probability sample who had a job: "Suppose you could receive just as much money as you earn now without going to work?" Six out of ten respondents indicated that they would rather go on working than receive their paycheques and stay at home (reported by Bartos, 1978:78).

TABLE 6.5

Desire to Work in the Absence of Economic Need

		% Yes	% No
Blue Collar	Men (n=99)	66.6	37.4
	Women (n=99)	47.5	52.5
White Collar	Men (n=100)	67	33
	Women (n=100)	77	23
Teachers	Men (n=100)	78	22
	Women (n=100)	84	16
Decision-Makers	Men (n=150)	89.3	10.7
	Women (n=150)	93.3	6.7
Housewives I (n=100)		57	43
Housewives II (n=100)		77	23

Source: Previously unpublished data from POW Project.

Likewise, a recent study exploring reasons for labour force participation of Canadian rural women found that when asked for the reasons for labour force participation (if employed part- or full-time, n=207) or their interest in labour force participation (if not employed, n=116), 11.5 percent responded that they needed money to provide necessities, 11.8 percent wanted money to improve their level of living, 46.1 percent wanted employment to satisfy personal needs, and the rest (30.6 percent) cited a combination of one of the two money reasons with personal need (Council on Rural Development Canada, 1979:83, t.12).[7]

In summary, then, we must consider wives' taking on paid employment as due to a number of variables. Economic considerations are very important but do not suffice to explain the dramatic increase in labour force participation. Other factors would include the industrialization of housework which has made it possible as well as desirable for many wives to seek a job. Finally, women clearly want to work at a job for some of the same reasons that move men to work at jobs: for the satisfaction involved, the social contacts that ensue, the status and prestige attached to having a paying job rather than being a dependent, and to have a measure of individual economic independence.

Private incomes are only one major source of income; government transfer payments are another. We will turn to this type of income next.

Government Transfer Payments

Government transfers of all kinds amounted to about 10 percent of all personal income in Canada in 1977–1978 (Canadian Intergovernmental Conference Secretariat, 1980:36). Altogether, this means that in this time period about seven million people, that is, 30 percent of the Canadian population, had direct or indirect access to benefits at some point during the year, *not* counting recipients of Family Allowance and provincial tax credits (ibid.:51). However, the importance of these monies varies greatly for different types of recipients. In general, the lower the private income, the higher the percentage of income that is generated through government transfers, with a sharp percentage drop at a relatively low level of income[8] due to the fact that the average payment per family does not vary substantially, irrespective of other income sources (McLeod, 1977). It is estimated that in 1977–1978 three to three and a half million persons, or 16 percent of the Canadian population, were completely dependent on this source of income (Canadian Intergovernmental Conference Secretariat, 1980:51). We are, therefore, dealing with a very important source of income for a significant minority of Canadians, and with an additional source of income for a majority of Canadians, if we include Family Allowance and provincial tax credits.

Overall, Canada has a very complex system of income security programmes. We can distinguish between three types of income security programmes: *demogrants,* which are made to a person irrespective of their financial situation (e.g., Family Allowance and Old Age Security); *social insurance programmes,* which make payments on the basis of previous earnings and contributions (e.g., workers' compensation, Unemployment Insurance, and the Canada/Quebec Pension Plan); and *income related programmes,* which make payments on the basis of established financial need (e.g., the Guaranteed Income Supplement and basic provincial and municipal social assistance).

Before 1900, government involvement with income security concerns was minimal:

> Under the influence of attitudes formed during the pioneer era, the Elizabethan poor laws, and in the case of Quebec the social doctrine and anti-statism of the Catholic Church, the economic security of individuals was largely seen as a private and local matter to be provided for those who could not be self-sufficient by family members, charities, religious organizations, and local governments. The prevailing attitude was that few persons should require assistance. Giving assistance

> fostered indolence and dependency. While some unfortunate instances of honest poverty deserving assistance did exist, public aid should be limited.
>
> Pre 1900 programming was thus characterized by limited local responsibility for the poor and indigent. Where assistance was provided, it was generally restricted to the sick, elderly, young, and women with dependent children only after all the family's financial resources had been exhausted and only where local residence was clearly established.[9]

At present, we have an income security system which is highly likely to touch every resident of Canada at some point of his or her life, starting with the Family Allowance to the Canada/Quebec Pension Plan and Old Age Security. However, jurisdiction over the various programmes is partially located at the federal level, partially at the provincial level, and yet others are under municipal jurisdiction. Eligibility criteria vary greatly, and what entitles a resident to a transfer payment from one programme may disentitle him or her from payment from another plan. After reviewing the entire system of income security programmes, a government conference came to the conclusion that the current system is beset by severe problems and shortcomings. The four major problems were identified as a confusion which makes the system immensely difficult for the public to understand; uncertainty because programme development tends to react to specific requirements rather than being based on a long-term integrated strategy; a lack of clear division of responsibilities between governments and an ensuing tendency for governments to act unilaterally without adequate consideration of what effects the individual decisions will have on the income security system as a whole; and administrative inefficiency (Canadian Intergovernmental Conference Secretariat, 1980:101).

To this list of problems we must add one more: horizontal inequity along interprovincial lines. A recent summary of social welfare payments across provinces shows huge differences for people in the same circumstances, as shown in Table 6.6

For instance, a mother with two children on family allowance received $533 per month in Newfoundland as compared to $929 in Alberta, or only 57.4 percent of what a comparable Albertan family received! The discrepancy is even more marked for a family of four on welfare, who would receive $505 in Sydney, Nova Scotia as compared to $1,051 in Alberta, or only 48 percent of their Albertan counterparts. Another noteworthy feature of the current income security system is that without exception a mother with two children on family allowance receives less money per month than a couple consisting of two senior citizens.

Private income and government transfers intersect in the eligibility criteria for transfer payments. We will consider this issue next.

TABLE 6.6

Social Welfare Benefits Across Canada — 1982

	Mother, two kids on family allowance up to:	Family of four on welfare up to:	Seniors pension (effective April 1)	
			Single	Couple
Newfoundland	$533	$585	$466.86	$826.58
Prince Edward Island	$671	684	$466.86	$826.58
Nova Scotia	$650	$505(Sydney)	$466.86	$826.58
			plus $109 annual supplement, 1/2 property tax rebate or up to $90 monthly rent allowance.	
New Brunswick	$656	$727	$466.86	$826.58
Quebec	$571	$699.50	$466.86	$826.58
			plus up to $67.50 shelter allowance.	
Ontario	$606	$615	$515.74	$976.48
			plus annual $550 grants	
Saskatchewan	$761	$931	$491.86	$871.58
			plus up to $100 monthly shelter costs.	
Alberta	$929	$1,051	$551.86	$996.00
			plus up to $1,000 to shelter costs	
British Columbia	$710	$800	$495.24	$907.66
			plus up to $225 monthly to shelter costs.	

Note: Manitoba figures unavailable

Source: Reprinted with permission — *The Toronto Star,* 1982 03 29, p. A4.

The Intersection of Private Income and Government Transfer Payments

Whenever a means, needs, or income test — of whatever sort — is applied, private incomes may mean disentitlement of a resident from a government transfer programme. In general, programmes which have some sort of means test are meant to be available only to residents whose private incomes are judged to be inadequate according to some standard. These standards may vary greatly, as do the payments (see Table 6.6). The nature of the intersection between private income and government transfers is, however, not only determined by the fact that there is some means test, but also by the assumptions concerning family structures that underlie these tests. Figure 6.2 summarizes some of the characteristics that are tested under major income security programmes.

FIGURE 6.2

Some characteristics tested under various major income security programs.

Program	Disability	Employment availability	Income	Family structure	Age 65+	Age 18	Employment history
Social assistance	X	X	X	X			
Workers' compensation	X						X
Prov elderly suppl			X	X	X		
Family Allowance				X		X	
Child Tax Credit			X	X		X	
Unemployment insurance		X			X		X
Veterans' Benefits	X	X	X	X			
CPP QPP	X				X		X
OAS					X		
GIS SPA			X	X	X°		

Note: An X in the box indicates that a given characteristic is generally treated as part of the eligibility requirements for a program.

°In case of Spouse's Allowance the eligible age group is actually 60–64.

Source: Canadian Intergovernmental Conference Secretariat, 1980, p. 112.

If we look at the columns marked as family structure and income we find that where family structure is taken into account, income is likewise taken into account, with the exception of the Family Allowance. This means in practice that eligibility to these programmes (i.e., social assistance, provincial supplements for the elderly, the Child Tax Credit, Veterans' Benefits, and the Guaranteed Income Supplement, as well as the Spouse's Allowance) are based on an income test of *family* income rather than individual income. By contrast, workers' compensation, Unemployment Insurance and the Canada/Quebec Pension Plans are based on individual characteristics rather than family characteristics, while Old Age Security is paid to every individual irrespective of income and family status.

Going back to our classification of types of income generation units (Figure 6.1) this means that for the purposes of major social security programmes all families are treated as if they were breadwinner families, rather than two-earner families, irrespective of whether this is an appropriate assumption given the family's history or not. This is one of the factors which contribute to the familism-individualism flip-flop (see Chapter 4).

There is an ongoing debate as to the effect of public assistance on marital stability. One school of thought suggests that public assistance leads to increased marital instability (e.g., Bishop, 1980; Bahr, 1981) while another school of thought suggests that marital instability leads to the need for public assistance but that public assistance has only a small if any effect on marital stability (e.g., Draper, 1981a and b). Both schools of thought seem to accept the primacy of the value of marital stability over other possible values, such as a life in dignity for every individual. As will be seen in the next chapter, unhappy marriages tend to be more deleterious in their effects for the adults *and children* involved than a divorce. Marriages which are held together *only* because of economic necessity are unlikely to be very beneficial for the people involved. On the other hand, if marriages are being destroyed or prevented by requirements of some income security programme (see examples given in Chapter 4) this is certainly an extraordinarily undesirable effect.

Overall, government transfer payments have vastly different meanings for different types of families and for different members of families. For families which have little or no private income, government transfers are the only or the major source of income. For families which do have a substantial private income, government transfers are likely to be a very small portion of their total income. For some such families, transfers may be more important as a safeguard in the case of an emergency than as an actuality. Finally, in breadwinner families with dependent children in which the husband is the breadwinner and the wife is a housewife, the family allowance and the refundable child tax credit may be the only monies which come directly to the wife in her own name. Although in terms of total family income the amount may be very small, the importance of these transfer payments for the wives may be extraordinarily high, given that these may be the only monies that they have actual control over.

This brings us to the issue of control over family finances, which will be considered next.

Financial Arrangements Within Families

There is extraordinarily little knowledge about how money is allocated *within* families, undoubtedly at least partially due to the fact that the family rather than the individual is usually treated as the consuming and spending unit. The most important consequence of this general lack of knowledge is that there is a widespread assumption that by and large monies are distributed equitably within families. Indeed, this assumption is one of the cornerstones on which the notion of horizontal equity, which takes the family rather than the individual as the smallest unit of analysis, rests (cf. discussion on equity in Chapter 4).

However, this assumption is no more than that: an unsubstantiated assumption. Due to the extreme scarcity of literature (there is, to my knowledge, not a single Canadian study which examines spending patterns *within* families) a recent small-scale Australian study is of interest here. In this study, fifty families were questioned in detail about their money arrangements. The study introduced a crucial distinction in the beginning; namely a distinction between "management" and "control" of money:

> Management of finance is akin to the implementation of functions performed within any enterprise — the carrying out of decisions which have already been made. The manager of family finances would handle family money and would make the actual payments. However, he/she may not in fact have a major role in financial decision-making, and might be given directions from other family members as to what to buy.
>
> 'Control' refers more to the decision-making aspect of family finances. It is akin to the policy-making functions of any enterprise. The person(s) in control of family decision-making would be influential in all but minor purchasing decisions.[10]

This study found that in the majority of families wives either managed family finances or shared management with their husbands; however, the majority of husbands either controlled or shared control of the family finances.

Whether or not a wife controlled — together with her husband — the family finances, was greatly affected by whether she generated an income herself. ". . . a large proportion of women in paid employment, full-time or part-time, were found to have joint control of finances. This was not the case for women without paid employment: nine of the thirty women in paid employment had husbands controlling the finances but eleven of the twenty women not in paid employment were so placed" (Edwards, 1981:69).

It is interesting to note that in some cases finances were controlled by the husband even though the wife had an independent income. Having two earners in a family therefore obviously does not suffice to lead to a symmetrical lifestyle, but it greatly increases the likelihood that the wife will have some control over family finances.

The study also found that more husbands than wives received personal spending money, and that husbands received more money than did their wives (Edwards, 1981:101). This is a significant empirical finding, in spite of the small sample size of the study, since it provides empirical evidence that increasing the resources of *one* family member need not automatically increase the resources of *all* family members.[11] This was also borne out in other parts of the study.

A somewhat surprising finding of the study was that personal spending money of husbands was relatively constant regardless of their or the family's income level. Wives' acceptance of their husbands' spending patterns "was such that the women looked on their husbands' personal spending money as an item of expenditure to be set aside, like money for urgent bills, before the amount available for housekeeping was determined" (Edwards, 1981:99). Betting on horses and spending at the pub were two common expenses of these husbands:

> While a lengthy period of paid employment was likely to lead to women managing their own incomes, lengthy periods of employment did not necessarily ensure that women would have an equal say in how total family income would be spent. It was, however, likely that a woman who had not worked since her first child was born, or had worked only intermittently since then, would be subordinate in financial decision-making.
>
> Overwhelmingly, wives used their incomes to raise the standard of living of all members of their families. However, there was some evidence that wives whose incomes contributed only a small proportion of total family income were more likely than were other women to spend that money on themselves. Incomes of wives were more often earmarked for housekeeping than were husbands' incomes. . . .
>
> The majority of women in paid employment considered it important to have their own income, mainly for the feeling of independence it gave them. This was particularly so for women who did not have a joint say in family financial decisions. On the whole, women without paid em-

> ployment disliked not having an independent source of income — this was especially so for women who had little say in either the management or control of finances.[12]

Correspondingly, wives tended to evaluate the effect of the family allowances as more important than did their husbands, since for some of them this was the only money over which they had control.

It would be extraordinarily desirable to have some reliable information on how individual members within Canadian families actually spend their money, who manages and who controls the money, what effects can be discerned with respect to money control depending on whether a family belongs to the two-earner type of family or to the breadwinner type of family, and what effects government transfers to women have on families who are not living at or below the poverty line. In the absence of such knowledge, it seems prudent to assume that money is not necessarily distributed equitably among all family members, and that it is quite possible that there may be hidden individual poverty in families who, according to their income levels, should be well above the poverty line.

Consequences of the Shift from Breadwinner to Two-Earner Families

As stated, we are presently witnessing the shift from a breadwinner type of family to a two-earner type of family, which has now replaced, in the case of husband-wife families, the breadwinner family as the modal type of family in Canada. Nevertheless, although statistically this statement is true, it somewhat underrepresents the complexity of the situation. For we are still truly in the process of transformation, and this process is unlikely to be completed before at least another thirty years have elapsed.

What we do have in Canada at present is a true mix of families with respect to income generation patterns. If we look at the existing mix of family types at one point in time, we note that there is still an extremely significant minority of families which conform to the breadwinner type. If we look at the mix of family types over time, we will note a different pattern. Looking at the wife's labour force participation over a lifetime, we will be able to identify women who held down paying jobs without interruption even though they married and may or may not have had children. On the other hand, we will be able to identify women who interrupted their paid work either upon marriage or upon the birth of their first children, and who may or may not have taken on paid work again. Those women who in 1979 were relatively young and *not* in the labour force (of the 20- to 24-year-olds 36.2 percent and of the 25- to 34-year-olds 44.7 percent; see Table 6.2) will continue to display the consequences of a mixed pattern throughout their lifetimes, simply by virtue of the fact that they will not have been in the labour force for some time, even if all of them return to or enter the labour force at some later age in their lives. The effects of not having had paying jobs will continue to affect, for instance, pension entitlement, seniority, the relationship between work experience and chronological age, and other factors throughout their lifetimes.

Taking one hypothetical case, the existing mix in income generation patterns can vacillate back and forth more than once. One type of sequence, for instance, could look like this[13]: a young single woman finds herself a job (type I). She marries and continues to work in her job (type Va). She has her first child and drops out of the labour force (type IVa) but returns to the labour force a few years later (type VIa). She divorces, maintains custody of her child, and continues to work (type II) and eventually remarries and continues to work for pay (type VIa). Some type of mix of income generation types is therefore certain to be with us for at least as long as the working age of young women who are not now in the labour force extends. Nevertheless, the likelihood of every married individual finding himself or herself at some point in a two-earner family has greatly increased and is likely to increase further. Consequences of this shift are extraordinarily important and vary greatly for women, men, children, the family as a unit, the state and society at large.

Consequences for Women

The move of married women into the labour force is taking place at a time in which we still have a strong segregation of labour by sex (cf. Armstrong and Armstrong, 1978). In addition, we find a systematic and continuing income differential between male and female workers. In 1972, for instance, full-time native-born females received only 62 percent of the income of full-time native-born male workers (Boyd and Humphreys, 1979). If we compare the income of all women who work for pay with that of all men who work for pay the differences become even greater (see Canada, Women's Bureau, 1979:44, t.8A).

In addition to working in general for less pay than men in comparable jobs, women continue to be asymmetrically responsible for housework and childcare. This tends to be true even for highly educated, professional couples (for a case study of married psychologists, see Williams et al., 1980; for the general point, see Benenson, 1981). This adds up to a considerable burden in terms of simple work load. One might therefore argue that because of the combination of low wages, generally less attractive jobs which are open to women, and the continuation of household and family duties women are actually worse off when they hold paying jobs than when they are housewives (cf. Meissner et al., 1975:426). Nevertheless, there seems to be no doubt that the majority of married women prefer to have paying jobs over being housewives and that furthermore, in general it is good for them.

The effects of taking on paid employment for women who were previously housewives may, of course, vary greatly by type of job, type of family structure, and class position of the family. Luxton (1981:16) provides some empirical evidence of the differences. When comparing wives from middle class and working class households in a small community in Manitoba, she found that working class women on the average increased household incomes through their pay by 32 percent while middle class women (who had husbands with much higher incomes) only increased household income by an average 20 percent. While this cannot be taken as typical for Canada, it does make the point of variable effects well.

In addition, middle class wives experienced a much greater increase in working time than working class women, which is explained by three factors: working class women accepted lower standards with respect to household improvements than middle class women, who felt strongly that they had to continue to improve the quality of their houses; middle class men actually reduced the amount of time they spent on domestic labour when their wives took on paid work, while working class men increased their contributions marginally; and middle class wives were expected to subsidize their husbands' jobs through maintaining appropriately furnished homes, producing acceptable social events such as dinner parties, and accompanying their husbands to social occasions organized by others, while working class wives were not expected to do this.

There is some evidence that working wives have a higher self-esteem than housewives (cf. Mackie, n.d.), and that strain as evidenced by suicide rates is higher for housewives than for employed wives (Cumming et al., 1975). Women with jobs seem to be in better physical and emotional health than housewives, hold more positive attitudes towards life in general and marriage in particular (Burke and Weir, 1975:11). There also seems to be a difference in the personalities of members of two-earner families as compared to members of breadwinner families, with people in dual-career families being more self-sufficient, self-reliant individuals than members of single-career families:

> . . . whereas the working wife may be characterized as more assertive than housewives, husbands of working wives can be characterized as less assertive and less concerned with power and authority than hus-

> bands of housewives. The data . . . showed the housewives to be the most submissive . . . in their interpersonal relating. They appeared more willing to give up power and authority to others and showed a greater preference for others to take charge of, and responsibility for decision-making. They also indicated the strongest needs for affectionate and intimate relationships, and for inclusion and acceptance by others.[14]

The causal relationship for such findings is, of course, unclear: it is possible that couples in which the wife is more assertive and the husband less power oriented are more likely to fall into the two-earner type of family for that reason, and it is also possible that the characteristics outlined are a consequence of following a two-earner type of lifestyle, or that there is a mutually reinforcing interconnection between the two factors.

Wives with jobs tend to be more satisfied with their marriages than housewives (Lupri and Frideres, 1981). A rather intriguing, very small-scale study from Halifax suggests that employed wives may actually have more control over their time than housewives. Contrary to common usage, this researcher let leisure time be individually defined by her respondents, such that the same activities could by different people be defined as either work or leisure. Using this criterion, she found that employed males had the most leisure (a conventional finding), housewives the least, and employed females in between employed males and housewives. This may be due to the fact that the housewives feel themselves to be "constantly on call" and experience this as work, even when no actual work is being done (see Shaw, 1981).

Overall, then, wives who have jobs are in general likely to have less attractive jobs than their husbands, with less pay and prestige; they are likely to continue to do the major share of housework and childcare; and they are likely to have less leisure time than their husbands. Nevertheless, all indications are that in terms of mental health, self-esteem, and marital happiness wives with paying jobs fare better than housewives. How is that possible?

Structurally speaking, housewives are asymetrically personally dependent on their husbands (see Eichler, 1973 and 1981). When a wife has a paying job, she ceases to be totally economically dependent on her husband. Even if her salary is only half his, for example, $9,000 a year, to $18,000 a year for him, $9,000 is enough to support oneself if necessary.

Earning money through her work means that the wife has taken at least part of her fate into her own hands, and can thereby gain a new dimension of self-actualization (although this will depend on the type of job she has—in some cases, housewifery may be the more attractive alternative to having a low-paid, unsatisfying job).

As the wife gains a measure of economic independence from her husband by earning a wage or salary of her own, so the husband loses some of his power over her, which is likely to lead to an overall improvement of her mental health. There remains the structural incongruity between the wife's job and her also carrying the major work load of the household and childcare. This is likely to eventually lead to a dissatisfaction with the domestic division of labour, which can be expected to reveal itself in pressure on the husband to take on a fairer share of household and childcare duties. In cases in which the husband can adjust his own behaviours and expectations, the marriage may be greatly enriched; in cases in which he is unable and/or unwilling to do so, the marriage may become extremely strife-ridden. Divorce statistics suggest that wives[15] seem to be increasingly less willing to tolerate a bad or unsatisfactory marriage. Conversely, husbands who receive fewer personal services may also be less willing to maintain a bad or unsatisfactory marriage. On the other hand, marriages may be greatly improved by transcending the constraining expectations attached to sex roles which are likely to inhibit the self-actualization of both men and women, although there is no *guarantee* that a wife's job will lead to great changes in other aspects of marital relations except the financial one; it is merely that the likelihood of this occurring is greater when the wife has a paying job than when she does not.

Consequences for Men

Men have long been socialized to think of themselves as the breadwinners of their families. When a wife takes on a paying job, the role of being the sole breadwinner is suddenly taken away from the man.

Just as a housewife's work contributions have been partially devalued through the industrialization of housework, so has the husband's economic provider role been partially devalued through the increasing labour force participation of wives. Increasing labour force participation of wives is therefore likely to produce some disorientation among husbands. This is likely to be especially the case where a wife takes a job without the husband's consent or even against his passive or active resistance. To the degreee that his self-esteem and feeling of well-being is premised on having control over his wife, he will experience the wife's partial independence as something disagreeable; to the degree that he enjoys interacting with his wife as an equal, he is likely to experience her taking (or keeping) a job as a positive event.

There is some evidence from American studies that marital satisfaction tends to be slightly higher when the wife is not employed (Bahr and Day, 1978). Similarly, Burke and Weir found that "Husbands of working women when compared with husbands of housewives were in poorer health, and, in addition, were less content with marriage, work, and life in general. The implications of these findings are that men whose wives work are subject to greater stress, than men whose wives are not working and they appear to be having more difficulty coping effectively with this pattern of daily living."[16] However, this finding is flatly contradicted by a more recent finding by Lupri and Frideres (1981). They found that in their sample of Calgary couples 50 percent of the husbands who had employed wives reported their marriages to be very happy, while only 38 percent of the husbands with non-employed wives reported their marriages to be very happy. Controlling for family life cycle stage, the authors found that "husbands of *employed* wives consistently reported higher marital satisfaction over the entire family life cycle than husbands of non-employed wives."

> Both the magnitude of the difference and their consistency over the family life cycle prompt us to contend that paid employment both enhances working women's self-esteem, self-confidence, and personal independence and increasingly constitutes an important economic family resource. Moreover, wives' paid work is one of the most significant determinants of *husbands'* marital satisfaction.[17]

Since Burke and Weir (1975) used a sample of professional men of three professions their contradictory findings may reflect idiosyncratic aspects of this particular group of men. Another possible explanation for the discrepancies in findings is that even a few years may make a difference in how men react: as more and more wives enter the labour force and this trend ceases to be seen as a negative reflection on the men's economic capacities, men may be more able to see the positive aspects of sharing financial responsibilities with their wives.

Once men get used to considering marriage as a relationship of equals rather than unequals, and of seeing personal services as something that can be exchanged among equals but to which nobody has a right by virtue of gender, labour force participation of wives is likely to be experienced as a matter of course, or, alternatively, if the couple decide that one of them will stay at home to look after the children and/or household-related matters, that work is likely to be valued as important work. Until such reorientation has occurred, however, for individuals as well as for men as a group, it is likely that there will be a strain on most contemporary marriages, whether they fall into the breadwinner model or the two-earner model.

Consequences for Children

The major consequence for children when their mothers work at a paying job while they are young is that they will be looked after by somebody other than their mother for substantial periods of their waking time. Since the issue of day care will be discussed at length in Chapter 8, the emphasis here will be on several supplementary effects.

There is a rather substantial literature on the effect of maternal employment on the development of children (there is hardly any literature on the effect of paternal employment on the development of children). The only thing that emerges very clearly from the literature is that maternal employment has no *one* effect on the development of children. Rather, it is a variable that does affect children's development, but the effects are mediated through a host of other variables, including the sex of the child, whether or not the mother enjoys her work, the socio-economic position of the family, and the father's attitudes and behaviours.

A very thorough review of the (mostly American) literature on the effects of maternal employment up to 1973 concluded that "maternal employment is associated with less traditional sex role concepts, more approval of maternal employment, and a higher evaluation of female competence" (Hoffman, 1974:210). With respect to academic achievement, the results are equivocal: there is some evidence that maternal employment is positively associated with high school children's college plans, but the opposite relationship has also been occasionally shown. Girls seem to profit from their mothers' employment, while boys are more likely to suffer somewhat, but "in the lower class . . . better academic performance is associated with maternal employment for both sexes" (Hoffman, 1974:225).

Canadian findings are similar. One recent study which looked at the effects of maternal employment on ten-year-old children and their parents found that "In general, the employed mothers are very much more content with their roles than the non-employed mothers, and it appears that the employed mothers who are most content with their roles have children with the most egalitarian sex-role concepts" (Gold and Andres, 1978a:82). Another study looking at first and second grade children found the children of employed mothers to be less rigid in their sex role stereotyping than the children of non-employed mothers (Jones and McBride, 1980).

While the overall adjustment of sons of employed and non-employed mothers was found to be the same, working class boys with employed mothers did have some adjustment difficulties, and middle class boys scored a bit lower on mathematics and language achievement tests. However, when fathers were more involved with their children (which they are more likely to be when the wife has a paying job) the sons' academic performance tended to improve. Girls' academic performance was not affected by the employment status of their mothers (Gold and Andres, 1978a).

Another study involving 110 nursery school children also found a somewhat poorer cognitive performance by boys of employed mothers, but better adjustment for children of employed mothers:

> Fathers of employed wives report more involvement with their daughters and more pro-feminist attitudes than do fathers who have daughters and non-employed wives.
>
> However, the involvement of fathers with their sons is not increased by the employent status of the mothers. It is the sons of employed mothers who, more than the other children, perceive their fathers as punitive and indicate less same-sex preference. Therefore, it appears that these fathers do not become more positive models that facilitate the boys' gender identification.[18]

A comparable study involving francophone rather than anglophone children found that francophone fathers reported more involvement in family activities, including more interaction with children, and more often shared household tasks with their wives. Overall, "Parents were happier with the mother's roles, reported the father as being more involved with the children, perceived themselves as behaving more similarly in the home, and held more pro-feminist attitudes when the mother was employed" (Gold and Andres, 1980:238).

Overall, then, the effects of maternal employment on the development of children seem to be less drastic and pervasive than could have been expected, especially on the basis of old theories of child development (see Rapoport, Rapoport and Strelitz, 1977, for a review and critique of these theories). It is possible that to try to isolate effects of maternal employment is too simplistic an approach[19], and that a different image would emerge were we to focus on the day care children receive while both their parents are at work as well as on the daily life of children whose mothers stay at home. Both positive and negative effects can be imagined. It would be useful to detail the daily life of children in different types of care situations, so that we can isolate the various factors which help or impede the emotional, intellectual, and physical development of children.

Consequences for the Family as a Unit

One obvious consequence of a wife's job is that a family has more money at its disposal than it would if the wife did not earn money. How exactly that money is spent we do not know. One study which tried to isolate whether or not there is a different consumption style in two-earner families as compared to breadwinner families failed to find a distinct style for two-earner families. The wife's labour force status had an effect on consumption patterns through her income effect, rather than through developing a distinct style of consumption altogether. The authors note that "We have found no similar study in Canada upon which to gauge the validity of our results" (Brière and Théorêt, 1978:45).

When we look at the average expenditures of couples in which the wife is either not employed, or part-time employed, or full-time employed, we find that in general the expenditures for two-earner couples are higher than those of breadwinner couples. That is not surprising, since the income in two-earner couples was, in 1976, on average higher than that in breadwinner couples: in 1976, a couple in which the wife was employed full-time had an average income of $25,763.40, a couple in which the wife was employed part-time had an average income of $21,854.10 and a couple in which the wife was not employed had an average income of $19,088.30.[20] No drastic differences in lifestyle emerge from the expenditure patterns (for instance, 60.5 percent and 56.6 percent respectively of the couples with full- and part-time employed wives were homeowners as compared to 65.8 percent of the couples in which the wife was not employed). A slight difference did emerge with respect to food consumption, however. Couples in which the wife worked full-time spent more money on food and spent a greater proportion of it on food that was not prepared at home; couples in which the wife worked part-time spent less money on food than the first type of family but more than the breadwinner couple, and also spent an intermediate proportion on food not prepared at home, as can be seen from Table 6.7. This suggests that two-earner families do consume more food that is not prepared by their own members than do breadwinner families.

Expenditure patterns are, of course, only one aspect of familial interactions that can be expected to be affected by the labour force status of the wife/mother. Another area concerns the participation of chil-

TABLE 6.7

Average Expenditures on Food by Employment Status of Wife, Canada, 1976

Food	Wife employed full-time		Wife employed part-time		Wife not employed	
	$	%	$	%	$	%
Prepared at home	2,555.30	73.8	2,584.50	77.9	2,610.40	83.1
Not prepared at home	907.80	26.2	732.50	22.1	531.90	16.9
Total spent	3,463.10*	100	3,317.00*	100	3,142.30	100

*slight differences from item 1-12 in unpublished table, probably due to rounding error.

Source: Unpublished Statistics Canada data.

dren in household chores. It would be reasonable to expect that children of two-earner couples would participate to a greater degree in household chores. However, to date there is no evidence that this is the case. If a systematic study was to confirm that indeed children in two-earner households participate no more in household chores than do children in breadwinner households, this would suggest the existence of a structural discrepancy in parent/child relations which would parallel the discrepancy in husband/wife relations in two-earner couples in which the husband participates to a considerably lower degree in household labour than the wife. At present, a reallocation of roles seems to be taking place between husbands and wives. It would seem reasonable to expect that in the future a similar process will take place with respect to parents and children, with children being asked to do a greater share of the work involved in keeping the household running. This is an area which warrants watching and in which some research would be highly desirable.

One of the most important issues that emerges in two-earner couples concerns job mobility. Where two marital partners hold paying jobs, the physical mobility of both of them is circumscribed. While the pattern until now has been that wives subordinated their jobs to those of their husbands (which may be changing — see Tiger, 1974), even in that case physical mobility is problematic. Once a couple is used to having two salaries, a move would have to involve a very substantial advancement to offset the loss of one job and to overcome the resistance of the spouse whose job might be sacrificed. Employers will likely have to change their hiring and promotion patterns to adjust to this changed situation.

While job mobility may be more restricted for two-earner couples, on the other hand the very fact that both marital partners do have jobs may make both of them more choosy with respect to overall job conditions. The increase in two-earner couples could thus have a profound effect on general working conditions — however, as long as unemployment is very high, this effect is not likely to occur.

The most important issue which arises in two-earner families is the question of childcare, not just for young children, but also for over ten-year-olds and even teenagers. In breadwinner families, it has usually been seen as the task of the wife/mother to be available on a full-time basis to look after her children. As she takes on a paying job, she can look after her children only on a part-time basis. Even if husbands desired to participate fully in childcare, this would not take care of the problem of childcare since in many cases both spouses will be working at the same time at their jobs and will therefore not be able to spell each other throughout the day. With a predominance of breadwinner families, childcare in all its various facets had been seen as a private matter. Now that the majority of families fall into the two-earner category, it is high time to start to reconceptualize childcare as a public matter. This issue will be discussed in full in Chapter 8.

Summary and Conclusion

We started out by considering the distinction of private incomes and government transfers. As far as private incomes are concerned, the most important recent change concerns the transition from the breadwinner type of family to the two-earner type of family. Reasons for this shift include the industrialization of housework and the generally perceived greater attractiveness of working at a paid job rather than being a housewife due to increased financial independence, social contacts, greater public esteem, and increased self-esteem.

Government transfers constitute about 10 percent of all personal income, but these 10 percent have a very different meaning for different people. In general, the higher the private income, the lower the importance of government transfer payments. Private incomes intersect with government transfers in eligibility criteria to public programmes, as well as in their administration and effects on families. Some recent Australian research has provided the beginning of empirical evidence that money is not necessarily distributed equitably or equally within family units, thus suggesting that taking the family unit as a basis for eligibility to social programmes may be an inherently flawed approach.

Consequences of the shift from the breadwinner to the two-earner family are generally positive for the wives who take on jobs in terms of their personal feelings and their public status, and may be experienced as either positive or negative by the husbands. To the degree that husbands' feelings of well-being are premised on having people around him who are economically and otherwise dependent on him, he may experience the increased independence of the wife as negative. To the degree that he gladly shares the burden of breadwinning and enjoys a relationship of equals rather than unequals, he is likely to see it as a positive phenomenon. Children seem not to be *directly* affected by the employment status of their mothers in terms of their development, but an exploration of the drawbacks and benefits of different types of care situations with respect to the daily life of the children remains to be undertaken.

Labour force participation of wives/mothers affects the lifestyle of the entire family in a host of ways. Two-earner couples spend somewhat more money on food which is not prepared within their own homes than do breadwinner couples, but once more a detailed comparison of the lifestyles of all members of a breadwinner family with those of a two-earner family needs as yet to be made.

We have addressed a number of important issues in this chapter, but others have not been considered. Kanter (1978), for example, notes the effects that paid work has on family lifestyle. For instance, the nature of the work performed, its timing, work-related travel, and the various subcultures that develop around particular jobs all have an effect on family life. Where we deal with two jobs instead of one, these effects would multiply, of course.

The greatest problem that emerges is the issue of childcare. As a society, Canada has not yet adjusted to the fact that the majority of couples now are two-earner couples. This leaves parents to cope with childcare in a situation when the care of its youngest members is only grudgingly and inconsistently recognized as an issue which affects the entire society. This question will be addressed in Chapter 8. Before turning to this question, however, we will examine discrepancies between marital and parental roles which considerably complicate the whole issue of childcare.

Notes

1. Pension income does not fit neatly into this categorization. Public pensions are partially to be considered a government transfer while private pensions constitute a private income.
2. Previously (in Chapter 2) we discussed the increased labour force participation of women. In Chapter 8 we will discuss the increased labour force participation of mothers. It must be kept in mind that these groups are not identical. Not all women are wives and/or mothers, nor are all wives mothers, nor all mothers wives.
3. Poverty was defined as income below the official Statistics Canada poverty line.
4. From *Last Hired, First Fired: Women and the Canadian Labour Force* by Mary Patricia Connelly reprinted by permission of Women's Educational Press, Toronto, 1978, p. 73.
5. Meg Luxton, "Taking on the Double Day," *Atlantis*, Vol. 7, No. 1 (1981):14.
6. Source: previously unpublished POW data.
7. That there has been some change in the attitudes of girls and women is suggested by a recent study comparing attitudes of girls in two private schools towards paid work and family involvement. While in 1966 only .8 percent of the girls at the Protestant school and 7.9 percent of the girls at the Roman Catholic school said they intended to work full-time after marriage and having children, in 1976 24.4 percent of the girls at the Protestant school and 20.2 percent of the girls at the Roman Catholic school said they intended working full-time under these circumstances. While in fact a higher percentage of girls is likely to be in the labour force, the change in attitude is quite marked, considering that only ten years divide the first and second survey (Maxwell, 1981:20, t.5).
8. In 1974, families with incomes under $5000 received only 30.7 percent of their income from earnings and 61.2 percent from government transfers, while families

with incomes between $5000 and $10 000 received 69 percent of their income from earnings and 10.8 percent from government transfers (McLeod, 1977:3, t.1–2).

9. Canadian Intergovernmental Conference Secretariat. The Income Security System in Canada. Report prepared by the Interprovincial Task Force on Social Security for the Interprovincial Conference for Ministers Responsible for Social Services. Ottawa: CICS, 1980.
10. Meredith Edwards, Financial Arrangements Within Families. A research report of the National Women's Adivsory Council, [Canberra], 1981, p. 4.
11. Stearns (1973) provides a historical example of British working class households at the turn of the century which suggests that resources were distributed unequally within families. "What seemed to be happening was that as wages advanced men took the bulk of the gain for themselves and abandoned the traditional pattern of turning most of their income over to their wives for family use" (Stearns, 1973:116).
12. Edwards, 1981, p. 129.
13. The types refer to those identified in Figure 6.1.
14. Ronald J. Burke and Tamara Weir, "Some Personality Differences Between Members of One-Career and Two-Career Families," *Journal of Marriage and the Family*, Vol. 38, No. 3 (1976):457. Copyright 1976 by the National Council on Family Relations. Reprinted by permission.
15. Wives are more likely to petition for divorce than husbands.
16. Ronald J. Burke and Tamara Weir, "Relationship of Wives' Employment Status to Husband, Wife and Pair Satisfaction and Performance." Paper presented at the Canadian Psychological Association Meeting, 1975, p. 12.
17. "The Quality of Marriage and the Passage of Time: Marital Satisfaction over the Family Life Cycle," Reprinted from The Canadian Review of Sociology and Anthropology, Volume *6.3(69)* by permission of Eugen Lupri and James Frideres and Canadian Sociology and Anthropology Association (emphasis in the original).
18. Dolores Gold and David Andres, "Relations between Maternal Employment and Development of Nursery School Children," *Canadian Journal of Behavioural Science*, Vol. 10, No. 2 (1978): 126–127.
19. Indeed a recent study which surveyed the literature on this topic concluded: ". . . a special plea is made that we do not cover the same ground three times. Two cumulations, representing 52 studies and spanning almost half a century, have arrived at a single, stable conclusion. Maternal employment is unrelated to child development. Perhaps we can now get on to other things" (Adams and Hedley, 1982).
20. All figures concerning this matter are taken from an unpublished detailed version of Table 18, *Summary of Family Expenditures by Employment Status of Wife; Eight Cities, 1979*, found in Canada, Statistics Canada 1979, p. 34.

References

Adams, Susan M. and R. Alan Hedley, "Latchkey Children Revisited: 1970–1980," paper presented at the meeting of the Canadian Sociology and Anthropology Association, Ottawa, 1982.

Armstrong, Pat and Hugh Armstrong, *The Double Ghetto, Canadian Women and Their Segregated Work*. Toronto: McClelland and Stewart, 1978.

Bahr, Stephen J., "Welfare and Marital Dissolution: A Reply," *Journal of Marriage and the Family*, Vol. 43, No. 2, 1981, pp. 300–301.

Bahr, Stephen J. and Randal D. Day, "Sex Role Attitudes, Female Employment and Marital Satisfaction," *Journal of Comparative Family Studies*, Vol. 9, No. 1, 1978, pp. 53–67.

Bartos, Rena, "What every Marketer should know about Women," *Harvard Business Review*, Vol. 56, 1978, pp. 73–85.

Benenson, Harold, "Family Success and Sexual Equality: The Limits of the Dual-Career Family Model," paper given at the American Sociological Association meeting, Toronto, 1981.

Bishop, John H., "Jobs, Cash Transfers and Marital Instability: A Review and Synthesis of the Evidence," *Journal of Human Resources*, Vol. 15, No. 3, 1980, pp. 301–334.

Boyd, Monica and Elizabeth Humphreys, *Labour Markets and Sex Differences in Canadian Income.* (Discussion Paper No. 143) Ottawa: Economic Council of Canada, 1979.

Brière, Normand and Claude Théorêt, *The Incidence of the Employment Status of the Wife Upon Some Expenditure Categories.* (SWP–7803). Ottawa: Long Range Planning, Policy Research and Strategic Planning Branch, Dept. of National Health and Welfare Canada, 1978.

Burke, Ronald J. and Tamara Weir, "Relationship of Wives' Employment Status to Husband, Wife and Pair Satisfaction and Performance," paper presented at the Canadian Psychological Association Meeting, 1975.

Burke, Ronald J. and Tamara Weir, "Some Personality Differences Between Members of One-Career and Two-Career Families," *Journal of Marriage and the Family*, Vol. 38, No. 3, 1976, pp. 453–459.

Canada. Statistics Canada. *Urban Family Expenditures, 1976*. Catalogue 62–547. Ottawa: Minister of Industry, Trade and Commerce, 1979.

Canada. Statistics Canada. *Income Distribution by Size in Canada, 1980*. Catalogue 13–207. Ottawa: Minister of Supply and Services, 1980.

Canada. Statistics Canada. *The Labour Force, December 1980*. Catalogue 71–001, Vol. 36, No. 12. Ottawa: Minister of Supply and Services, 1981.

Canada. Statistics Canada. *The Labour Force, December 1981*. Catalogue 71–001, Vol. 37, No. 12. Ottawa: Minister of Supply and Services, 1982.

Canada. Women's Bureau, Labour Canada. *Women in the Labour Force. Facts and Figures. 1977 ed.*, Part II: Earnings of Women and Men. Ottawa: Minister of Supply and Services, 1979.

Canada. Women's Bureau, Labour Canada. *Women in the Labour Force, 1978–1979*, Part I: Participation. Ottawa: Minister of Supply and Services, 1980.

Canadian Intergovernmental Conference Secretariat, *The Income Security System in Canada*. Report prepared by the Interprovincial Task Force on Social Security for the Interprovincial Conference for Ministers Responsible for Social Services. Ottawa: CICS, 1980.

The Changing Dependence of Women: Roles, Beliefs and Inequality. (Research Report No. 5). Ottawa: Health and Welfare Canada, Policy Research and Long Range Planning, 1978.

Ciuriak, Dan and Harvey Sims, *Participation Rate and Labour Force Growth in Canada.* (Series of papers on medium- and long-term economic issues) Canada: Dept. of Finance, 1980.

Connelly, Mary Patricia, *Last Hired, First Fired: Women and the Canadian Labour Force.* Toronto: Women's Educational Press, 1978.

Council of Rural Development Canada, *Rural Women: Their Work, Their Needs, and Their Role in Rural Development.* (CRDC Study Report). Ottawa: Council on Rural Development Canada, Jan. 1979.

Cumming, Elaine, Charles Lazer, and Lynne Chisholm, "Suicide as an Index of Role Strain among Employed and Not Employed Women in British Columbia," *Canadian Review of Sociology and Anthropology*, 1975, Vol. 12, No. 1 (Part I), pp. 452–470.

Draper, Thomas W., "On the Relationship between Welfare and Marital Stability: A Research Note," *Journal of Marriage and the Family*, Vol. 43, No. 2, 1981a, pp. 293–299.

Draper, Thomas W., "Reply to Bahr," *Journal of Marriage and the Family*, Vol. 43, No. 2, 1981b, p. 302.

Edwards, Meredith, *Financial Arrangements Within Families*. (A Research Report of the National Women's Advisory Council) N.p.:1981.

Eichler, Margrit, "Women as Personal Dependents. A Critique of Theories of the Stratification of the Sexes and an Alternative Approach," in Marylee Stephenson (ed.), *Women in Canada*. Toronto: New Press, 1973, pp. 38–55.

Eichler, Margrit, "Power, Dependency, Love and the Sexual Division of Labour. A Critique of the Decision-Making Approach to Family Power and an Alternative Approach with an Appendix: On Washing my Dirty Linen in Public," *Women's Studies International Quarterly*, Vol. 4, No. 2, 1981, pp. 201–219.

Fox, Bonnie J. and John Fox, "The Female Reserve Army of Labour," paper presented at the Canadian Sociology and Anthropology Association meeting, Halifax, 1981.

Gold, Dolores and David Andres, "Developmental Comparisons between Ten-Year-Old Children with Employed and Nonemployed Mothers," *Child Development*, Vol. 49, No. 1, 1978a, pp. 75–84.

Gold, Dolores and David Andres, "Relations between Maternal Employment and Development of Nursery School Children," *Canadian Journal of Behavioural Science*, Vol. 10, No. 2, 1978b, pp. 116–129.

Gold, Dolores and David Andres, "Maternal Employment and Development of Ten-Year-Old Canadian Francophone Children," *Canadian Journal of Behavioural Science*, Vol. 13, No. 3, 1980, pp. 233–240.

Hoffman, Lois W., "Effects of Maternal Employment on the Child — a Review of the Research," *Developmental Psychology*, Vol. 10, No. 2, 1974, pp. 204–228.

Horner, Keith and Neil McLeod, *Changes in the Distribution of Income in Canada*. (Staff Working Papers). Ottawa: Health and Welfare Canada, Policy and Long Range Planning (Welfare), 1975.

Jones, Linda M. and Joanna L. McBride, "Sex-Role Stereotyping in Children as a Function of Maternal Employment," *The Journal of Social Psychology*, Vol. III, 1980, pp. 219–223.

Kanter, Rosabeth Moss, "Jobs and Families: Impact of Working Roles on Family Life," *Children Today*, Vol. 7, No. 2, 1978, pp. 11–15+45.

Lupri, Eugen and James Frideres, "The Quality of Marriage and the Passage of Time: Marital Satisfaction over the Family Life Cycle," *Canadian Journal of Sociology*, Vol. 6, No. 3, 1981, pp. 283–305.

Luxton, Meg, "Taking on the Double Day," *Atlantis*, Vol. 7, No. 1, 1981, pp. 12–22.

Mackie, Marlene, "The Domestication of Self," unpublished paper. Calgary: n.d.

Maxwell, Mary Percival, "Women and the Elite: Educational and Occupational Aspirations of Private School Females 1966/76," paper given at the Canadian Sociology and Anthropology Meetings, Halifax, 1981.

McLeod, Neil, *Incomes of Single-Parent and Multi-Earner Families*. (Staff Working Paper). Ottawa: Health and Welfare Canada, Policy Research and Long Range Planning, 1977.

Meissner, Martin et al., "No Exit for Wives: Sexual Division of Labour and the Cumulation of Household Demands," *Canadian Review of Sociology and Anthropology*, Vol. 12, No. 4, Part I, 1975, pp. 424–439.

National Council of Welfare, *Women and Poverty*. Ottawa: National Council of Welfare, 1979.

Rapoport, Rhona and Robert N. Rapoport, and Ziona Strelitz, *Fathers, Mothers and Society, Towards New Alliances*. New York: Basic Books, 1977.

Shaw, Susan M., "The Sexual Division of Leisure: The Development of a Model," paper presented at the Canadian Sociology and Anthropology Association Meeting, 1981.

Stearns, Peter N., "Working-Class Women in Britain, 1890–1914," in Martha Vicinus (ed.), *Suffer and Be Still, Women in the Victorian Age.* Don Mills: Fitzhenry and Whiteside, 1973, pp. 100–120.

Swan, Carole, "Women in the Canadian Labour Force: The Present Reality," paper presented at the SSHRCC Seminar on Women and the Canadian Labour Force, 1980.

Tiger, Lionel, "Is This Trip Necessary? The Heavy Human Costs of Moving Executives Around," *Fortune*, September 1974, pp. 139–141+182.

Williams, Tannis MacBeth, Merle L. Zabrack, and Linda F. Harrison, "Some Factors Affecting Women's Participation in Psychology in Canada," *Canadian Psychology*, 1980.

CHAPTER 7

Discrepancies between Marital and Parental Roles

Introduction

In Chapter 1, we noted that due to the still prevailing monolithic bias, we tend to underestimate the degree of non-congruity between dimensions of familial interaction. We tend to make assumptions of congruity rather than examining the existing types of congruities and non-congruities. One of the most important types of non-congruity is a discrepancy between marital and parental status. Of course, everybody is aware that there are certain types of non-congruities in this context, such as when couples adopt children, or when a divorced parent remarries. However, there is at present no certain method that would allow us to assess what proportion of the population is actually experiencing some type of discrepancy between marital and parental status. Given the prevalence of emphasis on parenthood in the context of marriage and family, this seems astounding.

In this chapter, we will try to delimit the boundaries of the major forms of discrepancies involving parental and marital roles in order to arrive at an estimate concerning the approximate prevalence of non-congruities in this area and the significance of any demonstrated non-congruities for women, men, children, and society at large.

We can distinguish between simple forms of discrepancy and complex forms of discrepancy. A simple discrepancy involves the presence of only one role due to non-existence of some of the people in the equation. A complex discrepancy involves children whose parents are not married to each other though both parents are alive. Simple forms of discrepancies include (1) childless couples and (2) death of one parent. Complex forms of discrepancies include (3) unmarried parenthood, (4) divorce of parents, (5) permanent separation or desertion in families with children, (6) marital adultery resulting in offspring, (7) artificial donor insemination, (8) adoption, and (9) remarriage families. Each form of discrepancy will be discussed in turn, by estimating first its incidence (where possible) and considering second its implications for women, men, children, and society (where applicable).

Childless Couples

Were it not for the fact that in our society marriage and parenthood go together in the minds of most people (cf. Veevers, 1974), this type of discrepancy would not have been included in this chapter. As it is, some comments seem in order.

In the case of childless couples, a discrepancy between parental and marital roles exists only at the normative level, since there are no parental roles. This assumes, of course, that neither spouse has any children with any other partner. If either or both of them do have children outside the current conjugal unit, the discrepancy becomes complex and is dealt with in one of the following sections.

Childlessness is to some degree associated with sterility; however, the correlation is by no means perfect. Couples in which both partners are sterile may adopt a child or children, thus ceasing to be childless. Couples in which one partner is sterile and the other is fertile, may either adopt or have (a) child(ren) through artificial donor insemination, especially in cases in which the husband is sterile but the wife is fertile.

Nor do all couples in which both partners are fertile necessarily have children. Over the past thirty years it has generally been estimated that half of all childless couples were childless by choice. In Canada and the U.S., the incidence of voluntary childlessness among ever-married women was estimated at around five percent for the late seventies (Veevers, 1979:8) but this proportion is expected to increase in the future.

Veevers (1980:157) predicts that "in the immediate future we would expect voluntary childlessness to characterize between ten and 15 percent of all couples — approximately three times as many as were found in the 1960's." Grindstaff projects that by the year 2001, 20 percent of ever-married women in Canada aged 30 to 34 will never have borne a child (Grindstaff, 1975:21). This coincides with Veevers' estimate, since Grindstaff does not distinguish between voluntary and involuntary childlessness in his estimate. Both authors base their estimates on current trends in fertility and cite the "increasing participation of women in all aspects of Canadian life, and more opportunities for self-fulfillment outside of motherhood" (Grindstaff, 1975:21) as reasons for such a projected increase in the incidence of childlessness.

For the couple, childlessness probably means greater physical and mental health and a higher degree of marital satisfaction (Renne, 1976; for Canadian data see Lupri and Frideres, 1981). Counter to previous expectations, childlessness does not increase the likelihood of divorce of the couple, provided recent demographic analyses of British data can be generalized to Canada (see Gibson, 1980). In the case of childless couples, we are likely dealing with a two-earner marriage in which there is probably more egalitarianism between husband and wife than in families with children, since children tend to introduce a more traditional element in terms of division of labour and in other terms into a marriage (LaRossa and LaRossa, 1981). However, according to U.S. data, childless persons aged 65 and older are more likely to be socially isolated than persons of that age with living children, although this applies only for those in poor health and those from a working class background. If persons of age 65 and over have few health problems or come from non-manual backgrounds, the association between social isolation and childlessness is not found, suggesting that this latter group maintains a rather high level of contact with non-kin (Bachrach, 1980).

For society as a whole, one may hypothesize that the fewer children born to people who do not desire to have children, the better for everybody — provided that this does not mean that the childless become a political pressure group which will argue for the abolition of the few benefits currently in existence for families with children, or that they will be unwilling to support the creation of other necessary and desirable services and benefits for families with children.

Death of One Parent

Another simple form of discrepancy between marital and parental roles comes into being when one parent dies. This section has been entitled "death of one parent" rather than "widowhood," since not all cases in which a parent dies will involve parents who had been married to each other. Usually, however, this issue would be dealt with under the heading of widowed parents, since parents who are not living in the same household with their children and the children's other parent are normally treated as non-parents.

Unfortunately, statistics on death by parental status are not available. We have therefore to approach the issue by looking at the incidence of death by marital status and within specific age cohorts. As Table 7.1 shows, widowhood during normal parenting age is more likely to be a female than a male phenomenon, but there are men who are in a likely age category for having dependent children at home who do become widowers.

Overall, in 1980, 3849 married men of the age range 15 to 44 died, leaving therefore widows who would still be likely to have dependent children at home. In the same year, 2194 married women of the same age died. (Calculated from Statistics Canada, 1982).

TABLE 7.1

Percentage Widowed by Sex and Age, Canada, 1978

Age	Males	Females
15–19	—	0.1
20–24	0.1	0.2
25–29	0.1	0.4
30–34	0.2	0.7
35–39	0.3	1.3
40–44	0.5	2.5

Source: *Estimates of population by marital status, age and sex, Canada and provinces, 1977 and 1978.* Cat. 91–203, p. 42, t.2. Reprinted by permission of Statistics Canada.

When a married parent dies, not only is the surviving parent bereft of his or her spouse, but (s)he suddenly finds her/himself having to organize a one-parent household. In the case of a man, this will often mean having to cope with household tasks and childrearing tasks in which he had only been slightly involved before. Not only that, but he has to do so under aggravated circumstances, assuming that both he and the children are upset by the death of the wife/mother. On the other hand, a widower is quite unlikely to find himself suddenly destitute, since most men have paying jobs.

By contrast, when the husband/father dies, the most likely thing to happen is that the widow is not only bereft of her husband and the children of their father, but in addition the family is likely to become very poor. Most private pension plans do not provide adequately for the families of deceased participants. If the mother had a paying job before the death of her husband, her income is likely to be too low to support an entire family comfortably, given the large female/male wage differentials in Canada. If the mother did not have a paying job before the death of her spouse, her situation is likely to be even more desperate. The family finds itself not only lacking one member, but is highly likely to join the ranks of the poor. This situation is exacerbated by the likelihood of the deterioration of the social support system that existed during the life of both parents (see Vachon, 1981).

In spite of the obvious trauma of losing a spouse, recent American research suggests that compared to divorce, widowhood — in spite of a public image to the contrary — seems somewhat easier to endure. Widows, when compared with divorcees of the same age, seem to receive more support from other people than divorcees. The status of the widow also seems to have a clearer definition than the status of divorcee, both for self and for others, and widows (as well as reluctant divorcees who did not wish for a divorce) tend to have a more positive image of their husbands than most divorcees.

> Despite the perception that death of a loved one *should* be harder to adjust to than divorce from a previously loved one, data on the physical and mental health status of the widowed and divorced indicate that there is generally more physical and mental health disturbance among the divorced than the widowed.[1]

We are totally ignorant of the incidence as well as of the consequences of the death of a parent who was not married at the time of death to the other parent. Official statistics would classify such a parent either as single or as divorced, depending on whether the children were the offspring of a non-marital union or a divorced marriage. If the parent had remarried, (s)he would be listed as married. In spite of the fact that statistically a non-custodial parent would not be recognized as a parent, his or her death may still represent a heavy loss to the children, who may have had a close relationship with such a parent. It can also be assumed to have some effect on the ex-spouse or ex-partner, although to my knowledge nobody has ever studied this question, and we are therefore ignorant of any possible consequences. Where an ex-partner (whether previously married to the other parent or not) paid any child support, his or her death may also mean a financial loss to the custodial parent and the children. Again, no data on this question exist.

If a custodial parent dies, children may suddenly come into the custody of the other, previously non-custodial parent. This is more likely to happen in the case of children from a divorced marriage than from a non-marital union. Again, this would represent a tremendous change in lifestyle for the children as well as for the other parent, and once again, no data concerning this issue exist.

Unmarried Parenthood

Fertility has declined very drastically in the past twenty years in Canada, as we saw in Chapter 2. However, this is predominantly a decline in marital fertility. While overall married women are having fewer children, more unmarried women are having children. Between 1960 and 1980, the number of children born to unmarried mothers almost tripled, and the percentage of children born to unmarried women as a percentage of all children born within a specific year rose from 4.3 percent to 12.8 percent, as can be seen from Table 7.2.

Of the unmarried mothers, the majority are over 20 years of age, but the age group which has proportionately and absolutely the highest number of births to unmarried mothers is the age group 15 to 19 years old; that is, teenagers (see Table 7.3). Nevertheless, this does not mean that teenagers are more likely to give birth at present than in earlier years. Quite the contrary is true. If we go back to Table 2.2 which

TABLE 7.2

Births to Unwed Mothers, Canada, 1960–1980

Year	Numbers	Percent of Total Live Births
1960*	20,413	4.3
1961	21,490	4.5
1962	22,443	4.8
1963	24,458	5.3
1964	26,556	5.9
1965	28,078	6.7
1966	29,391	7.6
1967	30,915	8.3
1968	32,629	9.0
1969	34,041	9.2
1970	35,588	9.6
1971	32,693	9.0
1972	31,257	9.0
1973	31,005	9.0
1974**	19,183	5.9
1975	24,846	8.7
1976	25,995	10.2
1977	37,801	10.8
1978	39,508	11.4
1979	42,311	11.9
1980	46,014	12.8

Sources: Statistics Canada, catalogue 84–204, Vital Statistics, Vol. 1, Births for years 1973, p. 67, t.11; 1974, p. 26, t.9; 1975–76, p. 25, t.8; 1977, p. 31, t.8; 1978, p. 9, t.6; 1979, p. 11, t.7; 1980, p. 12, t.8.

*Figures for 1960–1973 represent illegitimate births, meaning parents who reported themselves as not having been married to each other at the time of birth or registration. In the case of Ontario, figures refer to those mothers whose marital status was reported as "single."

**For years 1974–1980, figures have been computed by adding together the births to mothers whose marital status was reported as single, widowed or divorced, and computing this figure as a percentage of all births in which the marital status of the mother was known.

looks at age-specific fertility rates, we find that the fertility rate for 15- to 19-year-olds declined from 59.8 in 1960 to 27.6 in 1980 that is, proportionately fewer teenagers than before are giving birth to children. What has changed, then, is that a greater proportion of them are unmarried.[2]

Not only are women who give birth more likely to be unmarried, but these mothers are also more likely than previously to keep these children rather than to give them up for adoption. The figures cited for retention ratios usually range between 70 to 85 percent (see Schles-

TABLE 7.3

Number of Live Births to Single Mothers by Age of Mother, Canada, 1974–1980

Age of Mother	1974	1975	1976	1977	1978	1979	1980
Under 15 years	217	300	291	296	308	297	260
15–19 years	9,653	12,497	12,869	16,800	16,806	16,671	17,188
20–24 years	5,378	6,872	7,371	11,645	12,610	14,059	15,770
25–29 years	1,707	2,235	2,331	4,008	4,336	5,259	6,035
30–34 years	544	687	722	1,365	1,536	1,812	2,119
35–39 years	175	207	240	367	426	442	478
Over 40 years	46	48	42	69	83	77	84
Total	17,723	22,849	23,869	34,634*	36,149**	38,633***	41,955****

Sources: Statistics Canada, catalogue 84–204, Vital Statistics, Vol. I, Births, for year 1974, p. 26, t.9; for 1975–76, p. 26, t.9; for 1977, p. 31, t.9; for 1978, p. 10, t.7; for 1979, p. 12 –13, t.8; for 1980, pp. 12–13, t.8.

*Includes 84 cases of age not stated.

**Includes 44 cases of age not stated.

***Includes 16 cases of age not stated.

****Includes 32 cases of age not stated.

inger, 1979:88); a retention rate of 80 percent seems to be the current rule of thumb.

In terms of the overall discrepancy between marital and parental roles, then, we find that approximately 13 percent of all children born in Canada are born to unmarried mothers. Assuming that the father and mother of the child do not marry after the birth of the child[3] this means that approximately 26 percent of households have either an adult who does not parent his or her child (in almost all cases this would be true for the fathers, whether the child is given up for adoption or lives in a one-parent household with the mother) or a child who lives with one parent only (this would apply to the approximately 80 percent of children who live with their mothers).

The consequences of unmarried parenthood for mothers, fathers, and children are maximally different. There is almost no literature about unwed fathers.[4] A recent American study interviewed 140 men who were collectively responsible for 176 extramarital pregnancies. The most striking finding is that although the men acknowledged their behaviour to be rule-violating, they lacked a sense of themselves as deviant and they successfully avoided being formally identified as deviant (Pfuhl, 1978).

This is not so for the woman involved. The woman must either have an abortion if she finds herself pregnant outside of marriage, or else give birth to the child and either give it up for adoption or raise it in a one-parent household. Any of the three possible pathways involve fundamental decisions which are likely to have their effects on her for life.

Obtaining a therapeutic abortion in Canada is a chancy and humiliating business for a woman. Therapeutic abortions must be approved by therapeutic abortion committees at hospitals, and many hospitals simply do not have such committees. Where there is no committee to which to apply for an abortion, no therepeutic abortions can be performed. In effect, then, for many women in Canada access to therapeutic abortions is not a reality. When women do seek abortion, they tend to seek out physicians very quickly, but they are then faced with long delays (an average interval of eight weeks, see Report of the Committee on the Operation of the Abortion Law, 1977:31) until the abortion is in fact performed. This makes the abortion medically more dangerous, and imposes an enormous psychological strain on the woman.

When a woman decides to give birth to the child she conceived in a non-marital union, she will, in the large majority of cases, start a one-parent household with her child, and in a minority of cases, give up her child for adoption.

If the woman forms a one-parent household with her child(ren), she is highly likely to be poor. If she is a teenage mother, she will probably not complete her high school education, since there are few facilities that allow teenage mothers to continue to attend school and to care for their children. If she goes on welfare, she may very well start a cycle of poverty that may be repeated by her own children.

If she gives up her child for adoption, she will probably carry with her a lifelong regret. Current adoption practices do not give the birth parents any information about their children once they have been legally adopted, just as they give adopted children little information about their birth parents. This issue will be discussed further in the adoption section.

Since we neglect to focus on unwed fathers not only in terms of research, but also in terms of social policy, the entire or at least the major financial burden of raising the children involved tends to be carried by society and by the mother. Giving birth to a child outside of marriage has therefore a truly life-altering impact on the woman concerned, but only a minimal impact on the father with respect to altering his life chances, although it may have a psychological effect on him which has simply not been studied.

As far as the children are concerned, until recently illegitimate children were not only socially but also legally discriminated against. In Ontario, New Brunswick, and Quebec, the legal distinction between legitimate and illegitimate children was removed with the enactment of the Family Law Reform Acts and the revision of the Civil Code, respectively. Nevertheless, children born to unmarried mothers are likely to grow up greatly underprivileged, due to the very great likelihood that they will grow up in poverty.

Growing up in a one-parent household is not by itself necessarily negative for children. Indeed, Howarth (1980), when testing 170 female and 142 male undergraduates, found that children brought up by both parents were more dependent than those reared by single parents. It is the combination of poverty with the lack of a social support system that disadvantages them. None of these factors needs to obtain, for instance, in the case of an older professional woman who plans to have a child outside of marriage, who is able to support the child and herself well, and who has the educational and financial means at her disposal to adequately meet the needs of the child as well as her own needs. There is no reason to believe that the child, or indeed the mother, need in any manner be deprived. However, the responsibility and involvement of the father remains an open question even in such a situation.

One atypical case that must be briefly mentioned is the situation of children who are officially born to single mothers but where, in fact, the mother lives together with the father in a stable common-law relationship. In such cases there is no reason to believe that the situation of the children would be different if the parents were legally married.

In the United States, the number of people cohabiting nearly doubled between 1970 and 1977, reaching almost two million. This represents 4.2 percent of all couple households. Of those cohabiting, approximately 20 percent had one or more children in their households (Newcomb, 1979). In how many cases these children were born to both cohabitants is unclear. One would expect that in the majority of cases they are the biological children of only one of the cohabitants.

One interesting Canadian study compared "keepers" (unmarried mothers who kept their children) with those who gave their children up for adoption. Both "keepers" and "adopters" (a misnomer, since we are dealing with the mothers who are giving their children up for adoption, not adopting one) were all residents in maternity homes (probably an atypical population of unmarried mothers since usage of these homes is shrinking in spite of an increase in births to unmarried mothers). Nevertheless, the results are interesting. The researchers found that on average, "keepers," compared with "adopters," were more likely to have reported serious illness or handicaps and were three times as likely to have undergone psychiatric treatment in the past.[5] "Keepers" were more likely than "adopters" to come from one-parent households themselves and more likely to be in continuous contact with the putative fathers than adopters (Lightman and Schlesinger, 1980).

As already stated, this may be an atypical population. A study comparing one-parent households with two-parent households in Metropolitan Montreal in 1976 found, for instance, that women who headed one-parent households were *not* more likely to have been raised in one-parent households themselves than were the married women[6] (Fortin, Charron and Hotte, 1979:117–127). This same study found that more than half of the one-parent households were below poverty level, and that even if the woman had a paying job, her income was inadequate. The majority of these families had no savings, and few of them had access to any luxury goods.

The study furthermore found that the mental health of women in one-parent and two-parent households was comparable, even though the women in one-parent households reported more suicide attempts than the women in two-parent households. Nor were the women in one-parent households more socially isolated than their counterparts in two-parent households; however, their sexual lives tended to be non-existent or sporadic, since they largely moved in a social circle composed of women, children, and adolescents.

A second study based on the same data set and focussing on the children found that there was no difference in the academic achievement of children from one-parent and two-parent households. However, mothers in one-parent households had less time to devote to their children than parents in two-parent households. Fathers were largely absent in the case of one-parent households, but the researchers noted that the fathers in two-parent households were also conspicuous by their absence. "En effet, pour plus de la moitié, les pères sont en interaction moins de 10 heures par semaine avec leurs enfants. Bien souvent, les enfants ne connaîtront de leur père que son rôle de pourvoyeur"[7] (Caouette and Gosselin, 1979:64).

The question remains as to why we have the increase in unmarried births that is manifested in Table 7.2. There are two issues that must be kept in mind. We have already noted that there is no overall increase in fertility for any age group, including teenagers, but rather a decline. That is, the increase in births to unmarried mothers is not due to an overall increase of births to teenagers. Second, we do not know whether more unmarried women get pregnant than previously, we only know that more unmarried women are *giving birth* than in previous years. This may simply mean that people are no longer willing to marry in case of an accidental pregnancy, whereas before they might have been. If this were the case, it would suggest that the increase in births to unmarried mothers is a part of the general trend of a loosening of the tie between parenthood and marriage.

Nor do we actually know whether premarital sex for teenagers has increased greatly. What can be observed is that there is more discussion of this activity, and that there is a somewhat greater acceptance of it. Nevertheless, unmarried teenagers who engage in sexual intercourse are faced with a situation in which they receive conflicting messages. On the one hand, there are now proponents who will publicly state that sex between unmarried people is natural; on the other, there is at the same time a strong moral condemnation of sex between unmarrieds, and specifically between unmarried teenagers. It is the moral ambiguity more than the lack of knowledge about contraception that must be seen as a culprit in leading to unwanted pregnancies. (This assumes that the majority of pregnancies experienced by unmarried teenagers are, in fact, unplanned and unwanted.) One study which looked at sex education in Ontario secondary schools found a range of problems with such instruction, which included instructional materials of poor quality, varying levels of maturity and knowledge among students, student and teacher embarrassment, and inadequate teacher preparation, as well as other problems (Herold and Benson, 1979).

Female teenagers see their parents as reacting negatively if they knew that their daughters had sexual intercourse (Herold and Thomas,

1978:311). They also tend not to wish to consult their family physicians under the assumption that this would make their parents aware of their activity (Herold and Goodwin, 1979:317–318).

In a social climate which on the one hand glorifies sexual relations, and on the other hand brands them as morally wrong, it is more likely that a lack of proper precaution will accompany unmarried intercourse between teenagers than if the activity was either a clearly and strictly prohibited act or a clearly permissible act.

The Montreal study which tried to explain the emergence of one-parent households by looking for specific characteristics on the part of the mother failed to come up with clearly distinguishable factors between women who head one-parent households and women in two-parent households. This suggests that maybe we have focussed too much attention on the mother and too little on the father. By focussing attention on the men who are also responsible for the formation of one-parent households by virtue of having fathered (a) child(ren) for which they do not take full or any responsibility, we might perhaps come up with more satisfying explanations. It might turn out that the most important determinant for the likelihood of children living in a one-parent household is the character of the adult male who is responsible for the formation of this type of household. We should therefore start examining the social and psychological background of these men, particularly so since they may be responsible for the formation of more than one one-parent household, if they have successive liaisons with different women which result in children.

Divorce

We noted in Chapter 2 that the incidence of divorce greatly increased during the seventies and have suggested that it is unlikely to decline during the eighties. In the context of this chapter, we are particularly interested in divorces that involve children, and particularly dependent children. With the increase in divorces, the number of children involved in divorces has also increased very considerably, as can be seen from Table 7.4. Between 1969 and 1980, the number of dependent children involved in divorce per year rose from 20 230 to 59 538. Between 1969 and 1980, a total of about 576 559 dependent children were involved in divorce.[8]

To calculate the chances of a child ending up with divorced parents is extremely difficult. In the United States

> An analysis of current data on living arrangements suggests that if current conditions persist, children born in the mid-1970s have about 45 chances in 100 of living in a one-parent family for a period of at least

TABLE 7.4

Divorces, by Numbers of Dependent Children, Canada, 1969–1980

Year		Number of Dependent Children 0	1	2	3	4	5 and more	Total Divorces	Average # of Children
1969	#	12,072	4,108	3,129	1,587	660	433	21,989	0.92
	%	54.9	18.7	14.2	7.2	3.0	2.0	100	
1970	#	13,714	6,013	5,025	2,624	1,180	682	29,238	1.11
	%	46.9	20.6	17.2	9.0	4.0	2.3	100	
1971	#	13,241	6,189	5,430	2,825	1,250	737	29,672	1.17
	%	44.6	20.9	18.3	9.5	4.2	2.5	100	
1972	#	14,305	7,078	5,956	2,963	1,294	768	32,364	1.15
	%	44.2	21.9	18.4	9.2	3.9	2.4	100	
1973	#	15,890	8,209	6,842	3,384	1,520	859	36,704	1.16
	%	43.4	22.4	18.6	9.2	4.1	2.3	100	
1974	#	18,588	10,277	8,817	4,349	1,850	1,138	45,019	1.22
	%	41.3	22.8	19.6	9.7	4.1	2.5	100	
1975	#	21,458	11,523	9,985	4,643	1,904	1,098	50,611	1.17
	%	42.4	22.7	19.7	9.2	3.8	2.2	100	
1976	#	23,996	12,272	10,523	4,726	1,793	897	54,207	1.10
	%	44.3	22.6	19.4	8.7	3.3	1.7	100	
1977	#	24,670	12,576	11,166	4,536	1,659	763	55,370	1.07
	%	44.6	22.7	20.2	8.2	3.0	1.3	100	
1978	#	25,657	12,994	11,983	4,517	1,395	609	57,155	1.04
	%	44.9	22.7	21.0	7.9	2.4	1.1	100	
1979	#	26,342	13,227	11,827	4,185	1,276	465	57,322	1.00
	%	46.0	23.0	20.6	7.3	2.2	0.8	100	
1980	#	29,205	14,021	12,877	4,371	1,168	377	62,019	0.96
	%	47.1	22.6	20.8	7.0	1.9	0.6	100	

Sources: Canada Yearbook 1974, p. 184, t.4.54, Statistics Canada, catalogue 84–205, vol. II, Marriages and Divorces, for 1977, p. 41, t.20; for 1978, p. 24–25, t.17; for 1979, p. 26, t.17; for 1980, p. 26, t.17.

several months before they reach the age of 18 years. However, because most young women remarry, a large proportion of these children will eventually spend part of their childhood in a two-parent family with a biological parent and a stepparent. In 1977, an estimated one-tenth of the children living with two parents were living with a stepparent, that is, were born before the natural parent they live with had remarried.[9]

This estimate has been estimated to reach 50 percent in 1990 (Glick 1979:176).

In Canada, the divorce rate is lower. Overall, the chances of a marriage ending in divorce are approximately one out of three in Canada. More than half of all divorces involve at least one dependent child (see Table 7.4). Between 1969 and 1980, the median proportion of divorces involving no dependent children was 45.4 percent, meaning that approximately 55 percent of all divorces involved dependent children. Assuming that about one third of all Canadian marriages result in divorce this means that about 18.3 percent of marriages with dependent children are likely to end in divorce. In order to arrive at an estimate of the effect of divorce on contributing towards marital/parental discrepancies in Canadian households, we have to multiply this figure by two, because the two parents will live in separate households, and a spousal/parental discrepancy will exist in the household in which the father lives as well as in the household in which the mother lives. A rough estimate then, of the proportion of households in Canada in which there exists some form of marital/parental discrepancy due to divorce for at least one member is 36.6 percent.

Very little in our social lore has prepared us for this type of situation. By assigning custody to one parent only courts encourage the fiction that the parental role for one parent must be severely restricted when marital roles end. Whereas before parents at least theoretically shared responsibility for their children, after divorce only one parent carries the responsibility, while the other is often denied an opportunity for meaningful interaction, and the parent with the responsibility is usually the mother.

As can be seen from Table 7.5, more than three quarters of all dependent children are given into custody of the mother, with about 15 to 16 percent given into the custody of the father. Counter to reports in the mass media and a widespread impression of the contrary, the proportion of fathers who receive custody of their children did not increase noticeably between 1971 and 1980. It remained remarkably stable. During the same time span, however, the likelihood of the mother receiving custody of the children has slightly increased. This is due to the fact that there is a decreased likelihood that no award of custody is made.

The effects of divorce are drastically different for children, mothers, and fathers. We will look at the consequences of divorce for children first. By now, there exist a number of American studies which try to assess the impact, both short-term and long-term, which divorce has on children. For the short term, children whose parents have divorced experience typically intense anger, fear, depression, and guilt (Wallerstein and Kelly, 1977; Hetherington, 1979). The negative effects

TABLE 7.5

Divorce with Dependent Children by Parties to Whom Custody Was Granted, Canada, 1971–1980

Year		To the husband	To the wife	To other person or agency	No award of custody made	Total
1971	#	2,584	12,610	72	1,718	16,984
	%	15.2	74.2	0.4	10.1	99.9
1972	#	2,777	13,906	96	1,968	18,747
	%	14.8	74.2	0.5	10.5	100
1973	#	3,310	16,279	76	1,986	11,651
	%	15.3	75.2	0.4	9.2	100.1
1974	#	3,956	21,036	135	2,447	27,574
	%	14.3	76.3	0.5	8.9	100
1975	#	4,510	23,522	133	2,184	30,349
	%	14.9	77.5	0.4	7.2	100
1976	#	6,344	33,299	155	2,405	42,203
	%	15.0	78.9	0.4	5.7	100
1977	#	6,216	33,547	111	2,199	42,073
	%	14.8	79.7	0.3	5.2	100
1978	#	9,291	46,752	152	3,241	59,436
	%	15.5	78.7	0.3	5.5	100
1979	#	9,116	45,562	137	3,041	57,856
	%	15.8	78.8	0.2	5.3	100
1980	#	9,554	46,607	132	3,307	59,600
	%	16.0	78.2	0.2	5.5	100

Source: Computed from Statistics Canada Catalogue 84–205, 1974, p. 39, t.22; 1977, p. 42, t.22; 1978, p. 22, t.15; 1979, p. 26, t.17, 1980, p. 24, t.15.

tend to be more marked for boys than for girls (Hetherington, 1979: 852–853) and the only child tends to feel more threatened than the child who shares the impact of divorce with siblings (Wallerstein and Kelly, 1979:470). However, as far as long-term consequences are concerned, the most thorough review of the literature available concludes that "findings to date are equivocal; they do not permit assertions that divorce has any single, broad-reaching impact on children" (Longfellow, 1979:287).

Nevertheless, divorce often does bring real problems, and it is probable that "the quality of the parent-child relationship itself is susceptible to some of the ill effects of divorce" (Longfellow, 1979:295).

"One significant change in children's lives following the parents' divorce may be that their mother's emotional well-being is in greater jeopardy. This in turn may cause a turn for the worse in the parent-child relationship" (Longfellow, 1979:295).

In addition, single parents tend to be socially isolated:

> Not only do children suffer from the direct effects of the marital strife of their parents, but they are also likely to endure deteriorating relationships with their single parents who may be depressed or anxious or overburdened by the emotional events in their lives. The problems are not only internal; divorce also intensifies the single mother's need for an external support system, while at the same time it throws up obstacles against her ability to build or maintain such a network. The loss of the benefits of a supporting network to the mother may well be a disadvantage for the child.[10]

Brandwein, Brown and Fox (1974:509) suggest that it may not be the father's absence which is most important but the mother's absence due to increased demands on her time and energy. They suggest that "Perhaps the appropriate comparisons should be made along the dimension of maternal deprivation, assessing the variables which would interfere with or enhance the mother's ability to provide adequate mothering."

The lack of a clear-cut impact of divorce on children suggests that we have perhaps been studying the phenomenon in the wrong manner. It is probably inappropriate to compare children of enduring marriages against children of divorced marriages. It might be more appropriate to compare children of enduring but conflict-ridden marriages with children of divorced marriages. An old study did just that and found that "at all socioeconomic levels, children from unhappy, unbroken homes reported more problems of adjustment than did children from single-parent homes" (Longfellow, 1979:293). A number of more recent studies suggest a similar relationship. Together, these studies propose that "living with two parents whose relationship is conflict-ridden is much more damaging to the child's adjustment than simply living with a single parent" (Longfellow, 1979:294).

Another study which examines several representative national samples from the U.S. confirms the general findings just cited. The researchers found few differences on global measures of adjustment for the children of divorce. Analysis by age suggested that young adults (21–34) from divorced backgrounds were significantly less likely to report being "very happy" than those from intact homes, but the differences dissipated as adults proceeded through the life course (Kulka and Weingarten, 1979:56). These researchers also supported the notion that coming from an unhappy, conflict-ridden family may be more harmful to the children than coming from voluntarily divorced families (Kulka and Weingarten, 1979:76). A recent Canadian study on the effects of separation found that mothers saw more improvement than deterioration in their children's psychological states following separation (Arnold, Wheeler and Pendrith, 1980:184).

However, a recent American study involving 560 divorced parents suggests that mothers may have a more positive view of the effects of divorce than fathers. This study found that 40 percent of the wives and 63 percent of the husbands felt that divorce had had a negative effect on their children (Fulton, 1979:135).

Overall, there is by now increasing evidence that divorce *per se* may not be half as significant for the children as had been thought — what matters are other factors which tend to be selectively associated with divorce, such as the relationships with both parents, poverty, mental health of the custodial parent, and others. Hess and Camara (1979), in pursuing this question analyzed children from sixteen divorced and sixteen intact American families. They found that "On such matters as communication between parents about child rearing, parental interest in and knowledge of the child's school and social life, and the amount of time parents spent with the child, *there was more variation within each group than between divorced and non-divorced groups*" (Hess and Camara, 1979:87, emphasis in the original).

Other research confirms that it seems to be the conditions rather than the *event* of divorce that matter. Jacobson, in examining children's adjustment, found that the most important factor was "The more time lost with the father, the higher the maladjustment of the child in the 12 month period after parental separation" (Jacobson, 1978a:356), and the greater the amount of interparent hostility prior to marital separation, the greater the maladjustment of the child (Jacobson 1978b:17). Finally, she found that the more attention children received from parents in dealing with separation, the more parents encouraged discussion of the event, and the more children brought problems to the parents for discussion, the better adjusted the children (Jacobson, 1978c:188).

Probing a different aspect of the conditions attending divorce, Colletta (1979) examined the relative importance of father absence and poverty on childrearing practices. For that purpose, she compared childrearing practices of seventy-two mothers who varied along the dimensions of father absence, income, sex of child, and number of children. She found that when families differed only in father absence, there were no significant differences in their childrearing practices. The greater demands low income divorced mothers tend to make of their children are therefore probably a function of strains inherent in living on a very small budget, rather than a direct function of belonging to a one-parent household.

Overall, then, it is unclear exactly what effect divorce has on children. So far, researchers have tried primarily to document the absence or presence of *negative* psychological effects by focussing on such variables as adjustment (and lack thereof), aggression, hostility, deterioration in scholastic performance, and the like. Perhaps the lack of consistent findings is due to the combined effects of (a) comparing children of divorced parents with children from intact marriages, rather than comparing children of unhappy marriages with children of divorced parents (b) focussing on the event of divorce rather than on the process within *both* marriages and divorces, and (c) searching for negative psychological outcomes rather than examining structural variables. Examining structural variables could have two major aspects: (c_1) parcelling out the effects of factors commonly associated with divorce such as poverty, social isolation of the custodial parent, etc., and (c_2) examining the structure of the household and of familial relations both during an ongoing marriage and after divorce has occurred and evaluating their impact on social relations.

One recent study has started to move in the latter direction. Weiss (1979) examined children growing up in one-parent households and noted that the fact that there is only one parent fundamentally changes the authority structure from that of an echelon structure to that of a partnership between the parent and the child(ren). He noted that children in this type of situation had to "grow up a little faster," and concluded "It would seem accurate to say that most children of single parent families, though they may be pleased that they proved able to meet the challenge of new expectations, also regret having had to do so" (Weiss 1979:107).

Levitin makes a similar point:

> . . . the adolescent whose after-school job is a vital source of family income, whose assistance with household tasks ensures that the household is maintained, who participates in important decisions about the family, and whose opinions are seriously and routinely sought may not feel alienated and may find transition to young adulthood less abrupt and less demanding of new skills and judgement. *For many adolescents the problems engendered by parental divorce may, ultimately, be out-weighed by the advantages of growing up earlier.*[11]

We have so far been concentrating only on assessing those research findings which have been concerned with the effects of divorce on children. Of course, both ex-spouses, their families, and indeed, society at large are affected by divorce as well. For both spouses, divorce tends to be an extremely stressful event (as indeed it is for children, irrespective of any ultimate positive or negative effects). Divorce involves loss of a spouse — even if interaction preceding divorce had been minimal — and it seems that it is experienced as a more stressful event than death of a spouse (see Deckert and Langelier, 1978:384 for some Canadian data, and Kitson et al., 1980, for some American data to this effect).

One immediate consequence of divorce is economic in nature. American studies show that between 1968 and 1974, the real income of married couples increased 21.7 percent, while the real income of divorced women decreased by 29.3 percent and of divorced men by 19.2 percent (Espenshade, 1979:617). Reasons for this decline in income for divorced people include loss of economies of scale (two adults can live together more cheaply than if they live separately), the fact that divorce is selective of couples less well off to begin with (there is an inverse relationship between socio-economic status and marital instability), the increased likelihood of women receiving welfare, and very little, if any, child support and alimony payments for women (Espenshade, 1979).

> In general, wives are left off worse than their former husbands. Not only are they usually the ones awarded custody of the children without commensurate financial help from fathers, but they generally face other impediments in the labor market to higher pay and adequate employment opportunities.[12]

In spite of the generally negative economic consequences of divorce, those who have gone through the process tend to prefer it to a continuing unhappy marriage. Renne (1970:55, no. 4) found that unhappily married people were worse off financially, socially, and in terms of psychological and physical health than those who have been divorced. She found that divorced people were less isolated than the unhappily married, and less likely to display the kinds of neurotic symptoms characteristic of the unhappily married (Renne, 1970:66, n. 25).

In their study of late divorced female Canadians Langelier and Deckert (1980:406) found that only one third of the late divorced females were usually employed at the time of divorce, earning an average of $9400 per year. The majority were housewives with husbands earning an average of $23 700. Not astonishingly, financial problems loom big for divorced women.

It seems that a non-traditional attitude towards sex roles makes it easier for women to cope with the after-effects of divorce. Brown and Manela (1978) found by studying 253 black and white women living in Detroit and its suburbs that "during divorce women with traditional sex role attitudes are more vulnerable to psychological distress and low self-esteem regardless of their age, race, education, or working status" (Brown and Manela, 1978:326). A Canadian study found that marriages in which the partners have non-traditional sex roles are more likely to be happy than those with traditional ones, and post-divorce adjustment for women was better when they had non-traditional sex roles than when they had traditional sex roles (Deckert and Langelier, 1978). The effect of non-traditional sex roles on men is less clear-cut. Chiriboga and Thurnher (1980:388), in examining 298 U.S. women and men in the process of divorce found that "it was deviation rather than conformity to traditional sex role expectations that was linked with better post-separation adjustment."

By now, we can make some tentative assessment of the effects of divorce on the women, men, and children involved. Under all circumstances it seems to be a very painful process for all those involved. The after-affects are different for ex-spouses and children, but in spite of the extreme stress experienced divorce seems to be preferable to the alternative — namely, continuing an unhappy marriage — for all parties.

This being the case, the most sensible reaction on the part of society would seem to be to accept that divorce is a present-day reality and is likely to be with us for a while. The effort should thus be concentrated on minimizing the negative effects of divorce. This includes especially two aspects: decreasing the negative economic effects and creating and fostering social support networks for the recently divorced (adults as well as the children involved).

The downward economic plunge which divorced wives and children take is not only significant because it constitutes a relative loss in simple economic terms, but because more often than not this translates to a loss of stability of environments and social contacts. Often, a mother heading a one-parent household needs to move with her children because the house has been sold or she no longer can afford the rent of the apartment. This means that both she and the children lose their neighbours and those friends whose friendship is based on physical proximity, the children may have to switch schools, and the mother may have to take a job if she did not work for pay before. A large number of highly significant and disrupting changes are therefore likely to occur at once, magnifying the distress experienced, the uncertainty, and the isolation. Maintaining more stability in living environments would in most cases probably be highly beneficial, as would minimizing the economic loss. Creating support groups for recently divorced people (for both men and women as well as for children) — for instance in the form of self-help groups — might also help to minimize the negative impact of divorce on all concerned.

As far as research into the effects, conditions, and process of divorce are concerned, most of the studies cited were American. There is a great paucity of information on this subject area in Canada. In particular, there are no studies at all about the effects of divorce on kin relationships, especially seen from the viewpoint of children. While ex-spouses may wish to sever their ties with former in-laws, these same in-laws remain relatives of the children involved. We do not know under what circumstances kin do or do not remain in touch with children whose parents are divorced. For instance, in what cases do grandparents whose child does not have custody of their grandchild remain in touch with the grandchild? When one parental tie is either disrupted or threatened, kin relationships may take on added importance for the children. To investigate actual patterns, and what factors impede and facilitate maintenance of kin ties beyond divorce is surely a highly important research topic, which, at this point in time, however, is virtually unexplored.

Permanent Separation and Desertion in Families with Children

In the 1971 Census of Canada about five percent of ever-married women classified themselves as married with husband absent or separated (Boyd, 1977:52). It is unclear how many of these women will remain permanently separated and how many have been or will eventually be divorced.

Until 1968, the domicile of a married woman as well as of a common-law wife was that of her husband. Since a divorce can only be filed in the jurisdiction of one's domicile, this meant in practical terms, that until 1968 a wife could not file for divorce if the husband had deserted her, either because she did not know his address, or because she did not have the means to move there. This factor could lead to permanent separations which would not end in divorce.

With the 1968 passage of the Divorce Act this particular impediment to divorce was abolished. A wife can now establish her own domicile, irrespective of her husband. A deserted spouse can now file for divorce for reasons of marriage breakdown after three years, and the deserter can file for divorce after five years. Therefore, those permanent separations which were due to restrictive legal requirements for divorce should have diminished since that time.

On the other hand, it is possible that some people simply do not bother to file for divorce. Where there is no intention to remarry, it may make little difference whether a couple is legally divorced or merely separated. Further, legal costs may act as an impediment. Since the educational level of separated women is lower than that of divorced women (Boyd, Eichler and Hofley, 1976:49) and since lower educational levels tend to correspond to lower socio-economic levels, financial considerations may be important.

However, we do not know who opts for which reasons not to go through a legal divorce although a separation had been on-going for many years and is regarded as permanent by both or at least one of the parties involved. Obviously, here is another fruitful field for research, and just as obviously, considering *only* divorce statistics as an indicator of marital breakdown means to underestimate the true amount of breakdown by some unknown factor.

Marital Adultery Resulting in Offspring

This is another area in which we have neither figures nor any other research. Personal acquaintances have informed me that adultery by married persons which results in offspring but not in divorce *does* exist. If we are dealing with a married man who has a child by an unmarried woman, the birth will be listed as a birth to an unmarried woman, and the child will in all likelihood live with the mother or be given up for adoption. In cases in which we are dealing with a married woman who has a child by a married or unmarried man who is not her husband, the child will be legally regarded as the child of her husband, unless there is proof positive that the husband is not the father. Statistically, the child will be counted as a birth to a married woman. Once more, here would be an interesting group to study which so far has been totally neglected.

Artificial Donor Insemination

Artificial insemination by a donor (AID) involves insemination of a woman by technical means with the sperm of a man whose identity is usually unknown to the woman (and occasionally unknowable, if a mix of sperm of several men has been used for insemination). This excludes artificial insemination with the husband's sperm.

Overall, there seems to be no research in existence that examines the consequences and effects of artificial donor insemination for the woman who has been inseminated, the child(ren) who have been conceived and born, the husband of the woman who is usually regarded as the father of the child(ren), the donor, and the medical personnel involved in the process. Nor has anybody kept count of the number of children so conceived and born.

Rioux and Ackman (1980:31) have estimated that "there have been at least 1500 births by artificial insemination over the last decade" in Canada. This seems like an extremely low estimate. They note that there are currently about fifteen non-profit university affiliated centres which practise artificial insemination, and that four of these centres possess a liquid nitrogen bank and use frozen sperm.

According to an older newspaper article, Dr. Jerald Bain was quoted as saying that "hundreds to thousands of babies are born by this method every year in Canada — but it's impossible to say exactly" (Thousands of babies, 1978:C1). According to a more recent newspaper article, donors "are responsible for at least 1,000 births a year. Dr. Michael Jewett, who works in the fertility unit at Wellesley Hospital, thinks the number is closer to 6,000" (Orr, 1981:15). The Royal Commission on Family and Children's Law estimated that two hundred to four hundred couples request AID per year in British Columbia alone (British Columbia: The Family and Children's Law Commission, 1975:2).

There seem to be four distinct motivations for seeking AID:

(a) If a fertile woman is married to a sterile husband and desires to give birth to a child, the couple may decide to have a child via AID. This seems to be the most common reason.
(b) A woman may wish to become a mother without wishing to be involved with a man, and without wishing to share the parenting with a man.
(c) A couple may decide to upgrade the genetic stock of their family by using the sperm of some "superstar." This, at least, is the idea behind the highly controversial sperm bank of Nobel Prize winners which has been started in the U.S.
(d) Finally, the phenomenon of the surrogate mother represents a new type of artificial donor insemination, in which a woman agrees to bear a child for a couple in which the wife is infertile, and for that purpose lets herself be inseminated with the man's sperm. The child is then adopted at birth by the couple. There are now some verified cases of this practice.

Numerically, probably only the first type of AID is significant. However, because of their social importance, all four types will be briefly considered.

An outstanding aspect is the consensus that the child should be left ignorant of his or her genetic origin, and that the woman's husband should pretend to be the genetic father of the child. In the absence of any empirical evidence, the general assumption has usually been that this pretense is unproblematic. For instance, in the commission appointed by the Archbishop of Canterbury, it was stated

> Doctors who have observed the family life in which A.I.D. children are being brought up report that the husband and wife quickly appear to assume the roles of normal parents and the episode of insemination soon becomes unimportant.[13]

This type of unsystematic casual observation by outsiders is emphatically not sufficient to state that indeed "the episode of insemination soon becomes unimportant." The current research on adoption has demonstrated the deep-seated desires of people to know their biological parents, even if they are perfectly happy with their adoptive family and have no desire to *live* with their birth parents. One would expect that any problems which adopted children experience around these issues would be magnified in the case of AID (see also Sorosky, Baran and Pannor, 1979:222–226).

Reflection suggests that having to maintain what essentially amounts to a lie would impose an extreme burden on any familial unit. Should there be additional problems, one would expect them to be worsened by having to maintain a false front. Given the importance of this type of medical interference in social relationships, it would seem useful to have some empirical evidence on which to assess the success of a policy of secrecy. The recent B.C. commission examining this issue recommended explicitly that "The child should not have the fact of his origin by artificial insemination divulged to him" (British Columbia: The Family and Children's Law Commission, 1975: Summary of Recommendations, point 7).

The fact of the matter is, however, that there is not a single empirical study published that measures what happens to children who learn inadvertently or deliberately that they were conceived through AID and that they will never know who their biological father is. We do not know what the strain imposed on a marital relationship is by having to maintain silence on such a basic issue in front of the children, nor do we know anything about the father-child relationship in such cases and especially what happens if the child is seen as problem-producing by one or both of the parents. Nor do we know what strain is imposed on the marriages of donors when their wives learn that their husbands are likely to have several children by other women.

Indeed, we know as little about the donors as we know about the recipients of semen: donors tend to be medical or dental students (Rioux and Ackman, 1980). A newspaper article which interviewed some seven donors suggested that the main motivation is to make a modest amount of money — the fee quoted per sperm donation was ranging from $25 to $50 (Orr, 1981:15).

In the second type of AID, a woman may desire to bear a child without involvement with a male. This may be the case, for example, because the woman simply does not know a suitable man who could father a child and/or because she is a lesbian who prefers not to have a co-parenting relationship with a man. One recent newspaper article suggested that "Dozens of unmarried lesbians in the San Francisco Bay area will give birth this year to infants through artificial insemination by donor (AID) in a variation of the technique which has become known as the 'turkey-baster baby method'" (Reed, 1980:11).

How widespread this practice is is, of course, unknown. Presumably, if children are conceived and born under these circumstances, one of the strains attending AID could conceivably be removed — there would be no need to pretend that a particular man is the genetic father of the child. Nevertheless, the problem remains that if a child has a natural curiosity about his or her father that this cannot be satisfied. One might speculate that this would be especially hard for boys, who, as they grow older, will start to appreciate that some man has effectively been used as a stud in order for them to be conceived. Again, it would be highly interesting to see what image of the father role these boys would eventually develop for themselves, as well as what ideas about relating to men the girls will eventually have.

The third type of AID involves the use of a sperm bank for upgrading the genetic stock of a family. This has become an issue with the founding of the so-called Nobel Sperm Bank by Robert K. Graham. This bank stores sperm of distinguished men, including some Nobel Prize winners, after they have been checked as being free of hereditary diseases. The sperm is made available only to married women who are highly intelligent. At some point, the founder of the bank required that the women all be members of Mensa, an organization for people with unusually high IQs, but he has since indicated that he will expand his search for recipients beyond Mensa members. Apparently there are not many female Mensa members who are married and who wish to use the services of his bank (see Chambers, 1980: also Dalby, 1980; "Hundred 'super tots'," 1980; "Sperm bank using mails," 1980; "No test-tube genuises," 1980; Hollobon, 1980; "Sperm bank's founder denies racial goal," 1980).

Most critics would agree that as a scientific experiment the sperm bank will be useless. Others have charged that there is an inherent racial bias (most Nobel Prize winners are white). Since donors and recipients are customarily matched not just for race but for physical characteristics, this does not make the bank different from other banks. However, other problems include that Nobel Prize winners are typically not young, and that therefore the chances of a Downs' Syndrome baby may increase. It is also unclear whether the traits that donors are selected on are genetically transferable, whether they are highly desirable to start out with, and in what manner genetic and environmental factors combine to produce certain traits in people.

The last type of AID involves surrogate motherhood. This became an issue only in 1980 in the United States, when Mrs. Kane (a pseudonym) went public with her story that she was for a fee bearing a child for a couple in which the wife was infertile (see Hall, 1980). Her case captured the imagination of the mass media, and since that time, a few other cases have come to public attention.

Numerically, at this point, surrogage motherhood is insignificant. We are dealing only with a few cases. Socially, legally, and in terms of social policy, however, it seems that we have crossed a threshold, and that surrogate motherhood will transform our prevailing notions of the value of giving birth and of the meaning of parenthood. It is for this reason that this type of AID is discussed in this context at some length, in spite of its numerical insignificance.

At the time of this writing, the legal situation was such that there were no rules and regulations in place that would either prohibit or foster surrogate motherhood. However, this can be expected to change soon, since the first Canadian case of surrogate motherhood came to public attention in the fall of 1982. In this case, a Metro Toronto couple who had tried unsuccessfully to have a child heard of surrogate motherhood through a television programme and approached Michigan lawyer Keane to arrange a surrogate mother for them. He did find an American woman who was then artificially inseminated with the husband's sperm. In order to facilitate adoption procedures the American mother came to Toronto to give birth to the child in Canada. However, since Canadian law prohibits the sale of babies, she did not receive her $10 000 fee for carrying the baby, as originally agreed upon. She gave birth to a healthy boy and left the day after her delivery to return to her husband in Florida. At this point the Children's Aid Society stepped in. Under Ontario law, the surrogate mother's husband rather than the sperm donor was considered the father of the child. However, eventually the natural father was recognized as the legal and biological father of the child, and the Children's Aid Society formally dropped their protection proceedings on behalf of the child.

As a consequence, Frank Drea, Minister of Community and Social Services in Ontario, announced that he would ask the Ontario Law Reform Commission to study the moral, social, and legal aspects of surrogate motherhood. It is therefore likely that some Ontario government guidelines will be set up sometime in 1983 concerning surrogate motherhood (cf. Tesher, 1982).

The same newspaper article which summarized this first Canadian case mentioned that "fifteen Canadian women are now waiting to be chosen as hired wombs" (Tesher, 1982:A4), and these may not be all of the cases. For instance, in the fall of 1981, a woman placed an ad in a newspaper which read:
"Healthy woman wants to carry pregnancy for infertile couple." She intended to charge $15 000 for the service, with which she wanted to pay her way through nursing school. According to the newspaper,

> "In essence, I am selling a baby," she said, "But I don't feel bad about it. I'm doing someone a service. I love kids, but this isn't my baby, it's someone else's. I'm just growing it for them, renting out — for a high fee — my uterus."[14]

In order to analyze the importance of such events, we need to separate them into two different components. One aspect is the fact that a woman offers to carry a child for another woman and for a man with whom she has no personal connection; the other is that she charges a fee for it. As far as the first aspect is concerned, there is nothing substantially different about it than when women give up their children for adoption, except that the pregnancy was deliberately planned. However, putting a price tag on giving birth to a child fundamentally alters the meaning of one of the basic human capacities. It puts a price tag not just on the labour involved, but in effect on human life itself. Babies thereby become a purchasable commodity, possibly available only to the rich.

One can profitably look at the question of blood donations, organ donations, and semen donations as parallel. In Canada, blood is donated, not sold. In the U.S., by contrast, it is sold. As a consequence, the quality of blood in Canada is apparently higher than the quality of U.S. blood. Likewise, the sale of human organs for transplantation purposes is prohibited in Canada. If newspaper articles can be trusted, however, some very poor people in Latin America are selling parts of their body — for example, one eye, or one kidney — in order to make enough money to survive. With respect to semen donation, the B.C. commission recommended that

> a prospective donor should receive full and adequate recompense for his time, expenses and the loss of any revenue that he may sustain in making himself available for sperm donations, sufficient to enlist his co-operation. However, it would seem inadvisable to pay him a price for the seminal fluid itself.[15]

If we fail to pass some legislation that prohibits the sale of babies — or the renting out of wombs — it is possible that we may move towards a society in which some women are reduced to the status of breeders, while others (rich ones) can buy children for themselves.

One other possibility must be considered. There have been, by now, several successful *in vitro* conceptions (misleadingly often referred to as test tube babies). It is conceivable that, given this possibility, and given the possibility of "renting a womb," some fertile women may decide that they do not wish to go through the bother of childbirth and will therefore ask for an *in vitro* fertilization, have the fertilized egg implanted in some woman who has agreed to carry the pregnancy to term for a fee, and in this manner may have children born to them.

The problem with surrogate motherhood, then, is not the discrepancy between biological and social parenthood that it entails, but the issue that it reduces childbirth to a commodity. Obviously, the whole area of AID merits detailed study of its effects on donors, recipients, their spouses, the children, and the technical personnel involved.

Adoption

Slightly more research exists concerning adoption than concerning some of the previous types of marital and parental discrepancies, but here also we are dealing with the issue of assessing exactly how many families are affected. Since adoptees receive a new birth certificate at the time of adoption and become the legal children of their adoptive parents, once this legal fiction has been completed, identification of adopted children, and of birth parents, rests on self-disclosure.

Table 7.6 provides some information on the incidence of adoption; however, we must consider the meaning of the figures.

TABLE 7.6

Adoption Completions in Canada (Excluding Northwest Territories and Yukon) as Percentage of the Child Population Aged Under One Year, 1959–60 to 1976–77

	A No. of Completed Adoptions (thousands)	B All Children Under 1 Year (thousands)	A as percentage of B
1959–60	12.8	479.2	2.7
1960–61	13.5	478.5	2.8
1961–62	13.7	475.7	2.9
1962–63	13.6	469.7	2.9
1963–64	14.3	465.8	3.1
1964–65	15.4	453.0	3.4
1965–66	16.4	418.6	3.9
1966–67	17.1	387.7	4.4
1967–68	17.9	370.8	4.8
1968–69	19.1	364.3	5.2
1969–70	20.3	369.6	5.5
1970–71	20.5	372.0	5.5
1971–72	20.2	360.3	5.6
1972–73	18.9	357.9	5.3
1973–74	17.3	347.7	5.0
1974–75	16.7	341.0	4.9
1975–76	14.6	336.6	4.0
1976–77	16.2	347.7	4.7

Source: Adapted from H. Philip Hepworth, *Foster Care and Adoption in Canada*, Reprinted by permission of Canadian Council on Social Development, 1980, p. 135.

These figures do not represent the total of all families that are in some way or other affected by adoption. First of all, it only lists adoptions of children under one year[16] and therefore underestimates the total number and percentage of children involved. More important, the table only gives us the number of *children* adopted, thus underestimating the number of families affected by adoption. Obviously there is a discrepancy between marital and procreative roles when a family adopts the child. Not quite as obviously, there is the reverse type of discrepancy in the families of the birth mother and the birth father, who are highly likely also to have married (not each other but somebody else) and who are not parenting their biological child. Assuming then that approximately five percent of the children in Canada are adopted, and that both birth parents form their own families, we need to multiply five percent of adopted children by three in order to arrive at a better estimate of the degree to which adoption affects, in one way or another, families in Canada and results in a discrepancy between parental and spousal roles. Were we to add to this percentage the adults who were themselves adopted as children, one could increase this estimate further. Adoption is, therefore, far from being a socially insignificant or marginal issue, in that it involves an important minority of families in Canada.

Recently, some attention has been focussed on adoption due to a growing concern of people involved in the adoption triangle — birth parents, adopted child, and adoptive family — to open up the until now totally closed files. In the last few years, a number of adopted children have embarked on a public search for their birth parents. Special organizations have sprung up to help this search, the most important one of them being Parent Finders. The attendant publicity has led to a reconsideration of the way in which adoptions are being handled, with some legislative changes occurring. The right of adopted children to know their birth parents is being weighed against the presumed right of adoptive parents not to have birth parents interfere in their parental relationship, and the presumed right of birth parents to their privacy. Until recently, there was almost no information on the feelings of birth parents. Recent research has demonstrated that we may have incorrectly attributed feelings of need for privacy on the part of birth parents. In the United States, increasing numbers of birth parents are returning to social agencies seeking information about the children they relinquished and wanting to update information about themselves (Pannor et al., 1978:330). This seems to be the case in Canada as well.

A large-scale American research project asked participants in adoption (i.e., birth parents, adoptees, and adoptive parents) to contact the researchers. Over 1000 letters were reported to have been received by 1978, with more coming in (ibid. p. 331). They were preponderantly from birth parents. One letter, which the researchers suggest is typical for many hundreds of others, reads as follows:

> After reading about your research in the newpapers, I realized that I could at least tell my story and hope that it would be of help to others.
>
> After two years of high school, at age 16, I found myself pregnant, young, inexperienced, and scared. Reality was kicking me in the stomach. My 17-year-old boyfriend had fantasies about marriage but was really more interested in his car.
>
> My parents eventually found out and sent me to a maternity home. I did a lot of lonely meditating during those eight months. My only companion was my baby inside. We cried together. I grew older by a hundred years. My parents said that keeping the baby would ruin my life. The social worker agreed. No one really thought about what it meant to me to give her up.
>
> Labor lasted six hours. I felt that someone was ripping my insides. My body, heart, and soul were no longer whole. As soon as she was out, they whisked her away. I was so shattered, I figured I had no right to even see her. The next morning I had papers poked under my nose. I was assured of a good home for the baby. That made me feel better.
>
> Today, at age 35, I look back at those memories, and tears well in my eyes. I am happily married, with two lovely children — John, who will be ten in January, and Sue, who just turned eight. I am a teacher and work with preschool children. I love children. I used to cry every time I saw a baby at someone's breast.
>
> I have since recovered my equilibrium, and the guilt is slowly disappearing, but the feeling of a child conceived in my body and given away will never disappear. The sorrow of a lost child, and the mother crying out at night is imprinted in my heart.
>
> I would be most happy if I could ever see my daughter. As far as demanding her back, I forfeited that right the morning I signed those papers. I hope she is happy with her adoptive family and wish them well. I am grateful to them for raising her. I would never want to harm them or interfere with their life in any way. I would like her to know, though, when she is an adult, that if she wishes to see me, she would be welcome. My husband knows about her and feels as I do. We plan to tell our children about her when they are older.[17]

Opening up the adoption record in some form or other remains a difficult and sensitive issue. Obviously, some adoptive children desperately want to know about and sometimes want to meet their birth parents. Some birth parents desperately want to know how their child is doing and sometimes would like to meet the child. Apparently many adoptive parents tend to feel threatened both by the desire of their adopted children to meet their birth parents as well as by the thought of an actual meeting. It seems that in this issue the age of the child is an important factor.

In an absolutely ideal society, it should be possible for a couple to adopt a child and for the child nevertheless to know both birth parents. In the less than ideal world in which we live, the notion that this might lead to conflicts about the raising of the child, and the possibility that the child might be caught in a cross fire, cannot be ignored. None of these objections, however, obtain once a child has reached adulthood. At a minimum, therefore, it would seem desirable to facilitate exchange of information via a third party about birth parents and their children, where desired by both parties, while the children are small, and to facilitate a meeting, where desired on both sides, when the children have reached adulthood.

Were it not that we, as a society, still seem to stigmatize adopted children as being less the children of their adoptive parents than biological children, and were it not for the stereotype that it is better for parents to have their "own" children and for children to be raised by their "own" parents, one would expect that the conflicts would be less severe.

The benefits of a more open exchange of information could be very considerable. For instance, medical information that was not collected — because nobody thought of doing so — before the child was placed in adoption may become important while a child grows up.

Perhaps the increasing number of divorces which result in such large numbers of children who are *visibly* rather than invisibly (as in the case of artificial donor insemination and adoption) growing up in a situation in which there is some incongruence between the procreative and spousal dimensions for their parents will help to further desensitize the issue of adopted children. Adopted children may cease being considered second-class children; their parents may cease being considered second-class parents; and birth parents may be spared the pain of being denied all knowledge about the well-being of their children. Finally, it could mean that adopted children would not be denied basic knowledge of themselves or later find themselves at the mercy of bureaucracies that decide whether or not adults are fit to learn some of the most fundamental and personal information about themselves.

Remarriage Families

The number of marriages which involve at least one previously married partner has been constantly rising during the last ten years. In 1980, 26.5 percent of all marriages involved a previously married partner. The single most important factor responsible for this trend is the in-

TABLE 7.7

Marital Status of Brides, by Marital Status of Grooms, Canada, 1967–1980

Year		Marital Status: single bride/ single groom	single bride/ widowed groom	single bride/ divorced groom	widowed bride/ single groom	widowed bride/ widowed groom	widowed bride/ divorced groom	divorced bride/ single groom	divorced bride/ widowed groom	divorced bride/ divorced groom	TOTAL MARRIAGES
1967	#	145,462	1,800	4,226	2,499	3,720	1,028	3,922	725	2,497	165,879
	%	87.7	1.1	2.5	1.5	2.2	0.6	2.4	0.4	1.5	99.9
1968	#	150,633	1,758	4,392	2,586	3,865	1,021	4,090	729	2,692	171,766
	%	87.7	1.0	2.6	1.5	2.3	0.6	2.4	0.4	1.6	100.0
1969	#	154,689	1,732	6,269	2,330	3,900	1,631	5,834	1,196	4,602	182,183
	%	84.9	1.0	3.4	1.3	2.1	0.9	3.2	0.7	2.5	100.0
1970	#	158,453	1,661	7,307	2,288	3,881	1,786	6,526	1,248	5,278	188,428
	%	89.0	0.9	3.8	1.2	2.1	0.9	3.5	0.7	2.8	99.9
1971	#	159,626	1,665	7,781	2,231	3,861	1,809	7,087	1,333	5,931	191,324
	%	83.4	0.9	4.1	1.2	2.0	0.9	3.7	0.7	3.1	100.0
1972	#	166,888	1,604	8,663	2,094	3,933	1,886	7,555	1,411	6,436	200,470
	%	83.2	0.8	4.3	1.0	2.0	0.9	3.8	0.7	3.2	99.9
1973	#	163,017	1,477	9,641	2,057	3,799	1,859	8,281	1,562	7,371	199,064
	%	81.9	0.7	4.8	1.0	1.9	0.9	4.2	0.8	3.7	99.9
1974	#	159,761	1,513	10,833	1,949	3,761	1,943	8,968	1,577	8,519	198,824
	%	80.4	0.8	5.4	1.0	1.9	1.0	4.5	0.8	4.3	100.1

Year											
1975	#	155,285	1,406	12,126	1,795	3,614	2,047	9,942	1,595	9,775	197,585
	%	78.6	0.7	6.1	0.9	1.8	1.0	5.0	0.8	4.9	99.8
1976	#	143,746	1,276	12,390	1,815	3,343	1,968	10,118	1,615	10,573	186,844
	%	76.9	0.7	6.6	1.0	1.8	1.1	5.4	0.9	5.7	100.1
1977	#	142,594	1,269	12,991	1,646	3,324	1,965	10,666	1,618	11,271	187,334
	%	76.1	0.7	6.9	0.9	1.8	1.0	5.7	0.9	6.0	100.0
1978	#	139,269	1,141	13,606	1,555	3,128	1,893	11,060	1,657	12,214	185,523
	%	75.1	0.6	7.3	0.8	1.7	1.0	6.0	0.9	6.6	100.0
1979	#	139,502	1,127	14,353	1,480	3,087	1,770	11,749	1,646	13,097	187,811
	%	74.3	0.6	7.6	0.8	1.6	0.9	6.3	0.9	7.0	100.0
1980	#	140,409	1,116	15,393	1,377	3,004	1,777	12,352	1,768	13,873	191,069
	%	73.5	0.6	8.1	0.7	1.6	0.9	6.5	0.9	7.3	100.1

Sources: Statistics Canada, Catalogue 82-205, Vol. II, Marriages and Divorces, 1971, p. 81, t.13; for 1972, p. 81, t.13; for 1973, p. 69, t.13; for 1974, p. 24, t.9; for 1975, p. 25, t.8; for 1976, p. 25, t.9; for 1977, p. 25, t.9; for 1978, p. 8, t.5; for 1979, p. 8, t.5; for 1980, p. 8, t.5.

crease in divorce. While the marriages involving one single partner with one widowed partner and the marriages involving two widowed partners have actually decreased, all types of marriages involving at least one divorced partner have increased, as can be seen from Table 7.7.

Where there are children involved, remarriages will result in a further type of discrepancy between parental and spousal roles. This does not, however, add to the overall proportion of families in which there is some discrepancy between marital and parental roles, since prior to remarriage the discrepancy would already have existed, either in the form of a divorced or widowed family, or in the form of unmarried parenthood.

Remarriage as a large-scale phenomenon is, of course, quite recent, since it is premised on the increase in divorces which took place during the seventies. Consequently, as in the other cases, research on remarriage families is extremely scarce. Not only is research scarce, but indeed the phenomenon is so novel that we have not even developed a terminology to describe the various relationships that may come into existence because of a remarriage, particularly as far as children are concerned. The terms "stepmother" and "stepfather" were originally employed to denote the spouse of a widower or widow with children. In such a case, one natural parent of the children concerned is dead, and the other parent's spouse was commonly expected to play a parent role.

In the case of remarriages which involve children from previous unions, the children do have two living parents, but they usually share the residence of one of them — most often of the mother — for a large portion of the time and visit with the other parent. The fact of the existence of two parents therefore influences the relationship a parent's spouse may have with the children. Then, there are differences in possible relationships depending on whether the remarried parent has custody or not. We have not developed terms to describe the possible relationships which are: my wife's children of whom she has custody, my wife's children of whom she does not have custody, my husband's children of whom he has custody, and my husband's children of whom he does not have custody.

Seen from the perspective of children, familial relationships become even more complex. There are, at present, no commonly agreed upon terms to describe the parent's spouse who is not a biological parent of the child. The situation gets more complicated by considering the generation above and parallel to the child. Presuming that a child lives with his or her mother who has remarried, are the mother's huband's parents in a grandparental relationship to the child or not? If either the biological father or mother have other children with another partner, these children are the half-siblings of the child of the original union. But what about the children a mother's or father's spouse may have brought into the new marriage? Are they siblings or not? Are they siblings in cases in which the children live in the same household only? Or are they also siblings in cases in which the child goes and visits the non-custodial parent, his or her spouse, and the spouse's children as well?

The answers to these questions can only be given in an empirical context. If these people feel themselves to be family members, and if they behave in such a manner as if they were, then, in sociological terms, they are family members — siblings, grandparents, etc. However, to date we are largely ignorant of the most basic aspects of family organization in remarriage families (see Gross, 1981) although this type of family is increasing more rapidly than any other form.

There is some American evidence which shows that remarried people see themselves as being more happy in their second marriages than in their first (not surprisingly, since that marriage ended in divorce), but that also they see themselves as more happily married than other people they know (Albrecht, 1979). However, correlates of happiness and sources of conflict seem to be different in first and second marriages. For first marriages, respondents listed infidelity of the spouse, loss of love for each other, emotional problems, and financial problems as the four most important sources of conflicts, with the first two accounting for 55 percent of the first-listed reasons for marriage failure.

By contrast, they listed financial problems as of first importance in their remarriage, with emotional problems being second, sexual problems being third, and spouse's former marriage being fourth. This particular study also found that presence of children had a rather mixed impact on remarriages. Other literature suggests that children from a previous marriage tend to be a major source of problems for the remarriage (Schlesinger, 1976 and 1980; Messinger, 1976; Walker, Rogers and Messinger, 1977; Visher and Visher, 1978; Walker and Messinger, 1979).

There is too little research available to sort out the differential effect that remarriage has on the women, men, and children involved, especially as remarriages may vary greatly by previous marital experience as well as by the presence or absence of children of one or both marital partners as well as of the new partners. Table 7.7 lists eight different forms of remarriage (single bride with widowed groom, single bride with divorced groom, etc.). If we were to introduce children as a further differentiating factor, we would end up with the variations in family structure seen in Figure 7.1

Multiplying the parent-child relationship by previous marital status

FIGURE 7.1

Possible Child-Parent Relationships in Remarriage Families

	Husband's child(ren) of previous union		Wife's child(ren) of previous union		Husband's and Wife's Children
Type	Living with family	*Not* living with family	Living with family	*Not* living with family	Living with family
I	X				
II		X			
III			X		
IV				X	
V					X
VI	X		X		
VII	X			X	
VIII	X				X
IX		X	X		
X		X		X	
XI		X			X
XII			X		X
XIII				X	X
XIV	X		X		X
XV	X			X	X

of the husband and wife, we arrive at 8 × 15 types of families, that is, 120 different types of families. It must be noted that several simplifying assumptions were made to arrive at this number. For instance, we have treated husbands and wives as if there had been only *one* preceding marriage, although there may have been more than one. With respect to the children, the same assumption has been made. Lastly, it was assumed for the purpose of the figure that children either live with a parent or that they do not live with the parent. The situation is more complicated in reality, since in divorces in which there is more than one dependent child involved, *each* parent may have custody of at least one of them. Had we taken this possibility into account as well, the final number of possibilities would have been greater yet.

The point is, however, clear as it is: we know too little of remarriage families to know which of these differences in composition would make for what types of systematic differences. Clearly the topic is rather complex. Indeed, we do not know how many families would fall into each category. We must further take into consideration that in these families as in others there may be further discrepancies, such as adopted children, conceived through artificial insemination, and the like. Obviously, this is once more an area of family relationships which urgently requires research.

Conclusion

In this chapter, we have considered some of the major forms in which discrepancies between parental and spousal roles within one household may occur. The overview is not complete — for instance, children placed in foster care were not considered at all, primarily because this is meant to be a temporary solution (although such temporary solutions sometimes turn out to be quite lengthy).

In order to assess in how many households some form of discrepancy obtains, we are not only faced with the problem that for each type of discrepancy we usually had to make an estimate, but with the further problem that these estimates cannot simply be added together, since they may be mutually overlapping. For instance, a child born to an unmarried mother may be adopted. It is therefore with extreme caution that we must attempt to arrive at an overall estimate as to how many households experience *some* type of parental-spousal discrepancy, leaving out childless couples and widowed parents (e.g., simple types of discrepancies) altogether from our calculations.

Starting out with adoption, we estimated that about 15 percent of all households are involved in this type of discrepancy, either through parenting an adopted child, or through *not* parenting a biological child. This assumes that birth parents do not marry each other. Since this accounts only for children adopted before they reach the age of one year, the overall discrepancy was somewhat underestimated.

To this type of discrepancy we can add children born to unmarried mothers. In 1980, births to unmarried mothers accounted for 12.8 percent of all births. About 80 percent of these mothers kept their children; the others gave theirs up for adoption. This means that we can take 80 percent of 12.8 percent = 10.24 percent and multiply this by two to take into consideration the unmarried fathers who do not share a household with their children. This brings the total amount of discrepancies to 15 percent + 20.5 percent = 35.5 percent.

Approximately one third of all Canadian marriages end in divorce, and approximately 55 percent of them involve at least one dependent child. This means that approximately 18 percent of all families with dependent children go through a divorce.

Adding this estimate to the previous one, we arrive at a total 53.5 percent. In the latter calculation, there will have been some overestimation, due to the fact that some of the divorced families will have already been included in the first two types of discrepancies, and that some people divorce more than once. This overestimation, however, is offset by the fact that adoption was underestimated, that permanent separation and desertion of families with children, marital adultery resulting in offspring, artificial donor insemination, as well as widowed parents who remarry and children in foster care were ignored altogether. In addition, the number of discrepancies resulting from births to unmarried women is probably underestimated, since presumably 100 percent of the fathers (rather than 80 percent as assumed above) live in a separate household, away from their children.

Approximately half of all Canadian households, then, experience some form of parental-spousal discrepancy, either in the form of children living in a husband-wife family not being the biological children of one or both of the spouses, or of children living in one-parent households, or of an adult being a parent of a child who does not live in his or her household. It must be noted that as far as the adults are concerned, the discrepancies are much more likely to take place for the men than for the women. Women are more likely to have custody of their children after divorce, and more likely to form a one-parent household after the birth of a child outside of marriage.

A remarkable feature of the seventies is that during that decade we witnessed the birth of a new social movement with respect to the rights of adopted children to know their birth parents, as well as some public concern about artificial insemination by a donor and a public concern about unmarried mothers. One possible explanation for these developments is that due to the increase in divorce and the subsequent rise in remarriages there has been an increase in forms of parental-spousal discrepancies which are socially *visible*. This in turn makes it possible to discuss discrepancies which have so far been largely socially *invisible*, such as adoption and AID.

One of the effects of divorce and remarriage may be, in the long term, that we as a society, as well as researchers, may come to acknowledge the diversity of family relationships, and recognize that good parenting relationships may exist between children and adults who are not related by blood, while at the same time acknowledging that a blood tie does constitute a special type of relationship that might at least carry with it the right of the various participants to know each other.

Notes

1. Gay C. Kitson et al., "Divorcees and Widows: Similarities and Differences," *American Journal of Orthopsychiatry*, Vol. 5, No. 2 (1980):299.
2. If we compare the figures in Tables 7.2 and 7.3 we note that the total number of births to unmarried women is higher in Table 7.2 than in Table 7.3. This can be explained by the fact that for Table 7.2 all categories of unmarried mothers were counted together (namely, mothers who were single, widowed, or divorced when giving birth), while Table 7.3 only lists single (i.e., never married) mothers.

3. Such a situation might occur occasionally, but one would expect it to be statistically insignificant since presumably the partners would marry before the birth of the child if they were so inclined.
4. See Chapter 3 for some references on unwed fathers.
5. Unfortunately, no figures are given on these averages, so that the interpretation and evaluation of the statements made is very difficult. This detracts significantly from the overall value of the study.
6. It must be kept in mind that the two studies refer to different populations of women. The Lightman/Schlesinger study deals only with unmarried mothers, the Montreal study deals with women heading one-parent households; that is, women who may have come to this position via becoming unmarried mothers, or via divorce or (rarely) widowhood.
7. These ten hours of interaction include sitting at the same table while eating meals, which may or may not entail interaction between fathers and children.
8. Calculated from Table 7.4 by multiplying the average number of children by total divorces for each year.
9. U.S. Department of Commerce. From *Divorce, Child Custody and Child Support* in the Current Population Reports, P–23, No. 84. Washington: Bureau of the Census, Population Division, June 1979, p. 3.
10. "Divorce in Context: Its Impact on Children," from *Divorce and Separation: Context, Courses and Consequences* by Cynthia Longfellow, ed. George Levinger and Oliver C. Moles © 1979 reprinted by permission of Basic Books, Inc., p. 297.
11. From "*Children of Divorce*" by Teresa E. Levitin which appeared in *Journal of Social Issues*, vol. 35, No. 4, p. 14. © 1979 reprinted by permission of Journal of Social Issues and the author, emphasis added.
12. Thomas J. Espenshade, "The Economic Consequences of Divorce," *Journal of Marriage and the Family*, Vol. 41, No. 4 (1979):623.
13. Julien D. Payne, "Artificial Human Insemination," *Northern Ireland Legal Quarterly*, Vol. 12 (1958):254.
14. "Student offers to rent womb for school fees," *Toronto Star*, 1981 09 02, p. A3.
15. British Columbia, *Ninth Report: Artificial Insemination* (Vancouver: The Family and Children's Law Commission, 1975), p. 23.
16. Hepworth lists in his table adoptions as a percentage of children under five years of age. In order to decrease the cases in which a child is adopted by the spouse of a natural parent (which is more likely to be the case with older children) this has been ignored here.
17. "Birth Parents Who Relinquished Babies for Adoption Revisited." From *Family Process*, Volume 17, No. 3, by Reuben Pannor, Arthur D. Sorosky, Annette Baran reprinted by permission of *Family Process*, Inc., 1978, p. 332.

References

Albrecht, Stan L., "Correlates of Marital Happiness Among the Remarried," *Journal of Marriage and the Family*, Vol. 41, No. 4, 1979, pp. 857–867.

Arnold, Robert, Michael Wheeler, and Frances B. Pendrith, *Separation and After: A Research Report*. Ontario: Ministry of Community and Social Services, 1980.

Bachrach, Christine A., "Childlessness and Social Isolation Among the Elderly," *Journal of Marriage and the Family*, Vol. 42, 1980, pp. 627–637.

Boyd, Monica, "The Forgotten Minority: The Socioeconomic Status of Divorced and Seperated Women," in Patricia Marchak (ed.), *The Working Sexes*. Vancouver: Institute of Industrial Relations, University of British Columbia, 1977, pp. 46–71.

Boyd, Monica, Margrit Eichler, and John Hofley, "Family: Functions, Formation, and Fertility," in Gail C.A. Cook (ed.), *Opportunity for Choice*. Ottawa: Statistics Canada in Association with the C.D. Howe Research Institute, 1976, pp. 13–52.
Brandwein, Ruth A., Carol A. Brown, and Elizabeth Maury Fox, "Women and Children Last: The Social Situation of Divorced Mothers and Their Families," *Journal of Marriage and the Family*, Vol. 36, No. 3, 1974, pp. 498–514.
British Columbia. The Family and Children's Law Commission, *Ninth Report: Artificial Insemination*, Vancouver, 1975.
Brown, Prudence and Roger Manela, "Changing Family Roles: Women and Divorce," *Journal of Divorce*, Vol. 1, No. 4, 1978, pp. 315–360.
Canada. Dominion Bureau of Statistics, *Vital Statistics 1967* (9004–505). Ottawa: Queen's Printer, 1969.
Canada. Dominion Bureau of Statistics, *Vital Statistics 1968* (9004–505). Ottawa Queen's Printer, 1970.
Canada. Dominion Bureau of Statistics, *Vital Statistics 1969* (9004–505). Ottawa: Information Canada, 1972.
Canada. Statistics Canada, *Vital Statistics 1970* (9004–505). Ottawa: Information Canada, 1973.
Canada. Statistics Canada, *Estimates of Population by Marital Status, Age and Sex, Canada and Provinces, June 1, 1977 and 1978*, Catalogue 91–203. Ottawa: Minister of Supply and Services, 1980.
Canada. Statistics Canada, *Vital Statistics, Vol. I, Births 1973*, Catalogue 84–204. Ottawa: Information Canada, March 1975.
Canada. Statistics Canada, *Vital Statistics, Vol. I, Births 1974*, Catalogue 84–204. Ottawa: Ministry of Industry, Trade and Commerce, 1976.
Canada. Statistics Canada, *Vital Statistics, Vol. I, Births 1975 and 1976*, Catalogue 84–204. Ottawa: Ministry of Industry, Trade and Commerce, 1978.
Canada. Statistics Canada, *Vital Statistics, Vol. I, Births 1977*, Catalogue 84–204. Ottawa: Treasury Board, 1979.
Canada. Statistics Canada, *Vital Statistics, Vol. I, Births and Deaths 1978*, Catalogue 84–204. Ottawa: Minister of Supply and Services, 1980.
Canada. Statistics Canada, *Vital Statistics, Vol. I, Births and Deaths, 1979*. Ottawa: Minister of Supply and Services 1981.
Canada. Statistics Canada, *Vital Statistics, Vol. I, Births and Deaths, 1980*. Ottawa: Minister of Supply and Services, 1982.
Canada. Statistics Canada, *Vital Statistics, Vol. II, Marriage and Divorces 1977*, Catalogue 84–205. Ottawa: Information Canada, 1979.
Canada. Statistics Canada, *Vital Statistics, Vol. II, Marriages and Divorces 1978*, Catalogue 84–205. Ottawa: Minister of Supply and Services, 1980.
Canada. Statistics Canada, *Vital Statistics, Vol. II, Marriages and Divorces 1979*, Catalogue 84–205. Ottawa: Minister of Supply and Services, 1981.
Canada. Statistics Canada, *Vital Statistics, Vol. II, Marriages and Divorces 1980*, Catalogue 84–205. Ottawa: Minister of Supply and Services, 1982.
Caouette, Diane Boyer and Lisa Gosselin, *Les Enfants de la Famille Monoparentale Matricentrique* (unpublished thesis for M.P.s-Ed. at the Université de Montréal), 1979.
Chambers, Bette, "The Nobel Sperm Bank Revisited," *The Humanist*, Vol. 40, No. 5, 1980, pp. 27–30 + 56.
Chiriboga, David A. and Majda Thurnher, "Marital Lifestyles and Adjustment to Separation," *Journal of Divorce*, Vol. 3, No. 4, 1980, pp. 379–390.
Colletta, Nancy Donohue, "The Impact of Divorce: Father Absence or Poverty?" *Journal of Divorce*, Vol. 3, No. 1, 1979, pp. 27–35.
Dalby, Paul, "Nobel baby plan called 'worthless,'" *Sunday Star*, 1980 03 02, p. A2.

Deckert, Pamela and Régis Langelier, "The Late-Divorce Phenomenon: The Causes and Impact of Ending 20-Year-Old or Longer Marriages," *Journal of Divorce*, Vol. 1, No. 4, 1978, pp. 381–390.

Espenshade, Thomas J., "The Economic Consequences of Divorce," *Journal of Marriage and the Family*, Vol. 41, No. 4, 1979, pp. 615–625.

Fortin, Carole, Louise Dumais Charron, and Jean-Pierre Hotte, *Situation des Femmes Parents Uniques de la Region Metropolitaine de Montreal*, (unpublished thesis for a Master's degree in Psycho-Education), Université de Montréal, 1979.

Fulton, Julie A., "Parental Reports of Children's Post-Divorce Adjustment," *Journal of Social Issues*, Vol. 35, No. 4, 1979, pp. 126–139.

Gibson, Colin, "Childlessness and Marital Instability: A Re-Examination of the Evidence," *Journal of Biosocial Science*, Vol. 12, No. 2, 1980, pp. 121–132.

Glick, Paul C., "Children of Divorced Parents in Demographic Perspective," *Journal of Social Issues*, Vol. 35, No. 4, 1979, pp. 170–182.

Grindstaff, Carl F., "The Baby Bust: Changes in Fertility Patterns in Canada," *Canadian Studies in Population*, Vol. 2, 1975, pp. 15–22.

Gross, Penny, "Kinship Structure in the Remarriage Family," unpublished paper delivered at the Canadian Sociology and Anthropology Association Meeting, Halifax, 1981.

Hall, Sarah Moore, "An Illinois Woman Decides to Bear a Stranger's Child as Surrogate for his Infertile Wife," *People*, 1980 04 21, pp. 38, 41, 42.

Herold, Edward S. and Rita M. Benson, "Problems of Teaching Sex Education: A Survey of Ontario Secondary Schools," *The Family Coordinator*, April, 1979, pp. 199–203.

Herold, Edward S. and Marilyn Shirley Goodwin, "Why Adolescents Go to Birth-Control Clinics rather than to their Family Physicians," *Canadian Journal of Public Health*, Vol. 70, Sept./Oct. 1979, pp. 317–320.

Herold, Edward S. and Roger E. Thomas, "Sexual and Contraceptive Attitudes and Behaviour of High School and College Females," *Canadian Journal of Public Health*, Vol. 69, July/Aug. 1978, pp. 311–314.

Hess, Robert D. and Kathleen A. Camera, "Post-Divorce Family Relationships as Mediating Factors in the Consequences of Divorce for Children," *Journal of Social Issues*, Vol. 35, No. 4, 1979, pp. 79–96.

Hetherington, E. Mavis, "Divorce: A Child's Perspective," *American Psychologist*, Vol. 34, No. 10, 1979, pp. 851–858.

Hollobon, Joan, "Plan to mate genes of Nobel Prize Winners with very smart women is silly scientists say," *Globe and Mail*, 1980 03 07, p. 13.

Howarth, Edgar, "Birth Order, Family Structure and Personality Variables," *Journal of Personality Assessment*, Vol. 44, No. 3, 1980, pp. 299–301.

"Hundred 'super tots' a year is aim of sperm bank," *Sunday Star*, 1980 03 02, p. A2.

Jacobson, Doris S., "The Impact of Marital Separation/Divorce on Children: I. Parent-Child Separation and Child Adjustment," *Journal of Divorce*, Vol. 1, No. 4, 1978a, pp. 341–360.

Jacobson, Doris S., "The Impact of Marital Separation/Divorce on Children: II. Interparent Hostility and Child Adjustment," *Journal of Divorce*, Vol. 2, No. 1, 1978b, pp. 3–19.

Jacobson, Doris S., "The Impact of Marital Separation/Divorce on Children: III. Parent-Child Communication and Child Adjustment, and Regression Analysis of Findings from Overall Study," *Journal of Divorce*, Vol. 2, 1978c, pp. 175–195.

Kitson, Gay C. Helen Znaniecka Lopata, William M. Holmes, and Suzanne M. Meyering, "Divorcees and Widows: Similarities and Differences," *American Journal of Orthopsychiatry*, Vol. 50, No. 2, 1980, pp. 291–301.

Kulka, Richard A. and Helen Weingarten, "The Long Term Effects of Parental Divorce on Adult Adjustment," *Journal of Social Issues*, Vol. 35, No. 4, 1979, pp. 50–78.

Langelier, Régis and Pamela Deckert, "Divorce Counselling Guidelines for the Late Divorced Female," *Journal of Divorce*, Vol. 3, No. 4, 1980, pp. 403–411.

LaRossa, Ralph and Maureen Mulligan LaRossa, *Transition to Parenthood: How Infants Change Families* (Vol. 119 of the Sage Library of Social Research). Beverly Hills: Sage Publications, 1981.

Levitin, Teresa E., "Children of Divorce: An Introduction," *Journal of Social Issues*, Vol. 35, No. 4, 1979, pp. 1–25.

Lightman, Ernie S. and Benjamin Schlesinger, "Non-married Mothers in Maternity Homes," unpublished paper given at the American Orthopsychiatric Association Meeting, Toronto, 1980.

Longfellow, Cynthia, "Divorce in Context: Its Impact on Children," in George Levinger and Oliver C. Moles (eds.), *Divorce and Separation: Context, Causes and Consequences*. New York: Basic Books, 1979, pp. 287–306.

Lupri, Eugen and James Frideres, "The Quality of Marriage and the Passage of Time: Marital Satisfaction over the Family Life Cycle," *Canadian Journal of Sociology*, Vol. 6, No. 3, 1981, pp. 283–305.

Messinger, Lillian, "Remarriage between Divorced People with Children from Previous Marriages: A Proposal for Preparation for Remarriage," *Journal of Marriage and Family Counseling*, 1976, pp. 193–200.

Newcomb, Paul R., "Cohabitation in America: An Assessment of Consequences," *Journal of Marriage and the Family*, Vol. 41, No. 3, 1979, pp. 597–603.

"No test-tube geniuses, please!" *Toronto Star*, 1980 03 01, p. B2.

Orr, Fay, "Sperm donated mainly for money," *Globe and Mail*, 1981 04 24, p. 15.

Pannor, Reuben, Annette Baran, and Arthur D. Sorosky, "Birth Parents Who Relinquished Babies for Adoption Revisited," *Family Process*, Vol. 17, No. 3, 1978, pp. 329–337.

Payne, Julien D., "Artificial Human Insemination," *Northern Ireland Legal Quarterly*, Vol. 12, 1958, pp. 252–265.

Pfuhl, Erdwin H., Jr., "The Unwed Father: A 'Non-Deviant' Rule Breaker," *The Sociological Quarterly*, Vol. 19, 1978, pp. 113–128.

Reed, Christopher, "'Turkey-baster babies' kept secret in lesbian world," *Globe and Mail*, 1980 08 09, pp. 11.

Reed, Christopher, "U.S. is caught unprepared for surrogate motherhood," *Globe and Mail*, 1981 06 24, p. 13.

Renne, Karen S., "Correlates of Dissatisfaction in Marriage," *Journal of Marriage and the Family*, Vol. 32, No. 1, 1970, pp. 54–67.

Renne, Karen S., "Childlessness, Health and Marital Satisfaction," *Social Biology*, Vol. 23, No. 3, 1976, pp. 183–197.

Report of the Committee on the Operation of the Abortion Law. Ottawa: Minister of Supply and Services, 1977.

Rioux, Jacques E. and C.D.F. Ackman, "Artificial Insemination and Sperm Banks: The Canadian Experience," in George David and Wendel S. Price (eds.), *Human Artificial Insemination and Semen Preservation*, Plenum Publ. Corp., 1980, pp. 31-34.

Schlesinger, Benjamin, "Children in Reconstituted Families," *Stepparent Forum*, Sept./Oct. 1976, pp. 4–6 and Nov./Dec. 1976, p. 6.

Schlesinger, Benjamin, "One Parent Families and their Children in Canadian Society," in *The Family and the Socialization of Children*, Report of the October 1979 Workshop directed by David Radcliffe and Spencer Hall under the sponsorship of SSHRC. Ottawa: The Social Sciences and Humanities Research Council of Canada, 1980, pp. 82–114.

Schlesinger, Benjamin (ed.), *One in Ten: The Single Parent in Canada*. Toronto: University of Toronto Guidance Centre, 1979.

Sorosky, Arthur D., Annette Baran, and Reuben Pannor, *The Adoption Triangle: The Effects of the Sealed Record on Adoptees, Birth Parents and Adoptive Parents*. Garden City, NY: Anchor Books, 1979.

"Sperm Bank using mails, lawyer says," *Globe and Mail*, 1980 09 23, p. 2.

"Sperm bank's founder denies racial goal," *Globe and Mail*, 1980 03 03, p. 14.

"Student offers to rent womb for school fees," *Toronto Star*, 1981 09 02, p. A3.

"Surrogate mom wins custody," *Toronto Star*, 1981 06 06, p. A15.

Tesher, Ellie, "Surrogate baby won by parents," *Toronto Star*, 1982 09 01, pp. A1 and A4.

"Thousands of babies owe life to lab," *Toronto Star*, 1978 10 09, p. C1.

U.S. Department of Commerce, Bureau of the Census, *Divorce, Child Custody and Child Support* (Current Population Reports. Special Studies Series, P–23, No. 84). Washington: Bureau of the Census, Population Division, June 1979.

Vachon, M.L.S., "The Importance of Social Relationships and Social Support in Widowhood," unpublished paper presented at the Canadian Sociology and Anthropology Meeting, Halifax, 1981.

Veevers, Jean E., "The Parenthood Prescription," *Alternatives: Perspectives on Society and Environment*, Vol. 3, 1974, pp. 32–37.

Veevers, Jean E., "Voluntary Childlessness: A Review of Issues and Evidence," *Marriage and Family Review*, Vol. 2, No. 2, 1979, pp. 1 + 3–26.

Veevers, Jean E., *Childless by Choice*. Toronto: Butterworths, 1980.

Visher, Emily B. and John Visher, "Common Problems of Stepparents and their Spouses," *American Journal of Orthopsychiatry*, Vol. 48, No. 2, 1978, pp. 252–262.

Walker, Kenneth N. and Lillian Messinger, "Remarriage after Divorce: Dissolution and Reconstruction of Family Boundaries," *Family Process*, Vol. 18, No. 2, 1979, pp. 185–192.

Walker, Kenneth N., Joy Rogers, and Lillian Messinger, "Remarriage after Divorce: A Review," *Social Casework*, Vol. 58, No. 5, 1977, pp. 276–282.

Wallerstein, Judith S. and Joan B. Kelly, "The Effects of Parental Divorce: Experiences of the Child in Later Latency," in Arlene S. Skolnik and Jerome H. Skolnik (eds.), *Family in Transition: Rethinking Marriage, Sexuality, Child Rearing, and Family Organization*. Toronto: Little, Brown and Co., 2nd ed., 1977, pp. 412–427.

Wallerstein, Judith S. and Joan B. Kelly, "Children and Divorce: A Review," *Social Work*, Vol. 24, No. 6, 1979, pp. 468–475.

Weiss, Robert S., "Growing Up a Little Faster: The Experience of Growing Up in a Single Parent Household," *Journal of Social Issues*, Vol. 35, No. 4, 1979, pp. 97–111.

CHAPTER 8

Changing Patterns in Childcare

Introduction

There are some inherent difficulties in trying to compare childhood and parenting patterns over time, due partially to the fact that every generation raises its children only once. Involvement with one's grandchildren, or with other people's children is a substantially different matter from raising one's own children. Any differences that people observe with respect to childcare practices, for instance, are therefore hard to interpret. To address the issue of changes in childcare patterns we must therefore orient ourselves towards changes in the social environment within which children are being raised.

Looking at the overall situation, we can note several important factors which in their totality constitute a situation with respect to childcare that is substantially different from that of only twenty or thirty years ago. For one, fertility has decreased substantially. Then, an ever-increasing number of mothers of pre-school and school-age children are actively participating in the labour force, resulting in a pattern of shared childcare. As we saw in Chapter 7, births to unmarried mothers and divorce rates have increased dramatically, resulting in more children who, at some point in their lives, form part of a one-parent household. Due to the increase in divorces, there is a concomitant increase in the proportion of remarriages, resulting in a new and complex pattern with respect to childcare. The costs of raising a child to adulthood are very high, although cost comparisons with earlier times are difficult to make and may not be very meaningful. And finally, the mass media, and particularly television, must be seen as a most potent force which has become increasingly important in the socialization of children.

Of all these patterns, the increased labour force participation of mothers is perhaps the most important one, although all of the factors mentioned are clearly important. In the following we will consider the nature and effects of some of these changes.

Decreased Fertility

Overall, we can note that since the early sixties fertility in Canada has declined steadily (see Table 2.2). Such a decline in fertility can come about in various ways. One possibility is that fewer women choose to have children at all, or that those women who do have children have, on average, fewer of them.[1] ". . . more young couples seem to be choosing to remain childless, and those *with* children are having smaller families" (Wargon, 1979:15). The net effect of fewer children per mother as well as of closer spacing of children is that the child-bearing period for women has been compressed. For children this means that a smaller proportion of them are growing up with many siblings, and a larger proportion of them with no, one, or two siblings.

There seem to be a lot of negative stereotypes attached to the notion of an only child. A recent American survey of the literature *cum* research project suggests that such stereotypes may be misplaced. The literature suggests that, overall, only children have higher I.Q.s, a larger vocabulary, and better verbal skills than children from multi-children families. Not surprisingly, only children tend to be successful students, and in addition they tend to be self-confident and resourceful. "In general, from preschool through adulthood only children display more self-reliance and self-confidence than their peers with siblings" (Hawke and Knox, 1978:216). They are consistently the most popular group among elementary students, possibly because they have more time, energy, and need to invest in friendship, not having siblings at home. However, most of the studies which came to these conclusions did not control for socio-economic factors, and since a disproportionate number of only children are found in middle- and upper-class families, maybe one should restrict the conclusions to mean that results mentioned are likely to be found in only children of a middle or upper class background (ibid.).

As far as parents are concerned, "Having one child is . . . related to increased personal and marital happiness when compared to having several" (Hawke and Knox, 1978:216). There is more time available for both the parents and the child, since one child makes less work. As a unit, the family has more money at its disposal than a comparable family with more children, for the simple reason that one child costs about half of what two children cost. In addition, decision-making tends to be more democratic than in a multi-child family.

"The disadvantage most plaguing to parents of only children is the tightrope they must walk between healthy attention and over-indulgence" (Hawke and Knox, 1978:218). Another potential problem concerns a two-against-one situation which can emerge in single child families. If these findings were to be replicated for Canada, one could hypothesize that an increasing number and proportion of families with only one child would in general constitute a positive rather than a negative phenomenon.

On the other hand, if more financial assistance and social services were available to families on the basis of the number of children they had, the situation might be substantially altered. Another consideration is whether only children are growing up in one-parent or in two-parent households. In 1971 and 1976, proportions of husband-wife families with one child at home were much lower than for one-parent households (Wargon, 1979:42).

Overall, Canada is moving towards the two-child family as the modal family. What effect this has on children's development as well as on their parents is an unanswered question. There can be, however, no doubt that the experience of growing up with one sibling must be substantially different from the experience of growing up with many siblings. Children are important socializing agents for each other. It is likely that age homogeneity will be increased where there are fewer siblings (see Chapter 2). The fewer people there are in a family, the fewer people with whom one is likely to share a household. This reduces the likelihood of crowding, and suggests that there is probably more money and material goods available than there would be if the same family had more children. One could also hypothesize that the fewer members there are in the family, the more intense the relationships are likely to be, for better or worse.

Implications of the number of siblings one has carry on over one's lifetime and into the next generation. A child of an only child will have no uncles or aunts from that parent's side, and consequently no cousins. An adult who was an only child will have no direct nephews and nieces. If more and more people are born into smaller families, this will eventually result in a contraction of blood relative networks. On the other hand, as more and more families are involved in divorce, this may result in the acquisition of potential kin by second marriage.

On the whole, the implications of declining fertility for families are largely unexplored, but obviously extremely important since they are very far reaching.

Labour Force Participation of Mothers

Until recently, there was a strong correlation between labour force participation of women and decreased fertility. Women in the labour force were more likely to have no or fewer children than women who were full-time housewives (Boyd, Eichler and Hofley, 1976:41–44).

It seems that this traditionally strong correlation has recently been

Myth

substantially weakened. Until about the mid-seventies, fertility continued to decline, and the involvement of women in the labour market continued to increase. However, in the mid-seventies the decline in fertility levelled off, while the labour force participation of women continued to rise.

Between 1971 and 1976, the participation rate of women with children at home increased, in absolute as well as in relative terms, more rapidly than the labour force participation rate of those women who had no children at home.

> More importantly, the participation rate of wives with children under six years old increased at least as much in absolute terms and significantly more in relative terms, than the rates of women whose children were all aged six or over.[2]

This same study concludes that there is no reason why the labour force involvement of mothers would not continue to increase. ". . . it would be invalid to project a flattening out of the labour force participation rate of women in the childbearing age groups, solely because the fertility rate is not expected to decline significantly in the future" (Ciuriak and Sims, 1980:20–21).

The implications of this trend for childrearing are extremely important. In the sixties, the "typical" woman married and continued working in the labour market until she started her family, at which time she dropped out of the labour market to care for her children. When the last child entered school, increasing numbers of women went back into the labour market (Ostry, 1968:19).

The newly emergent pattern seems to be that increasing numbers of mothers continue to remain in the labour force even after the birth of their first child. As has been suggested, the labour force participation of mothers has been increasing rapidly. In 1976, about 33 percent of all children under six years of age in husband-wife families had both parents in the labour force, about 43 percent of the children aged 6 to 14 had both parents in the labour force, and about 47 percent of all children aged 15 to 17 years had both parents in the labour force, as Table 8.1 shows.[3]

As can also be seen from Table 8.1, the increase in mothers' labour force participation has not been matched by a concomitant decrease in fathers' labour force participation. In other words, the fathers will not be able to pick up the slack with respect to childcare when the mothers enter the labour force.

More recent Canadian figures suggest that the increase in mothers' labour force participation was unabated between 1975 and 1981 (see Table 8.2), such that in 1981 about 54 percent of mothers with children under the age of 16 were in the labour force.

TABLE 8.1

Children in Husband-Wife Families by Age Showing Labour Force Activity of Father by Labour Force Activity of Mother, Canada, 1976

	Under 6 years		6–14 years		15–17 years	
	#	%	#	%	#	%
Total Children	1,909,303	100	3,298,995	100	1,160,210	100
Father and Mother in labour force	636,245	33.3	1,426,455	43.2	540,450	46.6
Father only in labour force	1,142,110	59.8	1,609,685	48.8	511,910	44.1
Mother only in labour force	17,835	0.9	41,160	1.2	19,695	1.7

Computed from unpublished Statistics Canada data from 1976 Census.

TABLE 8.2

Labour Force Participation Rates of Women by Presence of Children, Canada, 1975 and 1981

	Participation Rates	
Women	**1975**	**1981**
with preschool age children (age 0–5)	34.7	47.2
with school-age children only (age 6–15)	48.0	60.8
with children under age 16	41.4	54.1

Source: Statistics Canada Labour Force Survey Research Paper #31, 1982, p. 11.

We are witnessing the birth of a new pattern of mothering: one in which the mother can no longer be assumed to be a full-time caregiver even when her children are very small. To what degree this has led to a different pattern of fathering is unclear. The implications of this change are truly enormous, and, considering their importance, have to date not received the attention they deserve.

It is clear that we can no longer regard a childcare pattern in which the children are cared for by their mothers until they start public school, or one in which mothers are at home to feed their children during lunch break and to greet them when they come home from school as *the* pattern of childrearing in Canada. Instead, the *majority* of Canadian children will experience some form of shared childcare during substantial portions of their waking time.

Shared Childcare Patterns

Incidence

In February 1981, Statistics Canada conducted its first national survey on childcare arrangements. This survey provides us with the first set of comprehensive figures on this issue. Overall in 1981, 47.8 percent of all preschool children (age 0 to 5) were cared for exclusively by their parents, while 52.2 percent were cared for in some shared childcare arrangement, including 22.3 percent in nursery schools or kindergartens, 5.8 percent in day care centres, 18.6 percent in their own homes by somebody other than a parent, and 18.6 percent in another private home (computed from Statistics Canada, 1982, p. 16, t. 1. Shared arrangement figures add up to more than 52.2 percent, since children may experience more than one type of shared childcare arrangement).

The figures are a bit more difficult to interpret for school-age children, since the survey groups all of them together (i.e., age 6 to 14). In fact, there is, of course, a great difference in the type of care needed by a six-, seven-, or eight-year-old as compared to the needs of a thirteen- or fourteen-year-old child. The Statistics Canada survey tells us that of the children aged 6 to 14 only 43.9 percent have lunch at home, and that the majority (52.6 percent) eat lunch at school while the rest are cared for elsewhere during lunchtime. However, the majority of school-age children, namely 70.9 percent, are looked after by one of their parents in their own home after school, while 16.1 percent look after themselves and the rest are cared for in a variety of ways (computed from Statistics Canada, 1982, p. 16, t. 1). We would require a more refined age breakdown than the one provided in order to make much sense out of this information, since we cannot equate a six-year-old looking after himself or herself with a fourteen-year-old doing so.

While the figures for the school-age children are thus somewhat confusing, nevertheless one fact emerges very clearly: by now, the *majority* of preschool children experience some form of shared childcare, as do the majority of school-age children, at least during lunchtime.

In other words, it is at present the normal pattern rather than the exception that a child is taken care of by somebody other than the mother during significant periods of his or her waking time. The obvious question which now arises is: who is looking after these children and in what setting?

Types of Childcare Used

When we think of childcare, we tend to think of day care centres. In fact, only a small minority of children who experience shared care attend day care centres. A national estimate for 1979 suggests that 4.0008 percent of infants under the age of two whose mothers were in the labour force attended a day care centre, and that 15.46 percent of children aged 2 to 6 whose mothers were in the labour force attended a day care centre. Put together, this suggests that an estimated 10.57 percent of children up to age 6 with mothers in the labour force attended a childcare centre in 1979 (National Day Care Information Centre, 1980:6--7). Since, as we have seen, children need care for reasons other than the mother's employment, (cf. Lightman and Johnson, 1977:12 for a sample of Toronto mothers in 1976, and Davis and Solomon, 1980:489 for some American figures) this means that actually less than 10 percent of children under the age of six who experience some form of shared care attended day care centres. This estimate is confirmed by a recent Metropolitan Toronto study which estimated that in 1979 6.8 percent of children up to 9 years of age were in some type of licensed day care in Metropolitan Toronto[4] (Metropolitan Toronto:1980).

The numbers are even lower when we express them as percentages of the total child population of a given age rather than of children with mothers in the labour force. Overall, in 1982, only 3.5 percent of all children aged 0 to 9 years were in day care centres (see Table 8.3).

One problem with the various figures which can be obtained is that they tend to refer to different age groups, so that we are left with percentages referring to children 0 to 5 years of age, or 0 to 9 years of age, or 6 to 14 years of age, etc. When trying to reach an overall estimate, it is important to keep in mind that the ages referred to shift from one set of figures to the next. Another problem in interpreting the available scarce information is that probably most children will experience a succession of different arrangements during the years in which they need constant care and supervision.

Overall, it seems that care in licensed day care centres is an important type of shared care pattern for a relatively small minority of parents and children, and that the majority of children are looked after in unlicensed, privately organized types of arrangements. We will look briefly at both forms of shared childcare.

Shared Childcare in Licensed Centres

Although licensed day care centres are utilized at present only by a small minority of parents, they would seem to constitute the preferred

TABLE 8.3

Interprovincial Comparison of Day Care Spaces and Need for Day Care Spaces, 1982

Province	No. of Spaces	% of total Canadian day care spaces	% of total Cdn. child population 0–9 years	% of prov. child pop. accom. in day care
B.C.	13,268*	10.5%	10.7%	3.5%
Alberta	22,186	17.6%	10.2%	6.1%
Sask.	3,065	2.4%	4.5%	1.9%
Manitoba	7,864	6.2%	4.4%	5.0%
Ontario	47,416	37.7%	34.0%	3.9%
Quebec	24,281	19.3%	25.7%	2.7%
N.B.	2,355	1.9%	3.1%	2.1%
N.S.	4,015	3.2%	3.6%	3.2%
P.E.I.	465	.4%	.5%	2.3%
Nfld.	533	.4%	3.0%	.5%
Yukon	382	.3%	.1%	9.4%
NWT.	0**	0.0%	.3%	0.0%
Canada	125,830	100.0%	100.0%	3.5%

Child population figures are for June 1st, 1981 from Statistics Canada 1981 Census. All calculations by the authors.

*1980 figure for spaces in B.C.; 1982 figures not available at publishing date.

**There are no licensed regulated daycare spaces in the North West Territories. There are, however, some subsidized spaces.

Source: Day Care Research Group, "The Day Care Kit," Toronto, 1982, p. 6, t. 5.

type of care for perhaps half the parents who need some type of childcare. In the Toronto study of 1976, parents were asked "Supposing you needed child care and you could have exactly the kind of care for your child or babysitting arrangement you wanted. What would your ideal daycare arrangement be?" By far the most frequently chosen option was a day care centre. Of all the respondents, 48.8 percent indicated that as far as they were concerned, this was the ideal arrangement (Johnson, 1977:224). In reality, only 13.9 percent of them used a full-time day care centre or school (Lightman and Johnson, 1977:19, t. 7). A recent study which conducted a telephone interview with a random sample of Saskatchewan families with children under 13 years of age found that day care centres, which in this case included private nurseries, lunch, and after-school programmes, was chosen as the preferred type of shared childcare arrangement by 39 percent of all respondents (Day Care Need Study, 1979:28). In fact, only 6.2 percent used a day care centre, and .9 percent a private nursery school (Day Care Need Study, 1979:20, t. 12).

It must be noted that in this particular study, older children were included for whom the parents might prefer arrangements other than day care centres. In addition, the respondents had the alternative of answering "Mother should care for children," which was chosen by 12 percent of the respondents, irrespective of whether or not this was a viable option. In order to assess the discrepancy between demand for day care and its availability, another summary of the same study calculated the estimated total number of children in the province for whom day care centres would be the preferred form of care versus the availability of such places. The discrepancy is rather staggering. The estimate arrived at 2921 children under nineteen months of age, 14 542 children 19 months to 5 years, and 18 733 children of school age for whom this type of care was desired on a full- or part-time basis. This compares to 2200 neighbourhood day care spaces actually available in the province, plus an additional 525 spaces in family day care homes (Saskatchewan Survey, 1980:10). In other words, there were 2725 spaces available for an estimated desired 36 196 spaces. This implies that about 92.8 percent of the needed and desired day care spaces were not available in Saskatchewan in 1980.

The Saskatchewan situation seems to be similar to the national situation which found that there were spaces in either day care centres or licensed family care for 12.04 percent of the children up to the age of 6 who had employed mothers (National Day Care Information Centre, 1980:5–7).

In spite of the fact that the majority of parents seem to prefer day care centres for their children, there are, of course, good centres and bad centres as far as the quality of care is concerned. Howard Clifford, the day care consultant for the federal Department of Health and Welfare has suggested that about 50 percent of all day care centres in Canada which are presently licensed should not be licensed and should, in fact, be closed because of poor quality (reported in the CSPCC Journal, Vol. 3, No. 1, 1980:5). The issue, then, is not just one of availability of day care centre spaces, but also of the quality of the existing centres. In this context it is interesting to look at the sponsorship of day care centres, described in Table 8.4.

It is interesting to note that between 1975 and 1979 the total number of day care spaces increased in Canada, although this was not a linear increase, since there was an actual decline in the number of available spaces in 1977 and 1978. Since the number of mothers in the labour force continued to rise in those years, the decrease in day care spaces is likely an effect of fluctuating funding which is quite unrelated to the need for day care spaces. It is even more interesting to note that the rise in available spaces that occurred between 1978 and 1979 is almost totally due to an increase in the number of spaces in commercial

TABLE 8.4

Sponsorship of Day Care Centres, 1975–1979, Canada

Type of Sponsorship	1975			1976			1977			1978			1979		
	Centres	Spaces	% of Spaces	Centres	Spaces	% of Spaces	Centres	Spaces	% of Spaces	Centres	Spaces	% of Spaces	Centres	Spaces	% of Spaces
Public	145	6 513	9.98	195	9 882	12.64	209	9 834	12.92	219	10 140	13.61	171	6 215	7.39
Community Board	708	22 405	34.32	839	31 087	39.78	822	30 783	40.44	877	28 349	38.04	900	33 119	39.39
Parent Co-op	155	5 677	8.69	112	3 293	4.21	121	4 443	5.84	110	3 638	4.88	107	3 200	3.81
Commercial	831	30 686	47.01	809	33 891	43.36	810	31 057	40.80	844	32 389	43.47	1 306	41 549	49.41
	1 839	65 281	100.00	1 955	78 153	99.99	1 962	76 117	100.00	2 050	74 516	100.00	2 484	*84 083	100.00

*Includes 5430 Centre spaces that serve Lunch and After School children.

Source: From *Status of Daycare in Canada 1979* (c) 1980 reprinted by permission of the Department of National Health and Welfare Canada, p.10, t. 4.

day care centres, and that spaces in public and parent co-op centres actually *decreased* between 1978 and 1979 while community board centre spaces increased. In 1980 and 1982, spaces in non-profit centres increased to 50 228 and 54 230, respectively, while spaces in commercial centres dropped to 39 515 in 1980 and increased to 43 164 in 1982 (Day Care Research Group, 1982, p. 6, t. 4).

The growth in commercial day care centres presents a somewhat disturbing trend. By definition, commercial centres are profit-oriented. They therefore try to keep expenses down, in order to maximize profits. Expenses involve staff salaries, facilities, equipment, food, and activity-related expenses for children. None of these is an item on which savings would be desirable if our criterion was the best interest of the children. This is not to say that all commercial centres are of a poor quality, or, for that matter, that all non-commercial centres are of a high quality. It remains, however, a troubling thought that decisions affecting the growth and development of children will be made increasingly in a profit-oriented manner rather than in a child-oriented manner.

Clifford has characterized the North American perspective on day care as that of a "Banana Republic:"

> . . . when a society is in the process of becoming monitized, there is a natural breakdown in historical perceptions. The banana republic model states that at one time, while energy was required to look after the bananas, to pick them, and to deliver them, they were considered free.
>
> However, when the process became monitized, someone had to be paid for doing each of these functions and the consumer was stunned at the cost of bananas, because before they had always been free. Likewise with day care, individuals have always spent a great amount of time and energy in nurturing children, and it only seemed free because the activity had not been monitized. Now it is, and it takes considerable readjustment to cope with this cultural reality. Of course we are being phased in rather gently. The average Canadian centre is open 10 hours a day at a cost of about $1 an hour. As day care completes the transformation process more fully from a "Banana Republic" to a monitized system, the adjustments in our perceptions will have to change even more.[5]

Another problem with Canada's approach to day care is the welfare orientation that is integrally tied to our day care system. Approximately half of all day care spaces in Canada are subsidized (National Day Care Information Centre, 1980:11). Subsidies, however, are tied to income, and the assessment procedure tends to be integrated with the welfare services. This results in a segregation of children on the basis of family composition and socio-economic status, particularly so since the subsidies are concentrated in non-profit centres. Approximately 95 percent of all the children in non-profit centres are subsidized (National Day Care Information Centre, 1980:11).

Clifford comments upon this issue as follows:

> Isn't it strange that, when our theoretical knowledge tells us that the strengthening of a person's self-concept is essential to a good prognosis, we insist that a family accept a self-definition of being a 'problem' before we will give a needed service? In families on average incomes three-quarters of the wife's earning would be expected to go to day care. As day care becomes more expensive, more and more families choose alternate care arrangements. Yet I walk through centres where almost 100 percent of the children are from one-parent families. I have observed children in the drama corner where they literally could not play the role of an adequate father.[6]

In spite of these problems, a *good* day care centre may provide optimal care for a child. There are many reasons why a child may benefit: (s)he has the opportunity to interact with other children which is particularly beneficial to children who would otherwise be socially isolated. Furniture, toys, equipment, etc. are geared towards children and not adults. Good centres teach a large variety of skills that can be highly beneficial for the development of a child. Many of the staff have a warm, loving nature and genuinely care for the children. The range of experiences of a child is likely to significantly expand through a centre experience.

However, day care centres should not be seen as the best possible solution for *all* children and for *all* families. Some children may not be physiologically and/or emotionally suited to be constantly together with a rather large number of other children. For some families with children at different ages, day care centres which only take children of particular ages may be unsuitable, because the organizational problems become too complex. And a continual problem exists in the case of illness. If centres accept sick children with a contagious illness, the other children as well as the staff are liable to catch the illness. Besides, sick children need different care than healthy children, and most centres are not equipped to handle sick children, who would in any case most likely be better off in their own homes. This last problem is a problem for almost all types of shared childcare, and requires a separate solution, such as rotating caregivers who will come into the houses of sick children and look after them until they are well again.

Overall, cost, location, and transportation, operating hours, programming, equipment, facilities, staffing, and the general atmosphere that prevails within individual centres will all combine to create more or less desirable environments for small children, and provide a better or poorer service to parents.

It is clear that the present availability of day care spaces does not even start to approximate the demand for them. Therefore, the majority of parents have to turn to other, informal, privately arranged, unlicensed and unsupervised types of care.

Shared Childcare in Private Arrangements

Besides licensed centres, there are a whole range of other types of childcare arrangements. Basically, they can be broken down along two axes: the child may be looked after in his or her own home or in the sitter's home, and the caregiver may be a relative or unrelated to the family. This gives us a fourfold category system of arrangements in which (a) the child is cared for in his/her own home by a relative, (b) the child is cared for in the relative's home by the relative, (c) the child is cared for in his/her own home by an unrelated sitter, and (d) the child is cared for by an unrelated sitter in the sitter's home. Of these arrangements, the latter two seem to be the most frequent ones (see Statistics Canada, 1982, p. 16, t. 1).

When a child is cared for in his or her own home by a relative it involves no daily break in the child's living pattern and may or may not be a very desirable type of care arrangement, depending on the relative who does the caring. The same applies to the third type of arrangement. These tend to be situations in which people in general see no need for licensing, for educating the caregiver, for investigating physical hazards for children, and the like.[7] These questions are raised primarily (if at all) in the context of the fourth alternative, care of an unrelated sitter in the sitter's home. Of the privately arranged types of care this is socially the most significant one, since it involves the largest number of children and families utilizing non-institutionalized forms of day care (see ibid.).

As has already been an unhappy refrain in this book, our information on the quality of care is extremely limited. The set of Toronto studies previously cited is relevant here, since it gives some empirical insight into the situation of children being taken care of in unlicensed informal babysitting arrangements as well as investigating the effects of such arrangements on the caregivers. Overall, the picture that emerges is not very encouraging. The care provided by sitters in their own homes seems often to be substandard in terms of nutrition, stimulation provided for the children, warmth, affection towards the children, the amount of television that children are permitted to watch, the stability of arrangements, and other factors (Johnson, 1978). This is not to deny that some of these arrangements may be extremely beneficial to the child and may show the opposite characteristics.

One of the important aspects of shared childcaring is that where there is more than one major caretaker there is room for disagreement between them. For the child this means that it is necessary to learn to adapt to more than one standard of behaviour, which may potentially be a very valuable skill. On the other hand, on some very basic issues it would seem desirable to have some consistency between the various caretakers. This may not always be the case, as the Toronto studies show. One area in which such disagreement seems particularly important is that of discipline.

When caregivers were asked whether or not there was agreement between themselves and the parents concerning discipline, the large majority (77.6 percent) reported that they believed their ideas about discipline to be generally similar to those of the child's parents, but 22.4 percent responded negatively. This is a rather substantial minority, encompassing almost a quarter of all caregivers. For those who reported a difference of opinion concerning discipline, 61.7 percent reported that they saw themselves as more strict than the parents. An *additional* 8.8 percent stated that while they used corporal punishment, the parents did not do so (Johnson, 1978:160–163). Since caregivers tend to be of a lower socio-economic status than parents whose children they look after (Li, 1978:19) we may here be dealing with the effects of differences in educational attainment of parents and caregivers.

When parents in the same study were asked about their satisfaction with respect to four characteristics of care provided by the caregivers, 85 percent of the parents declared themselves completely satisfied with respect to the reliability and dependability of caregivers, 74.2 percent were completely satisfied with the amount of affection and warmth the caregiver showed for the child, 60.6 percent declared themselves totally satisfied with the amount of time the caregiver spent playing with the child, and only 52 percent of the parents were completely satisfied with the caregivers' disciplinary techniques (Johnson, 1977:183, t. 5.9). This suggests that caregivers may have underestimated the amount of disagreement between themselves and the parents concerning discipline.[8] After all, 48 percent of the parents were *not* completely satisfied with the disciplinary techniques of the caregivers.

To move to another setting, in the Saskatchewan study cited, 63.1 percent considered the arrangements made for their children not to be what they would have preferred! The degree of dissatisfaction varied by the age of the child: of those parents with children under 19 months of age, 58.1 percent were dissatisfied with their arrangements, of those with children nineteen months to five years, 68.4 percent were dissatisfied, and of those with children 6 to 12 years, 58.3 percent were dissatisfied. In all age groupings, the largest number of dissatisfied users were found among those parents who used an "out of home sitter" (Day Care Need Survey, 1979).

In terms of overall agreement as to the important aspects of a childcare arrangement, some lesser discrepancies were found in the Toronto studies. In the study, both parents and caregivers were asked to rank five qualities of childcare arrangements in terms of their importance. The five qualities were affection (assuring an affectionate, loving environment for the child), safety (assuring the safety and health of the child), stimulation (assuring a stimulating environment for the child, and basic learning like colours, the alphabet, numbers, etc.), sociability (assuring that the child learns to get along well with other children and adults), and arrangement dependability (being dependable — the care is available when the parent needs it and it never breaks down).

Both caregivers and parents agreed that affection and safety ranked first and second, respectively, within a care arrangement. Parents ranked stimulation as next in importance; sociability was ranked fourth, and arrangement dependability last, while caregivers ranked sociability third, arrangement dependability fourth, and stimulation last (Li, 1978:81).

> The item on arrangement dependability shows the greatest proportion of disagreement. There are relatively more caregivers (44%) ranking this attribute higher than parents (34%). This may indicate a greater number of caregivers than parents consider child care as a custodial type of service for the parent, rather than as a service for the child in care. They thus tend to rank dependability — which essentially means convenience for the parent — as more important than the other attributes.
>
> The second largest proportion of disagreement is found regarding the stimulation factor. A considerably larger number of parents (52%) rank this item higher than do caregivers (19%). This reveals a marked distinction between the view of parents and that of caregivers of child care. Parents tend to regard child care arrangements as an educational experience for their children, whereas caregivers tend to assign this less importance, and instead, view child care arrangements as primarily a custodial service for parents.[9]

Not only is there substantial disagreement between parents and caregivers on the major functions of caregiving, but in addition "Both groups appear unaware of these discrepancies" (Li, 1978:100).

In spite of the disagreements as documented, one might argue that this is of relatively slight importance compared with the fact that most parents and caregivers seem to agree with the notion that all five items are of some importance. It would be highly interesting and important to go beyond the values as specified and examine the methods whereby parents and caregivers aim to realize them. It can be supposed, from the information on disciplinary techniques, that more differences in opinions and practices between parents and caregivers would emerge.

The greatest problem in this type of care arrangement is perhaps that the amounts of money which change hands for such an extremely important activity as looking after children is tiny. The average weekly payment received for caring for a child was found to be $23.04 in the Toronto study (Johnson, 1978:79). In 1981, the average weekly cost for care by a non-relative in a private home other than the child's was $28.68 for all of Canada (Statistics Canada, 1982, p. 20, t.7). Indeed, the Toronto study concluded, when taking into account the cost of caring for children in their homes, that if caregivers "were to do a realistic accounting of costs incurred in caregiving, many caregivers would show a net loss from caregiving" (Johnson, 1978:95). This judgement, however, ignores the fact that in most cases it will be the husbands who will bear the costs (via general household expenses) but the wife who will earn the income as a personal income. For the wives — whom we can assume to be housewives and therefore without any other source of income in the large majority of cases — it may therefore be worthwhile to engage in childcare for even very small amounts of money.

Some Implications of Contemporary Shared Childcare Arrangements

One currently popular theory on the historical development of families contends that in order to understand contemporary families, we must understand the movement to domesticity that characterized families in the past and current century and which involved the couple's almost complete withdrawal from routine community life and the corresponding strengthening of their ties to parents and close relatives — and to each other (Shorter, 1975).

> What really distinguishes the nuclear family — mother, father, and children — from other patterns of family life in Western society is a special sense of solidarity that separates the domestic unit from the surrounding community. Its members feel that they have much more in common with one another than they do with anyone else on the outside — that they enjoy a privileged emotional climate they must protect from outside intrusion, through privacy and isolation.[10]

With the large-scale entry of mothers into the labour force, we have clearly entered a new stage. While *couples* may be privatized in their social relations, when we look at the family from the perspective of children, there has been an opening up in quite an unparallelled manner in a direction which is opposite to any privatization trend. Children are given into the care of strangers for significant portions of time. This involves a double process of opening up: the family that releases the child for a part of the day thereby also exposes the child to different sets of rules and standards, to intimate insight into how other families function, and the entire family must cope with the results of the opening up process. When the child is taken into another home to be cared for, that family also is opening up to admit one more member on a regular, although timewise restricted basis into their family.

One must assume that the impact on the caregivers will also be considerable. In the Toronto study, it was found that 84 percent of the caregivers were married (Johnson, 1978:26, t. 2.1) and the majority of them (69.1 percent) had at least one child of fifteen years or under living with them (Johnson, 1978:28, t. 2.3). Since in the majority of cases the caregiving took place in the home of the caregiver, the presence of one or more small children must inevitably have some effects on other family members, and as we have just seen, in the vast majority of cases, there are other members, adults as well as children.

When asked "Does caregiving have any good effects on your family life?" 72.9 percent of the caregivers responded positively. Of these, 28.3 percent said that it provided company or a playmate for their own child(ren); 27.6 percent stated that they liked something specific about an arrangement or that they liked to be home with their own kids, for their husbands, etc., or that the family liked a particular child; 16 percent stated they they enjoyed caregiving, that it made them happy, or that they enjoyed having children around the home; 10.7 percent said that it provided company for them, something to fill the day (including helping to organize the family routine and scheduling), and the rest gave other reasons.

On the other hand, 17.8 percent of the caregivers answered affirmatively to the question "Does caregiving create problems in your family life?" Of these, 33.1 percent stated that caregiving interfered with family life (hours too long, restrictions on activities), 18.5 percent said that caregiving was a difficult job, 16.7 percent stated that caregiving imposed a strain on personal relationships with other adult members of the household, and 13 percent stated that the caregiver's child(ren) were jealous (Johnson, 1978:211–214).

We do not know how many of the children who experience childcare have siblings and how a pattern of shared childcare affects sibling relationships. If children are being taken care of in different settings, shared childcare could conceivably reduce sibling contacts, perhaps with an ensuing enriched ability of children to form friendship ties with non-siblings. Again, this is an open question. The sitters, finally, share their homes for prolonged periods of time with the children of strangers. When they have children themselves, these children may acquire a set of quasi-siblings through their mother's caregiving. There may be rivalries for toys, space, and attention, and there are the possibilities of friendships, sociability, and more attention because the mother concentrates on the children rather than on other tasks. Again, this is an area that needs systematic investigation.

Whether the consequences of caregiving are good or bad, it is reasonable to see caregiving as a modern form of de-privatization of the family (in a social rather than in an economic sense) which centres around a family's children. This coincides with a contemporary renewed interest in children's rights, child abuse, and particularly sexual abuse of children.

Historically, many children have always been abused, in Canada as well as in most other Western countries. Even today, teachers and parents have the right to use physical punishment as a means of discipline. The current concern about various forms of child abuse does therefore *not* mean that child abuse is on the increase; on the contrary, it signals a greater concern for children. There is no good way of assessing the actual numbers and proportions of abused children since registries provide, at best, knowledge about the tip of an iceberg. Since 1979 individuals in Ontario who in the course of their professional duties encounter instances of possible child abuse are required by law to report suspected abuse to a Children's Aid Society. Looking at child abuse statistics for that province (see Table 8.5), this law has not led to an increase in the proportion of cases registered. However, it signals that child abuse is no longer seen as a socially accepted behaviour, contrary to previous times.[11]

Similarly, in the late seventies there were some expressions of public interest in the problem of incest, as expressed in attempts to revise federal legislation on this point and in a number of publications, scholarly as well as more popular, on this issue (e.g., Finkelhor, 1979 and 1980; Forward and Buck, 1979; Nakashima and Zakus, 1977;

TABLE 8.5

Child Abuse Cases Reported to the Central Registry in Ontario, from all Sources (1966–1981)[a]

Year	Number of Cases	Year	Number of Cases
1966	225	1974	562
1967	380	1975	769
1968	269	1976	746
1969	370	1977	1045
1970	407	1978	1762
1971	422	1979	1186
1972	491	1980	506
1973	598	1981[b]	506

[a] Source: Unpublished records dept by the Central Register, as reported in Webster, 1981:8

[b] This statistic is only for the period from January 1st to October 31st, 1981.

Kempe, 1978; Rush, 1980; MacFarlane, 1978; Butler, 1978; Geiser, 1979; and Herman, 1981; an excellent overview of the recent major publications on this issue is contained in Bagley, forthcoming).

While it is not here suggested that childcare should either reduce child abuse or even lead to greater detection at an official level (sitters too may abuse children), I am suggesting that the move to have children cared for by strangers either in the stranger's home or in centres should be seen as part of an overall de-privatization of parent-child relations. Another contributing factor to this general trend is the rise in divorce rates and the ensuing custody battles, in which judges have to make decisions as to who receives custody and what type of visitation rights should be granted to the non-custodial parent. This involves a consideration of the parenting skills and efforts of parents, which in effect amounts to a public scrutiny of parenting practices. In the long run, this can be expected to have implications for parenting standards in general, even in the case where there is no disruption of marital ties or discrepancy between parental and spousal roles.

The Cost of Raising Children

In agrarian societies, children are usually economic assets, because they constitute cheap labour. In urban industrialized societies, children are usually economic liabilities, because looking after their well-being costs money. A recent Canadian estimate is that to raise a child on a modest budget to the age of 18 costs around $84 000, in 1981 dollars. This seems to be what it is billed as: a non-frills standard. The estimates are based on the assumption that the child is part of a family consisting of two adults and two children living in a rented home without a car and earning $20 000 a year. Table 8.6 provides a breakdown by item of expense.

A recent article written from a middle-class perspective puts the price tag at somewhere around $200 000 per child by comparison (Lilley, 1981). It is interesting to note that day care accounts for about 34 percent of the total costs in Table 8.6.

While parents do not, as a rule, see their children primarily in economic terms and as liabilities, costs are an important consideration, especially for low-income families. For instance, one matter that becomes clear when comparing Table 8.6 with Table 6.6 is that the amounts paid in social welfare across Canada are insufficient to meet basic living costs of families with children.

This is also the major problem with respect to the current increases in births to unmarried women and in divorce. The majority of female-headed families in Canada is poor (National Council of Welfare, 1976). Even in the best of cases, poverty tends to have devastating effects

TABLE 8.6

Cost of raising a child to age 18 (in 1981 dollars)

Age Grouping			Food	Clothing	Personal Care	Transport	School Needs	Receation	Housing	Household Items	Day Care (incl. B.S.)	Baby Sitting	TOTAL (with day care)	TOTAL (without day care)
Infant Costs			423	779					648	237	3,354		5,441	2,087
1 to 3	Average Per Year	BOY	709	172	45	6		72	648	237	4,050	550	5,939	2,439
		GIRL	709	185	45	6		72	648	237	4,050	550	5,952	2,452
4 to 6	Average Per Year	BOY	838	202	56	16	19	72	648	237	3,151	464	5,239	2,552
		GIRL	838	216	56	16	19	72	648	237	3,151	464	5,253	2,566
7 to 9	Average Per Year	BOY	998	259	60	19	56	203	684	237	2,454	292	4,970	2,808
		GIRL	998	304	60	19	56	203	684	237	2,454	292	5,015	2,853
10 to 12	Average Per Year	BOY	1,173	277	66	23	57	218	720	237	195	195	2,966	2,966
		GIRL	1,173	338	96	23	57	218	720	237	195	195	3,057	3,057
13 to 16	Average Per Year	BOY	1,388	349	78	161	84	274	720	237	—	—	3,291	3,291
		GIRL	1,219	466	169	161	84	274	720	237	—	—	3,330	3,330
15 to 18	Average Per Year	BOY	1,585	422	127	161	142	328	720	237	—	—	3,722	3,722
		GIRL	1,165	589	208	161	142	328	720	237	—	—	3,550	3,550
	TOTAL	BOY	20,496	5,823	1,296	1,156	1,073	3,500	13,068	4,503	32,904	4,502	83,819	55,417
	TOTAL	GIRL	18,729	7,073	1,903	1,156	1,073	3,500	13,068	4,503	32,904	4,502	83,909	55,607

Costs for day care include additional costs for babysitting. Total cost with daycare assumes a two-parent family with both parents working, whereas total cost without daycare assumes that one of the parents remains at home to help raise the family.

Source: Reprinted with permission — *The Toronto Star*, 1982 02 23, p. A6.

which are likely to last a lifetime. In 1976, one-quarter of all children in Canada were growing up in poverty (Canadian Council on Children and Youth, 1978:31).

If Canada as a society believes that every citizen deserves an equal opportunity to become a productive member of society, more resources will have to be made available to families with children.

We have so far looked at shared childcare which is primarily (although not exclusively) due to increased labour force participation of mothers and at costs involved in raising a child. One factor which is quite independent from these aspects but extremely important when discussing childcare patterns is the mass media. We will turn to this issue next.

Childcare and Television

The mass media exert a powerful influence on all members of our society, due to their pervasiveness and their effectiveness. Of all the mass media, TV is probably the most important one, and this section will therefore restrict itself to a short consideration of the effect of TV on childcare.

By and large, TV is universally accessible to children in Canada. In 1979, 98 percent of all Canadian households had at least one TV in their possession (Canada, 1979a, p. 30, t.29). Of course, the presence of a TV in a household is not enough to infer that children actually watch it. However, studies on the utilization of the mass media indicate that TV is watched regularly by the vast majority of Canadian children and that, indeed, TV watching is the number one leisure activity of Canadians in general (Canada, 1979b).

When discussing the effect of TV on childcare, at least three variables need to be considered: the amount that is watched, the content of what is watched, and the context within which TV is watched.

As far as the amount of TV children watch on average is concerned, it is truly enormous, as indicated in Table 8.7.

As can be seen, the average number of hours watched by children varies somewhat by age, sex, and language spoken in the home, but with the exception of 2- to 6-year-old boys of neither English nor French language background and of 2- to 6-year-old anglophone girls it is above twenty hours per week per child. The amount watched by school-age children is generally even higher than for pre-school children. TV must therefore be seen as an extraordinarily important factor in the lives of the children, and it is reasonable to suppose that it plays a considerable role in moulding the personalities and opinions of the children who watch it.

This leads us to the question of content. Overall, it seems unfor-

TABLE 8.7

Average number of hours of TV watching by Canadian children, age 2–17*

		Age	Average hours/week	Reach***	% reach
Males	English**	2–6	20.9	356,100	96
		7–11	20.8	823,400	98
		12–17	23.6	776,800	97
	French**	2–6	21.9	129,500	99
		7–11	23.4	271,600	97
		12–17	24.8	271,500	96
	Other**	2–6	15.3	22,000	100
		7–11	29.0	29,400	97
		12–17	23.7	40,800	98
Females	English**	2–6	19.8	315,300	99
		7–11	21.4	814,500	97
		12–17	22.7	903,400	97
	French**	2–6	21.4	116,200	96
		7–11	22.3	255,500	97
		12–17	25.4	287,400	96
	Other**	2–6	17.4	8,500	98
		7–11	29.1	28,000	98
		12–17	31.4	45,000	93

*Source: BBM Spring Survey 1978, computed from data dictated by John Gordon. Reprinted by permission of Statistics Canada.

**Language spoken at home.

***Reach = number of persons who watched at least 15 minutes during the week.

tunately fair to say that TV programmes in Canada are American-dominated, sexist, violent, and consumer-oriented.

As far as the origin of TV programmes watched by Canadian children is concerned, the majority of programmes are on Canadian rather than American channels (see Table 8.8).

However, due to the fact that many Canadian channels broadcast American programmes for a good portion of their time, Canadians view predominantly American-originated programming. Indeed, in 1976, 71.1 percent of all programming that was viewed in Canada on all English-language stations was of foreign origin, as was 35.2 percent of the programming on all French-language TV stations (Canada, 1979b:24, t.X). Since Canadians watch a fair number of American channels, it seems that the majority of programmes watched by Anglophone children and a minority of programmes watched by francophone children is of American origin.

With the exception of some educational channels, a thread of con-

TABLE 8.8

TV channels watched by Canadian children

			English/Canad. TV		French/Canad. TV		U.S. TV		All TV	
		Age	Aver. hours	% reach	Aver. hours	% reach	Aver. hours	% reach	Aver. hours	% reach
Males	English	2–6	13.5	96	1.7	6	10.6	66	20.9	96
		7–11	13.9	98	2.6	4	10.3	64	20.8	98
		12–17	15.9	97	2.5	4	11.4	64	23.6	97
	French	2–6	5.5	56	18.0	99	4.7	17	21.9	99
		7–11	5.0	50	20.0	97	4.4	22	23.4	97
		12–17	5.9	48	20.9	96	4.7	20	24.8	96
	Other	2–6	8.3	100	1.2	5	8.9	78	15.3	100
		7–11	16.9	97	5.5	13	14.1	79	29.0	97
		12–17	16.2	98	6.3	11	10.0	66	23.7	98
Females	English	2–6	14.6	96	2.0	3	8.8	55	19.8	99
		7–11	14.5	97	2.6	4	10.3	65	21.4	97
		12–17	15.6	97	2.9	1	10.7	64	22.7	97
	French	2–6	4.6	50	18.5	96	2.9	17	21.4	96
		7–11	5.4	46	18.9	97	4.5	18	22.3	97
		12–17	5.5	54	21.1	96	5.5	19	25.4	96
	Other	2–6	13.6	98	1.0	28	5.6	61	17.4	98
		7–11	14.5	98	10.1	7	15.6	87	29.1	98
		12–17	17.0	93	9.0	14	14.6	82	31.4	93

Source: BBM Spring Survey 1978. Reprinted by permission of Statistics Canada.

tinuing violence is the one predominant feature in TV programming (see Ontario, 1977). Programmes, especially advertising, are generally sexist (Courtney and Whipple, 1978) and due to the constant interruption of the majority of programmes for advertising purposes the message to consume various items is almost constantly reinforced (Wartella, 1979).

While there is a fair debate regarding the manner and the degree to which TV influences the development of children, it must certainly be seen as a major factor in their social environment, against which parents continually have to react. Since the values propounded by the majority of TV programmes are profoundly anti-social, one would assume that TV basically has a negative effect on the personality development of children — although this need not be the case where programming is of a good quality, where the amount watched is controlled in a reasonable manner, and where parents discuss with their children what they have seen.

A small study conducted by the Canadian Teachers' Federation (1980) suggests that children use what they see on television to learn, among other things, about sex roles and family roles. If the content were of a better quality, this might be a very good source of information. As things stand, this is quite deplorable.

Summary and Conclusions

Childcare has been greatly affected by the fact that more mothers than ever before are now in the labour force. This has resulted in a pattern of shared childcare which did not exist in this form and to this degree a generation ago. It is impossible to speculate on all the consequences of this change, since there has been little research that has looked at the various caring arrangements. From the evidence that exists, it is obvious that only a small minority of children are cared for in day care centres, although this seems to be the preferred type of care arrangement for at least half of the parents. Nor are all centres of the same quality, or even of a good quality.

In general, parents seem to be unhappy about the care arrangements they are able to find for their children. Legislation and social policy in this area are greatly behind the times, considering that more than half of all Canadian children spend a significant portion of their time in such care arrangements, and that more than half of all parents need this kind of service.

One obvious answer to the problem is that mothers go back into the home. This is not a feasible possibility, since many families could not afford to lose the mother's salary, and a significant minority of children are from one-parent households to begin with. But even if this were not the case, it would not be a possible solution to the problem, since it would coerce women into the home against their wishes and will. An unhappy mother at home is certainly not desirable for the children, and it would constitute an abrogation of a basic right of women, namely the right to a paying job. Even with the inferior care arrangements in existence today, we have not been able to demonstrate negative effects on children who are exposed to such arrangements, probably because in general it is beneficial for the mother's well-being to have a job, and this is likely to have a carry-over effect on the child(ren).

On the other hand, women's liberation should not be carried out on the backs of children, and rather than looking for the absence of negative effects of group care on children we should consider it a possibility to create positive environments for children. It seems that a comprehensive national policy for childcare is highly desirable and, indeed, necessary.

Such a national policy on childcare would have to consist of a mix of various policies which concern the parental behaviour of mothers as well as fathers along with such issues as the quality of group care arrangements and finances. Desirable components of such a national policy could include, for instance:

— a generous parental leave policy, which allowed fathers as well as mothers to care for infants, both those born to them or adopted.

— a financial assistance plan which would transfer money to every child. This is being done right now on a very modest scope with the family allowance. A vastly expanded family allowance programme, which starts approximating the real costs of childcare, would seem to be the ideal solution. In order to ensure progressivity, such an expanded family allowance plan would, of course, have to be fully taxable.

— if enough money were made available, group care arrangements of good quality and of different types could be expected to spring up. A variety of them, including small and big centres, licensed family care, drop-in centres, etc. should be encouraged and periodically inspected.

— employers could be required by law to provide a rotating homemaker service which would be available to employees with sick children (or other sick family members). Small employers could share the services of one agency.

— alternate work loads should be facilitated for parents, by guaranteeing fringe benefits on a pro-rated basis for part-time employees, by facilitating various types of part-time employment, for women as well as for men, and by counting part-time work for purposes of seniority.

Overall, we must start to rethink childcare as a responsibility which is shared between parents and the state, and support parents to the degree possible in the task of raising children.

Notes

1. Other factors, such as the number of women of childbearing age, may also contribute to changes in fertility, but in our context, these other factors are of less importance and are therefore ignored.
2. Dan Ciuriak and Harvey Sims, *Participation Rate and Labour Force Growth in Canada* (Ottawa: Department of Finance, 1980), p. 17.
3. It must be noted that the table does *not* represent the number and proportion of all children with both parents in the labour force, since it excludes children from one-parent households.
4. Metropolitan Toronto, Day Care Planning Task Force, *Future Directions for Day Care Services in Metro Toronto* (Toronto: Department of Social Services, 1980).
   It should be noted that none of the figures cited in this section are strictly comparable, for two reasons: the age brackets of children shift and the reference groups of parents shift. Sometimes the figures refer to children of all parents, sometimes to those of employed mothers, and sometimes to those parents who use some type of care arrangement.
5. Howard Clifford, "Day Care in Times of Economic Uncertainty — Part II — The Solution," *Rapport*, Vol. 3, No. 3 (November 1980):1.
6. Howard Clifford, "Changing Canadian Cultural Values and Their Relationship to Early Childhood Programs," paper given at the National Seminar on Early Childhood Services, Banff, 1975, p. 5.
7. This is, of course, a very serious fallacy. As Bégin (1981:2) has noted,

   > Accident rates for children and youth in Canada are higher than in most western countries. In 1974 Canada had the worst record of accidents among 18 countries in the 5–14 age group, and rated only slightly better in the 10–14 [should probably read: 1–4] age group. In 1978 there were 6,516 children aged 14 years and under who died in Canada. Of these, 1,420 or 22 percent died as a result of accidents, poisonings, and violence.
   >
   > Next to traffic accidents, the home is where most of fatal accidents occur with falls, burns, poison ingestion and crib deaths due to strangulation as the major causes. Most people are aware of the effectiveness of detergents, bleaches, birth control pills, insecticides, polishes, solvents, aspirins, disinfectants and hundreds of other common household items when they are used for their intended purpose. What they often forget is that drugs, medication, cleaners, petroleum products and even plants are potentially dangerous to young children.

   From notes for an address at the 1st National Conference on Childhood Accidents and Prevention, April 14, 1981 (c) 1981 reprinted by permission of Health and Welfare Canada.

8. It must be noted that the populations of parents in this report (Johnson, 1977) and the ones that "caretakers" are referring to in the previously cited report (Johnson, 1978) are not identical. In the previously cited report, only caretakers

who looked after children to whom they were not related were considered; in this report, all parents who use caregivers, including relatives, are included. Presumably, the level of disagreement might be different — probably higher — if only parents who utilized care by non-relatives had been considered.

9. From *Between Neighbours, Between Kin: A Study of Private Child Care Arrangements in Metropolitan Toronto* by Selina Li (Toronto: Social Planning Council, 1978), p. 82.
10. From *The Making of the Modern Family* by E. Shorter © 1975 reprinted by permission of Basic Books, Inc., p. 205.
11. Of the 506 cases reported for January to October of 1981, 235 were cases of sexual abuse. (Oral information supplied by Ontario Child Abuse Registry, reported in Lungen, 1981).

References

Bagley, Chris, "Childhood Sexuality and the Sexual Abuse of Children. A Review of the Monograph Literature 1978 to 1982," *Journal of Child Care*, Vol. 1, No. 3, forthcoming.

Bégin, Monique, "Notes for an Address at the 1st National Conference on Childhood Accidents and Prevention, April 14, 1981." Ottawa: Office of the Minister, Health and Welfare Canada, 1981.

Boyd, Monica, Margrit Eichler, and John R. Hofley, "Family: Functions, Formation and Fertility," in Gail C.A. Cook (ed.), *Opportunity for Choice. A Goal for Women in Canada*. Ottawa: Statistics Canada in association with the C.D. Howe Research Institute, 1976, pp. 13–52.

Butler, Sandra, *The Conspiracy of Silence: The Trauma of Incest*. San Francisco: New Glide Publications, 1980.

Canada. Statistics Canada, *Household Facilities and Equipment, May 1979*, Cat. 64–202. Ottawa: Minister of Supply and Services, 1979a.

Canada. Statistics Canada, *Culture Statistics. Radio and Television 1978*, Cat. 87–630. Ottawa: Minister of Supply and Services, 1979b.

Canada. Statistics Canada, Labour Force Survey Research Paper # 31, 1982.

Canadian Council of Children and Youth, *Admittance Restricted: The Child as Citizen in Canada*. Ottawa: Canadian Council of Children and Youth, 1978.

Canadian Teachers' Federation, *Survey of Students' Choice of Television Programs. Report*. Ottawa: Canadian Teachers' Federation, 1980.

Ciuriak, Dan and Harvey Sims, *Participation Rate and Labour Force Growth in Canada*. (Series of papers on medium- and long-term economic issues). Ottawa: Department of Finance, 1980.

Clifford, Howard, "Changing Canadian Cultural Values and Their Relationship to Early Childhood Programs." Paper given at the National Seminar on Early Childhood Services, Banff, 1975.

Clifford, Howard, "Day Care in Times of Economic Uncertainty — Part II — The Solution," *Rapport*, Vol. 3, No. 3, Nov. 1980, pp. 1, 7–9.

Courtney, Alice E. and Thomas W. Whipple, *Canadian Perspectives on Sex Stereotyping in Advertising*. Ottawa: Advisory Council on the Status of Women, 1978.

Davis, Joseph and Phyllis Solomon, "Day Care Needs among the Upper Middle Classes," *Child Welfare*, Vol. 59, No. 8, 1980, pp. 497–499.

Day Care Research Group, The Day Care Kit, Toronto, 1982.

"The Daycare Need Study — A Summary." Regina: Department of Social Services, Planning and Evaluation Branch, 1979.

Finkelhor, David, *Sexually Victimized Children*. New York: Free Press, 1979.

Finkelhor, David, "Psychological, Cultural and Family Factors in Incest and Family Sexual Abuse," In Joanne Valiant Cook and Roy Tyler Bowles (eds.), *Child Abuse. Commission and Omission*. Toronto: Butterworths, 1980, pp. 263–269.

Forward, Susan and Craig Buck, *Betrayal of Innocence. Incest and Its Devastation*. Harmondsworth: Penguin, 1979.

Geiser, R.L., *Hidden Victims. The Sexual Abuse of Children*. Boston: Beacon Press, 1979.

Hawke, Sharryl and David Knox, "The One-Child Family: A New Life-Style," *The Family Co-ordinator*, Vol. 27, No. 3, 1978, pp. 215–219.

Herman, Judith L., *Father-Daughter Incest*. Cambridge: Harvard University Press, 1981.

Johnson, Laura Climenko, *Who Cares? A Report of the Project Child Care. Survey of Parents and their Child Care Arrangements*. Toronto: Social Planning Council, 1977.

Johnson, Laura Climenko, *Taking Care. A Report of the Project Child Care. Survey of Caregivers in Metropolitan Toronto*. Toronto: Social Planning Council, 1978.

Kempe, C. Henry, "Sexual Abuse, Another Hidden Pediatric Problem: The 1977 C. Anderson Aldrich Lecture," *Pediatrics*, Vol. 62, No. 3, 1978, pp. 382–389.

Li, Selina, *Between Neighbours, Between Kin: A Study of Private Child Care Arrangements in Metropolitan Toronto*. Toronto: Social Planning Council, 1978.

Lightman, Ernie S. and Laura C. Johnson, *Child Care Patterns in Metropolitan Toronto*. (Project Child Care Working Paper #2). Toronto: Social Planning Council, 1977.

Lilley, Wayne, "The Bottom Line on Baby," *The Financial Post Magazine*, Oct. 1981, pp. 14 – 17 + 20.

Lungen, Adeena, "Father Daughter Incest: A Feminist Analysis." Unpublished seminar paper, O.I.S.E., 1981.

MacFarlane, Kee, "Sexual Abuse of Children," in Jane Roberts Chapman and Margaret Gates (eds.), *The Victimization of Women*. Beverly Hills: Sage Publications, 1978, pp. 81–110.

Metropolitan Toronto, Day Care Planning Task Force, *Future Directions for Day Care Services in Metro Toronto*. Toronto: Department of Social Services, 1980.

Nakashima, Ida I. and Gloria E. Zakus, "Incest: Review and Clinical Experience," *Pediatrics*, Vol. 60, No. 5, pp. 569–701.

National Council of Welfare, *One in a World of Two's*. A Report by the National Council of Welfare on One-Parent Families in Canada. Ottawa: National Council of Welfare, 1976.

National Day Care Information Centre, *Status of Day Care in Canada 1979. A Review of the Major Findings of the National Day Care Study 1979*. Ottawa: Minister of National Health and Welfare, 1980.

Ontario. Royal Commission on Violence in the Communications Industry, *Report*, Vol. 1, Approaches, Conclusions and Recommendations. Toronto, 1977.

Ontario. Women's Bureau, Ministry of Labour, *Women in the Labour Force*. Toronto, 1981.

Ostry, Sylvia, *The Female Worker in Canada*. (One of a series of labour force studies in the 1961 Census Monograph Programme). Ottawa: Dominion Bureau of Statistics, 1968.

Rush, Florence. *The Best Kept Secret: The Sexual Abuse of Children*. Englewood Cliffs NJ: Prentice Hall, 1980.

"Saskatchewan Survey of Child Care Preferences," *Rapport*, Vol. 3, No. 2, July 1980, pp. 1, 9, 10.

Shorter, Edward, *The Making of the Modern Family*. New York: Basic Books, 1975.

Wargon, Sylvia T., *Children in Canadian Families*. Cat. 98–810 Occasional. Ottawa: Statistics Canada, Minister of Supply and Services, 1979.

Wartella, Ellen (ed.), *Children Communicating: Media and Development of Thought, Speech, Understanding*. Beverly Hills: Sage Publications, 1979.

Webster, Rhonda, "The Historical Development of Child Abuse as a Social Problem," unpublished seminar paper, O.I.S.E., 1981.

CHAPTER 9

Legal Policies

Introduction

In Canada, many aspects of family relations are regulated by law. Marriage, for instance, is a legally sanctioned ceremony which has important legal implications. Most people in Canada do get married at some point in their lives. Why they do so is not quite clear. As Larson has observed:

> There is no requirement to marry, nor for divorced and widowed persons to remarry. The social and economic advantages of married persons, compared to singles, are modest. The legitimation of sexual access, thought to be a widespread function of marriage by Stephens (1963) and certainly a basic principle in most of the major religious traditions, continues to have a measurable influence on the desire to marry. However as Hobart (1973) has demonstrated, sexual relationships are increasingly common among unmarried Canadian youth. It would seem that Canadians, like their Trobriand counterparts, marry because they value marriage.[1]

Marriage in Canada continues to be associated with love and sex (cf. Whitehurst and Booth, 1980:73–79; Ramu, 1979:6–8). Both love and sex are commonly seen to be intensely private, personal affairs. How then is it that the state regulates, through its judicial system, who may marry whom under what circumstances? Why does the state also regulate who may divorce whom and under what conditions? Why should it be a matter of *public* rather than *private* concern who lives together with whom, has sex with whom, shares household expenses, and the like?

Beyond marriage and divorce, the relationships between children and parents are also circumscribed by law. Although in general family affairs are usually seen as private, in fact the state regulates in some detail with respect to certain issues what these relationships should be.

In this chapter, we will look at current legal policies concerning marriage (legal as well as common-law), divorce, the rights and duties of parents towards children and of children towards parents, as well as legal policies concerning adoption and artificial insemination.

Marriage

In Canada, people may marry legally or they may live together as husband and wife without having gone through a civil or religious marriage ceremony, in which case their relationship may be designated as a common-law marriage. We will consider first legal marriage, and then briefly consider common-law marriage.

Legal Marriage[2]

Marriage laws in Canada are provincial laws. (By contrast, divorce law is federal law.) Although each province has a different set of laws regulating the various aspects of marriage, there are important commonalities. For instance, all the provinces and territories make provision for religious and civil marriage ceremonies. All the provinces stipulate a minimum age for marriage with and without parental consent, although the age limit varies quite a bit. It tends to be around eighteen years of age without parental consent (nineteen in Nova Scotia, the Northwest Territories, and the Yukon), and around sixteen with parental consent, and sometimes earlier for young women who are pregnant and when special permission has been obtained.

All provinces also prohibit marriage between certain people, including people of the same sex, people within prohibited degrees of consanguinity, and people already married to somebody else. All provinces also stipulate under what circumstances a marriage can be declared as invalid, through annulment. Reasons for annulment include prior and continuing marriage of one of the parties, non-consummation, impotence (but *not* sterility), non-compliance with statutory formalities, and lack of consent by reason of duress on the part of one of the parties.

Why is the state interested in marriage? One of the possibilities that comes to mind is that it wants to regulate sexual activities. However, in general, sexual intercourse between non-married consenting adults is not prohibited, nor can we assume that marriage is primarily meant to legally restrict sexual activity to the married couple only, although the sexual aspect of a marriage does have legal importance: as noted, a marriage can be annulled if it remains unconsummated (i.e., ordinary sexual intercourse has not been achieved), or if one partner is permanently impotent. Nevertheless, adultery (i.e., sexual intercourse of a married person with someone other than the spouse) is in general no longer illegal or prohibited, although it is recognized as a reason for divorce. On the other hand, if adultery has occurred and has been condoned by the other spouse, it is no longer a valid reason for divorce. An interest in regulating the sexuality of its adult citizens, then, is not a sufficient explanation as to why the state takes an interest in marriages.

Being married is a civil status that profoundly alters one's relationship to the state in a multitude of ways: entitlements to various social benefits depend on one's marital status (see Chapters 4 and 10); one's responsibility to one's spouse and children becomes legally defined and enforceable; and one's obligations towards the state are modified by one's marital status (e.g., a taxpayer may claim a dependent legal spouse for a deduction, but not a dependent common-law spouse).

Apparently, the state thinks that it is preferable to have its adult citizens married rather than divorced, since overall it is easier to get married than to get divorced. What, then, is it that makes it attractive to the state to have its citizens married?

It seems that the state benefits in two ways: spouses have an obligation to care for each other, and to provide each other with the necessities of life, and marriage places the children socially and makes two adults (rather than just the mother) responsible for the economic, social, emotional, and physical well-being of the children. To the degree that spouses are obliged to look after each other, the state is relieved of the task of looking after those adults who might otherwise need looking after; and to the degree that parents look after their children the state need not do so. Most children are born, raised, and cared for with only a minimal contribution from the state until they are six, and a greater public input after that age through the provision of free and universal education for children of age six (sometimes earlier) and over.

Of course, marriage laws are seldom written with an explicit discussion as to the benefits the state derives if people marry or remain married. Nor can we argue that the law focusses only on the two aspects just mentioned — the support function of spouses for each other and of parents for children — or that children and marriage are always linked together. For instance, while impotence and non-consummation of a marriage are reasons for annulment, sterility is not. Marriage is, therefore, not only conceived of as an institution for procreation and childrearing, but as an institution which has social significance and meaning even in the absence of children. Therefore, when we are discussing consequences of marriage for the state, such consequences need not be reflected in all aspects of legal practices.

Over time, the legal meaning of marriage in Canada has changed dramatically. Much of this change occurred in the late seventies and early eighties, as far as common-law jurisdictions are concerned, starting with Ontario's Family Law Reform Act of 1978.

Until that time, the legal conception underlying marriage was drastically different from what it is today. In general, wives and children were considered the economic and social dependants of their husbands/fathers, who in turn were entitled to services from their wives. The legal rights of wives were, until recently, restricted by their marital status. For instance, the domicile of a married woman was automatically with her husband, although for purposes of divorce she could establish her own domicile since the passage of the federal Divorce Act of 1968.

While most of the legal disabilities of married women with respect to civil rights were removed in the course of time, marriage remained in principle an unequal partnership until the last round of reform legislation, at which point it was made *in principle* (not necessarily *in fact*) an equal partnership between husbands and wives. For instance, the Ontario Family Law Reform Act states in its preamble that "it is necessary to recognize the equal position of spouses as individuals within marriage and to recognize marriage as a form of partnership." Consequently, the act provides in section 65

> For all purposes of the law of Ontario, a married man has a legal personality that is independent, separate and distinct from that of his wife and a married woman has a legal personality that is independent, separate and distinct from that of her husband.

Further, *in principle* (not in fact) the obligations and rights of husbands and wives are generally seen as identical within marriage.

Inequalities remain, of course. For instance, in the common-law provinces wives usually take the surname of the husband on marriage, although this is *not* a legal requirement (King, 1980:19). The exception to this general rule is Quebec, which has been taking a path-breaking lead in taking the concept of the equality of spouses one step further than the other provinces.

The Civil Code of Quebec (1981) specifies:

> Art. 441. The spouses have identical rights and obligations in marriage.
>
> They owe each other respect, fidelity, succour, and assistance.
>
> They must live together.
>
> Art. 442. In marriage, each spouse retains his surname and given names, and exercises his civil rights under this surname and these given names.
>
> Art. 443. The spouses together take in hand the moral and material direction of the family, exercise parental authority and assume the tasks resulting therefrom.
>
> Art. 444. The spouses choose the family residence together.
>
> Art. 445. The spouses contribute towards the expenses of the marriage in proportion to their respective means.
>
> Each spouse may make his contribution by his activity within the home.

As far as the children's names are concerned,

> Art. 56.1 A child is assigned, at the option of his father and mother, one or more given names, and the surname of one parent or a surname consisting of not more than two parts, taken from the surname of his father and mother.

The symbolic and practical importance of surnames can hardly be overestimated. "A name is a person's identity" (Hughes, 1971:1). Wives have customarily changed their surname to those of their husbands upon marriage, and therefore have been socially identified with their husbands. They have also had to change their various identification papers such as driver's licences, social insurance numbers, passports, etc., signalling a break in identity. In telephone books they could not be identified except through their husband's name. This has ramifications not only for one's own self-perception and the way one is perceived by others, but also for identification over time. For instance, someone who knew a woman before marriage but did not know her married name might find it difficult or impossible to locate her if a marriage had taken place in an interval of no interaction.

In terms of the placement function of marriage, wives were socially placed through their husbands, but not *vice versa*, and children were socially placed through their fathers rather than their mothers in terms of *immediate* identification.

Under the new Quebec law, a Quebecois family of, let us say, two spouses and two children may well have four different surnames: the father one, the mother another, the first child, for instance, a surname which combines in hyphenated form the surnames of both mother and father and the second child the same but hyphenated in reverse order. This will hopefully eventually necessitate that federal forms for all types of official interactions (e.g., income tax, application for federal grants, etc.) will allow space for different surnames for spouses as well as children. It should accustom officials to cope with such situations, and thereby facilitate the use of separate names for couples (and eventually children) in the other provinces.

It means that women will no longer have to change a fundamental aspect of themselves upon marriage, and for men it will symbolize that marriage no longer means the acquisition of a wife as property.

Overall, then, the legal implications of marriage have changed fundamentally in the late seventies and after, moving towards equality of husbands and wives (but not children and parents), in intention if not in fact.

Spouses, in general, are responsible for each other's support, and parents are responsible for the support of their children. To a lesser degree, adult children are responsible for the support of their indigent parents, but this is not a legal requirement that is, at present, generally enforced.

For the state, the most important aspect of marriage is the mutual support obligation of spouses, since it usually implies disentitlement from public support. What is noteworthy about this function that marriage plays for the state is the disjunction between the *effects* of being married and the *reasons* for getting married. People marry for love, to enjoy sexual relations with each other, to publicly express their desire to live together, to maintain a joint household and, possibly, to have children together, or because of social pressure. Marriage, however, also results in a new civil status with a new set of rights and obligations which for most people is probably only an incidental by-product of the decision to get married. Nevertheless, for the vast majority of people marriage is probably the most important contract they will ever sign during the course of their lives. It is therefore ironic that the minimum age for marriage (with parental consent) is lower than the voting age, and that people are able to marry (with consent) earlier than they can see some films (with parental consent). By and large, we can assume that people are largely ignorant of the legal consequences of getting married.[3]

Marriage also has important social and economic consequences. These tend to be more drastic for women than for men. Socially, if a woman does change her surname, it denotes the creation of a new social existence. In English, the distinction between Mrs. and Miss also indicates the importance of marital status for women, while the Mr. remains the same for married and unmarried men. It is for this reason that the title Ms., which does not require immediate identification of marital status for women, has become popular in recent years.

Patterns of sociability tend to be different for married and single people (cf. Stein, 1981). This applies to both men and women. Further, the entire lifestyle is likely to change significantly upon marriage for both people involved.

Marriage also has a direct and indirect economic effect, which varies for the sexes. ". . . marriage increases male earnings, and reduces female earnings" (Block, 1982:108). This is partially the case because marriage is still tied up (to a decreasing degree, but nevertheless still significantly) with the notion of the married man as the breadwinner for his family. Women, because of marriage or the expectation of marriage, may lower their occupational expectations by subordinating them to those of their husbands or husbands-to-be. If, for instance, a wife decides to move with her husband because of a job transfer or to become a housewife for a while because of the birth of a child she will pay a short-time penalty in having interrupted her own occupational pattern. This will carry on into the future (thus becoming an indirect long-term penalty) through reduced pension entitlements, lower seniority, lower unemployment insurance entitlements, etc. (To conclude from this fact that it is marriage and not sex which leads to economic disadvantages, as the Fraser Institute (1982) does, is, of course, rather ludicrous since it is only one sex that bears negative economic consequences of marriage and since over 90 percent of all women eventually do get married.)

There is, thus, a rather large discrepancy in the functions marriage serves for the state and for individuals. We will now turn to common-law marriages.

Common-Law Marriage

Canada has a tradition of common-law marriages which refer to relationships between a man and a woman which are like marital relationships but where no legal marriage has taken place. The nature of a common-law marriage has been described as follows in 38 *Corpus Juris*:[4]

> A common law marriage may be briefly described as a marriage without formal solemnization . . . . To constitute a marriage valid as common law, *that is, in the absence of a statute otherwise specifically providing*, it is not necessary that it should be solemnized in any particular form or with any particular rite or ceremony. All that is required is that there should be an actual and mutual agreement to enter into a matrimonial relation, permanent and exclusive of all others, between parties capable in law of making such a contract, consummated by their co-habitation as man and wife or other mutual assumption openly of marital duties and obligations.

Since 1978, there has been a move towards a limited legal recognition of common-law spouses. This typically only formalizes support obligations but does not include any right to matrimonial property. The Ontario Family Law Reform Act, for instance, defines as a spouse for the purpose of support obligation either a legal spouse *or*

> either of a man and woman not being married to each other who have cohabited,
> (A) continuously for a period of not less than five years, or
> (B) in a relationship of some permanence where there is a child born of whom they are the natural parents, and have so cohabited within the preceding year. . . .[5]

British Columbia includes in the definition of a spouse for all purposes except matrimonial property

> a man or woman not married to each other, who lived together as husband and wife for a period of not less than 2 years.[6]

Nova Scotia includes under the definition of spouse, (for support purposes)

> a man and woman who, not being married to each other, live together as husband and wife for one year.[7]

It should also be noted that Quebec Civil Law does not recognize a common-law spouse. However, most social welfare legislation, such as the Workmen's Compensation Act or the Crime Victims' Indemnity Act recognize a person who has cohabited with a person of the opposite sex for three years or more as *de facto* spouse or *conjoint de fait,* who can claim any indemnities due.[8]

These statutes suggest two things. First, the rights of individuals to support from a common-law spouse vary significantly depending on which province they live in. While in Nova Scotia one year's cohabitation would establish the right to be supported by a common-law spouse, in British Columbia it would take two years and in Ontario five, unless there was a joint child. Secondly, these statutes suggest a gradual move towards treating common-law spouses like legal spouses with respect to support obligations. Recent decisions (such as Becker v. Pettkus — see MacDougall, 1980) affirm this trend to treat cohabiting couples similar to the way legally married couples are treated, even with respect to property settlements. The prime motivating force towards legal recognition of cohabitation of common-law marriages has been identified as "a desire to fix liability on the persons living in a family-like situation, to avoid invidious comparisons with persons living in a lawfully established family, and to protect the community from the burden of supporting those who would otherwise be entitled to social assistance" (MacDougall, 1980:316).

Often, this move towards a limited (or even broad) recognition of common-law marriages is justified in terms of protecting women from exploitative relationships. However, there is need to pause for a moment. Another motivation behind recognition of common-law marriages is also, as quoted above, "to protect the community from the burden of supporting those who would otherwise be entitled to social assistance"; in other words, to disentitle people from public support. This is currently being done with welfare mothers (see examples in Chapter 4), and basically amounts to an official ban on sexual activity for poor women, but not for men or for non-poor women. Is this truly desirable?

As far as the individuals within a common-law relationship are concerned, we must assume that people cohabit without legal marriage out of choice rather than for other reasons, since a marriage is relatively simple to contract. Marriage, however, involves an economic partnership of a particular nature. For instance, the principal residence of a couple is usually designated as a matrimonial home and is considered the joint property of both spouses.

It seems reasonable to assume that if people do *not* marry but instead live together that this constitutes a deliberate choice which has been taken for specific reasons, and which may partially be based on the desire to live in a different type of economic relationship. To impose a marriage model on people who do not wish to live within such a framework seems therefore a basic derogation of rights. In general, the benefits associated with being married compared to cohabiting seem rather slight, and the disadvantages seem greater with respect to disentitlement from public benefits. If we argue for treating people as individuals rather than as family members for social policy purposes, this suggests that "marriage should become more like cohabitation and not the other way around" (Deech, 1980:303). Marriage, in that sense, would retain its *social* importance, but its *administrative* importance would be minimized. A parallel situation exists with respect to the distinction between illegitimate and legitimate children, which will be considered next.

Rights and Duties of Parents and Children

Parents have a rather clear and sweeping set of rights and duties with respect to their children, while children have a few rights which are legally enshrined with respect to their parents. In the following, we will consider the rights and duties of parents towards children born in and outside of marriage, and the issue of children's rights and duties.

Children Born Within and Outside of Marriage

Until recently, all provinces made a distinction between legitimate and illegitimate children. If children are born outside of marriage, they are considered related to the mother, but paternity must be established in a special procedure. Even where paternity has been established, the rights of illegitimate children are lesser than those of legitimate children with respect to inheritance and support obligations of the father. Since 1978, Ontario and later, New Brunswick, as well as Quebec, have abolished the distinction between children born outside and within marriage in terms of legal rights, a step that has been called "a revolutionary statement (for law in any case)" (Mohr, 1979:2). The concept of illegitimacy is therefore no longer applicable in these three provinces.

Where a distinction between children born inside and outside of marriage exists, the illegitimate child is generally disadvantaged from birth onward merely by the fact that his or her parents were not married at the time of birth. Where children are born to a married woman (as is the case for the majority of children), they are automatically presumed to be the children of her husband, whether or not that is indeed the case. The husband has to take extraordinary steps in order not to be deemed the father of the children of his wife.

The state has traditionally been more concerned with children born outside of marriage than inside a marriage. There is a tendency to more readily regard illegitimate children as "at risk" than children born in wedlock, and historically, mothers who had given birth to children outside of marriage often placed their children for adoption. In Ontario, for instance, only 30.1 percent of all unwed mothers kept their children in 1968. Only ten years later, in 1977, 88.3 percent of all unwed mothers kept their children — a dramatic change in behaviour (Ontario, 1979:19, t.8). Adoption creates a fictional legitimate birth (adopted children are considered legitimate children); the state ceases to be concerned with a completed adoption. We will return to the question of adoption later.

Parents' Rights and Duties

In general, parents have the obligation to maintain their children, and in exchange for this, children are under the authority of their parents until they reach the age of majority (usually at age eighteen). In the succinct words of the Civil Code of Quebec:

> Art. 645. Every child, regardless of age, owes respect to his father and mother.
>
> Art. 646. A child remains subject to the authority of his father and mother until his majority or emancipation.
>
> Art. 647. The father and mother have the rights and duties of custody, supervision and education of their children.
>
> They must maintain their children.
>
> Art. 648. The father and mother exercise parental authority together.
>
> If either parent dies, is deprived of parental authority or is unable to express his will, the other parent exercises parental authority. . . .
>
> Art. 650. No unemancipated minor may leave the family home without the consent of the person having parental authority.
>
> Art. 651. The person having parental authority has a right to correct the child with moderation and within reason.

The parents' duties vis-à-vis their children are very sweeping, as is their authority vis-à-vis their children. Parents are, in general, responsible not only for the maintenance of their children, but also for their actions. For instance, parents may be sued for damages that their children have caused. In return, children are under the almost complete authority of their parents, who have the right to correct them, determine in what religion they shall be raised, determine their daily behaviour and lifestyle to the minutest detail (for instance, how to wear their hair, what to eat when, how to speak to others, what clothes to wear, etc.).

When parents fail to care for their children properly, the state may intervene and take the children into care. Ultimately, parents may (in extreme cases) be totally deprived of their parental rights — for instance, when the child is given up for adoption because the parents have been ruled unfit parents by the Crown.

However, by and large, parents exert an extraordinary amount of control over children, without any institutionalized checks on the wise use of this control. It is still impossible to determine how many children are abused by their parents, which is basically due to the fact that children are regarded as their parents' property. In return, the state does very little to help parents in their task of raising children, as we saw in Chapter 8.

> Children remain the property of others, in law and in fact. It is on this account that even when we may be outraged at the verbal or physical abuse of a young person by his or her guardians, we are as inhibited from intervening as we would be from walking across their back gardens, or entering uninvited into their classrooms or homes. It is 'their business', and, if we transgress their proprietary rights, we are soon reminded of precisely this fact in precisely these terms. Indeed, the ownership relationship here may well be more strictly ensconced than with lawns or buildings, judging from the stricter taboo against interfering with what people do, or do not do, with their children. You may, it seems, more easily tell a person to look after his house than you can tell him not to assault his young.[9]

A newly emergent model of parenting, which is in contrast to the still prevailing model of children as parental property, is a guardianship model. This approach to parenting recognizes the biological and psychological factors of both dependency and growth.

> The guardian model divests prerogatives in specified areas as the child matures and becomes capable of exercising rights and meeting responsibilities. The model thus presumes the growth of the child, thereby providing notice for the adult withdrawal from the beginning.[10]

Socializing adults are, in this model, not seen as persons who have a natural right over the socialization process of the child as "the producers" but instead draw their authority from a mandate to raise and prepare members of the community.

> Individual parents would no longer exclusively determine the social responsibilities and rights of the young, and in the process impose idiosyncratic demands while insulating or releasing them from social obligation and participation.[11]

Ironically, we may be slowly moving in this direction as an unintended consequence of divorce and ensuing custody disputes between parents. Since *in principle* (not in fact) either parent is equally eligible to obtain custody of children in the case of a divorce, when custody is contested, the decision is supposed to be made in the best interest of the child. This involves an examination of the parenting skills and circumstances of each parent, and thereby introduces an element of public scrutiny into parental relationships, as well as the probably totally unintended and possibly unreflected setting of standards as to what constitutes acceptable parenting behaviour, through judicial decisions which are made with respect to custody and access. We will return to this question when dealing with divorce.

Children's Rights and Duties

Children have the right to be maintained by their parents, and in return owe respect and obedience to their parents. A recent review of children's rights in Canada concluded that, besides two statutes which confer limited rights to children, namely the Quebec Youth Protection Act, S.Q. 1977 (Bill 24) and the Ontario Child Welfare Act, S.O. 1978 (Bill 114), "there are virtually no legal rights for children in Canada. After examining possible sources for those rights, we find little remaining except myths and hopes about the legal status of the child. The existing law, besides lacking a basic statement of children's rights, has not even begun to tackle the vital criteria for true legal rights: practicability, responsibility, enforceability, and institutional action."[12]

Children's rights depend, at the most basic level, on the definition of a child. That is by no means a simple or straightforward matter in Canada — children reach adult status at different times for different purposes in Canada, and across provinces. As noted, children can marry at different ages — until 1981, a female of the age of twelve years and a male of the age of fourteen could get married with parental consent in Quebec! (It is now age eighteen for both sexes in Quebec.) The age of majority and accountability is usually eighteen years of age, but Saskatchewan recently raised the legal drinking age to twenty-one (Cruikshank, 1979:222, n. 18).

In theoretical terms as well, children's rights present real difficulties, comparable perhaps only to those of mentally handicapped persons. Compared with adults, children are not equal in competence and capabilities, they cannot always judge the consequences of their actions and can therefore not reasonably be held accountable for them, and they are not capable of bearing the responsibilities of adulthood. Complicating this situation is that their competences emerge at different ages for different activities, and not necessarily at the same age for all children. These factors make any concern for children's rights different from similar concerns for minority group adults, for instance. Nevertheless, the notion of children as property, either of their parents or of the state (as expressed in the term "wards of the Crown" — a ward being in earlier centuries a child who was bought and sold for his or her labour through "wardship courts" which were little more than auction sales, (cf. Cruikshank, 1979:213) seems outdated.

The recent British Columbia Royal Commission on Family and Children's Law proposed legislation that would contain a statement of twelve children's rights which would be universally applicable, practicable, and enforceable. The recommended statement reads as follows:

Statement of Children's Rights

1. The right to food, clothing and housing in order to insure good health and personal development.
2. The right to an environment free from physical abuse, exploitation and degrading treatment.
3. The right to health care necessary to promote physical and mental health and to remedy illness.
4. The right to reside with parents and siblings except where it is in the best interests of the child and family members for the child to reside elsewhere.
5. The right to parental and adult support, guidance and continuity in the child's life.
6. The right to an education which will ensure every child the opportunity to reach and exercise his or her full potential.
7. The right to play and recreation.
8. The right to be consulted in decisions related to guardianship, custody and a determination of status.
9. The right to an independent adult counselling and legal assistance in relation to all decisions affecting guardianship, custody, or a determination of status.
10. The right to a competent interpreter where language or a disability is a barrier in relation to all decisions affecting guardianship, custody, or a determination of status.
11. The right to an explanation of all decisions affecting guardianship, custody, or a determination of status.
12. The right to be informed of the rights of children and to have them applied and enforced.[13]

The first seven proposed rights set minimum positive standards of care that children ought to receive, while the last five set out rules for procedural fairness for children in administrative and judicial settings.

One might want to suggest that another right should be included in this list, namely the right to make meaningful contributions to society according to their capacity to do so, and to be rewarded in correspondence with the contributions made rather than their age. This would imply, for instance, that if a minor does an adult job, that (s)he be paid according to the job performed, and not according to age.

Passing legislation along these lines would go some distance to improve the current situation of children in Canada, in which they have practically no legal rights. So far, we have considered the lack of rights for children only. Their duties are another important matter.

By law, adult offspring are obligated to support their indigent parents, but in practice, this does not seem to be a duty that is strictly enforced. For instance, senior citizens can qualify for the Guaranteed Income Supplement on the basis of their income alone, even though their adult children may be well off. In this sense, adult offspring and their parents are in social practice to a large degree emancipated from each other. Besides the support function (which is not enforced, nor should it be), children have few duties except generalized obedience to parental authority. One principle which needs to be kept in mind when arguing for children's rights is that rights are customarily associated with responsibilities, and therefore, if we wish to argue for greater rights of children, we should at the same time argue for greater responsibilities. This, it should be noted, is the opposite logic of that used in the early 19th century when reformers were fighting for children's rights. For instance, one of the urgent aspects of 19th century reforms was to shield children from the rigours of the adult system of criminal justice, while nowadays there are critics who maintain — at least partially rightfully so — that such a separate system of justice leads to more stringent control of youth than of adults, especially where status offences and sexual behaviour of young women are concerned.

> . . . when one examines the development of attitudes towards children and their rights, as they evolved in Western European and North American society, one can say that over the past century, the discussion has in some ways come full circle. In the nineteenth century, reformers, working against considerable opposition, asserted the rights of children to be treated differently from adults, on the ground that children were different in nature from adults and had different needs. After much struggle, the views of these reformers were accepted and, in fact, have today come to dominate. In contrast, some twentieth-century radical reformers, while they do share the concern first widely expressed in the nineteenth century, that children deserve protection from abuse and neglect, are also concerned about the autonomy of children, and about their right to partake in the heritage of liberal individualism. This radical concern has led, in some cases, to an attack on the most fundamental of the nineteenth and twentieth century reforms.[14]

The issue of children's rights therefore goes beyond the question of parent-child relations, although the societal position of children as property (or chattel) of their parents (or guardians) is supported and reinforced by the lack of legal recognition of the individual personalities of children. Revising parent-child relationships with a view towards greater autonomy of children cannot be reasonably done unless society at large is willing to play a greater role in providing childcare than it does at present, including bearing more of the financial cost of raising children, and unless society is willing to reshape itself in such a manner that children can participate in life more freely. One simple example is traffic. In most urban areas, the hazard is so great that children must be restrained, forcibly, if necessary, from exposing themselves to possibly fatal danger. This can be done by forcing them to use seatbelts within cars, prohibiting them from crossing streets unattended, forcing them to attend to standard traffic rules, such as crossing only at crosswalks, obeying traffic lights, keeping them in enclosed areas, and the like. All of these solutions involve prohibiting children from walking freely on streets. Another theoretically possible approach would be to try to reduce the hazards of urban streets by re-structuring our traffic. Walking recently in Rome (Italy) in exceedingly narrow streets I was struck by the fact that small children walked without much concern by them or their adult attendants anywhere in the street. There were so many people on foot, from very young to very old, with baby carriages and without, that cars had to drive at a pace no quicker than the speed of a person walking. Without wishing to hold up Roman traffic as a model to be copied (it is quite horrible), I simply mention this example to make the point that giving priority to cars over people is not the only way streets can be used.

Ultimately, then, arguing for greater rights of children vis-à-vis their parents implies greater societal concern for the welfare of children. Boulding (1977:40) has argued that adult-child relationships offer a critical intervention point for breaking the vicious cycles of dominance behaviours that pervade public and international life. If society sets legal age limits which define certain people, on the basis of age, not on the basis of capacity, as incapable of participating in shaping their own lives and that of society around them, by denying them reasonable access to the resources that would make participation possible, "that society is protecting itself by legal means from having to incorporate young persons into full participation in society" (Boulding, 1977:40). (A parallel case can, of course, be made for the aged.)

Divorce

While marriage is under provincial jurisdiction in Canada, divorce is under federal jurisdiction. Legally, the issues that seem most important with respect to divorce are circumstances under which divorce can be obtained, property settlements after divorce and support payments for children and the ex-spouse, and custody of children. We will briefly look at these issues in turn.

Reasons for Divorce

Prior to 1968, the availability of divorce varied from province to province, usually with the law of England as a starting point. In Newfoundland and Quebec however, the courts had no jurisdiction over divorce decrees. Petitioners domiciled in these provinces could obtain divorces only by having private acts passed by the federal Parliament. Since 1968, with the passage of the federal Divorce Act, conditions for obtaining divorce have been uniform across Canada. In addition, reasons for divorce were extended in comparison to the former, very restrictive legislation. Divorce can now be granted on the basis of two separate types of grounds: matrimonial offences and marriage breakdown. Matrimonial offence grounds include: adultery, sodomy, bestiality, rape, homosexual acts, a form of marriage with another person, and mental or physical cruelty which renders continued cohabitation impossible.

When divorce is requested on the basis of marriage breakdown, the parties must be living separate and apart at the time the petition for divorce is presented.[15] Marriage breakdown grounds include: prolonged imprisonment, gross drug addiction with no expectation of rehabilitation, lack of knowledge of the petitioner of the whereabouts of the respondent for at least three years immediately preceding the petition, and having lived separate and apart for at least three years (five years if the deserting party petitions for divorce).

There are cases in which a divorce may be refused; namely when there has been collusion, condonation, or connivance. *Collusion* refers to an agreement or conspiracy on the part of the petitioner to subvert the administration of justice. *Condonation* applies only when divorce is sought on the basis of a marital offence, rather than on the basis of marriage breakdown. It has been defined as

> a blotting out of the offense imputed so as to restore the offending party to the same position he or she occupied before the offense was committed. Mere forgiveness is not condonation. To be condonation, it must completely restore the offending party, and must be followed by cohabitation.[16]

In one recent case, a wife's divorce petition on the grounds of cruelty was dismissed by the trial judge. In this case, the parties had been married for twenty years but the marriage had been gradually breaking down for a number of reasons. On one occasion, the husband had beaten up his wife for taunting him on his inability to perform his conjugal duty. The assault was so serious that the wife had to be hospitalized. However, the couple continued to cohabit for some time until the divorce petition. The trial judge based his refusal to grant the petition on the grounds that the husband's behaviour had been condoned by the wife. However, the appeal court granted the divorce, on the grounds that cruel conduct could only be condoned when it ceased to continue and was replaced by reconciliatory conduct, which was not the case.[17]

Connivance refers to a situation in which a person petitioning for divorce on grounds of adultery has consented or wilfully contributed to the commission of the adultery or has promoted it in some other way.

A divorce, once it is final, changes not only the civil status of a person from married to single, but it also involves a judgement concerning the division of property of the ex-spouses and, where children are involved, usually involves the award of custody of a dependent child to one of the parties only. In addition, there may be maintenance payments for the children and/or an ex-spouse.

Property Settlements

In earlier times, a married woman's right to property was very restricted. Today, a married woman may own and dispose of property as though she were a single person, although under the new family legislation either spouse may block the disposal of some family assets by the other spouse.

In general, although family law has moved in the direction of recognizing the individual legal personality of spouses, with respect to property such a move is not discernible. In the train of the recent reforms across provinces in family law, property relationships of spouses have been fundamentally revamped. The thrust of the new changes is that spouses, in some form or other, jointly own the matrimonial home (irrespective of in whose name the property is registered), while by-and-large business assets remain the property of the spouse in whose name these assets are registered, although in certain cases judges may order a division even of business assets. Joint ownership of the matrimonial home stems from the tradition of "dower rights" on the one hand (a life interest of a widow in one-third of all the real property which a husband had seized at any time during the marriage, except land that he held in trust) and so-called "homestead legislation" on the other hand. In Manitoba and Nova Scotia, the wife still retains her traditional dower rights, with the equally traditional rider that if she engages in uncondoned adultery she loses the dower rights.

Alberta, British Columbia, Manitoba, Saskatchewan, and the Northwest Territories have some form of "homestead legislation." In these acts, the residence of the spouses can only be disposed of with the written consent of the other spouse (or a judge's order dispensing with the consent). With the exception of the Saskatchewan act, these acts also give the surviving spouse a life interest in the residence after the death of the owner. In British Columbia and Saskatchewan, these rights are given only to the wife; in the other provinces, they apply to either spouse. Newfoundland and the Yukon do not have any legislation dealing with dower or homestead rights, and Ontario and Prince Edward Island have abolished dower in favor of joint ownership of the matrimonial home.

In Ontario and Prince Edward Island, the new reform legislation introduced a new species of matrimonial property, called "family assets." Upon divorce, family assets are to be divided equally between the ex-spouses, subject to certain discretionary powers of the court, while non-family assets remain the property of their respective owners.

Family assets include all property, real or personal, owned by either spouse or by both, and used or enjoyed by the family unit, including the children, for shelter, transportation, household, educational, recreational, social, or aesthetic purposes while the spouses are residing together. This definition clearly includes, in addition to the matrimonial home, a cottage, the family car, household furniture, paintings and other works of art in the home. It might not include the husband's boat if he alone goes sailing in it or the wife's coin collection if she alone has pursued the hobby. Further, included are any bank accounts in the name of either spouse which are ordinarily used to pay shelter, transportation, household expenses, or for any other family purpose.

The court may, however, order an unequal division of family assets if an equal division would, in its opinion, be inequitable. Subsection 4 (5) of the Family Law Reform Act of Ontario provides guidelines for the exercise of this judicial discretion. It emphasizes that marriage is a joint effort and that spouses may make their contribution not only by providing money, but also by managing the house and by caring for the children. It also enunciates the principle that "child care, household management and financial provision are the joint responsibilities of the spouses."

Recent decisions which divided family assets unequally include Devcic v. Devcic (1980) in which the marriage lasted only four months. In this case, the court awarded only a nominal share of the family assets to the wife. Similarly, in Hartling v. Hartling, the marriage lasted eighteen months, and the wife received a 25 percent share of the family assets. By contrast, in Irrsack v. Irrsack, the marriage lasted less than three years. However, the shortness of duration of the marriage was balanced against the fact that the wife gave up the prospect of advancement in her job for the sake of the marriage and that she prejudiced herself financially by selling her own home. The judge therefore concluded that the assets should be divided equally between the spouses.

Another relevant consideration is the extent to which a property is acquired by one spouse by inheritance or gift. In Gilbert v. Gilbert (1979) the matrimonial home was purchased three years after the marriage, but entirely on funds given to the husband by his parents. The wife did not have a paying job during the ten years that the marriage lasted. The husband received 75 percent of the home; 25 percent went to the wife.

What is so significant in the legislation and its interpretation is that housework and childcare actually entitle the performer to money or money's worth — a complete change from the principles enunciated in the infamous Murdoch case, for instance. In the Murdoch case, the wife had been doing heavy farm labour for five months of the year by herself, while the husband was away on other business, and was equally involved in running the farm during the rest of the year. However, she had made no direct financial contributions, and the court denied her an interest in the farm, a decision which was upheld by the Supreme Court of Canada in 1973 (see Eichler, 1978:142–143). It was partially the manifest injustice of this case which spurred the efforts at law reform which have since been instituted.

There have, by now, been several cases in which the wife was awarded either a greater share of the family assets or a portion of the husband's non-family assets on the basis of her contribution to the husband's business, both direct and indirect in the form of freeing him from his duty to do his share of the household labour and childcare. For instance, in Weir v. Weir (1978) the judge found that the wife had made a significant contribution to her husband's accumulation of substantial non-family assets by assuming almost the entire burden of childcare and household management. He concluded that the court could either recognize her contribution by making a division of the property that was not a family asset or by making a division of family assets in unequal shares. He awarded her sole ownership of the matrimonial home.

However, there are also cases in which it was argued that the assumption by one spouse of the major share of responsibility for childcare and household management does *not* justify an unequal division of labour. For instance, in Page v. Page (1980) the wife sought an increase in the award of $10 000 made in her favour, in respect of services which she had performed for her husband's management company. It was argued on her behalf that her contributions to childcare and household management enabled the husband to increase his assets more substantially than he could have if he had undertaken a more significant role in the management of the home. However, the judge who delivered the judgement stated that "A wife is not entitled to an award under s. 8 simply because she has been a zealous wife and mother, freeing the husband for the pursuit of great income and assets, which may become non-family assets."

One of the interesting aspects of the new family legislation is that, on the one hand, it assumes equal responsibility of both marital partners for childcare and household management as well as for the financial well-being of the family, thus going beyond the notion of the breadwinner family, while at the same time recognizing the economic value of unpaid work. With respect to legal marriages, the law has moved towards recognition of the equality of spouses. This aspect of family law is therefore more advanced (and more appropriate for current circumstances) than those social policies which are still based on the notion of the breadwinner family, such as welfare policies. It is regrettable, however, that at the same time the law has moved to make cohabitation similar to marriage. Since the current provincial family laws all have some important economic ramifications which are rather inflexible, especially with regard to the matrimonial home, people who opt to live in a different type of economic arrangement are very restricted in their ability to do so. Although marriage contracts are valid in a number of provinces and allow some variation in economic arrangements, most of them do not allow the division of the matrimonial home other than fifty-fifty. Where this is the major asset of one of the partners and the other keeps his or her money in other types of investment, this may create difficulties in terms of equity in the case of a divorce.

Another factor which must not be overlooked is that cases which are cited usually give a biassed impression of the size of family assets, since there is probably a correlation between the size of family and non-family assets and a contested decision. Most people do not have many assets to divide upon a divorce, and in spite of the new legislation it is still true that women tend to be immediately poorer upon a divorce than they were previously, while the same is not generally true for men. Besides property, custody of children is the other, and possibly much more important, issue in divorce. We will consider this next.

Custody

When a couple with dependent children get divorced, the general rule is that one of the parents (usually the mother, see Table 7.5) gets custody of the children while the other parent (usually the father) gets access to the children in the form of visitation rights. The custodial parent has the sole right to make decisions affecting the child's future, such as in which religion (s)he will be educated, what type of education (s)he will receive, etc. The non-custodial parent, therefore, is suddenly relegated to a status which is subordinate to that of the custodial parent with respect to decisions concerning the child's life. The rationale behind giving custody to one parent only is that in order to reduce conflict it is better for the child as well as for everybody else to have one clear authority figure rather than two.

While this seems like a reasonable policy at first glance, there are, however, internal contradictions in the award of custody to one parent and visitation rights to the other.

> Though judges may not recognize the internal contradiction in the award of custody to one parent and reasonable visitation to the other, this contradiction is felt by the parents. The custodial parent, although responsible for the children, must relinquish control over them for the interval of the visitation. Some custodial parents try to bridge the contradiction by presenting the visiting parent with directions regarding the children's care. ('Be sure they have their coats on if they go out to play.') Visiting parents, however, tend to resist the implication that they are now required to observe the custodial parents' directives.[18]

Depending on the type of visitation agreement and the circumstances surrounding the separation and subsequent divorce, non-custodial parents may retreat from their children. It has been argued that "an order for sole custody is a clear message to the family that only one parent need feel responsible for the child. Such a decision renders the other parent impotent, devalued, and less available to the child, and reinforces a structure in which shared communication and responsibility between parents is deemed unnecessary" (Greif, 1980:55).

By assuming that marital discord must automatically imply inability to co-operate as parents, the law takes an essentially monolithic view of family relationships (see Chapter 1). There is some research that suggests that it is possible for people to maintain positive relationships with their children even though there is discord between the parents, and that the crucial factor in mitigating the negative effects of divorce for children consists in keeping a positive relationship with both parents (Hess and Camara, 1979).

It seems clear what the most desirable outcome of custody arrangements for children is; namely, the protection of the child's relationship with both parents, easy access for the child to both parents, and a fostering of a relationship between the parents within which each is supportive of the other's parental efforts (Weiss, 1979:335), but how this outcome can best be achieved is an open question. It must also be noted that in exceptional cases a complete rupture of parent-child relations may be preferable to maintaining them, such as when one parent is severely disturbed and/or highly abusive.

One solution which has been proposed and tried in some cases is joint custody. In Canada, joint custody is so rare that there is not even a category for it in the Statistics Canada compilations of custody awards (see Table 7.5), but it does exist. Joint custody preserves, at all times (in contrast to a split or alternating order of custody) both parents' joint legal responsibility for the child's upbringing. Both parents continue to act as parents, and to share as equally as possible the authority and responsibility for the decisions that significantly affect the life of their child (Fineberg, 1979:433).

There are, to date, no reliable studies on the effect of joint custody versus sole custody for children, mothers, and fathers. Advocates for joint custody speak very highly about the benefits of joint custody (e.g., Galper, 1978). However, due to the fact that this group comprises at the present time only a tiny minority of divorced couples, and due to the further fact that the parents may have had to fight for this type of disposition in the face of judicial resistance, we are, by definition, dealing with an atypical group.

There is a small-scale American study which involves interviews with forty-one divorced parents, one year after the divorce, who had court-awarded joint custody. In San Diego County, where the study was conducted, physical custody is determined separately within the joint custody decision. This means that parents may share the responsibility for children without implying that the children necessarily live with both parents. Of the forty-one cases, eight (19 percent) had a system of alternating physical custody, two (5 percent) were awarded joint custody, and thirty-one (76 percent) had sole physical custody arrangements. However, in all cases both parents shared parental rights and responsibilities.

The majority of the parents (84 percent) reported that overall they were satisfied with their joint custody arrangement. Among those parents who were non-residential, there was great variety in terms of frequency and content of parent-child interactions. *About half* of the non-residential parents reported that they were more involved with their children at the time of the interview than either at the time of separation or in the marriage prior to the time at which they were considering divorce. Some parents, though, reported that they were less involved than before (Ahrons, 1980:194). Nor did joint custody mean equal involvement of both parents. Nevertheless, the study did demonstrate that "divorced parents can continue to share a parenting relationship while terminating, both legally and emotionally, a marital relationship" (Ahrons 1980:202; see also Hess and Camara, 1979:90–92).

There is, however, a problem with terminology. Some divorced parents manage to maintain good parental relationships even when one of them officially has sole custody. What seems to be a crucial variable for smooth relationships is free access of the non-custodial parent to the children and vice versa. In a very small-scale Toronto study, Dominic and Schlesinger (1980) found that fathers who had free access to their children expressed no discomfort in calling their children and cancelling a meeting if necessary, and they in turn did not feel rejected when their children called them to cancel a visit because of some other engagement. These were fathers who consistently saw their children at least twice a week, and some of them spent more time with their children than some of the fathers in Ahrons' (1980) study who officially had joint custody!

Further, Fulton (1979:133) found considerable post-divorce mobility for children between parents, which had not been previously described or documented. ". . . these data make the legal matter of deciding who shall be the custodial parent seem a little less 'final' and the matter of who is, at any given time, the custodial parent, a little more unclear."

In other words, some awards of sole custody may, in effect, approximate an award of joint custody. This can be the case when both parents are highly motivated to maintain their parental roles, and when the custodial parent thinks sufficiently highly of the parenting skills of the non-custodial parent that she is willing to co-operate with the non-custodial parent. "Paradoxically, the joint custody order appears to be best suited for parents who probably do not need a Court order to codify the arrangement" (Fineberg, 1979:439). Nor is there any indication so far that joint custody awards result in increased litigation (Fineberg, 1979:442), as is sometimes argued when people argue against joint custody.

One drawback of joint custody is that it usually requires close physical proximity of the two parents. Fineberg (1979:444) considers this a condition *sine qua non.* In addition, joint custody may be quite expensive, if both parents find that they need to maintain a suitable household for children, with extra clothing, toys, and space available for them. On the other hand, a joint custody arrangement is likely to reduce the costs for the parent who would otherwise be the sole custody parent, usually the mother, who would often live in poverty. In that respect, joint custody is likely to result in higher financial contributions of the father for the child(ren), and therefore to be beneficial.

Just as there is a bit of evidence that parents can continue to relate to their children beyond a marital break-up, so there is some evidence that children can continue to relate to their parents beyond a divorce.

"Children can relate positively to two psychological parents who are not in positive contact with each other" (Lowenstein and Koopman, 1978:205). This suggests that counselling should focus on encouraging ex-spouses to separate their marital and parental roles, and to encourage the custodial parent (where there is sole custody) to help maintain contact between the non-custodial parent and the children. This is also a finding that should be conveyed to non-custodial parents: that they continue to be important for the psychological well-being of their children.

In terms of minimizing the negative effects of divorce on children, it is also important to focus on parental interactions during the process of separation. Jacobson (1978:188) found that the more attention children received from their parents in dealing with separation, and the more parents encouraged discussion of the event, the better adjusted were the children. However, she notes that discussion with children may be difficult for parents who are themselves involved in the situation and who may be overwhelmed by the events. Since the incidence of divorce has increased so dramatically over the past few years, "Many parents are grappling with a situation they never expected to occur. And on the societal level, there are no rituals to help parents or children deal with a marital separation, such as the rituals surrounding a death in the family" (Jacobson, 1978:190). While this was written to describe the American situation, it applies equally well to Canada.

With respect to custody awards, it seems clear that where it works, joint custody is preferable over sole custody. The sole custody parent (usually the mother) tends to be overburdened, both economically and emotionally, while the non-custodial parent (usually the father) tends to feel underburdened and shut out. He has lost not only a wife but also his home and his children. Shared custody may therefore have benefits not only for the children, who maintain close contact with both parents, but also for the parents (see Fineberg, 1979:451).

On the other hand, one cannot assume that joint custody would work in all cases. "Is it better to have two antagonistic parents involved with the child, or to have a single, overburdened parent who may provide a semblance of consistency? Indeed, a question for Solomon" (Felner and Farber, 1980:344).

One last consideration in this context concerns procedural rather than substantive law. If the emphasis in custody decisions is on serving the best interests of the child rather than on the rights of the parents, then this involves a change from assessing past behaviours of parents ('which parent has behaved best') to an assessment of the future, "a process more ethereal than a review of historical occurrences" (Bayda, 1980:66). Given that such a dramatic shift in substantive law has occurred, Bayda argues that it must be accompanied by an equally dramatic shift in adjective law. "It has been found over the years that the technique most suited to coping with the future, with the formulation of plans and the like is not the adversarial approach but the investigative or scientific method" (Bayda, 1980:66). He therefore suggests that only two rules should apply in the future in an inquiry:

1. Anything reasonable that will assist in this search should be brought forward and examined, and
2. The setting should be one of informality, but a *predictable* informality.[19]

Custody decisions and arrangements are of course only one, although an extremely important, consequence of divorce. Support payments are another consequence.

Support Payments

It used to be the case that a wife was entitled to alimony upon divorce, especially if her husband had committed adultery and/or had deserted her. However, if she herself committed adultery, she was highly likely to lose her right to alimony. This type of legislation was based on two sets of assumptions: that a marriage is typically a breadwinner marriage in which only the man has a paying job, and secondly, that the wife is sexually the property of the husband. This assumption is most clearly expressed in laws which stipulate that an ex-wife loses her right to alimony if she has sexual relations with another man, even though her ex-husband may since have remarried!

Canada is moving away from the notion of alimony, although alimony legislation still exists in Alberta (which is the only province that allows a husband to sue for alimony; in the other provinces mentioned, only wives can sue for alimony), British Columbia, Manitoba, New Brunswick, Nova Scotia, Saskatchewan, and the Northwest Territories. In Newfoundland, there is no explicit law regulating alimony, but it can nevertheless be granted. In Ontario and Prince Edward Island, alimony has been explicitly abolished and replaced with a mutual support obligation, as is also provided for in the Civil Code of Quebec.

The law is moving towards a mutual support obligation of the spouses which depends on a variety of factors. For instance, the Manitoba Family Maintenance Act of 1978 spells out the following factors:

(a) The financial needs of each spouse.
(b) The financial means, earnings and earning capacity of each spouse.
(c) The standard of living of the spouses.
(d) Any obligation of a spouse for the support and maintenance of a child or a person other than the other spouse.

(e) Any contribution of a spouse within the meaning of subsection (2). [referring to the fact that conduct is in most cases irrelevant for support obligations]
(f) The amount of any property settlement made between the spouses.
(g) Where one spouse is financially dependent upon the other spouse, the measures available for the dependent spouse to become financially independent of the other spouse, and the length of time and cost involved in taking those measures.
(h) Any impairment of the income earning capacity and financial status of either spouse resulting from the marriage.
(i) Where one spouse is financially dependent upon the other spouse, whether and to what extent the dependent spouse is complying with the requirements of section 4. [referring to the onus on each spouse to take all reasonable steps to become financially independent of the other spouse]
(j) The length of time that the marriage has subsisted.

The courts are therefore moving towards an assumption that self-support after divorce is the expected course of action for the wives as well as for the husbands.

The treatment of common-law spouses does not seem to vary substantially any longer from that of legal spouses with respect to support obligations.

Support payments for an ex-spouse is only one type of maintenance payment; another concerns support payments for children. The two outstanding factors of support payments for children seem to be that they are generally very low — far too low to cover real costs — and that they have a very high chance to be defaulted upon. As always, available information is very spotty, but apparently up to 75 percent of support payments are at some point defaulted upon, while average child support payments are very low — usually much too low to pay even the average price for a day care centre, let alone food, clothing, and other necessities. For instance, a recent study which looked at recently separated mothers from the Hamilton-Wentworth, Burlington, and Brantford area found that of those cases in which husbands had been ordered by the court or had committed themselves to make payments (the highest percentage reached was 73 percent), 38 percent had agreed to pay or been ordered to pay between $1 and $99 for one child per month, and another 42 percent were committed to between $100 and $148 (i.e., 80 percent of those fathers who were committed to pay paid less than $150 per month for a child in 1978) (Arnold et al., 1980:136, t. 7–5). Of those who were committed to $0 to $99, 39 percent had either missed their payments or paid a lower amount, and 28 percent of those committed to $100 to $149 missed their payment or had paid a lower amount in the preceding month (Arnold et al., 1980:139, t. 7–8).

Another recent study found that in British Columbia, monthly awards made between 1976 and 1978 averaged approximately $71 per month. In spite of these very low award levels, default levels are extremely high. This same study noted that two-thirds of the active cases sampled in British Columbia in 1978 were in arrears, and that the Alberta Family Court at Calgary reported that 85 percent of support payments were in default. In Ontario, about 70 percent of men ordered to pay support were in default at some point (Burtch, Pitcher-LaPrairie, and Wachtel, 1980).

American studies show similar results. Fulton (1979:132) for instance, found that of 287 custodial mothers who were interviewed 94 percent had been awarded child support, but two years after divorce only 48 percent of the women said that they were receiving what the court ordered. Summarizing a number of American studies on the payment of child support, Espenshade (1979:621) concluded that if payments were made at all they were consistently extremely low. Only 3 percent of all eligible households in the Michigan Panel Study of Income Dynamics (PSID) received sufficient alimony/child support to raise them to or above the poverty level in any given year. A 1975 International Women's Year Study found that only 44 percent of divorced or separated mothers had been awarded payment, of whom less than half actually *received* child support on a regular basis (Espenshade, 1979:622).

To my knowledge, there is no study which correlates access of the father to the child(ren) and size and regularity of payments. One would assume that fathers who maintain regular and close contact with their children would be more inclined to pay, both because they would be more aware of the consequences of financial need, and probably be concerned about the well-being of the child(ren), and probably less hostile to the mother. This would be an important study to undertake at some point.

Mothers who are dependent on support payments which come irregularly or not at all are likely to be in a desperate situation. A better system could be to pay single parents an allowance from the state, which would then be retrieved (via wage garnishing) in part or fully, depending on capacity to pay, from the other parent. Quebec has pioneered a mechanism which assures just that. This means regular and adequate payment to the custodial parent, puts the force of the law behind extracting payments from the other parent, and might not be more expensive than the present system, due to the fact that the non-custodial parent has to pay according to ability.

So far, we have looked at various legal aspects of marriage, rights of children and parents, and divorce. In the case of divorce in which there are dependent children involved, we are dealing with one type of discrepancy between marital and parental roles. Other types of discrepancy involve adoption, artificial insemination, and surrogate motherhood. We will briefly consider legal issues in adoption and will then draw a parallel to artificial insemination and surrogate motherhood.

Adoption

Adoption involves usually that one or two natural parents give their consent that their child be placed for adoption, and that one or two other adults adopt the child as their own. The effect of adoption has been described as follows by Jenkins:

> . . . [to] extinguish all the rights, duties, obligations and liabilities of the parent in regard to the infant, to vest those rights, duties, obligations and liabilities in the adopter, and to convert the infant into the legal equivalent of a child born to the adopter in lawful wedlock, to whom the natural parent becomes in the eye of the law a mere stranger.[20]

Most adoptions involve children of divorced parents, one of whom has remarried (stepparent adoptions); children who have been found to be in need of protection and made permanent wards; and children whose parents are unable or unwilling to assume or continue their care and custody (for instance, children born out of wedlock and given up for adoption by their mothers).

In general, either single persons or couples may adopt as far as the law is concerned; however, Children's Aid Societies may have their own procedural rules. When there are more people willing to adopt than there are adoptable children (as is the case right now), special requirements may be added by agencies that place children for adoption.

In most jurisdictions the consent of both parents, or, in the case of one death, of the surviving parent, is required in order to free for adoption a child born in wedlock. In the case of children born out of wedlock, only the consent of the mother is required in Alberta, British Columbia, Manitoba, Newfoundland, Nova Scotia, Saskatchewan, and the Northwest Territories. In these jurisdictions, the natural father of a child may not be able to prevent an adoption of his child by somebody else.

By contrast, in New Brunswick, Ontario, Prince Edward Island, Quebec and the Yukon Territory, the consent of the natural father of a child may be required in certain circumstances. The conditions for consent vary, but generally hinge on the father having declared his paternity in a legally specified manner and having taken over some responsibility for the child.

Once a child is legally adopted, (s)he receives a new birth certificate which declares her/him to be the legitimate child of the adopting couple (or single adult). Adoption involves thus a fictional blood relationship, which is probably at the root of the problems surrounding adoption. Kirk (1981) argues strongly that the equation of adoptive kinship with consanguineal kinship is a mistake. "If the definition of adoptive kinship as the equivalent of consanguineal kinship is false, and if from that false definition derive undesirable consequences, such as lack of public understanding of the issues, then a first priority ought to be the attempt to redefine the nature of adoptive kinship so as to conform to realities."

By now, it tends to be the recommended policy to counsel adoptive parents to tell their children that they are adopted, rather than hide it as if it were an ugly secret. To this degree we have moved towards recognizing adoption as a special type of kin relationship. However, the relationship (or rather the denial of any relationship) between the adopted child and the birth parents remains a problematic area.

At present, according to the prevailing practice adopted children are denied access to identifying information about their birth parents, birth parents are given no information whatsoever about the well-being of their children once adoption has occurred, and the two do not usually meet. This is justified in terms of the best interest of the child as well as of the adoptive parents, and occasionally as well in the interest of the birth parents, who are supposed to be able to have forgotten that they ever had a child.

Recent research (see Chapter 7) has shown that certainly the last assumption seems to be false in many cases, and that adopted children seem to have a deep yearning to get to know their birth parents at some time in their lives. Before arguing for totally open records, however, it must also be recognized that if a child were known to and knew his or her birth parents, an emotional tug of war could occur between the birth parents and the adoptive parents, and that it is necessary to protect the child as well as the adoptive parents from later requests of the birth parent(s) to play a parental role. On the other hand, children do grow up, and at some point they should be able to make decisions about their own lives. In adoption policies, adoptive children essentially continue to be treated as children, even when they have reached adulthood.

> The 'needs of the child' — these may have been represented well by the adoption lobby, but at the same time the interests of the adults have been both forgotten and neglected, perhaps precisely because of the 'child' label. But if the agencies considered the needs of the parents to be secondary to the interests of the children, why were the professionals not able to see that children, including adopted ones, must be allowed

> to grow up and make adult choices if they are to become full members of society? When a person cannot legally obtain basic documents relating to his or her own life, then that person does not have the same basic rights and duties of adults as that term is defined in society.[21]

Ontario does have a register for voluntary disclosure of information about the birth parents, but the adoptive parents must agree for their child to have access to this information, even after the child has reached adulthood. This is, at best, half a step forwards. Since other children are free from parental authority once they reach adulthood, it seems somewhat paradoxical that the same should not apply to adopted children.

In general, nobody is proposing totally open records, or totally open contacts between adopted children and their birth parents. There are cases in which children must be protected from such contacts. An intermediate step, however, would be to allow periodic updating of records by birth parents, as well as encouraging adoptive parents to update information about their child (for instance, once a year at the child's birthday), so as to keep the birth parents informed about their child. Finally, after the child has reached adulthood, decisions on whether or not to seek a meeting with the birth parents should rest entirely with the child and with the birth parents.

Artificial Insemination

Artificial insemination is, at present, in a legally gray area. Quebec provides that children born by artificial insemination to a married woman with the consent of the husband are legitimate children. The presumption would be in most cases that children born in such circumstances are, in fact, legitimate children.

However, as in the case of adoption, the child has no means to ever find out the name or any information about his or her genetic father. The recent findings of the adoption literature would suggest that this is experienced by the children as a basic denial of a human right.

Since there are no laws regulating disclosure of the genetic father, there is also no law which would provide for a systematic follow-up on the various children a semen provider may have produced. Therefore, if through insufficient testing a semen provider with a genetic handicap were selected, he might go on being used over and over again, with little chance of the handicap being detected.

Since artificial insemination is an ongoing practice in Canada, it seems urgently necessary to create laws which protect the interests of all concerned, but particularly those of the children conceived by artificial insemination, including their natural right to know their natural parents. For instance, some physical tendencies are genetically determined. If there is no way to identify and contact the natural father, there will never be a possibility to construct adequate information on the medical backgrounds of both parents which may be relevant to determine the most appropriate treatment for the child.

A special subtype of artificial insemination involves surrogate motherhood.

Surrogate Motherhood

Surrogate motherhood is a very recent phenomenon. It involves the insemination of a woman, usually via artificial insemination, with a man's sperm, with the understanding that the child will be adopted by him and his wife at birth. A fee tends to be involved for the woman.

At present, there are no laws which regulate and/or prohibit this activity. However, selling children for adoption purposes is illegal, and this logic can be extended to cases of surrogate motherhood.

Summary and Conclusion

We have looked at some of the changes in family law that have occurred recently. With respect to both marriage and divorce, there have been very sweeping changes which make divorce more accessible to people, which allow divorce on the grounds of marital breakdown rather than only on grounds of a marital offence, while marriage has been redefined as an economic and social partnership of equals rather than as comprising a male head who is the provider for his family which consists of his dependants. This equalization is, however, not complete. There is also a tendency to treat common-law marriages like legal marriages, rather than the other way around. In its understanding of marriage as a partnership of two equals who are both responsible for housework and childcare as well as for the finances of the family, the law has therefore gone further than some social policies which are still based on the notion of the breadwinner family.

The rights of children in Canadian law are basically unprotected. Children are, by and large, still legally treated as the property of their parents. This is also reflected in adoption law which does not give adoptive children the right to know their birth parents, even where birth parents would like to have contact with their natural children after these children have reached adulthood. The same disregard for the rights of children is displayed in the treatment of children of artificial insemination in its various forms.

The law, then, has fundamentally revised what family membership means for spouses, but not for parents and children.

Notes

1. From *The Canadian Family in Comparative Perspective* by Lyle E. Larson © 1976 reprinted by permission of Prentice-Hall Canada Inc., p. 162.
2. Where statements are not specially referenced, in this and all subsequent sections, they are based on analyses or descriptions of cases in the *CCH Family Law Guide*, up until February 1982.
3. There is very little research on the legal knowledge of people who are affected by various laws. As far as family law is concerned, one small-scale unpublished study from Toronto looking at the legal knowledge of 112 high school students taking a driver education course in March 1981 suggests that their knowledge on family law is very limited indeed. For instance, 45 of the respondents did not know that both parents are legally obliged in Ontario to provide support for a child living at home until the child reaches age eighteen or marries — a rather basic aspect of parenthood (see Clifford, 1981:21).
4. See note 1.
5. R.S.A. 1980, c. 152, sec. 14.
6. R.S.B.C. 1979, c. 121, sec. 1.
7. S.N.S. 1980, c. 6, sec. 2.
8. Personal communication with Jennifer Stoddard.
9. John McMurtry, "The Case for Children's Liberation." Unpublished paper delivered at the Conference on Children's Rights, Carleton University, Ottawa, 1979, p. 4.
10. James E. Block, "Beyond Parenthood: Toward a Guardianship Model for Parenting," *Social Policy*, Vol. 10, No. 5 (1980):42. Reprinted by permission of *Social Policy* published by Social Policy Corporation, New York, New York 10036. Copyright 1980 by Social Policy Corporation.
11. Ibid., p. 44.
12. David A. Cruickshank, "The Right of Children," in *The Practice of Freedom, Canadian Essays on Human Rights and Fundamental Freedoms*, ed. R. St. J. Macdonald and John P. Humphrey (Toronto: Butterworths, 1979), p. 212.
13. David A. Cruickshank, "The Right of Children" From *The Practice of Freedom, Canadian Essays on Human Rights and Fundamental Freedoms*; ed. R. St. J. Macdonald and J.P. Humphrey, 1979. Reprinted by permission of Butterworth & Co. (Canada) Ltd.
14. Deborah Gorham, "A Discussion of the Exploitation of Children in Nineteenth-Century Britain, and of its Relevance to Contemporary Questions Concerning Children's Liberation." Unpublished paper delivered at the Conference on Children's Rights, Carleton University, Ottawa, 1979.
15. There are a few unusual exceptions to this rule called "same roof cases" in which it was recognized that the parties had not cohabited in spite of their continuing to live in the same dwelling, i.e., they had not had sexual relationships or otherwise communicated normally for the last ten years. Such cases are, however, very rare. (Based on personal communication with Jennifer Stoddard.)
16. Allin v. Allin, 1942, O.W.N. 444.
17. Aucoin v. Aucoin, 1976, 15 N.S.R. (2d) 399, 28 R.F.L. 43 (C.A.)
18. "Issues in the Adjudication of Custody When Parents Separate." From *Divorce and Separation: Context, Courses and Consequences* by Robert S. Weiss ed. George Levinger and Oliver C. Moles © 1979 reprinted by permission Basic Books, Inc., p. 333.
19. Edward D. Bayda, "Procedures in Child Custody Adjudication. A Study in the Importance of Adjective Law," *Canadian Journal of Family Law*, Vol. 3, No. 1 (1980):70. Emphasis in the original.

20. Re K., 1952 2 All E.R. 877, p. 884.
21. David Kirk, *Adoptive Kinship: A Modern Institution in Need of Reform* (Toronto: Butterworths, 1981).

References

Ahrons, Constance R., "Joint Custody Arrangements in the Post-divorce Family," *Journal of Divorce*, Vol. 3, No. 3, 1980, pp. 189–205.

Arnold, Robert, Michael Wheeler, and Frances B. Pendrith, *Separation and After: A Research Report*. Hamilton: Ministry of Community and Social Services, 1980.

Bayda, Edward D., "Procedures in Child Custody Adjudication. A Study in the Importance of Adjective Law," *Canadian Journal of Family Law*, Vol. 3, No. 1, 1980, pp. 57 and 70.

Block, James E., "Beyond Parenthood: Toward a Guardianship Model for Parenting," *Social Policy*, Vol. 10, No. 5, 1980, pp. 41 and 46.

Block, Walter, "Economic Intervention, Discrimination and Unforeseen Consequences" in *Discrimination, Affirmative Action and Equal Opportunity*. Vancouver: Fraser Institute, 1982, pp. 103–125.

Boulding, Elise, "Children's Rights," *Transaction*, 1977, pp. 39–43.

Burtch, Brian, Carol Pitcher-LaPrairie, and Andy Wachtel, "Issues in the Determination and Enforcement of Child Support Orders," *Canadian Journal of Family Law*, Vol. 3, No. 1, 1980, pp. 5–21.

CCH Canadian Ltd., *Canadian Family Law Guide*, Vol. 1&2. Don Mills, 1982.

Clifford, Linda, "Educational Implications of the Family Law Reform Act of 1978," O.I.S.E., unpublished seminar paper, 1981.

Cruickshank, David A., "The Rights of Children" in R. St. J. Macdonald and John P. Humphrey (eds.), *The Practice of Freedom, Canadian Essays on Human Rights and Fundamental Freedoms*. Toronto: Butterworths, 1979, pp. 209–223.

Deech, Ruth, "The Case Against Legal Recognition of Cohabitation," in John M. Eekelaar and Sanford N. Katz (eds.), *Marriage and Cohabitation in Contemporary Societies. Areas of Legal, Social and Ethical Change*. Toronto: Butterworths, 1980, pp. 300–312.

Dominic, Katherine Tasios and Benjamin Schlesinger, "Weekend Fathers: Family Shadows," *Journal of Divorce*, Vol. 3, No. 3, 1980, pp. 241–247.

Eichler, Margrit, "Social Policy Concerning Women," in Shanker A. Yelaja (ed.), *Canadian Social Policy*. Waterloo: Wilfrid Laurier University Press, 1978, pp. 133–146.

Espenshade, Thomas J., "The Economic Consequences of Divorce," *Journal of Marriage and the Family*, Vol. 41, No. 3, 1979, pp. 615–625.

Felner, Robert D. and Stephanie S. Farber, "Social Policy for Child Custody: A Multidisciplinary Framework," *American Journal of Orthopsychiatry*, Vol. 50, No. 2, 1980, pp. 341–347.

Fineberg, Anita D., "Joint Custody of Infants: Breakthrough or Fad?" *Canadian Journal of Family Law*, Vol. 2, No. 4, 1979, pp. 417–454.

The Fraser Institute, *Discrimination, Affirmative Action and Equal Opportunity*, Vancouver, 1982.

Fulton, Julie A., "Parental Reports of Children's Post-Divorce Adjustment," *Journal of Social Issues*, Vol. 35, No. 4, 1979, pp. 126–139.

Galper, Miriam, *Co-Parenting. A Source Book for the Separated or Divorced Family*. Philadelphia: Running Press, 1978.

Gorham, Deborah, "A Discussion of the Exploitation of Children in Nineteenth-Century Britain, and of its Relevance to Contemporary Questions Concerning Children's Liberation." Unpublished paper delivered at the Conference on Children's Rights, Carleton University, Ottawa, 1979.

Greif, Judith Brown, "Access: Legal Right or Privilege at the Custodial Parent's Discretion?" *Canadian Journal of Family Law*, Vol. 3, No. 1, 1980, pp. 43–56.
Hess, Robert D. and Kathleen A. Camara, "Post-Divorce Family Relationship as Mediating Factors in the Consequences of Divorce for Children," *Journal of Social Issues*, Vol. 35, No. 4, 1979, pp. 79–96.
Hobart, Charles W., "Attitudes toward Parenthood among Canadian Young People," *Journal of Marriage and the Family*, Vol. 35, No. 1, 1973, pp. 93–101.
Hughes, Marija Matich, "And then There were Two," *The Hastings Law Journal*, Vol. 23, No. 1, 1971 (A Warner Modular Publication, Reprint 197, 1973, pp. 1–15).
Jacobson, Doris S., "The Impact of Marital Separation/Divorce on Children: III. Parent-Child Communication and Child Adjustment, and Regression Analysis of Findings from Overall Study," *Journal of Divorce*, Vol. 2, No. 2, 1978, pp. 175–194.
King, Lynn, *What Every Woman Should Know About Marriage, Separation and Divorce.* Toronto: James Lorimer & Co., 1980.
Kirk, David, *Adoptive Kinship: A Modern Institution in Need of Reform*. Toronto: Butterworths, 1981.
Larson, Lyle E., *The Canadian Family in Comparative Perspective.* Scarborough: Prentice-Hall of Canada, 1976.
Lowenstein, Joyce S. and Elizabeth J. Koopman, "A Comparison of the Self-Esteem between Boys Living with Single-Parent Mothers and Single-Parent Fathers," *Journal of Divorce*, Vol. 2, No. 2, 1978, pp. 192–208.
MacDougall, Don, "Policy and Social Factors Affecting the Legal Recognition of Cohabitation without Formal Marriage," in John Eekelaar and Sanford N. Katz (eds.), *Marriage and Cohabitation in Contemporary Societies. Areas of Legal, Social and Ethical Change.* Toronto: Butterworths, 1980, pp. 313–322.
McMurtry, John, "The Case for Children's Liberation." Unpublished paper delivered at the Conference on Children's Rights, Carleton University, Ottawa, 1979.
Mohr, J.W., "Notes on Childhood as Stage and Status." Unpublished paper delivered at the Conference on Children's Rights, Carleton University, Ottawa, 1979.
Ontario. *The Family as a Form for Social Policy.* Toronto: Provincial Secretary for Social Development, 1979.
Ramu, G.N. (ed.), *Courtship, Marriage and the Family in Canada.* Toronto: Macmillan of Canada, 1979.
Stein, Peter J. (ed.), *Single Life. Unmarried Adults in Social Context.* New York: St. Martin's Press, 1981.
Stephens, William N., *The Family in Cross Cultural Perspective.* New York: Holt, Rinehart and Winston, 1963.
Weiss, Robert S., "Issues in the Adjudication of Custody When Parents Separate," in George Levinger and Oliver C. Moles (eds.), *Divorce and Separation: Context, Causes and Consequences.* New York: Basic Books, 1979, pp. 324–337.
Whitehurst, R.N. and G.V. Booth, *The Sexes. Changing Relationships in a Pluralistic Society.* Toronto: Gage Publishing Ltd. 1980.

CHAPTER 10

Governmental Policies

Introduction

This chapter will provide a brief historical outline of the emergence of family-oriented policies and of their underlying philosophy. We will then give an overview of the major current social programmes which are oriented towards families and subsequently utilize this overview to identify notions concerning family responsibilities underlying the various social policies. This will lead to an assessment of some of the problems in the current social security system, and proposals for solving some of them.

Historical Outline of Social Policies

The recent report on the income security system in Canada (Canadian Intergovernmental Conference Secretariat, 1980) which resulted from an interprovincial task force on social security identifies five phases in the emergence of the present income security system in Canada. The first phase comprises the period before 1900, and is characterized by very limited local responsibility for the poor and indigent. The general attitude of that period was that few persons should require assistance, since assistance fosters indolence and dependency. Consequently, help was only provided after all the financial resources of a family had clearly been exhausted, and only in cases in which local residence was clearly established.

The second phase, from 1900 to 1930, saw the emergence of the first provincial and federal responses to three categories of people: injured workers, older workers, and needy mothers with children. Workers' compensation came into operation in Ontario in 1915, and by 1921 all provinces except Prince Edward Island had enacted legislation based on the Ontario statute. Compensation for work injuries had thereby become a matter of right for workers, without the necessity of proving negligence on the part of the employer.

The end of the First World War also brought federal legislation providing pensions for war widows, and provincial legislation providing financial assistance for mothers with dependent children was enacted around the same time (Canadian Intergovernmental Conference Secretariat, 1980:9–12). Manitoba was the first province to enact such legislation in 1916, and by 1920 British Columbia, Ontario, Saskatchewan, and Alberta had similar legislation. This legislation was partially a response to the fact that women achieved the franchise during this period and thereby became an electoral constituency. The most generous of all these plans was that of British Columbia, which in its Mothers' Pensions Act covered indigent mothers or deserted wives, wives of men who were inmates of asylums or penal institutions, mothers whose husbands were unable to support their families because of illness or accident, and "any other person whose case, in the opinion of the Superintendent, is a proper one for assistance under the provisions of this Act" (quoted in Guest, 1980:55).

The context was a relatively non-demeaning one in British Columbia, since the Mothers' Pensions were administered through the Workmen's Compensation Board and the money was identified as a pension rather than as an allowance. Nevertheless, in order to put such *relative* generosity and non-degradation into context, it is important to realize that the applicants for such a pension had to be "of good character" in order to qualify for a pension. Guest provides one example of the effect of this stipulation:

> A woman with three children, one of whom was crippled, was granted a pension after the death of her husband. Three years later she remarried and her pension ceased forthwith. Although she had married her second husband in good faith, it turned out to be a bigamous union. Her second husband was jailed and on his release disappeared from the scene. With no means of support, the woman re-applied for a mother's pension but was told that in view of her bigamous marriage she was not a 'fit and proper person' to receive a pension.[1]

Assistance to the aged was provided, until 1927, if at all, through local relief measures or private charity. In 1927, the Old Age Pension Act was passed which provided for a means-tested, non-contributory payment to British subjects aged seventy or over, who had resided in Canada for at least twenty years. This was the first major cost-shared federal-provincial program (Canadian Intergovernmental Conference Secretariat, 1980:13).

The third phase, from 1930 to 1944, involved a number of federal responses to the problems generated by the Great Depression and the Second World War. It was the Depression which revealed the total inadequacy of the doctrine of seeing social assistance as a limited local responsibility. By 1933, 15 to 20 percent of the population were dependent on municipal social assistance, and over 25 percent of the male labour force were unemployed (Canadian Intergovernmental Conference Secretariat, 1980:14).

Municipalities were unable to cope with this flood of people in need. Consequently, between 1930 and 1935, the federal government enacted a series of ad hoc unemployment relief measures, which, however, proved inadequate. In 1935 the federal government introduced the Employment and Social Insurance Act, which provided for a system of nation-wide compulsory insurance, to be financed by contributions from employees, employers, and the federal government. In 1937, the act was declared *ultra vires* by both the Privy Council and the Supreme Court. Consequently, the federal government proposed a constitutional amendment which added unemployment insurance as an exclusive federal power to section 91 of the British North America Act. In 1941, the Unemployment Insurance Act became effective (Canadian Intergovernmental Conference Secretariat, 1980:15).

The fourth phase, from 1945 to 1960, saw the first steps towards a federal welfare state. In 1945, a universal Family Allowance programme was started, and in 1952 the Old Age Security Act came into effect. The year 1951 also saw the passing of the Blind Persons' Act and 1954 of the Disabled Persons' Act, which provide allowances to blind and disabled persons, respectively. The amounts paid out through all these schemes were very low: $40 a month for Old Age Security, and the same for totally blind or totally disabled persons, and $5 to $8 monthly per child, based on the child's age (Kesselman, 1979:662).

The fifth and last phase, from 1960 to 1980, "marked the beginnings of the piecemeal disintegration of the system of centralized federalism developed in the post war years" (Canadian Intergovernmental Conference Secretariat, 1980:21–22). During this period, amounts that were paid out under the various programmes were increased, and in 1966 the Canada Assistance Plan replaced a number of programmes. The assistance was to be provided by the provinces, with cost sharing by the federal government. In the late sixties and mid-seventies, an increase in provincial unilateral programmes took place, "and thus a geometric growth in the complexity of Canada's income maintenance system [ensued]" (Canadian Intergovernmental Conference Secretariat, 1980:28).

The development of social security is extremely complex to chart (and the above is *not* a complete summary of the major developments, but merely a presentation of some key factors) because of the complicated provincial-federal relations in this area. Another confusing element is introduced through the different philosphical stances underlying the various pieces of legislation. Guest has distinguished between two distinct approaches to social security: the residual concept of social security and the institutional concept of social welfare.

The residual concept of social security conceives of aid to those who find themselves in need as being of a gratuitious nature, since the recipient has no right to assistance. The "normal" channels of help are to seek alternate sources of income by finding another job, borrowing, or seeking credit, and when all these fail, to ask the help of a relative. For women in need it may mean to find another man who will provide for them, or to stay with a man, even though the two dislike each other. In this perspective, social security is understood as a matter for families, not as a matter for the state. Where people do receive assistance from some agency there tends to be a strong moralistic element:

> The apathy toward the condition of the poor in British North America may be related to the view, commonly held, that poverty was the result of some personal failing or character flaw. Certain elements of protestant theology provided support for this view by interpreting success as evidence of godly living and of God's grace. The corollary was, of course, that poverty was an indication of a sinful life and of divine retribution. Therefore such help as was extended to the poor was often accompanied by unsolicited and largely irrelevant advice on how the poor might regain God's grace through the exercise of those human qualities which He apparently admired and rewarded. The poor were urged to appreciate values of thrift, hard work, self-help, and self-discipline. Biblical tracts pointing the way to spiritual salvation were popular items for distribution to the poor.[2]

By contrast, the institutional concept of social welfare is premised on the notion that our collective way of living in an urban, industrialized society has certain risks attached to it that should be shared by the entire society. By consequence, if a person loses his or her job, for instance, the individual should be protected by a public programme that maintains the income, or a reasonable portion thereof, until he or she is re-employed.

> The conflict over an institutional as opposed to a residual role for social security programmes has been a significant and recurring theme in the history of Canadian social security. The forces supporting a residual role were most influential in the years prior to 1940, but the shift to the institutional role was unmistakeable at the close of World War II. Nevertheless, in every major social security issue since 1945 these two viewpoints have had their adherents, and both sides have been influential in shaping policy decisions.[3]

As long as poverty is defined as being caused by "thriftlessness, mismanagement, unemployment due to incompetence, intemperance, immorality, desertion of the family and domestic quarrels" (from a 1912 report of the Associated Charities of Winnipeg, as quoted in Guest, 1980:37) the residual approach to social welfare will seem justified to many. One of its correlates is an emphasis on abuse of programmes with attempts to catch cheaters. Unfortunately, this perspective is by no means dead today (cf. Hasson, n.d.).

Current Policies Relevant to Families

In the following, we will briefly outline some of the major programmes and policies that affect families today. This is not meant to be a comprehensive review of all the operating programmes, but merely a description of the *major* current programmes and/or policies, in order to provide a basis for a critical analysis of them. The presentation of the various programmes will follow a categorization that is somewhat unusual. Rather than follow a more usual breakdown, for example, into federal and provincial programmes, programmes will be grouped by type of recipients, in order to facilitate the subsequent analysis. Another point must be mentioned here. In general, income tax deductions and other preferential tax treatments tend not to be included in a discussion of social policy. Bergeron (1979), for example, in an analysis of social spending in Canada, completely ignores the "so-called 'back-door' spending which occurs through the granting of preferential tax treatment (exclusions of certain types of income, exemptions, deductions, and credits)" and which "is most commonly referred to as tax expenditures" (Maslove, 1981:232). Yet for 1978, tax expenditures through the personal income tax system exceeded $9 billion! (Maslove, 1981:239). Omitting income tax provisions would omit a very major aspect of the government's treatment of families. For this reason, it is important to consider tax provisions in conjunction with social welfare policies. The emphasis will be on federal rather than provincial policies.

The various policies will be presented as: (a) those which are oriented towards children, then (b) those which are oriented towards marital status, (c) income maintenance policies (i.e., transfers to people), and (d) indirect subsidies (i.e., transfers to institutions).

Child-oriented Policies

There are four major policies that are oriented towards children: the family allowances, the refundable child tax credit, the tax exemption for dependent children, and the childcare deduction.

As noted, family allowances have been in existence since 1945. In 1981, they amounted to $23.96 a month — $287.52 a year — for each dependent child under the age of 18. In Quebec, benefits vary according to the number of children in a family and their ages, and in Alberta, according to age; however, total payments for all children taken together average in all provinces $23.96. The allowances are paid to the mother irrespective of her own or her husband's income, and they are taxed by being included in the income of the parent who claims the tax exemption for the same children — usually the parent with the higher income; that is, usually the father.

The refundable child tax credit was first introduced in 1978. In 1981, it paid an additional amount up to $238.00 per child, depending on *family* income. The payments are made once a year to the mother, who must file a tax return in order to become eligible for the child tax credit even if she has no taxable income herself.

The tax exemption for dependent children reduces the amount of money a taxpayer must pay, provided (s)he can claim a child as being totally dependent on him or her. For the 1981 taxation year, the maximum allowable claim for a wholly dependent child under 18 years of age was $590, and $1090 for a wholly dependent child over 18. Individuals over 21 years of age must either attend school or be infirm before they can be claimed as dependants. The exemption for dependent children will usually be claimed by the parent with the higher income, since in that case the savings are greater. Since fathers tend to have higher incomes than mothers, it is therefore a saving that will usually come to the father.

By contrast, the childcare deduction can only be claimed by a "working" mother. Fathers can claim the childcare deduction only when they can prove that the mother either was not available (e.g., the father is a widower, or single, or he is divorced or separated and has custody and control of the children) or his wife was infirm or in an institution for a period of not less than two weeks. The maximum allowable deduction was, for the 1981 taxation year, $1000 per child, up to a maximum of $4000 or up to two-thirds of the claimant's earned income, whatever was *less*. Since eligibility to the childcare deduction hinges on the labour force status of the mother only, this leads to some asymmetries. For instance, a working mother can claim childcare expenses if her husband is unemployed or a student but if she herself is unemployed or a student, she *cannot* claim childcare expenses.

Marital-status-oriented Policies

There are four policies which result in direct savings or transfers on the basis of marital status: the married exemption, the equivalent-to-married exemption, the possibility of transfers of deductions between spouses, and the spouse's allowance.

For the taxation year 1981, the married exemption allowed a tax filer who was married to a spouse with an annual income of less than $490 to claim an exemption of $2780. In most cases, a husband will claim a wife, although a wife may claim a husband if she earns money and he does not. This exemption is available only to legally married people; a common-law spouse cannot be thus claimed, even if s(he) was totally dependent on the tax filer during the taxation year.

The equivalent-to-married exemption is available only to people who are not married; that is, to people who are single, separated, divorced, or widowed and who supported a relative — a parent, grandparent, sister, brother, aunt, or uncle, or the equivalent among in-laws — during the taxation year. The exemption is the same as the married exemption, and operates under the same set of rules. The equivalent-to-married exemption is applicable only to kin and in-laws; that is, it is also not usable for a common-law spouse, or for a totally dependent adult who is not a relative.

Deductions not used by one spouse can be transferred to and claimed by the other spouse. The following deductions can be so claimed: education deduction, disability deduction, pension income deduction, and interest, dividends and capital gains deduction. In this way, the amount of tax payable may be reduced for a taxpayer on the basis of his or her spouse's income.

Finally, the spouse's allowance is a direct transfer, and not a taxation device. It is a monthly payment to spouses (mostly wives) who are married to a pensioner in receipt of an Old Age Security pension. The spouse who wishes to receive the spouse's allowance must satisfy certain residency requirements and must be between the age of 60 and 65. (At 65, (s)he becomes eligible for her/his own Old Age Security pension.) This is an income-tested programme in which the income of *both* spouses is considered in order to determine eligibility for the spouse's allowance.

Income Maintenance Policies (Transfers to People)

The major income maintenance programmes in Canada are the Unemployment Insurance programme, Old Age Security, the Guaranteed Income Supplement, the Canada/Quebec Pension Plans, and social welfare. With the exception of welfare which is a provincial and/or municipal responsibility, these are federal programmes.

Unemployment Insurance is a universal programme under federal legislation for all waged or salaried workers. It provides income maintenance in the case of loss of job up to a certain maximum level (in 1981, the maximum *weekly* benefit was $189, or 60 percent of the average weekly earnings, whichever was less). Unemployment Insurance payments are income-related in the sense that they depend on previous earnings, up to a maximum ceiling. They are, however, not income tested (a person may have other income, for instance, from stocks and investments, and still receive Unemployment Insurance premiums) and they are paid to individuals irrespective of their family status.

Old Age Security makes monthly payments to every individual who has resided in Canada for a certain number of years and who is 65 years of age or over. This income is taxable (except the first $1000). It is, like the family allowances, a demogrant; that is, any individual who meets certain demographic criteria receives these pensions, irrespective of other factors such as income and family status. Amounts payable are adjusted four times a year. In April 1981, the monthly OAS payments for every individual were $208.20.

The Guaranteed Income Supplement, by contrast, is an income-tested supplement of Old Age Security, eligibility for which is determined on the basis of *family* income. In April 1981, maximum GIS payments for a single person were $209.03, and for a married person $161.16. This amounted to a guaranteed income for a single person over 65 years of age of $417.23 per month (as of April 1981) and of $738.72 for a couple, both of whom were over age 65 (as of April 1981.)[4]

The Canada/Quebec Pension Plans (C/QPP) provide for a retirement pension based on employee/employer contributions. This is a compulsory plan to which every employer and employee must contribute. The current intent of the plan is to replace no more than 25 percent of previous individual earnings. (Since the whole pension system is currently under reconsideration, one possible outcome might be an expansion of the C/QPP to have it replace 50 percent of an individual's wages, up to a certain maximum. This is only one proposal among many that have been made.)

Since the Canada Pension Plan reflects previous earnings, and since female earnings are significantly lower than male earnings in Canada, we find consequently a very marked sex difference in the level of pensions received from C/QPP.

For all C/QPP pensioners, average monthly payments by age and sex were distributed in December 1980 as shown in Table 10.1.

For our purposes, two other features of the C/QPP are of prime importance: survivor's benefits and pension splitting. We will first consider survivor's benefits.

Survivor's pensions are calculated on a complicated formula that takes into account the age of the beneficiary at the death of the pensioner, the presence or absence of dependent children, any personal pension entitlements that the survivor may have, and the pension previously payable to the pensioner. Overall, it amounts to approximately 60 percent of the previous pension, and is reduced when the survivor is personally entitled to a pension. Since the most important

TABLE 10.1

Monthly Average of Retirement Pensions by Sex and Age, December 1980

	Males		Females	
Age	**Numbers**	**Monthly Average**	**Numbers**	**Monthly Average**
65	53,242	$202.09	29,367	$130.98
66	55,745	$194.96	29,699	$127.86
67	51,915	$188.83	26,803	$124.36
68	48,735	$179.70	24,635	$119.70
69	44,446	$167.72	21,798	$112.66
70	41,899	$155.09	20,525	$104.66
71–74	153,353	$115.95	68,986	$ 80.25
75–79	100,357	$ 77.73	38,709	$ 56.65
80+	9,150	$ 50.20	3,375	$ 38.80
Total	558,842	$143.48	263,897	$ 99.99

Source: From Statistical Bulletin, Vol. 12, No. 4, t.16, p. 16, Dec. 1980. Reprinted by permission of Health and Welfare Canada.

factor in this calculation is the size of the pension of the deceased pensioner, male survivors get even lower benefits than female survivors, since female pensioners have, on average, lower pensions than male pensioners, as displayed in Table 10.1. Average survivor's benefits are quite low: they amounted in December 1980 to $71.81 for male beneficiaries of deceased female pensioners, and to $109.03 to female beneficiaries of deceased male pensioners (Canada: Health and Welfare, 1980, pp. 22 and 23).

In July of 1977 the Canada/Quebec Pension Plan was amended to allow for equal splitting between husband and wife of C/QPP credits earned during marriage if either spouse applies within three years of the divorce. However, the takeup rate in the case of pension splitting has so far been exceedingly low — indeed in 1978–1979 it was less than one percent of all eligible applicants. Out of 117 000 divorces that took place in that time period, there were only 900 applications for pension splitting[5] although application by *one* spouse is sufficient to insure pension splitting.

Welfare, finally, is under provincial and municipal legislation, although the federal government through the Canada Assistance Plan (CAP) contributes as much as 50 percent of total expenses (depending on whether provinces exceed their obligatory 50 percent contribution). Through regulations contained in the CAP agreement, the federal government exerts some control over how monies are disbursed, although the actual disbursements take place at lower levels of government.

Every province has different welfare regulations. We will here consider the case of Ontario. First, we must distinguish between General Welfare Assistance and Family Benefits. General Welfare Assistance is meant to be short-term, for people who are technically employable. However, many of the recipients are older women, who stay on general welfare assistance for years and years.[6] General Welfare Assistance is available to families as well as individuals. It is under all circumstances based on a needs test; that is, an estimate of expenditures (or the actual expenditures) and the available income. Cheques have to be picked up at the welfare office — they are not mailed — and only one person in a family receives a cheque. In a husband-wife family, the man is always the recipient, and the wife is always considered the dependant.

Family Benefits, the second major form of welfare, is, in contrast to General Welfare Assistance, meant to be a long-term form of assistance. Cheques are mailed, rather than having to be picked up. As in the case of General Welfare Assistance, only one cheque per family is made out, and in the case of a husband-wife family, always to the husband. The wife is always considered his dependant. (In the case of a one-parent household in which the parent is female, the cheques are made out to the mother, of course.)

Family Benefits are available to single women, to people who are disabled, blind, or permanently unemployable, and to mothers raising children alone, provided the candidate is not a patient in a psychiatric hospital or an inmate of a prison, or a recipient of General Welfare Assistance or Old Age Security or an allowance from the Ontario GAINS programme (Guaranteed Annual Income Supplement), although General Welfare Assistance may be a pathway to receiving Family Benefits. Two other exceptions will be cited in full from the handbook which explains the Family Benefits to potential users:

> The Family Benefits Act provides benefits for mothers raising children alone, therefore, if you are not living as a single person, you are not eligible for assistance.
>
> For the purposes of Family Benefits, if you are a married woman who is disabled, blind or permanently unemployable, and dependent upon your husband for support and maintenance, you cannot apply for Family Benefits as a recipient in your own right. If a father is permanently disabled, for example, he and his family can get Family Benefits, but if his wife only is disabled, this does not make the family eligible.[7]

Indirect Subsidies (Transfers to Institutions)

Normally, when social security or income maintenance programmes are discussed, the discussion is restricted to direct transfers. However, indirect transfers are an important aspect of the entire social security system and do indeed take a large share of the tax dollar. Health costs alone accounted for 7.5 percent of our GNP in 1981 (Dunlop, 1981:A1). Education is similarly expensive. Both health care and education are universal systems which are more or less freely available to all residents of the country, although the majority of people must pay insurance premiums for their health care, which, however, cover only a fraction of the costs incurred. Both public health care and public education are so well accepted that we tend to take them for granted and in fact tend not to see them as part of a social security system.

Two other transfers to institutions which are particularly relevant in this context concern subsidies to day care and to homes for the elderly. Day care centres can receive subsidies by reserving places for children from families below a certain income level. The subsidies bridge the gap between real costs and what the parents are charged. From the parents' perspective, this means that although they do not receive money directly for day care costs, they may instead gain access to a subsidized day care space. In Metro Toronto, the majority of day care centres operate with a combination of subsidized and non-subsidized children (Metropolitan Toronto Day Care Planning Force, 1980:9). This seems also to be the case for the rest of the country. Eligibility for a subsidized day care space depends on family income. A day care space in Metropolitan Toronto cost around $250 per month in 1979 (Metropolitan Toronto Day Care Planning Force, 1980:51). There is a shortage of spaces; waiting lists far outnumber vacancies (Metropolitan Toronto Day Care Planning Force, 1980:85). When no subsidies are received, the cost of a day care space may be prohibitive for many parents, especially if they have more than one child in need of day care.

As far as the elderly are concerned, all Canadian residents of 65 years of age or older receive some personal transfer monies, as we have seen. In addition, some homes for the elderly receive subsidies. Eligibility to subsidized spaces for the elderly is based on income. In June 1981, the Metro Toronto Housing Co. Ltd. (which serves the elderly) set maximum eligibility levels for access to subsidized housing at $950 per month ($11 400 per year for an individual) and at $1350 per month ($16 200 per year) for a married couple. Rents per apartment are also based on income. In 1981, they amounted to 20 percent of one's income with a minimum of $102 per month and a maximum of $212 per month. The recipient must be 60 years of age or disabled.[8]

As in the case of day care, then, and counter to the practice in the health services and public education, access to subsidized housing for the elderly is income tested on an individual basis (if the person applying is single) or a couple basis (if the person applying is married). Although the situation is somewhat different in every province, this general statement nevertheless describes the overall situation in Canada.

We have provided a very cursory look at the *major* transfers that are part of the Canadian social security system. This cursory overview is neither complete, nor does it adequately reflect the provincial variations, but it suffices as a basis for an overall assessment of the current social security system and the various conflicting notions of the family underlying it. In the following, the system will be analysed as a whole, by identifying the notions of responsibility, dependency, and interdependency underlying the various components of the system.

Notions Underlying the Various Social Policies

Family vs. Individual Entitlements

Every social policy has some sort of rationale on the grounds of which it can be justified. Such rationales may be founded on general philosophical stances, political expediency, budgetary restraints, or other bases. The analysis that follows is not concerned with any rationales presented at the point of time at which the various policies became law and/or practice, or even with interpretations that are presented by politicians and administrators concerning the philosophical basis of any given policy. Instead, the analysis will focus on the policies themselves, irrespective of any rationales given, and draw its conclusions simply by applying the same questions to all the policies briefly described thus far. It will therefore examine assumptions which are incorporated into the various policies, rather than assumptions that are held by the people administering the policies.

As Chart 10.1 shows, recipients vary by programme. Some programmes are clearly and exclusively geared towards individuals as beneficiaries. This is unambiguously true for Unemployment Insurance, Old Age Security, and public education, and describes more or less our health care systems, even though membership in any of the provincial health plans tends to be on a family basis. One could also add to this list family allowances. Although it is usually the mother — that is, a family member — who receives the allowance rather than the child, nevertheless the benefit is tied to the child, and the mother merely receives the money in lieu of the child. If the child changes parents (e.g., custody is switched from one parent to the other), the money follows the child to the next major caretaker. In that sense, family allowances can also be understood to have individuals as beneficiaries, although it is clearly a borderline case.

The first and most basic question to ask concerning social policies is who the eligible recipients of benefits are: individuals or family units.

CHART 10.1

Beneficiaries of Selected Social Programmes

Programme	Recipients
Family Allowance	Mother for every child
Refundable Child Tax Credit	Mother, on basis of number of children and family income, not her income alone if married.
Tax exemption for dependent children	Higher income parent, usually father.
Child care deduction	Earning mother, for childcare rendered by non-relative.
Married exemption	Earning spouse in breadwinner marriage, usually husband, irrespective of children.
Equivalent-to-married exemption	Unmarried head of household for one dependent relative in household.
Transfer of deductions between spouses	Earning spouse in breadwinner marriage, usually husband, irrespective of children.
Spouse's allowance	Dependent spouse between 60 and 64 years of age (usually wife) of pensioner.
Unemployment Insurance	Unemployed previous earner, irrespective of parental and marital status.
Old Age Security	Every individual over 65 years of age.
Guaranteed Income Supplement	Single individuals on basis of income, couples on basis of joint income.
Canada/Quebec Pension Plan	Any former income earner, regardless of family status, plus a surviving spouse who was not an earner on a pro-rated basis, plus dependent children in case of death of pensioner. Upon application, pension may be split between pensioner and ex-spouse following a divorce.
Social welfare:	
General Welfare Assistance	Any individual, based on needs test, or any family, based on needs test, taking *family* income into account.
Family Benefits	Disabled man and his family, single women with dependent children.
Health care	Any individual, although membership in a health plan is on a family basis.
Public education	Every child aged 6 to 16, and some older and younger ones.
Day care subsidies	Parents of pre-school children, based on needs test taking family income into account.
Homes for elderly subsidies	Any single person over 60 years of age, based on an income test, or any couple over 60 years of age, based on a family income test.

The Canada/Quebec Pension Plan is even more of a borderline case. One portion of the plan is geared towards individuals, another portion is geared towards family members. The primary pensioner receives his or her pension irrespective of family status, presence of dependants, or other factors. Level of pension payments depends on previous contributions, not on need. However, those aspects of the plan that provide for payment for survivors (surviving spouses as well as surviving dependent children) provide pensions on the basis of family status, rather than on the basis of previous *personal* contributions (although the pension level is determined by the contributions of the deceased pensioner). In the case of survivors' benefits, potential recipients of survivors' pensions may be partially or totally disentitled if they made their own pension contributions and therefore have built up their own individual pension entitlements, or if they earn sufficient money.

In all other programmes, entitlement to benefits depends on some aspect of family status, rather than on personal characteristics. The refundable child tax credit comes to mothers largely on the basis of their husbands' incomes (mentioned to be generally higher than women's, and therefore having a disproportionate impact on determining eligibility for the child tax credit). The exemption for dependent children goes usually to the father (i.e., the parent with the higher income), while the childcare deduction goes to the mother for costs incurred for children who are looked after part of the time by non-relatives. The married exemption and the transfer of deductions between spouses is available to a man (in most cases, although legally wives are eligible to claim these exemptions) simply by virtue of his marital status. This presupposes, however, that his wife has practically no income. The equivalent-to-married exemption goes largely to single mothers raising dependent children, on the basis of their being *not* married while the spouse's allowance goes to needy widowed or married women because of their marital status (single women of the same age and the same degree of neediness are not eligible for this pension).

The Guaranteed Income Supplement, social welfare, day care subsidies, and housing subsidies for the elderly all depend on family income and marital status, and in the case of social welfare, also on the sex of the applicant (male and female applicants of the same family income and family status are treated differently: a disabled man entitles the family to benefits; a disabled woman does not). Since all of the latter programmes mentioned are dependent on family status, it follows that a married person cannot participate in them as an individual. Either the whole family participates, or none of the individual members do.

Family-based programmes have some very important consequences.

For one, they show the paradox of the familism-individualism flip-flop in operation. Second, they are premised on and reinforce particular notions of the familial division of labour and family responsibilities. Third, they have a differential effect on women and men.

The Familism-Individualism Flip-Flop in Operation

The familism-individualism flip-flop is characterized by the paradox that policies, the overt intent of which is "to help families," usually end up actually disadvantaging some and sometimes all families. "Family policies," in spite of their name and their explicit rationale, therefore often work against families, rather than for them. This is at least partially due to the fact that in order to implement a family policy, one needs to have some policy definition as to what a family is. Once criteria which define a family have been adopted, these same criteria, by implication, rule out other groupings as non-families. Where there are conflicting claims, it may be necessary to distinguish between "real" families and other families, or at least decide on a ruling as to which family is the "primary" family.

An area in which such distinctions were traditionally made was with respect to legitimate and illegitimate children. In order to "protect the family" (meaning the legal wife with or without children) illegitimate children and their mothers were defined as non-families, and therefore not eligible for support. This seems to be the logic behind many of the older laws which draw a sharp distinction between the rights of legitimate and illegitimate children. Fortunately this distinction is on its way out in Canada (see Chapter 9).

An area in which we find similar attempts to distinguish between "primary" and "secondary" families, or "real" families and other families, and which is of increasing relevance today, concerns the support rights and obligations in cases of divorce and remarriage. Who has the primary right to the support of a husband and father — the first wife and mother, or the second wife and mother? (For a discussion of some of these issues, see Bhardwaj, 1980)

The familism-individualism flip-flop is in operation, then, when a policy — in the name of "the family" — actually discriminates against some or all families, or against individuals on the basis of their family status. In the following, we will briefly examine to what degree the familism-individualism flip-flop is operative in the social policies we have been examining so far.

Theoretically, a family policy could either advantage or disadvantage people on the basis of their family status. It is here postulated that *in practice,* family policy more often discriminates against marriage and certain types of families rather than being supportive of them.

Of the selected social programmes considered here, the married exemption, the possibility of transfer of deductions between spouses and the spouse's allowance advantage particular sets of married people over comparable sets of unmarried people. If, for instance, two unrelated people of the same sex, or even of opposite sexes, have a joint household, and one is for a particular taxation year totally dependent on the other, the one who earns money cannot claim a tax exemption for the other, as one can for a dependent spouse. Indeed, even if the two adults are a couple living together under common law, one common-law spouse cannot claim the other as a dependant. Likewise, eligible deductions can only be transferred between spouses, not between other people who may share a common household. The spouse's allowance, as already mentioned, is not available to single women between 60 and 64 years of age, although they may be as needy (or more needy) than wives or widows whose husbands either receive a pension or died at a point in time which qualifies them for the spouse's allowance.

In these cases, then, it is of advantage to be married rather than not married, and in these particular cases, a "family policy" does what people usually associate with the term: give some advantages to people on the basis of their marital status, provided the potential recipients of the various benefits also meet the other eligibility criteria. However, as we will see in the next section, only a particular type of family actually profits from these programmes.

In the case of the Guaranteed Income Supplement, Social Welfare (both General Welfare Assistance and Family Benefits), day care subsidies, and subsidies for housing for the elderly, which also constitute family-oriented policies, people are actually disadvantaged because of marital status. This is due to the fact that (a) all of these programmes define eligibility on the basis of *family* income (rather than individual income) and/or (b) benefits for a married couple are lower than for two single individuals. So, for instance, two elderly women living together, both of whom are eligible for GIS, will have a higher entitlement together than a married couple has. The same applies to social welfare. Since rates for individuals are proportionately higher than for couples, two individuals will together receive higher benefits than a couple. However, in the case of social welfare this is only true for two individuals sharing a household if they are of the same sex, since for eligibility purposes a man and woman living together, whether married or not, are treated as a married couple. This will be discussed further in the next section.

In the case of access to a subsidized space in a home for the elderly, the income limit for a married couple is lower than it is for two unmarried individuals who live together. The case of subsidized day care is somewhat more complicated. Parents tend to gain privileged access to subsidized day care if they already receive some other form of assistance such as Ontario's Family Benefits. The disadvantage to married couples therefore extends from eligibility to social assistance to access to subsidized day care.

All of the latter discussed programmes are *family* programmes in that they are explicitly geared towards families. Their rationale tends to be to *help* families. However, their effect is to *disadvantage* people on the basis of their marital status, so that programmes ostensibly designed to help families actually end up imposing a penalty on people for being married.

This is one of the manifestations of the familism-individualism flip-flop. Treating people administratively as family members rather than as individuals works, in general, against them. However, what about the policies that we considered first, in which people derived an economic advantage from being married? In order to see whether this is a contradiction to a general theory of a familism-individualism flip-flop, we need to reconsider these programmes by asking ourselves *what type* of family benefits from these programmes.

Notions of Dependency and Familial Division of Labour Underlying Family-oriented Policies

Notions of dependency, division of labour, and responsibility within families are inextricably bound together and are therefore here considered together. Basically, there are two fundamentally opposed conceptions of families co-existing at the present time, and they are both reflected in our social policies, namely the *breadwinner family* and the *two-earner family* (see Chapter 4 for a description of the differences).

A few of the selected policies are very clearly oriented towards the assumptions underlying the breadwinner model of the family. The married exemption is the clearest example. Insofar as a tax deduction constitutes a social benefit for those who are in a high enough tax bracket to profit from it, the married exemption is a benefit that transfers money to breadwinners. It is not a benefit that supports marriage in general — if this was so, every married couple could claim the exemption. However, it is only available to breadwinners with a dependent spouse. It is likewise not a benefit that transfers money to an individual who has taken over economic responsibility for another adult, since it is only available to a married person for the spouse, in spite of the fact that there are people who have adult dependants who are not their spouses (dependent common-law spouses cannot be claimed as dependants either).

The equivalent-to-married exemption can be claimed by an *unmarried* (including separated or divorced) person who supported a person of any age (adult or child) who is related by blood, marriage, or adoption. A taxpayer cannot claim both the married and the equivalent-to-married exemption. Therefore, if a taxpayer supported a dependent spouse and, for example, a dependent mother, (s)he can claim only one of them. (There was a possibility to deduct up to $1090 for the 1981 tax year for a close relative who was dependent on a taxpayer, provided the relative was either a child or was physically or mentally infirm.) The married exemption and equivalent-to-married exemptions, then, do not benefit families in general, but only those of the breadwinner type.

The childcare deduction is available only to "working" (i.e., money earning) mothers, or working fathers, provided the mother is unable to look after the child(ren) because she is dead, absent, or disabled. The childcare deduction is therefore *not* available to all parents who actually utilize and pay for childcare, but only to a portion of them. If the Toronto study is generalizable, (Johnson 1977 and 1978), about 14 percent of the parents utilizing day care do so for reasons *other* than mother's paid work, predominantly because the mother is a student, or has health problems, or does volunteer work. In the vast majority of these cases, neither parent can claim childcare expenses, although they may have incurred costs identical to those of parents who are deemed entitled to claim such expenses

The notion concerning familial division of labour and responsibility is clearly one according to which it is the mother's (but not the father's) responsibility to care for children. This explains why a couple in which the father is a student or unemployed and the mother earns money may claim childcare expenses, while a couple in which the mother is a student or unemployed and the father earns money cannot claim child care expenses. It also explains why couples in which the parents, for reasons other than the mother's paid work, have incurred childcare expenses, cannot claim the expenses they have incurred for childcare: the mother is supposed to look after the children on a full-time basis, irrespective of whether she does or does not do so. Furthermore, when the mother looks after her children, this is seen as a valueless activity in terms of money.[9]

The stipulation that only expenses paid to non-relatives can be claimed is another example of the familism-individualism flip-flop. Although there is a prevailing consensus that it is better for small children to be cared for by relatives, we deprive families that manage to arrange that type of care of benefits that they would receive were they to employ a non-relative.

Transfer of deductions from one spouse to the other ostensibly benefits *all* couples, irrespective of type, but in practice they only benefit breadwinner families. This is so because deductions will only be transferred from one spouse to the other after the taxable income of the spouse from whom the deductions are transferred has been reduced to zero.

Social welfare is also totally oriented towards a breadwinner family with a clear notion of division of labour by sex. The wife is treated as the husband's dependant (he gets one cheque for the whole family). Her loss of earning power does *not* entitle the family to benefits; his loss of earning power does. The mother is treated as a breadwinner in the absence of a man, but as soon as she lives together with a man she is treated as a dependant and is disentitled from her benefits. *Any* man with whom a woman on family benefits lives together is automatically considered responsible for the economic well-being not only of the woman, but also of all her dependent children. In effect this means that responsibility for the children is transferred to a man who is not their father. Here again we see the familism-individualism flip-flop in operation: although it is generally considered desirable by social welfare agencies that mothers be married, and that children consequently grow up in husband-wife families, men (or women) who are interested in living together with or marrying a single parent are discouraged from doing so by their disentitlement to family benefits. This is a paradox indeed, but one which is understandable (although not excusable) in light of the still existing assumptions about familial division of labour and responsibilities on the basis of sex.

The Spouse's Allowance is likewise premised on the breadwinner model of the family, since it is not simply the neediness of members of a particular age group that entitles them to this benefit, but the presumption that they are dependent because of their family status (equally needy single people cannot claim this benefit).

All the types of social benefits so far considered in this section, then, apply only to breadwinner families. By contrast, family allowances, unemployment insurance, old age security, health care insurance, and public education benefit *all* families, irrespective of their structure and internal organization.

The C/QPP presents an interesting borderline case. In as far as individual contributors receive pensions based on their previous contributions, the plan does not discriminate on the basis of family status. However, when we consider survivors' benefits, the same old picture emerges: the plan supports primarily breadwinner families. Dulude (1981:15) has noted that "as widows' benefits increase with husbands' incomes and are reduced or non-existent when the wife earned C/QPP credits of her own, the main beneficiaries of surviving spouses' benefits are not low-income widows, but rather the families of middle- and upper-income men who are so well off that their wives don't have to work outside their homes."

So far, we have mostly treated the family as a unit. However, this unit is neither stable, as we have seen before, nor are its members in equal positions, nor do policies benefit or disadvantage all members equally. In the following, we will briefly consider the differential impact of a few selected policies on women and men.

The Differential Impact of Selected Social Policies on Women and Men

We have already seen that the beneficiaries of the various social programmes vary. Taking into consideration only after-tax family allowances, the refundable child tax credit and tax savings from exemptions for a hypothetical two-parent family in Ontario with two young children and a full-time housewife, we find the allocation of benefits by income level shown in Table 10.2.

We can note several things. First of all, benefits received increase up to a family income of $18 000 and decrease thereafter. In other words, the poorest families presumably most in need do not receive most benefits, due to the fact that the tax savings from exemptions are higher the higher the income. (Tax exemptions are always regressive, giving higher benefits to higher income groups, while tax credits are progressive, provided they are taxed, giving higher benefits to lower income groups.) Secondly, the proportionate share of the wife decreases as the husband's income increases (the assumption is that the man is a breadwinner and the woman is a housewife). As the husband gets richer, the wife gets poorer. Although the wife presumably benefits from the husband's earnings, nevertheless, he is legally in control of his income, while she is only in control of such amounts as

TABLE 10.2

Child-Related Benefits Paid to Mother and Father, Ontario 1978

Family income	Benefits paid to the father	Benefits paid to the mother	Total received by family	% of all benefits paid to the mother
$ 7,000 or less	$ 0	$880	$ 880	100%
10,000	135	880	1,015	87%
15,000	157	880	1,037	85%
18,000	170	880	1,050	84%
22,000	176	680	856	79%
26,000	197	480	677	71%
30,000	224	480	704	68%
50,000	269	480	749	64%

Source: Adapted from Dulude, 1980, p. 3.

are paid directly to her. For the vast majority of wives earning income, their personal income including government transfers will be considerably below those of their husbands, due to wage differentials by sex.

Shifrin, in discussing the political calculations behind various social policies, asks himself

> Why, for example, is everyone so ready to volunteer the family allowance for restructuring rather than the children's tax exemption? Not only, on a family basis, is the allowance mildly progressive while the exemption is entirely regressive, but they have massively different male/female impacts as well.[10]

I wonder whether the fact that the vast majority of tax experts are men has something to do with the readiness to reduce or abolish the family allowance (which is paid to women) rather than the various exemptions (which are mostly paid to men).

We have seen that of the major social benefit programmes considered here a few (e.g., OAS, UI) treat people administratively as individuals. They therefore do not discriminate on the basis of marital status. Of those programmes that treat people administratively *not* as individuals, but as family members, most discriminate *against* family members (usually in the name of supporting the family) while those that confer benefits to marital couples do so only in the case of breadwinner families, but not in the case of two-earner families.

In breadwinner families, women are defined as the economic dependants of men. This is the one major reason why the majority of Canadian women become poor at some point in their lives. Having been defined as dependants, they have built up few individual entitlements to any social benefits in their own right. By contrast, their husbands have generally built up entitlements to social benefits over a lifetime. Creating or maintaining social policies that are oriented towards the breadwinner model of the family, then, contributes towards maintaining the dependency of women and the economic superiority of men. To elaborate the point, we will consider one example only: pensions.

At the present time, the Canadian pension system is in the process of being reformed. There is consensus on two issues: that the current system is inadequate and that women are the more poorly served sex.

In order to improve the performance of the system overall, a number of general proposals have been made which will here be ignored. In order to improve the performance of the pension system for women, two solutions are often proposed: to increase the survivor's benefits, and to further implement pension splitting. Both proposals stem clearly from a breadwinner model of the family with its attendant notions of female dependency, and could therefore serve to continue to reinforce dependency of wives on husbands and female poverty.

Let us consider the case of pension splitting first. Let us assume a couple was married for ten years and has two children. They divorce and the wife obtains custody of their two children and applies for pension splitting. She thus receives an entitlement to half of her husband's pension credits accumulated during their ten-year marriage. The husband remarries, the first wife does not (more divorced men remarry than women). When the man retires at age 65, his pension is split three ways, with an insignificant amount going to his first wife, while he and his second wife live on his pension minus that amount. Since a pension under the current system is meant to replace after 35 years of earnings only 25 percent of the average industrial wage, the credits accumulated during the ten years of the man's first marriage will result in a small payment indeed (cf. Table 10.1 for *full* pension payments). The first wife, meanwhile, continues to look after her children on a full-time basis for another five years. During this time she accumulates no pension credits whatsoever. After that she takes a job at rather low pay (since she is now middle-aged and no longer has skills currently in high demand) and accumulates pension credits for twenty-five years of work. In spite of pension splitting her pension will be extremely small. The same will be true for the second wife's survivor's pension after her husband dies.

The major problem with the notion of splitting is that the woman gets an entitlement after divorce not on the basis of what she has done, but on the basis of her marital status. Therefore, if she continues to raise children but no longer is a wife she will receive no credits.

Survivors' benefits are also clearly derived from the breadwinner model of the family. Since survivors' benefits are reduced or eliminated if a survivor has her own pension entitlement, they are, by definition, benefits which accrue only to a breadwinner family, in which, in other words, the wife is economically dependent on the husband. (Theoretically, either spouse may qualify for survivors' benefits, however, since men usually have their own pension entitlements, in practice survivors' benefits are widows' benefits, and occasionally orphans' benefits, if the breadwinner dies while he still has dependent children.)

One of the major problems with survivors' benefits is equity. Either the survivor receives a portion of the deceased's pension, in which case this will continue to be inadequate, or, if the survivor benefits are increased (maximally to 100 percent of the deceased's pension) a spouse (usually a wife) will receive a benefit simply for having been a wife that may be higher than the pension of a woman who has worked for pay all her life (since women's pensions are smaller than men's pensions due to wage differentials). Also, in the case of a married breadwinner couple, one contribution will, in effect, generate two pensions, while in the case of single persons or a two-earner couple, one contribution results in one pension.

A far better approach would seem to be to phase out survivor's benefits altogether, and use the money thus saved to create a second pension plan geared towards all non-earners (male and female) that would interlock perfectly with the contributory plan. If people do not earn money because they are raising children or caring for dependent adults, the state should make pension contributions for this extremely important and socially necessary work. If, on the other hand, a couple without dependent children or an adult in need of care, decide that one spouse (usually the woman) stay at home to look after the housework and the comfort of both spouses, the earning spouse (usually the man) should contribute regularly on a compulsory basis to his wife's pension plan, since he profits from her work in the home.

This way, every individual would build up an uninterrupted pension entitlement throughout adult life, irrespective of marital status, and the asymmetrical dependency and poverty of women and men in their later years could be largely overcome.[11]

The next section shall attempt an overall assessment of the social policies as they currently exist, including an identification of problems and gaps in policies.

Social Policies Affecting Families — An Assessment

Canada, as we have seen, has a wide range of social programmes. Indeed, there are so many of them, that there should not be a single person who should not be affected by at least some of them. Some of the programmes are universal, others are selective and based on income tests. Some pay transfers directly to individuals; others provide transfers to institutions that provide services to people. For some, individuals are the recipients; for others, the couple or the entire family is considered the smallest administrative unit. Some determine eligibility on individual criteria only, others modify criteria on the basis of marital status. What, then, are the overall characteristics of this medley of programmes?

First, it is important to note that in spite of the large-scale introduction of social programmes in the past quarter-century, the income distribution "in Canada has tended to be quite stable, or has perhaps worsened slightly. The bottom 20 percent of Canadian family units habitually receive around four percent of total Canadian income, and the top 20 percent habitually receive around 42 percent" (Ross, 1980:85).

Women as a group are much poorer than men as a group, "we find that women in each quintile receive an income between one-third and one-half that of their male counterparts' income, and that this has been stable since 1951" (Ross, 1980:85).

The poorest people are found among the elderly who are alone, and among them, the incomes of the women are lower than the incomes of the men (Poduluk, 1980:287). There is an increasing number of elderly women.

Equally horrifying is the fact that about one-quarter of all Canadian children are officially living in poverty (see National Council of Welfare, 1975; and Canadian Council on Children and Youth, 1978:31). In Canada's social security system, women and children are definitely last.

To put the poverty of the elderly and families with young children into perspective, it is instructive — and dismaying — to compare minimum payments for the elderly and Family Benefits for families with children.

In January of 1981, a single adult of 65 years of age or over was guaranteed a monthly payment of $453.96 per month in Ontario (a combination of OAS, GIS and GAINS). At the same time, a mother with one child between the ages of 10 and 15 was guaranteed a maximum allowance of only $438 per month; that is, less for two persons than one older person is entitled to! The maximum social welfare allowance for an individual was only $257. For a married elderly couple the guaranteed income was $852.92 in January 1981, while a couple with three children between the ages of 10 and 15 on Family Benefits was entitled to a maximum payment of only $650; that is, five persons of a younger age receive considerably less than two persons of an older age. Clearly, this constitutes a rather severe inequity, which is exacerbated by the fact that in order to qualify for GIS and GAINS, only an *income* test is conducted, but in order to qualify for Family Benefits, a *needs* test is conducted, which takes into account any assets an applicant may own. (For an overall picture comparing payments to the aged with payments to welfare families, see Table 6.6).

Overall, although the incomes of the elderly are far below what they should be, the situation of families who are wholly dependent on some sort of transfer payment is much worse as yet. Most of these families constitute female-headed one-parent households.

We have seen in the preceding analysis that programmes that determine eligibility to benefits on the basis of family status or family income tend to have a very negative effect on women, who tend to be disentitled from benefits on the basis of their husbands' incomes. The only cases in which so-called family policies actually advantaged people on the basis of their marital status were those of breadwinner families, in which the wife is economically dependent on the husband.

It is the economic dependence of wives that is a major factor in the disproportionate poverty among women as compared to men. In addition, it is a major reason for poverty among children, since a substantial proportion of poor children are members of female-headed one-parent households. Between 1971 and 1976, the number of families headed by women under 55 increased by 29 percent. Of all households headed by women, 42.6 percent were below the poverty line in 1961. In 1976, the percentage was 42.8 percent (Podoluk, 1980:287). During that time span, the situation of female-headed families has been deteriorating, comparatively speaking. While the average income of female-headed families in 1967 was 64 percent of the overall average family income, in 1975 it was only 52 percent (Podoluk, 1980:287). In the same year, 69.1 percent of all children living in one-parent households, were poor (National Council of Welfare, 1975:ii).

As a society, Canada treats its children and their mothers extremely poorly. Maternity leave provisions are far below those found in most European countries, and paternity leave provisions are almost nonexistent. To put this into perspective, three European examples may suffice: Sweden, for instance, has a "parenthood insurance" plan which allows employed parents to mutually apportion among them nine months of "child leave" at 90 percent of their regular income (Liljeström, 1978:41). Norway gives every employed woman an eighteen-week maternity leave (part of which may be taken by the father) at 90 percent of his/her wage (Henriksen and Holter, 1978:62). Hungary gives employed women a twenty- to twenty-five week maternity leave at full pay, an increase in the normal period of paid leave, reduced working hours during the breastfeeding period, up to sixty days per year of leave paid at the rate of illness benefits to allow parents to care for ill children under age three, and a childcare grant to those mothers who wish to stay at home for up to the time the child is three years old after their fully paid maternity leave has expired, which is paid for at approximately the level of half of an average salary for their cohort (Ferge, 1978:75).

In Canada, mothers are economically penalized for giving birth, fathers are largely precluded from caring for the children full-time at any point in time, and the country as a whole has in no way adequately responded to the dramatic effects of a labour force participation of wives and mothers which has by now become the norm.

In cases of divorce, desertion, death, or unwed parenthood, a large proportion of mothers are obliged to apply for some form of welfare which is even more inadequate than our payments to the elderly. Welfare payments are also humiliating and punitive due to the associated means or needs test.

The major problems with the current system of social policies then, are that the system as a whole is confusing and hard to understand. It does not redistribute wealth from the rich to the poor, it penalizes women for bearing and rearing children, and does not facilitate the integration of fathers into the childrearing process. Programmes that are geared towards families rather than towards individuals tend to discriminate against married couples, except where such couples fall into the breadwinner type of family, which is based on female dependency. Childcare is still largely seen as a private responsibility, with very poor public support, and that of a highly regressive nature (the childcare deduction). A quarter of Canadian children are growing up in poverty — a truly obscene figure considering the fact that Canada ranks among the countries with the highest per capita income in the world.

Overall, neither horizontal nor vertical equity are assured in Canadian social policies, notions of female dependency are still underlying a number of programmes, and we find the familism-individualism flip-flop in operation in a number of policies.

On the positive side, there are a few programmes which do not show these negative characteristics; notably Old Age Security and Family Allowances. Unemployment Insurance, as well as the public education system and the health care system, are also universal, but benefits tend to be higher for those with higher incomes, for different reasons. For instance, with respect to Unemployment Insurance, the National Council of Welfare (1978:10) found that "Incredibly, what low-income workers get for paying at the highest rate is the lowest coverage."

In the final section we will briefly put forward three proposals to improve the situation.

Three Proposals for Improving the Social Security System — Radical, Moderate, and Piecemeal Realistic

The Radical Solution — A Credit Income Tax

A radical solution to the majority of woes we encounter at present would be the introduction of a Credit Income Tax (CIT) which would transfer a certain amount of income to every individual in Canada — woman, man, child. It would be taxable on a flat-rate basis, such that it would be recouped in its entirety from all individuals above a certain income. This measure would with one swoop eliminate total dependency of wives on husbands, and eliminate children growing up in poverty. Even if we assume a rather moderate amount per person — let us say $3000 annually — a family of four would have a guaranteed income of $12 000. It would replace all social welfare programmes, as well as all tax exemptions discussed here, the Family Allowance, the

Child Tax Credit, Old Age Security and the Guaranteed Income Supplement. It would *not* replace the Canada/Quebec Pension Plan or Unemployment Insurance, which are based on employer/employee contributions.

Of course, such a scheme would involve substantial amounts of money. Some of it would be recouped through taxation, some saved by eliminating programmes that were made obsolete, but even then, a very substantial amount would certainly be left to be paid. The financing of a CIT would therefore involve an increase in personal income tax. If vertical equity is a goal in the sense that a decrease in the existing extreme income disparities is seen as desirable, this should be an acceptable route to take. The highest income individuals would be taxed most. Since no individuals would any longer be totally responsible for any other individuals during their entire lifetime, very large incomes could no longer be justified in terms of family obligations.

Unfortunately, the political climate is not such that this seems a feasible plan for the moment. Next, therefore, is a more moderate proposal which would solve *some* of the problems that were identified.

A Moderate Solution — A Child Care Tax Credit

A Child Care Tax Credit would consist of a monthly payment which corresponds to the average cost of a day care space — between $250 and $300 per child — to every mother for each child that had not yet entered the public school system. As a child entered the public school system (at age four, five, or six depending on when he or she enters Kindergarten) the payment would be pro-rated by those hours that the child did not need care, using an eight-hour, five-day week, twelve-month basis. These pro-rated payments would continue until such time as the child needs no lunch and after-school supervision or holiday supervision; for instance, until age fourteen.

The payments would be made through the Family Allowance system which is already in place, and would therefore entail no further administrative costs. The payments would be made to every mother, whether or not she held a paying job. If she was at home (or if the father stayed at home), the payments would be retained by the stay-at-home parent, while they would presumably be utilized to defray the costs of day care in case both parents (or the one parent in a one-parent household) worked. The Child Care Tax Credit would be fully taxable, thus ensuring that the plan would be progressive.

In addition, parents caring for dependent children or dependent adults at home would automatically become a part of the C/QPP, with the state paying contributions on their behalf. If, on the other hand, a spouse stayed at home in order to be a homemaker, but with no fully dependent children or adults in the household, the earning spouse would be required to make contributions on behalf of the homemaker spouse to the pension plan.

This programme would alleviate some of the current problems encountered in the social security system. It would transfer monies from families without children to families with children, reduce the poverty of children and poor families in general, and improve the situation of women.

It would replace the child care deduction, the married exemption, the refundable child tax credit (but only for those children up to fourteen), the equivalent-to-married exemption, the transfer of deductions between spouses, and subsidies to day care centres. The remaining net costs would have to be financed via the income tax, which would result, as stated, in the transfer of monies from families and individuals without children to those with children.

However, even such a moderate proposal is likely to run into some resistance at the present time. As a last alternative, therefore, a piecemeal but more realistic approach will be proposed that can be implemented in small and relatively easy steps.

The Piecemeal Realistic Approach to Social Policies

We have seen that it is a misperception that selective programmes are more redistributive than universal programmes — it depends on the interaction between the tax system and the transfer programme what the net distributional effects are. Universal programmes have therefore a large number of features to recommend them over selective programmes: they are cheaper and easier to administrate, they have a potentially high appeal since the large majority of people profit from them at least to a degree, they are non-demeaning in that they administer an income test through the income tax rather than through means or needs tests which are almost always humiliating, experienced as degrading, and which stigmatize their recipients in a manner in which universal transfers do not, they have a close to universal take-up rate, and, if they are paid to individuals irrespective of sex and marital status, they are not premised on any notion of female dependency and do not perpetuate existing sex inequalities. Existing examples are the Old Age Security and the Family Allowance.

As a general approach, then, the government should, whenever changes are contemplated, expand the universal programmes and/or convert selective programmes into universal programmes, in which all transfers are always taxed on the basis of the *total* income of every recipient. In practice, this would imply abolishing the child tax credit and putting it back into Family Allowance (from where it was originally taken; see Shifrin, 1980). This would *not* mean that poorer families would receive less and richer families would receive more, for that is purely a function of how the Family Allowances are taxed (see Kapsalis, 1980, and Kesselman, 1979).

More important, the greatest attention should be directed towards tax expenditures. The vast majority of them should be eliminated, and the money thus saved (in the area of around $9 billion) should be divided between the Family Allowances and Old Age Security. Likewise, the Guaranteed Income Supplement should be abolished and added on to Old Age Security. With the savings from the tax expenditures, the freed monies from the Child Tax Credit and the Guaranteed Income Supplement, both Family Allowances and Old Age Security could be very substantially increased.

This would result in a much more progressive social security system (since it is the tax expenditures which make an otherwise progressive income tax non-progressive), would reduce sexual inequalities, would transfer monies to those families and individuals who need them most, namely the elderly and families with young children, and would not cost an extra cent.

In addition, non-earners (both male and female) should be participants in some public pension plan, with their contributions being paid by the state if they stay at home in order to care for a person in need of care, possibly, a dependent child or an adult in need of care for physical or mental reasons. When wives (and occasionally husbands) stay at home in order to keep house for their spouses, the spouses should be obliged to contribute to a pension plan on their behalf. This would mean that practically every individual in Canada would build up a personal pension entitlement, which should greatly reduce the incidence of poverty among the aged.

Further, welfare agencies should eliminate the restriction that benefits cease if a man moves in with a woman with children who collects Family Benefits. This practice derives from an outdated model of the family, and imposes an impossible burden on the man as well as impeding women from developing — because of this burden — a relationship with a man who could potentially become a new mate. This would remove one of the most dramatic instances in which the familism-individualism flip-flop penalizes existing and/or emergent families.

These changes could be phased in gradually, and would at least point us into the right direction, although they would not solve all the problems that were identified.

Notes

1. From *The Emergence of Social Security in Canada* by Dennis Guest reprinted by permission of University of British Columbia Press, 1980, p. 16.
2. Ibid.
3. Ibid., p. 30.
4. Several provinces add further payments to these federal minima.
5. Based on information supplied via telephone by CPP sources in Health and Welfare Canada.
6. Personal communication from an official in the Ontario Ministry of Community and Social Services.
7. From *Your Family Benefits Handbook,* 1975 reprinted by permission of the Ministry of Community and Social Services. The Family Benefits Handbook is now entitled *For Your Benefit.* On 1981 11 01, section 5 (d) of Regulation 318 under the Family Benefits Act was repealed. The result of this repeal is that blind, disabled, or permanently unemployable married women are eligible for family benefits in their own right in the same way as any other applicant (from a written communication from the Ministry of Community and Social Services, dated October 4, 1982).
8. Based on personal communication from an official of the Metropolitan Toronto Housing Co. Ltd.
9. That childcare and housework in general are seen as totally valueless — in spite of the fact that there has been some vigorous work examining the value of unpaid work in the last decade (see Chapter 5 for some of the references) — becomes particularly obvious when reading arguments for family taxation. Typically, the argument is that couples in which both spouses work should pay exactly the same amount for tax for their combined incomes as would the breadwinner in another family who earned as much as the two earners in the first family (see, for example, Salyzyn, 1980:145). This suggests that the work that the wife does as a housewife is seen as totally without value, with no need for replacement purchases.
10. Leonard Shifrin, "The Meaninglessness of the Selectivity versus Universality Debate," *Canadian Taxation,* Vol. 2, No. 3 (1980):171.
11. The pension entitlement would not be totally equalized, for as long as there are wage differentials between women and men these are likely to be reflected in pension entitlements. However, the problem of unequal wages cannot be addressed by reforming the pension system. For that, other strategies are necessary. For a comprehensive discussion of the issues raised, see Dulude (1981) and Collins (1978).

References

Bergeron, Michel, *Social Spending in Canada. Trends and Options.* Ottawa: Canadian Council of Social Development, 1979.

Bhardwaj, Vijay K., "The Impact of Serial Monogamy and Living Outside Marriage on the Public and Private Law of Matrimonial and Child Support," in John M. Eekelaar and Sanford N. Katz (eds.), *Marriage and Cohabitation in Contemporary Societies. Areas of Legal, Social and Ethical Change. An International and Interdisciplinary Study.* Toronto: Butterworths, 1980.

Canada. Health and Welfare, Canada Pension Plan. *Statistical Bulletin,* Vol. 12, No. 4, 1980.

Canadian Council on Children and Youth. *Admittance Restricted: The Child as Citizen in Canada.* Ottawa: Canadian Council of Children and Youth, 1978.

Canadian Intergovernmental Conference Secretariat. *The Income Security System in Canada*. Report prepared by the Interprovincial Task Force on Social Security for the Interprovincial Conference for Ministers Responsible for Social Services, Ottawa, 1980.

Collins, Kevin, *Women and Pensions*. Ottawa: Canadian Council on Social Development, 1978.

Dulude, Louise, "Joint Taxation of Spouses — A Feminist View," *Canadian Taxation*, Vol. 1, No. 4, 1979, pp. 8–12.

Dulude, Louise, *Discussion Paper on Federal Income Security Programs for Families with Children*. Ottawa: Canadian Advisory Council on the Status of Women, 1980.

Dulude, Louise, *Pension Reform with Women in Mind*. Ottawa: Canadian Advisory Council on the Status of Women, 1981.

Dunlop, Marilyn, "Rising costs force Ottawa's hand: There's no new money for health," *Sunday Star*, 1981 06 14, pp. A1 and A14.

Ferge, Zsuzsa, "Hungary," in Sheila B. Kamerman and Alfred J. Kahn (eds.), *Family Policy. Government and Families in Fourteen Countries*. New York: Columbia University Press, 1978, pp. 68–90.

Garfinkel, Irwin, "Overview," unpublished manuscript.

Guest, Dennis, *The Emergence of Social Security in Canada*. Vancouver: University of British Columbia Press, 1980.

Hasson, Reuben, "The Cruel War: Social Security Abuse in Canada," unpublished paper, York University (Osgoode Hall Law School), n.d.

Henriksen, Hildur Ve and Harriet Holter, "Norway," in Sheila B. Kamerman and Alfred J. Kahn (eds.), *Family Policy. Government and Families in Fourteen Countries*. New York: Columbia University Press, 1978, pp. 49–67.

Hepworth, H. Philip, "The Child and Social Policy in Canada," unpublished paper, 1979.

Johnson, Laura Climenko, *Who Cares? A Report of the Project Child Care. Survey of Parents and their Child Care Arrangements*. Toronto: Social Planning Council, 1977.

Johnson, Laura Climenko, *Taking Care. A Report of the Project Child Care. Survey of Caregivers in Metropolitan Toronto*. Toronto: Social Planning Council, 1978.

Kapsalis, Constantine, "In Defense of Family Allowances," *Canadian Public Policy*, Vol. 6, No. 1, 1980, pp. 107–109.

Kesselman, Jonathan R., "Credits, Exemptions and Demogrants in Canadian Tax-Transfer Policy," *Canadian Tax Journal*, Vol. 27, No. 6, 1979, pp. 653–688.

Kesselman, Jonathan R., "Pitfalls of Selectivity in Income Security Programs," *Canadian Taxation*, Vol. 2, No. 3, 1980, pp. 154–163.

Kesselman, Jonathan R. and Irwin Garfinkel, "Professor Friedman, Meet Lady Rhys-Williams: NIT vs. CIT," *Journal of Public Economics*, Vol. 10, 1978, pp. 179–216.

Kirshna, Vern, "Selectivity in Tax-Transfer Programs and the Tax Unit Problem," *Canadian Taxation*, Vol. 2, No. 3, 1980, pp. 164–166.

Liljeström, Rita, "Sweden," in Sheila B. Kamerman and Alfred J. Kahn (eds.), *Family Policy. Government and Families in Fourteen Countries*. New York: Columbia University Press, 1978, pp. 19–48.

Maslove, Allan M., "Tax Expenditures, Tax Credits and Equity," in G. Bruce Doern (ed.), *How Ottawa Spends Your Tax Dollars. Federal Priorities in 1981*. Toronto: James Lorimer and Co., 1981, pp. 232–254.

Mendelson, Michael, "The Selectivity Mistake," *Canadian Taxation*, Vol. 2, No. 3, 1980, pp. 167–169.

Metropolitan Toronto Day Care Planning Task Force, *Future Directions for Day Care Services in Metro Toronto*. Toronto: Department of Social Services, 1980.

National Council of Welfare, *Poor Kids*, Report by the National Council of Welfare on Children in Poverty in Canada, Ottawa, 1975.

National Council of Welfare, *Bearing the Burden, Sharing the Benefits.* Report by the National Council of Welfare on Taxation and the Distribution of Income, Ottawa, 1978.

Ontario Ministry of Community and Social Services, *Your Family Benefits Handbook,* Toronto, 1975.

Organization for Economic Co-Operation and Development, *The Treatment of Family Units in OECD Member Countries under Tax and Transfer Systems,* Report by the Committee on Fiscal Affairs, Paris, 1977.

Podoluk, Jenny, "Poverty and Income Adequacy," in Economic Council, *Reflections on Canadian Incomes,* (Catalogue EC22-78/1980E). Ottawa: Minister of Supply and Services, 1980, pp. 275–298.

Ramey, James, "Experimental Family Forms — the Family of the Future," *Marriage and Family Review,* Vol. 1, No. 1, pp. 1, 3–9.

Ross, David P., *The Canadian Fact Book on Income Distribution.* Ottawa: Canadian Council of Social Development, 1980.

Salyzyn, Vladimir, "Savings, Labour Supply and Tax Equity," *Canadian Taxation,* Vol. 2, No. 3, 1980, pp. 142–148.

Schnepper, Jeff A., "A Tax on Marriage," *Intellect,* Vol. 106, No. 2395, 1978, p. 381.

Shifrin, Leonard, "The Meaninglessness of the Selectivity versus Universality Debate," *Canadian Taxation,* Vol. 2, No. 3, 1980, pp. 170–171.

Trost, Jan, "Cohabitation Without Marriage in Sweden," in John M. Eekelaar and Sanford N. Katz (eds.), *Marriage and Cohabitation in Contemporary Societies. Areas of Legal, Social and Ethical Change. An International and Interdisciplinary Study.* Toronto: Butterworths, 1980, pp. 16–22.

Watson, Roy E. L., "The Effects of Premarital Cohabitation on Subsequent Marital Adjustment," paper given at the Canadian Sociology and Anthropology Meetings in Halifax, 1981.

Appendix 1

The Participation of Women Project (POW Project)

The POW project is part of a larger international study on the participation of women in public life, involving four countries: Canada, Italy, Poland, and Romania. The principal investigators involved in this study are Mino Vianello (Italy), Renata Siemienska (Poland), and Tamara Dobrin and Pompiliu Gregoresco (Romania). The questionnaire was drawn up jointly by a larger group in 1977, and in Canada the data were collected in 1978.

The international group agreed on a joined instrument and on comparable samples, although every principal investigator was free to add more respondents (this was done in Canada) or to add some questions (this was not done in Canada). The international group agreed on the following sample:

(1) 100 male and 100 female blue-collar workers without subordinates from factories with at least 100 employees;
(2) 100 male and 100 female white-collar workers without subordinates from factories with at least 100 employees;
(3) 100 unemployed men;
(4) 100 housewives married legally or common-law to a man in a working class occupation without any independent source of income;
(5) 100 male and 100 female public school teachers in the public school system with a teaching rather than an administrative job.

All respondents in categories 1–5 were from the Metropolitan Toronto area. The next category, by contrast, was a national sample:

(6) 150 top female decision-makers from across the country to whom 150 male decision-makers were matched.

Decision-makers were defined as women in positions in power in government, the public service, trade unions, political parties, private business, educational institutions, and voluntary organizations. Decision-makers were identified in a variety of ways: by making systematic searches of various listings (party listings, government lists, *Who's Who in Canada*, the *Financial Post Directory of Directors*, *The Parliamentary Guide*, *Legislative Debates*, newspapers, etc.), as well as through snowballing. Once all women respondents had been identified, they were matched individually to a man in a comparable position: for instance, a female provincial cabinet minister would be matched with a male provincial cabinet minister with a similar portfolio in a province of comparable size; the female president of a large voluntary organization would be matched with a male president of another comparable organization; a female university president would be matched with a male university president of a similar-sized university; etc. The men were matched to the women since there are much fewer women in decision-making positions. The final breakdown for decision-makers (both males and females, of course) was as follows: 32 elected and appointed government officials at the federal level, 33 elected and appointed government officials at the provincial level, 20 elected and appointed government officials at the local level, 31 business executives, 6 labour union officials, 18 political party officials, and 9 officials of educational institutions and big voluntary organizations.

In Canada, in addition, we added to the sample

(7) 100 housewives who were married to husbands with professional or managerial jobs.

The research was supported by OISE grant #3474 and SSHRCC grants #410-78-0300 and #410-78-0302. Aisla Thomson co-ordinated the data collection process. The following people served as interviewers: in Toronto, Marsha Cressy, Morris Freedman, Carolyn Eisen, Margaret Gee, Doug Hart, Barbara Lamb, Patricia McKay, Patricia Marshall, Carl Stieren, Helen Sussman, Adaline Thomson, Hanneke Vonk. In Ottawa, Elizabeth Bateman, Janine Brodie, Marilyn Burnett, Catherine Crear, Mr. Singh. In Halifax, Pat Connelly, Carmelle Le Gendre. In Montreal, Nancy Robinson. In Regina, Milnor Alexander, Audrey Dewit. In Edmonton, Bill Becker, Patricia Brand, Rosalind Sydie. In Vancouver, Maureen Martin, Roxana Ng. Doug Hart did the necessary computer runs.

So far, two papers have been published from the Canadian data set: Margrit Eichler, "Sex Equality and Political Participation of Women in Canada. Some Survey Results," in *Revue Internationale de Sociologie,* Series II, Vol. 15, Nos. 1–3, April-December 1979, pp. 49–75; and Margrit Eichler, "Sex Role Attitudes of Male and Female Teachers in Toronto," *Interchange,* Vol. 10, No. 2, 1979–80, pp. 2–14.

Appendix 2

The Atypical Families Project

I first started to play around with the idea of a dimensional approach to families in 1978. In order to push my thoughts further, I decided to engage in some empirical pilot work, which eventually evolved into the atypical families project. In the summer of 1978, I sought out, starting with personal contacts and using a snowballing technique, ten families which in some way or another deviated from the stereotypical nuclear family consisting of a wife and husband both in their first legal marriage, and their biological children, all sharing the same residence, without other people present.

The ten families I eventually interviewed are the following ones: #1, a homosexual couple (interviewed both women); #2, a divorced family (interviewed co-resident mother and daughter); #3, a co-operative household (interviewed four members); #4, a group marriage (interviewed the two men and the woman involved); #5, a widower with a young wife (interviewed only the wife, the interview with the husband did not materialize); #6, a couple with tenants in their imperfectly partitioned home (interviewed the wife and the husband); #7, a common-law couple (uncle and niece) with five adopted children (interviewed man, woman, and the eldest adopted daughter); #8, a remarriage family (interviewed wife, husband, and husband's oldest son who was non-resident); #9, a lesbian mother with four children, still legally married and co-parenting but separated from her husband; and #10, a commuting couple, in which the wife had a business in New York and the husband in Toronto (interviewed wife and husband).

Each interview was conducted in the home of the respondents, with the exception of case #5, in which I interviewed the wife in her parents' home, where she was visiting, #6, in which the husband came over to my home for the interview, and #8, where the child came to my office. In every case, each respondent was interviewed separately and assured (and given) confidentiality. I used a focussed approach to interviewing. Each interview lasted about an hour, was taped, and afterwards transcribed.

Questions focussed on personal data, on how the current relationship got started and its current quality. If there were preceding, step- or concomitant relationships, these were discussed as well. The main body of the interview focussed on the residential, economic, sexual, emotional, parental, social, and legal dimensions as well as the time perspective of respondents with respect to their family relationships and their personal definitions of their own family.

So far, these data are unpublished, except for the excerpts used in this book, where I have drawn occasionally on cases #6 and #8. However, the interview experience was very significant for myself in informing my thinking, and I owe a large debt of gratitude to the people who so generously shared their time and their personal lives with me.

Epilogue

When looking at the bewildering array of issues, perspectives, and changes affecting families today, one factor jumps out of them as of fundamental importance: families are slowly moving towards becoming voluntary rather than non-voluntary units for their *adult* members. I am not trying to exaggerate the degree to which this process has progressed: I see the transformation of families into voluntary rather than involuntary units as a long-term process which has just started and which is certainly not complete, nor, indeed, likely to be completed for at least another thirty years, and possibly longer. Nevertheless, even the first manifestations are starting to have an effect on our social structures and on our collective and individual self-understanding.

I am, of course, thinking about the increase in the divorce rates, but this is only one factor. Due to the increase in the labour force participation of women, which nowadays tends to persist even when women become wives and/or mothers, economic dependency no longer serves as the iron bond that glues spouses together, although economic issues continue to be important. Due to the industrialization of housework, single people, men as well as women, find it feasible to keep their own household while also holding down a job. Social legislation, inadequate as it is, does prevent starvation and other horrible outcomes for people who find themselves without familial support. Sex roles have already changed somewhat, are continuing to change, and are likely to go on changing until hopefully some day in the far future they will have all but disappeared.

The increase in the volitional nature of families makes it easier to recognize families as social rather than as "natural" units. However, families have at least two very important components: one involves the relationships between two adults, commonly in some form of marriage, and the other involves the relationship between parents and children. These two relationships are of a fundamentally different nature. While marriage (or its equivalent) is a purely social relationship (and always has been), parenthood is a social as well as a biological relationship. As *marriage* becomes more volitional, parent-child relationships may be involuntarily disrupted, even though both parents are alive. Voluntary marriage may thus be complemented by involuntary loss of a parent by a child (or loss of a child by a parent), unless we start to learn to separate the parent-child relationship from the spousal relationship and learn to consider each on its own merits.

This would require a fundamental shift in our thinking. One way to help us along this route might be to focus our attention, for a while, on those families in which there is some discrepancy between parental and marital roles, of whatever kind. This might help us to recognize and become more comfortable with the essentially social nature of marriage, while also helping us to recognize and become comfortable with the mixed social/biological nature of the parent-child relationship.

Overall, the move towards family membership as voluntary membership is, of course, a very positive one, including the increase in divorce — for what is more desirable: to keep people in unhappy unions or to allow them an out? Nevertheless, it is also a profoundly disorienting, painful, and confusing change. Where we were brought up to believe that there is certainty, we now find uncertainty; where we thought to find shared understanding, we now discover that people are miles apart in their expectations and behaviours.

With comparative new freedom come new problems for which we, as a society, simply have not yet invented the solutions. How does one combine the notion of autonomous individuals with that of long-time commitment? How can we create social structures in which individuals find personal freedom as well as personal security? How can we co-operate as equals when most of us have spent (and continue to spend) most of our time in hierarchical structures? How can there be equality of the sexes within families in a basically sexist society? How can we teach our children what we ourselves have not yet learned?

I believe that we must start reconceptualizing families not as discrete social units with clear boundaries, but instead as complex networks with overlapping but nevertheless in most cases non-congruent sets of relationships, further complicated by potential non-congruity in various dimensions of familial interaction. This would allow us to start thinking about mechanisms with which to retain some of the relationships within a network, even when one of them is disrupted.

INDEX